LIFE AT THE MARGINS IN
EARLY MODERN SCOTLAND

St Andrews Studies in Scottish History

Series Editor
Professor Emeritus Roger Mason (Institute of Scottish Historical Research, University of St Andrews)

Editorial Board
Professor Dauvit Broun (University of Glasgow)
Professor Michael Brown (Institute of Scottish Historical Research, University of St Andrews)
Dr David Ditchburn (Trinity College, Dublin)
Professor Emerita Elizabeth Ewan (University of Guelph)
Dr Clare Jackson (Trinity College Cambridge)
Dr Catriona MacDonald (University of Glasgow)
Dr Malcolm Petrie (Institute of Scottish Historical Research, University of St Andrews)

Sponsored by the Institute of Scottish Historical Research at the University of St Andrews, St Andrews Studies in Scottish History provides an important forum for the publication of research on any aspect of Scottish history, from the early middle ages to the present day, focusing on the historical experience of Scots at home and abroad, and Scotland's place in wider British, European and global contexts. Both monographs and essay collections are welcomed.

Proposal forms can be obtained from the Institute of Scottish Historical Research website: www.st-andrews.ac.uk/ishr/studies.htm. They should be sent in the first instance to the chair of the editorial board at the address below.

Professor Emeritus Roger Mason
Institute of Scottish Historical Research
St Andrews University
St Andrews
Fife KY16 9AL
UK

Previous volumes in the series are listed at the back of this book

LIFE AT THE MARGINS IN EARLY MODERN SCOTLAND

Edited by
Allan Kennedy and Susanne Weston

THE BOYDELL PRESS

© Contributors 2024

All Rights Reserved. Except as permitted under current legislation
no part of this work may be photocopied, stored in a retrieval system,
published, performed in public, adapted, broadcast,
transmitted, recorded or reproduced in any form or by any means,
without the prior permission of the copyright owner

First published 2024
The Boydell Press, Woodbridge

ISBN 978 1 83765 023 1

The Boydell Press is an imprint of Boydell & Brewer Ltd
PO Box 9, Woodbridge, Suffolk IP12 3DF, UK
and of Boydell & Brewer Inc.
668 Mt Hope Avenue, Rochester, NY 14620–2731, USA
website: www.boydellandbrewer.com

A catalogue record for this book is available
from the British Library

The publisher has no responsibility for the continued existence or
accuracy of URLs for external or third-party internet websites referred to in
this book, and does not guarantee that any content on such websites is, or
will remain, accurate or appropriate

Contents

List of Illustrations vii
Contributors viii
Acknowledgements x
List of Abbreviations xi

Introduction: Centring the Margins 1
ALLAN KENNEDY AND SUSANNE WESTON

Part I
Social Margins

1 Disability and the Domestic Sphere in Early Modern Scotland 17
   CHARLOTTE HOLMES

2 Relieving the Poor in Mid-Seventeenth-Century East Fife 32
   SAMANTHA HUNTER AND ALLAN KENNEDY

3 The Marginalisation of Gypsies in Scotland, 1573–c. 1625 47
   THOMAS M. TYSON

4 Burgesses on the Edge 62
   KEVIN HALL

5 Enslaved and Formerly Enslaved Young People in Eighteenth- and Nineteenth-Century Scotland 79
   MATTHEW LEE

Part II
Occupational Margins

6 Working on the Margins: Freemen, Unfreemen, and Stallangers in Early Modern Scotland 97
   AARON M. ALLEN

7 The Life of the Lockman 114
   LAURA I. DOAK

CONTENTS

8 'Huirdome and Harlettrie': Female Sex Workers in Early Modern
   Edinburgh, 1689–1760   130
   SUSANNE WESTON

9 Navigating Marginality: The Coal Mine Workers of Seventeenth-
   Century Scotland   145
   ROBERT D. TREE

Part III
Contemplating Marginality

10 Migrants, Itinerants, and the Marginality of Mobility in
   Seventeenth-Century Scotland   163
   ALLAN KENNEDY

11 Seeking the Lord, Seeking a Husband: Navigating Marginality in
   the Diary of Rachel Brown (1736–8)   179
   MARTHA MCGILL

12 Queering the Castalian: James VI and I and 'Narratives of Blood'   194
   LUCY R. HINNIE

Afterword   210
Index   215

Illustrations

1 Sculptured stone panel showing Adam and Eve, with a paraphrase of Genesis 3:19: 'In sudore vultus tui vesceris pane tuo'. From the Netherbow, Edinburgh, sixteenth century. NMS, H.KG 41. Image © National Museums Scotland   98

2 Iron girdle for baking oatcakes, thought to be of the Culross type. National Trust for Scotland, 2017.2422. Reproduced by kind permission of the National Trust for Scotland   100

3 Howie's depiction of a cobbler working under a stair. ECA, Howie Prints, 'A Cobbler in his Stall, John Knox's corner, the last of the race in Edinburgh', vol. 2 (c. 1850), 17. By kind permission of City of Edinburgh Council   108

The editors, contributors and publisher are grateful to all the institutions and persons listed for permission to reproduce the materials in which they hold copyright. Every effort has been made to trace the copyright holders; apologies are offered for any omission, and the publisher will be pleased to add any necessary acknowledgement in subsequent editions.

Contributors

Aaron M. Allen is an independent scholar whose research focuses on the economic and social history of work. Having recently completed a monograph on the building trades, *Building Early Modern Edinburgh* (2018), he is currently undertaking archival scoping work for the Edinburgh Incorporation of Bonnetmakers and Dyers and the Edinburgh Incorporation of Baxters.

Laura I. Doak was formerly Research Fellow with the Scottish Privy Council Project (Leverhulme Trust) at the University of Dundee. She is an historian of early modern Scottish political culture and is particularly interested in how ordinary people could be engaged in political debate, publishing elsewhere on public executions, print, and royal pageantry.

Kevin Hall is a PhD student in Scottish History at the University of Edinburgh. His publications include 'The Famine of 1622–3 in Scotland', in H. Cornell, J. Goodare and A. MacDonald (eds), *Agriculture, Economy and Society in Early Modern Scotland* (Woodbridge, 2024).

Lucy R. Hinnie (she/her) completed her PhD at the University of Edinburgh in 2019. From 2019 to 2021 she was a white settler scholar on Treaty Six Territory and the Homeland of the Métis at the University of Saskatchewan, where she was a Postdoctoral Fellow of the Department of English and the Centre for Medieval and Renaissance Studies. From 2023 to 2024 she was a Postdoctoral Fellow at the Institute for Advanced Studies in the Humanities at the University of Edinburgh.

Charlotte Holmes completed her PhD from the University of Edinburgh on domestic medicine in early modern Scotland in 2022. She currently works at the Royal College of Physicians of Edinburgh and is developing her research on disability.

Samantha Hunter is a PhD student at the University of Dundee. Her thesis examines the effects of national political, social, and economic disruption on the resilience of local governance in North-East Fife (1640–80).

CONTRIBUTORS

Allan Kennedy is Lecturer in Scottish History at the University of Dundee. He specialises in the political and social history of the early modern period, and he also serves as Consultant Editor of *History Scotland* magazine. His publications include *Governing Gaeldom: The Scottish Highlands and the Restoration State* (2014) and *Serious Crime in Late-Seventeenth-Century Scotland* (forthcoming).

Matthew Lee completed his PhD at the University of Aberdeen. His research focuses on Scotland's historic connections to Atlantic slavery.

Martha McGill is a British Academy Postdoctoral Fellow at the University of Warwick, where she is working on a project titled 'Bodies, Selves and the Supernatural in Early Modern Britain'. She is the author of *Ghosts in Enlightenment Scotland* (2018) and the co-editor of *The Supernatural in Early Modern Scotland* (2020).

Robert D. Tree is double graduate of the University of Glasgow and currently a third year PhD researcher at the University of Stirling. His thesis is focused on the Scottish Privy Council's role in church and civil government from 1689 to 1708. It is funded by the Leverhulme Trust as part of the Scottish Privy Council Project across the Universities of Stirling and Dundee. His main interests lie in the politics, religion, and government administration of seventeenth-century Scotland, in addition to the social and cultural implications of collier 'serfdom' between around 1606 and 1799.

Thomas M. Tyson is a final year PhD student at the University of Cambridge and Scouloudi Doctoral Fellow at the Institute of Historical Research, London. His research considers the history of 'Egyptians', or Gypsies, as a prism through which to better understand some of the key developments in early modern Scottish history, including the Reformation, state building and Atlantic imperialism. He is also interested in the history of antiquarianism, historical anthropology and Romanticism.

Susanne Weston is a PhD student at the University of Dundee. Her work centres on social control and social policy in the early modern era, with a particular focus on the period 1689–1708 and the role of the privy council.

Acknowledgements

The editors would like to thank Roger Mason and Caroline Palmer for their help, encouragement, and guidance throughout the preparation of this volume. The anonymous peer reviewer provided a great deal of thoughtful feedback, for which we are very grateful. Thanks are also due to Graeme Morton, Alan MacDonald, and Alastair Mann for their support, and to our families for putting up with our periodic absorption in the project. The editors would also like to thank all the contributors for their dedication and hard work in bringing the book to fruition.

Abbreviations

Aberdeen Recs.	Extracts from the Council Register of the Burgh of Aberdeen (4 vols, Aberdeen/Edinburgh, 1844–71)
Argyll and the Isles	J. Cameron and J. Imrie (eds), *The Justiciary Records of Argyll and the Isles, 1664–1742* (2 vols, Edinburgh, 1949–69)
Criminal Trials	Robert Pitcairn (ed.), *Ancient Criminal Trials in Scotland* (3 vols, Edinburgh, 1833)
DAC	Dumfries Archive Centre, Dumfries
Dumbarton Recs.	Dumbarton Burgh Records 1627–1746 (Dumbarton, 1860)
DSL	*Dictionary of the Scots Language*, available online at: www.dsl.ac.uk/
ECA	Edinburgh City Archives, Edinburgh
ELCALHS	East Lothian Council Archive and Local History Service, John Gray Centre, Haddington
EUL	Edinburgh University Library, Edinburgh
Edinburgh Recs.	M. Wood et al. (eds), *Extracts from the Records of the Burgh of Edinburgh* (9 vols, Edinburgh, 1927–67)
Elgin Recs.	W. Cramond (ed.), *The Records of Elgin* (2 vols, Aberdeen, 1908)
Glasgow Recs.	J.D. Marwick et al. (eds), *Extracts from the Records of the Burgh of Glasgow* (8 vols, Glasgow, 1876–1913)
Inverness Recs.	W. Mackay & H.C. Boyd (eds), *Records of Inverness* (2 vols, Aberdeen, 1912)
Old Aberdeen Recs.	A.M. Munro (ed.), *Records of Old Aberdeen* (Aberdeen, 1899)
NLS	National Library of Scotland, Edinburgh
NMS	National Museum of Scotland, Edinburgh
NRS	National Records of Scotland, Edinburgh
ODNB	*Oxford Dictionary of National Biography*
OLA	Orkney Library and Archives, Kirkwall
OSA	*Old Statistical Account of Scotland*
PJC	*Records of the Proceedings of the Justiciary Court Edinburgh, 1661–1678* (2 vols, Edinburgh, 1905)
PKA	Perth and Kinross Archives, Perth

ABBREVIATIONS

RPCS, 1st Series	J.H. Burton and D. Masson (eds), *The Register of the Privy Council of Scotland, First Series* (14 vols, Edinburgh, 1877–98)
RPCS, 2nd Series	D. Masson and P.H. Brown (eds), *The Register of the Privy Council of Scotland, Second Series* (8 vols, Edinburgh, 1899–1908)
RPCS, 3rd Series	P.H. Brown et al. (eds), *The Register of the Privy Council of Scotland, Third Series* (16 vols, Edinburgh, 1908–70)
RPS	K.M. Brown et al. (eds), *The Records of the Parliaments of Scotland to 1707*, www.rps.ac.uk
SA	Shetland Archives, Lerwick
SCA	Stirling Council Archives
SHR	*Scottish Historical Review*
Stirling Recs.	R. Renwick (ed.), *Extracts from the Records of the Royal Burgh of Stirling* (2 vols, Glasgow, 1887–89)
TNA	The National Archives, Kew

Introduction
Centring the Margins
Allan Kennedy and Susanne Weston

In his controversial polemic published in 1996, *An Intelligent Person's Guide to History*, John Vincent argues that the main concern of historians should be 'the role of power in society'. Force and compulsion were, for Vincent, the primary drivers of human development, and for that reason, the heart of all historical study should be the use and negotiation of power. Or, as he put it, co-opting a phrase associated with his intellectual opponents, 'king and battles' must remain the order of the historiographical day.[1] Vincent's assertion encapsulates the 'traditional' view of what 'History' as a discipline should be. It is a view stretching back to the very emergence of academic History in the days of Leopold von Ranke: it should concern itself with great men (and occasionally women), high-level developments, and above all, politics and diplomacy. That such a formulation now sounds impossibly quaint is down, in no small part, to the development in the mid-twentieth century of social history, a sub-discipline which insisted that the structures and rhythms of society, as well as affairs of state, were legitimate targets of the historian's interest. Prominent within the initial ferment of social history was the concept of 'history from below', a phrase particularly associated with the Marxist-inspired work of E.P. Thompson. Deployed to its fullest effect in Thompson's seminal *The Making of the English Working Class*, 'history from below' posits that ordinary people should be centred within historical analysis, and from this premise contends that the power to shape history lies just as much with the teeming masses as it does with great men or abstract processes.[2]

Working within, or inspired by, the 'history from below' tradition has allowed scholars to open up whole new areas of historical inquiry; it is, for example, hard to see how scholarship of the 'kings and battles' mould could have allowed for recent growth in the field of emotion history.[3] At the same time, 'history from below' has helped to demonstrate that non-elite actors have always played a crucial part in 'big' historical developments. In a British context, this is perhaps most obvious with regard to the Civil

---

[1] J. Vincent, *An Intelligent Person's Guide to History* (London, 1996), p. 37.
[2] E.P. Thompson, *The Making of the English Working Class* (London, 1963). Vincent, unsurprisingly, was excoriating about both social history and 'history from below', viewing them as dilettantish distractions at best, Leftist interlopers at worst. Vincent, *Guide to History*, chapter 13.
[3] K. Barclay and P.N. Stearns (eds), *The Routledge History of Emotions in the Modern World* (London, 2022).

Wars of the 1630s to 1650s, research on which – particularly their English dimensions – now pays a great deal of attention to the experiences and importance of ordinary and middling folk.[4] Other themes, if not generating quite the same volume of 'history from below', have nonetheless benefited from some attention; an obvious Scotland-focused example is the ecclesiastical struggles of the Restoration (1660–89), current understandings of which have been greatly enriched by moving beyond high politics and exploring more popular religiosity.[5]

But as well as helping 'ordinary' people reclaim their historical influence, a 'history from below' approach demands that attention be given to those who lacked any real agency at all – people who were confined to the very edges of society, enduring lives marked by degradation and disempowerment. Some scholars have made a social-justice argument for such an approach, suggesting that recovering sidelined experiences can (or should) become almost a collective act of atonement for the initial disenfranchisement.[6] But even in more narrowly intellectual terms, there are clear advantages to centring the once sidelined. Studying such people expands our understanding of the past, in the process likely complicating many dearly held canards. It also helps shed light on the underlying dynamics of past society; understanding social exclusion necessarily involves mapping out and deconstructing the concept of the 'mainstream'. English historians have proved particularly alive to all this potential, resulting in illuminating studies of pedlars, vagrancy, migrants, enslaved people, cultural minorities, and much more besides.[7]

---

[4] C. Hill, *The World Turned Upside Down: Radical Ideas during the English Revolution* (London, 1972); D. Purkiss, *The English Civil War: A People's History* (London, 2006); M. Braddick, *God's Fury, England's Fire: A New History of the English Civil Wars* (London, 2009); J. Rees, *The Leveller Revolution: Radical Political Organisation in England, 1640–1650* (London, 2014).

[5] The 'high politics' approach to this topic is exemplified by J. Buckroyd, *Church and State in Scotland 1660–1681* (Edinburgh, 1980); J. Buckroyd, *The Life of James Sharp, Archbishop of St Andrews 1618–1679* (Edinburgh, 1987); I.B. Cowan, *The Scottish Covenanters 1660–88* (London, 1976). For more 'popular' approaches, see E. Hymen, 'A Church Militant: Scotland 1661–1690', *Sixteenth Century Journal*, 26:1 (1995), 49–74; N. McIntyre, 'Saints and Subverters: The Later Covenanters in Scotland c.1648–1682 (unpublished PhD thesis, University of Strathclyde, 2016); J.M. Macdougall, 'Covenants and Covenanters in Scotland 1638–1679' (unpublished PhD thesis, University of Glasgow, 2018).

[6] V. Bahl, 'What Went Wrong with "History from Below"?', *Economic and Political Weekly*, 38:2 (2003), 11–17.

[7] See, for example: M. Spufford, *The Great Reclothing or Rural England: Petty Chapmen and their Wares in the Seventeenth Century* (London, 1984); A.L. Beier, *Masterless Men: The Vagrancy Problem in England, 1560–1640* (London, 1985); R. Vigne and C. Littleton (eds), *From Strangers to Citizens: The Integration of Immigrant Communities in Britain, Ireland and Colonial America, 1550–1750* (Brighton, 2001); T. Hitchcock, *Down and Out in Eighteenth-Century London* (London, 2004); N. Goose and L.B. Luu (eds), *Immigrants in Tudor and Early Stuart England* (Brighton, 2005); L.B. Luu, *Immigrants and the Industries of London, 1500–1700* (Aldershot, 2005); M. Stoyle, *Soldiers and Strangers: An Ethic History of the English Civil War* (New Haven, CT 2005); J. Selwood, *Diversity and Difference in Early Modern London* (Farnham, 2010); M. Kaufmann, *Black Tudors: The Untold Story*

INTRODUCTION

On first sight, many of these disadvantaged social categories might appear to have little in common – what meaningful connection can there be, after all, between, say, 'women' and 'religious nonconformists', two categories that might easily incorporate affluent or otherwise privileged individuals, and 'beggars', which manifestly would not? Yet the linkages between all these groupings can be made clear by deploying the concept of 'marginality'. This is an idea developed by social scientists in the mid-twentieth century, originally as a means of unpacking the experiences of populations or individuals who found themselves straddling more than one culture group, such as immigrants. Over the years, the concept has evolved, and more recently has generally been used to explore the persistence of extreme poverty in the modern world. 'Marginality', in this sense, is defined as any form of – usually involuntary – exclusion from social, political, or economic systems, with the effect of limiting full participation, typically to detrimental effect.[8] This conceptual expansiveness has its drawbacks, of course, not least because it could conceivably be stretched to cover just about anybody – even kings and emperors might be seen as to some degree 'marginalised' because their august positions inhibited them from doing the same things as their subjects. By the same token, however, the great advantage of applying 'marginality' as an analytical lens is that it accommodates complexity, allowing scholars to explore the multiplicity of pressures or obstacles that can, cumulatively, place people in a position of acute structural disadvantage.[9]

Whether consciously or otherwise, historians of early modernity have tended to embrace the concept of 'marginality', in the sense that they have been increasingly concerned with uncovering the interconnected ways in which disadvantaged groups were placed at, and kept on, the sidelines. As one example of many, we might take David Hitchcock's recent work on vagrancy in post-Civil Wars England. This period saw the legal disadvantage of the itinerant poor become ever more entrenched; a succession of punitive acts of parliament – thirty-two between 1653 and 1731 – forced such people to live under a crushing legislative burden. But for Hitchcock, that is only part of the story, since England's anti-vagrancy laws did not evolve, or operate, in a vacuum. Instead, a plethora of other pressures also worked to marginalise the

---

(London, 2018); D. Cressy, *Gypsies: An English History* (Oxford, 2020); S.P. Newman, *Freedom Seekers: Escaping from Slavery in Restoration London* (London, 2022).
[8] J.A. Del Pilar and J.O. Udasco, 'Marginality Theory: The Lack of Construct Validity', *Hispanic Journal of Behavioural Sciences*, 26:1 (2004), 3–15; R.J. Dunne, 'Marginality: A Conceptual Extension', in R.M. Dennis (ed.), *Marginality, Power and Social Structures: Issues in Race, Class, and Gender Analysis* (Amsterdam, 2005), 11–27; F.W. Gatzweiler, H. Baumüller, C. Ladenburger and J. von Braun, 'Marginality: Addressing the Root Cause of Extreme Poverty', *Zentrum für Entwicklungsforschung Working Paper Series* 77 (2011), 1–24.
[9] F.W. Gatzweiler and H. Baumüller, 'Marginality – A Framework for Analyzing Causal Complexities of Poverty', in J. von Braun and F.W. Gatzweiler (eds), *Marginality: Addressing the Nexus of Poverty, Exclusion and Ecology* (Heidelberg, New York and London, 2014), 27–40.

vagrant. Ideals of community and settlement, however weakly they accorded with social reality, continued to cast vagrancy as a normative challenge. Stagnant or falling real wages, combined with subsistence crises, created a socio-economic context that ensured hostility to the wandering poor. Even more broadly, developments in economic orthodoxy repositioned joblessness as a drain on the nation's collective wealth, a sense that was reinforced by empire; as an imperial nation, England could not afford to let the labouring potential of the vagrant go untapped, either at home or in the colonies. At the same time, changing ideas about the role and capacity of the state rendered vagrants 'improvable' – they came to be seen as a defective cog in the national machine that could, and must, be repaired. Running alongside all of this was a crucial cultural development, whereby the malignant, malingering figure of the 'vagabond' became a stock character in English culture, especially ballads. In Hitchcock's reading, all of these pressures – legislative, social, economic, intellectual, and cultural – interacted dynamically with one another, merging into a complex and shifting discourse that allowed to vagrants no legitimate place in English society. 'Vagrancy', then, was not simply a disadvantageous lifestyle; it was 'an economic, social, and cultural experience of displacement'.[10] Hitchcock's approach is, of course, not unique, but he stands as one of the more overt – and eloquent – recent examples of how the holistic concept of 'marginality' can help scholars develop a fuller, more nuanced understanding of the lives of the historically underprivileged.

Marginality and Early Modern Scotland

It is a perennial complaint of historians interested in the non-elite components of the pre-modern world, let alone the marginalised, that sources are hard to find. It is unquestionably true that the overwhelming weight of documentation available to us was generated by governments or elites, and that such material necessarily preserves marginalised experiences only second-hand, and typically through a thick shroud of prejudice. Yet, when we turn our attention to Scotland specifically, the situation does not appear irrecoverably grim, since the source base, for all its imperfections, is rich. The dense network of public and private courts that made up the criminal justice system has, for example, left a huge amount of documentation that, by its very nature, speaks to the sort of deviance that was very often the end-point of marginalised experiences. Administrative records, too, often offer glimpses into marginal lives, with things like town council minutes, institutional papers, and justice of the peace materials being especially likely to capture interactions between the marginal and the mainstream. Taxation records, too, can offer valuable insights (as demonstrated by Helen Dingwall's

---

[10] D. Hitchcock, *Vagrancy in English Culture and Society, 1650-1750* (London, 2016). Quote at p. 150.

forensic examination of the hearth and poll tax returns of 1690s Edinburgh), as can the rich and varied types of documentation preserved in the archives of landed estates.[11] A diverse array of literary sources – ballads, prose fiction, self-writing, newspapers, poetry (typically in English, Scots, Latin, or Gaelic), and so on – can provide more generalised and abstract insights into the marginal experience. Of course, and as we have already observed, all of these record-types were generated either by officialdom or elites, and there are few documentary mechanisms for accessing the voices of marginalised peoples unmediated. Used carefully and sensitively, however, these materials present tremendous opportunities for scholars – as, indeed, the contributions to this volume amply attest.

The jewel in Scotland's documentary crown, however, is the ecclesiastical record. The minutes, registers, and other materials produced by the dense hierarchy of church courts that constituted the Church of Scotland from the late-sixteenth century onwards add up to a veritable mountain of paperwork. Not only that, but the highly local nature of the documents' creator organisations, particularly the parish-level kirk sessions, mean that the ecclesiastical archive is both genuinely national in coverage, touching all corners of the country from Shetland to Selkirk, from Stornoway to Stonehaven (albeit not evenly in terms of survival rate), and richly intimate in character. Kirk records naturally reveal a huge amount about religious practice and culture, but their great interest for social historians lies in the information they preserve about ecclesiastical discipline; in attempting to correct the moral and behavioural shortcomings of the faithful, Church authorities ended up recording, often in astonishing detail, how ordinary people – including the marginal – conducted their lives. Church materials are, of course, not unproblematic, not least because they are inevitably infused with the assumptions and prejudices of Scotland's prevailing Calvinist orthodoxy. Nonetheless, thanks to its size, eclecticism, and granularity, the ecclesiastical record provides historians of Scotland with a uniquely powerful tool for reconstructing the day-to-day rhythms of early modern society. When added to the range of other surviving records outlined above, this makes the study of social marginality a far less hopeless prospect in Scotland than it might be in many other places.

Despite the potential (if contingent) richness of the sources, marginal groups within early modern Scottish society only began to command significant scholarly attention with the publication in 1969 of T.C. Smout's ground-breaking *A History of the Scottish People*. Building upon only the most rudimentary historiographical base, supplemented with significant primary-source familiarity, Smout effectively established the field of Scottish social history by presenting a sweeping yet remarkably detailed panorama of Scottish life between the Reformation and the end of the Georgian era. He took in such themes as work, poverty, leisure, material culture, food and drink, popular piety, deviance, family life, lordship, and much else besides.

[11] H. Dingwall, *Late 17th-Century Edinburgh: A Demographic Study* (Aldershot, 1994).

Many of Smout's conclusions are now thoroughly out-of-date, in some cases – for example in his discussion of witchcraft – painfully so, and his overall thesis was notably simplistic in its Whiggishness.[12] Yet *A History of the Scottish People* still stands as a milestone in Scottish historiography, and might perhaps be regarded as the most important work of Scottish History published during the twentieth century. The trail blazed by Smout was soon followed by a number of other scholars, perhaps most prominently Rosalind Mitchison, but also people like Leah Leneman, Margaret Sanderson, Rab Houston, Ian Whyte, Chris Whatley, Michael Graham, Margo Todd, and others[13] – who collectively established Scottish social history as a vibrant and vigorous field.

The expansion of social history scholarship since the 1970s has, naturally, involved bestowing welcome attention on marginalised groups, albeit unevenly. Probably the best-served such group has been women. Building on early general surveys,[14] women have now received welcome attention as political, religious, intellectual, and, especially, economic actors.[15] The deployment of gender as an analytical prism has allowed for further valuable insights, particularly around perceptions of femininity and women's

---

[12] T.C. Smout, *A History of the Scottish People, 1560–1830* (London, 1969).

[13] See, for some of the more significant examples, E. Foyster and C.A. Whatley (eds), *A History of Everyday Life in Scotland, 1600–1800* (Edinburgh, 2010); M.F. Graham, *The Uses of Reform: 'Godly Discipline' and Popular Behaviour in Scotland and Beyond, 1560–1610* (Leiden, 1996); R.A. Houston and I.D. Whyte (eds), *Scottish Society 1500–1800* (Cambridge, 1989); L. Leneman (ed.), *Perspectives in Scottish Social History: Essays in Honour of Rosalind Mitchison* (Aberdeen, 1988); L. Leneman, *Alienated Affections: The Scottish Experience of Divorce and Separation, 1684–1830* (Edinburgh, 1998); R. Mitchison and L. Leneman, *Sexuality and Social Control: Scotland 1660–1780* (Oxford, 1989); R. Mitchison and P. Roebuck (eds), *Economy and Society in Scotland and Ireland, 1500–1939* (Edinburgh, 1988); M.H.B. Sanderson, *A Kindly Place? Living in Sixteenth-Century Scotland* (East Linton, 2002); M. Todd, *The Culture of Protestantism in Early Modern Scotland* (New Haven, CT and London, 2002); C.A. Whatley, *Scottish Society 1707–1830: Beyond Jacobitism, Towards Industrialisation* (Manchester, 2000); I.D. Whyte, *Agriculture and Society in Seventeenth-Century Scotland* (Edinburgh, 1979).

[14] Sanderson, *A Kindly Place?*, chapter 8; R.A. Houston, 'Women in the Society and Economy of Scotland, 1500–1800', in Houston and Whyte, *Scottish Society*, pp. 118–47.

[15] E.C. Sanderson, *Women and Work in Eighteenth-Century Edinburgh* (London, 1996); E. Ewan and M.M. Meikle (eds), *Women in Scotland c.1100–c.1750* (East Linton, 1999); J. Stevenson, 'Reading, Writing and Gender in Early Modern Scotland', *The Seventeenth Century*, 27:3 (2012), 335–74; D. Simonton and K. Barclay (eds), *Women in Eighteenth-Century Scotland: Intimate, Intellectual and Public Lives* (London, 2013); N. Cowmeadow, '"Your Politick, self designing sister": The Role of Katherine, first Duchess of Atholl in the Scottish Parliamentary Elections of 1702', *Parliaments, Estates and Representation*, 33:1 (2013), 1–19; N. Cowmeadow, 'Simply a Jacobite Heroine? The Life Experience of Margaret, Lady Nairne (1673–1747)', in A.I. Macinnes and D.J. Hamilton (eds), *Jacobitism, Enlightenment and Empire, 1680–1820* (London, 2014), pp. 29–42; A. Raffe, 'Female Authority and Lay Activism in Scottish Presbyterianism, 1660–1740', in H. Smith and S. Apetrei (eds), *Religion and Women in Britain, c.1660–1760* (London, 2014), pp. 61–78; C. Spence, *Women, Credit, and Debt in Early Modern Scotland* (Manchester, 2016); J.R. Baxter, 'Elizabeth Melville, Lady Culross: New Light from Fife', *Innes Review*, 68:1 (2017), 38–77.

relationships – especially intimate and familial relationships – with men.[16] As a result of all this work, we now know much more about early modern women in Scotland than we used to, and it has become clear that they were able to exercise a good deal more agency, and claim a more significant public role, than has traditionally been thought – although it should be noted that the bulk of the extant research focuses on the better-documented eighteenth century, and the women of earlier ages still await fuller assessment. The big exception to this chronological bias lies in witchcraft studies. Following some pioneering work from Christina Larner in the 1980s, this sub-specialism really took off from the 1990s onwards, thanks in no small part to the efforts of Julian Goodare. The resulting corpus touches on a huge array of issues, not least around beliefs, mentalities, and state-formation, but it has also emphasised the close interplay between witch-hunting and gender; witchcraft as a concept, it is now clear, overtly contributed towards the policing of women's speech, sexual behaviour, and working lives, especially in the seventeenth century.[17]

The flowering of witchcraft scholarship links women to another marginal group that has done relatively well in terms of academic attention: criminals. The work of Anne-Marie Kilday has been crucial here, not least in uncovering *longue durée* patterns in the nature of deviance and its prosecution, but we have also benefited from a number of local studies, or investigations into specific offences, that have provided useful insights into the causes, performance, and consequences of criminal behaviour.[18] The criminality of

---

[16] K.P. Walton, *Catholic Queen, Protestant Patriarchy: Mary, Queen of Scots, and the Politics of Gender and Religion* (London, 2007); K. Barclay, 'Negotiating Patriarchy: The Marriage of Anna Potts and Sir Archibald Grant of Monymusk, 1731–1744', *Journal of Scottish Historical Studies*, 28:2 (2008), 83–101; K. Barclay, *Love, Intimacy and Power: Marriage and Patriarchy in Scotland, 1650–1850* (Manchester, 2011); D. Barret-Graves, 'Mermaids, Sirens, and Mary Queen of Scots: Icons of Wantonness and Pride', in D. Barret-Graves (ed.), *The Emblematic Queen: Extra-Literary Representations of Early Modern Queenship* (London, 2013), pp. 69–100; D.L. Simonton, '"To Merit the Countenance of the Magistrates": Gender and Civic Identity in Eighteenth-Century Aberdeen', in K. Cowman, N.J. Koefoed, and Å.K. Sjögren (eds), *Gender in Urban Europe: Sites of Political Activity and Citizenship, 1750–1900* (London, 2014), pp. 17–32; R. Mason, 'Women, Marital Status, and Law: The Marital Spectrum in Seventeenth-Century Glasgow', *Journal of British Studies*, 58:4 (2019), 787–804.

[17] C. Larner, *Enemies of Gods: The Witch-Hunt in Scotland* (London, 1981); C. Larner, *Witchcraft and Religion: The Politics of Popular Belief* (Oxford, 1984). Among the wider literature, see, in particular, J. Goodare (ed.), *The Scottish Witch-Hunt in Context* (Manchester, 2002); J. Goodare, L. Martin and J. Miller (eds), *Witchcraft and Belief in Early Modern Scotland* (Basingstoke, 2008); J. Goodare (ed.), *Scottish Witches and Witch-Hunters* (Basingstoke, 2013).

[18] A.-M. Kilday, *Crime in Scotland 1660–1960: The Violent North?* (Abingdon, 2019); G. DesBrisay, '"Menacing their persons and exacting their purses': The Aberdeen Justice Court, 1657–1700', in D. Stevenson (ed.), *From Lairds to Louns: Country and Burgh Life in Aberdeen, 1600–1800* (Aberdeen, 1986), pp. 70–90; J.G. Harrison, 'Women and the Branks in Stirling, c.1600 to c.1700', *Scottish Economic and Social History*, 18:2 (1998), 114–31; F. Bigwood. 'The Courts of Argyll, 1664–1825', *Scottish Archives*, 10 (2004),

women, especially but not exclusively through the prism of infanticide, has received particularly strong attention.[19] As welcome as all this research is, it is strikingly uneven: the geographical coverage is haphazard; male criminality is less well-served than female; organised crime has been almost completely ignored; and material on the seventeenth century in particular is very thin. Yet if there is clearly much more to do, solid criminal-history foundations have nevertheless been laid.

Also comparatively well-served in scholarly literature have been religious minorities. Thanks to the centrality of sectional disputes to the historical development to post-Reformation Scotland, scholars have found value in unpicking the ideals, aims, and activities of religious 'out' groups, especially Roman Catholics, Presbyterians, and Episcopalians. This body of research has served to underline the importance of religious belief and practice as a mechanism for self-definition, and also a vector of marginalisation; in a Scotland inclined to associate all forms of religious nonconformity with sedition, adhering to anything other than the state Church tended to bring with it both social ostracisation and legal vulnerability.[20] Other, smaller sects have

---

27–38; J.G. Harrison, 'The Justices of the Peace for Stirlingshire 1660 to 1706', *Scottish Archives*, 12 (2006), 42–52; B.P. Levack, 'The Prosecution of Sexual Crimes in Early Eighteenth-Century Scotland', *SHR*, 89:2 (2010), 172–93; J.R.D. Falconer, *Crime and Community in Reformation Scotland: Negotiating Power in a Burgh Society* (London, 2013); W.W.J. Knox, 'Homicide in Eighteenth-Century Scotland: Numbers and Theories', *Journal of Scottish Historical Studies*, 94:1 (2015), 48–73; A. Kennedy, 'Crime and Punishment in Early Modern Scotland: The Secular Courts of Restoration Argyllshire, 1660–1688', *International Review of Scottish Studies*, 41 (2016), 1–36; C. Falconer, *Justice and Society in the Highlands of Scotland: Strathspey and the Regality of Grant (c.1690–1748)* (Leiden, 2022); A. Kennedy, 'Deviance, Marginality, and the Highland Bandit in Seventeenth-Century Scotland', *Social History*, 47:3 (2022), 239–64.

[19] Y.G. Brown and R. Ferguson (eds), *Twisted Sisters: Women, Crime and Deviance in Scotland since 1400* (East Linton, 2002); E. Ewan, 'Impatient Griseldas: Women and the Perpetration of Violence in Sixteenth-Century Glasgow', *Florilegium*, 28 (2011), 149–68; J.R.D. Falconer, '"Mony Utheris Divars Odious Crymes": Women, Petty Crime and Power in Later Sixteenth Century Aberdeen', *Crime and Misdemeanours*, 4:1 (2010), 7–36; C. Hartlen, 'Catching Fire: Arson, Rough Justice and Gender in Scotland, 1493–1542', in S. Butler and K.J. Kesselring (eds), *Crossing Borders: Boundaries and Margins in Medieval and Early Modern Britain* (Leiden, 2018), pp. 153–73; A.-M. Kilday, '"Monsters Of the Vilest Kind": Infanticidal Women and Attitudes to their Criminality in Eighteenth-Century Scotland', *Family & Community History*, 11:2 (2008), 100–16; A.-M. Kilday, *Women and Violent Crime in Enlightenment Scotland* (Woodbridge, 2007); A.-M. Kilday, *A History of Infanticide in Britain c.1600 to Present* (Basingstoke, 2013).

[20] R.S. Spurlock, '"I do disclaim both ecclesiasticke and politick popery": Lay Catholic Identity in Early Modern Scotland', *Records of the Scottish Church History Society*, 38 (2008), 5–22; A. Raffe, *The Culture of Controversy: Religious Arguments in Scotland, 1660–1714* (Woodbridge, 2012); J. Stephen, *Defending the Revolution: The Church of Scotland 1689–1716* (Farnham, 2013); T. Mcinally, 'Support Networks for the Catholic Mission in Scotland', *Innes Review*, 65:1 (2014), 33–51; A.T.N. Muirhead, *Reformation, Dissent and Diversity: The Story of Scotland's Churches, 1560–1960* (London, 2015); R.S. Spurlock, 'The Tradition of Intolerance in the Church of Scotland', in H.J. Selderhuis and J.M.J.L. van Ravenswaay (eds), *Reformed Majorities in Early Modern Europe* (Leipzig, 2015), pp. 215–312; C. McMillan, '"Scho refuseit altogiffer to heir his voce": Women and

received more limited attention, but some valuable work does exist, most importantly focused on the Cromwellian interlude of the 1650s.[21] Scholars' attention has so far focused mostly on elite nonconformity, or on high-level argument and organisation, and there is a pressing need for further work on popular experiences, certainly outside the Covenanting movement. Yet our understanding of the marginalising effect of religious dissent remains comparatively well-developed.

The poor represents a fourth marginal group that has commanded relatively substantial volumes of scholarly attention. Much of the credit for this state of affairs lies with Rosalind Mitchison, whose pioneering work on poor relief, culminating in her *The Old Poor Law in Scotland*, largely established poverty studies as a viable and credible field in Scotland.[22] Mitchison tended to portray poor relief as chaotic and ineffectual, and it is largely in response to this thesis that a stream of new work has emerged in the twenty-first century. Much of this research took the form of local studies exploring the dynamics of poverty and poor relief in defined, typically urban areas, including Aberdeen, Dundee, Edinburgh, and Ayrshire, or following distinct demographical shocks like the famines of the 1620s and 1690s.[23] More recently, emphasis has been placed on the importance of informal relief and interpersonal relationships in ameliorating want.[24] The most significant counterpoint to Mitchison, however, has come from John McCallum, whose exhaustive survey of poor relief practice in the century after the Reformation has not only suggested that the system was – at least in normal times – far more effective than Mitchison allowed, but has also shown that its capacity for flexibility and compassion meant that the poor were often treated far more generously than might be expected.[25] It will be noted from this survey that almost all of the extant work

---

Catholic Recusancy in North East Scotland', *Records of the Scottish Church History Society*, 45 (2016), 36–48; A. Raffe, 'Archibald Pitcairn and Scottish Heterodoxy, c.1688–1713', *Historical Journal*, 60:3 (2017), 633–57.

[21] R.S. Spurlock, *Cromwell and Scotland: Conquest and Religion 1650–1660* (Edinburgh, 2007); R.S. Spurlock, '"Anie Gospell Way": Religious Diversity in Interregnum Scotland', *Records of the Scottish Church History Society*, 37 (2007), 89–119; R.S. Spurlock, 'The Politics of Eschatology', *Baptist Quarterly*, 43:6 (2010), 324–46.

[22] R. Mitchison, *The Old Poor Law in Scotland: The Experience of Poverty, 1574–1845* (Edinburgh, 2000).

[23] R.E. Tyson, 'Poverty and Poor Relief in Aberdeen, 1680–1705', *Scottish Archives*, 8 (2002), 33–42; K. Wilbraham and C. Lodge, 'Responses to Poverty in Ayrshire, 1574–1845', *Scottish Archives*, 8 (2002), 57–70; L. Stewart, 'Poor Relief in Edinburgh and the Famine in 1621–24', *International Review of Scottish Studies*, 30 (2007), 5–41; K. Cullen, *Famine in Scotland: The 'Ill Years' of the 1690s* (Edinburgh, 2010); J. McCallum, 'Charity and Conflict: Poor Relief in Mid-Seventeenth-Century Dundee', *SHR*, 95:1 (2016), 30–56.

[24] A. Glaze, 'Sanctioned and Illicit Support Networks at the Margins of a Scottish Town in the Early Seventeenth Century', *Social History*, 45:1 (2020), 26–51; K. Barclay, *Caritas: Neighbourly Love and the Early Modern Self* (Oxford, 2021); C.R. Langley, *Cultures of Care: Domestic Welfare, Discipline and the Church of Scotland, c.1600–1689* (Leiden, 2019).

[25] J. McCallum, *Poor Relief and the Church in Scotland, 1560–1650* (Edinburgh, 2018). See also J. McCallum, 'Charity Doesn't Begin at Home: Ecclesiastical Poor Relief beyond

on poverty and the poor approaches the topic through the prism of poor relief; the actual experience of being poor, as distinct from such people's treatment by those in authority, remains a weakness in the scholarship, largely because of the nature of the primary-source base. Nonetheless, we now know more about the poor of early modern Scotland than we do about most other marginalised groups.

If women, criminals, religious nonconformists, and the poor have, comparatively speaking, been 'winners' in the game of commanding scholarly attention, numerous other marginal groups remain notably under-served. The most curious such omission, arguably, is the migrant. There has, especially in the last twenty years or so, been a huge amount of research into the mobile Scot, but almost exclusively this has concentrated on emigration. Studies abound of Scots in America, Europe, Ireland, and more recently England, but migrants and itinerants within Scotland, whether themselves Scottish or otherwise, have received pitiful levels of attention.[26] A few isolated studies, for example of apprentice migration to Edinburgh or the evidential value of ecclesiastical testimonials, have served to highlight what might be achieved by a greater focus on the itinerant, and models can also be found in the far larger stock of work dealing with internal mobility in the modern era.[27] For the present, however, migrants as a marginal group remain woefully under-researched.

Racial and cultural difference represents another glaring hole in the scholarship of Scottish marginality. Enough work has been done to say for certain that early modern Scotland was not culturally monolithic: foreign immigrants, Romani communities, and Jewish settlers are all known to have existed long before 1700, as did a small population of Black people, but none of

---

the Parish, 1560–1650', *Journal of Scottish Historical Studies*, 32:2 (2012), 107–26; J. McCallum, '"Fatheris and Provisioners of the Puir": Kirk Sessions and Poor Relief in Post-Reformation Scotland', in J. McCallum (ed.), *Scotland's Long Reformation: New Perspectives on Scottish Religion, c.1500–c.1650* (Leiden, 2016), pp. 69–86.

[26] K.M. Brown and A. Kennedy, 'Land of Opportunity? The Assimilation of Scottish Migrants in England, 1603–c.1762', *Journal of British Studies*, 57:3 (2018), 709–35; K.M. Brown, A. Kennedy, and S. Talbott, '"Scots and Scabs from North-by-Tweed": Undesirable Scottish Migrants in Seventeenth- and Early Eighteenth-Century England', *SHR*, 98:2 (2019), 241–65; T.M. Devine, *Scotland's Empire 1600–1815* (London, 2004); D. Edwards (ed.), *The Scots in Early Stuart Ireland: Union and Separation in Two Kingdoms* (Manchester, 2016); A. Grosjean and S. Murdoch (eds), *Scottish Communities Abroad in the Early Modern Period* (Leiden, 2005); M. Harper and M.E. Vance (eds), *Myth, Migration and the Making of Memory: Scotia and Nova Scotia, c.1700–1990* (Halifax and Edinburgh, 1999); D.J. Hamilton, *Scotland, the Caribbean and the Atlantic World, 1750–1820* (Manchester, 2005); N.C. Landsman, *Scotland and its First American Colony, 1683–1765* (Princeton, NJ, 1985).

[27] A.A. Lovett, I.D. Whyte and K.A. Whyte, 'Poisson Regression Analysis and Migration Fields: The Example of the Apprenticeship Records of Edinburgh in the Seventeenth and Eighteenth Centuries', *Transactions of the Institute of British Geographers*, 10:3 (1985), 317–32; R. Houston, 'Geographical Mobility in Scotland, 1652–1881: The Evidence of Testimonials', *Journal of Historical Geography*, 11:4 (1985), 379–94; C.W.J. Withers, *Urban Highlanders: Highland-Lowland Migration and Urban Gaelic Culture 1700–1900* (East Linton, 1988).

these groups has so far attracted anything more than exploratory attention.[28] One cultural minority has, however, been subjected to significant study: Gaels. The complexities of Gaelic culture and the nature of its interactions with the Anglophone world; evolutions in social and economic structures; Gaelic engagement with the developing systems of the Scottish and British states; the imperial Gael – work in all of these areas, and others, has allowed scholars to develop a nuanced understanding of Gaelic distinctiveness, and has emphatically underlined that early modern Scotland was not, and cannot meaningfully be treated as, culturally or ethnically homogenous.[29] Moreover, this work has underlined the importance of race and culture as an axis of marginality in early modern Scotland – Gaelicness, after all, was rarely perceived or experienced as an asset in the Lowlands – and it is thus all the more notable that the country's other cultural minorities have as yet not received sustained attention.

If various forms of social marginality remain under-explored in the extant literature, the same might be said for the economic margins. Surprisingly little research has been done on patterns of work and employment in the early modern period, but there is enough for it to be clear that there existed a wide array of economic roles which, either because they offered limited financial rewards or because they carried significant social penalties (or, indeed, both), tended to exercise a marginalising influence. Among these might be included service, both agricultural and domestic, unlicensed craft and retail work, peddling, and general labouring, and while these – and other – marginalising occupations have not been totally overlooked, the under-developed state of the existing scholarship means that our understanding of marginalised (and marginalising) work has not yet reached beyond the outline stage.[30]

---

[28] D. Alston, *Slaves and Highlanders: Silenced Histories of Scotland and the Caribbean* (Edinburgh, 2021), chapters 7–8; S. Daiches, 'The Jew in Scotland', *Records of the Scottish Church History Society*, 3:3 (1929), 196–209; D. MacKinnon, 'Slave Children: Scotland's Children as Chattels at Home and Abroad in the Eighteenth Century', in J. Nugent and E. Ewan (eds), *Children and Youth in Premodern Scotland* (Woodbridge, 2015), pp. 120–35; D. MacRitchie, *Scottish Gypsies under the Stewarts* (Edinburgh, 1894); J. Turnbull, 'Venetian Glassmakers in the Prestonpans Area in the Seventeenth Century', *Scottish Archives*, 23 (2017), 103–13.

[29] See, for example, D. Broun and M. MacGregor (eds), *Mìorun Mòr nan Gall, 'The Great Ill-Will of the Lowlanders'? Lowland Perceptions of the Highlands, Medieval and Modern* (Chippenham and Eastbourne, 2009); R. Clyde, *From Rebel to Hero: The Image of the Highlander 1745–1830* (East Linton, 1998); M. Hechter, *Internal Colonialism: The Celtic Fringe in British National Development* (London, 1975); A. MacCoinnich, *Plantation and Civility in the North Atlantic World: The Case of the Northern Hebrides, 1570–1639* (Leiden, 2015); A.I. Macinnes, *Clanship, Commerce, and the House of Stuart, 1603–1788* (East Linton, 1996); A. Mackillop, *'More Fruitful than the Soil': Army, Empire and the Scottish Highlands, 1715–1815* (East Linton, 2000); M. Newton, *Warriors of the Word: The World of the Scottish Highlanders* (Edinburgh, 2009); C.W.J. Withers, *Gaelic Scotland: The Transformation of a Culture Region* (London, 1988).

[30] I.D. Whyte, 'The Occupational Structure of Scottish Burghs in the Late Seventeenth Century', in M. Lynch (ed.), *The Early Modern Town in Scotland* (London, 1987), pp. 219–44; Dingwall, *Late 17th-Century Edinburgh*, chapters 5–7; R.E. Tyson, 'People in the

New Horizons

Building upon existing foundations, but also attempting to address the lacunae outlined above, the essays in this volume seek to explore the diverse experiences of marginalised Scots from the sixteenth to the eighteenth centuries. Both the chronology and the thematic coverage have been left deliberately broad, the intention being to highlight the huge array of themes that can be explored and, thus, signpost opportunities for further research and discussion. The book is divided into three parts. In Part I, the focus is on 'Social Margins' – that is, groups whose marginality was rooted in social factors like ethnicity, status, or physical difference. Charlotte Holmes commences proceedings with a discussion of the link between disability and domesticity, uncovering networks of care and support that, while often working to enclose people with disabilities within a private, domestic sphere, also permitted them to live fuller lives. Attention then turns to the poor, with Samantha Hunter and Allan Kennedy offering a focused case study of ecclesiastical poor relief in rural East Fife. They demonstrate the flexibility and relative compassion underpinning treatment of the poor and, by extension, the opportunities available to them for mitigating marginal status. We then turn to issues of race. Thomas Tyson in Chapter 3 explores the persecution of Romani people under James VI, arguing that this transformed the social position of Scottish 'Egyptians', confining them more firmly than ever before to the social and legal periphery. Kevin Hall then asks what happened when social standing was lost, a dynamic he explores by reconstructing the lives of two Edinburgh burgesses caught up in reputation-shredding scandals. Finally in this part, Matthew Lee reconstructs the experiences of enslaved and formerly enslaved young people, and shows how, despite their acutely challenging circumstances, they often made strenuous efforts to exert autonomy.

The book's second part concentrates on 'occupational margins'; that is, on experiences of social marginality rooted in economic function. Aaron Allan's essay on 'unfree' workers explores the liminal space that allowed skilled but unlicensed individuals to make a living in the context of a corporatist economic model. This ambiguity of status – accepted, but only within strict limits – is carried forward into Laura Doak's study, which uses a trio of case studies to explore the lot of arguably the most reviled (but also indispensable) workers of the age: public executioners. Deepening this

---

Two Towns', in E.P. Dennison, D. Ditchburn and M. Lynch (eds), *Aberdeen Before 1800: A New History* (East Linton, 2002), pp. 111–28; K.J. Cullen, C.A. Whatley and M. Young, 'Battered but Unbowed – Dundee during the Seventeenth Century', in C. McKean, B. Harris and C.A. Whatley (eds), *Dundee: Renaissance to Enlightenment* (Dundee, 2009), pp. 84–110; C. Whatley, 'Work, Time and Pastimes', in Foyster and Whatley, *A History of Everyday Life in Scotland*, pp. 273–303; A. Allen, *Building Early Modern Edinburgh: A Social History of Craftwork and Incorporation* (Edinburgh, 2018).

theme of socio-economic unacceptability, Susanne Weston examines sex work, an occupation that was anathema to early modern values, but which also afforded some women rare opportunities for economic stability and the development of independent support networks. Finally, Robert Tree explores coal mine workers, a cohort labouring under a uniquely restrictive legal framework, but which, as Tree notes, still found ways to express autonomy and engage actively with the world around them.

Part III – 'contemplating marginality' – adopts a more conceptual style, offering three contrasting explorations of the ways that marginality as an idea was constructed and negotiated. Allan Kennedy focuses on the issue of mobility, tracing the inherent 'othering' of itinerant people in early modern society, but stressing as well how this impulse stood in constant tension with a desire to welcome the (im)migrant and profit from their skills or contributions. A quite different approach is adopted by Martha McGill, who provides a close reading of the somewhat eccentric spiritual diary of Rachel Brown (b. 1712). Brown, in McGill's analysis, used her diary as a space to negotiate her identity and to challenge – albeit with limited real-word impact – the marginalised position of women in early modern society. The part – and volume – is brought to a close by Lucy Hinnie, who presents a queer reading of James VI and the poetic circle around him. This exercise, Hinnie contends, not only helps us recover often-hidden queer experiences, but also allows for a fuller understanding of James, both as man and king.

Collectively and individually, these studies significantly expand our understanding of marginal populations in early modern Scotland, providing new insights into both the rationale for confining certain groups to the social periphery, and the mechanisms by which this was achieved. At the same time, the limits of marginality, and the myriad ways in which deprived peoples were able to wield agency, is a recurring theme of the book. This is not, of course, the last word on early modern marginality in Scotland; instead, the authors hope that the new vistas opened up in this volume will stimulate further research, allowing scholars to recover still more of the lives and experiences of those lowly, downtrodden, or disadvantaged Scots who have so long been overlooked.

Part I

Social Margins

1

Disability and the Domestic Sphere in Early Modern Scotland

Charlotte Holmes

The domestic sphere was the basis of early modern Scottish society. It was the place where a person ate, drank, worked, prayed, and slept. To complete the ordinary tasks of living, members of the household negotiated the space of the house and the surrounding area. The heads of the household, usually a husband and wife, held responsibility for their dependants, including the provision of care, which fell mostly to the housewife to accomplish. Depending on the wealth and needs of the household, dependants could comprise children, servants, animals, or all three. It was where people lived, including people with disabilities.

Discussions of disability have influenced British historical studies from at least the 1990s.[1] Since then, disability historians have worked to bring people with disabilities into the historical narrative. A large amount of the resulting disability history focuses on the nineteenth century with its increased documentation and urbanisation.[2] Scholars have looked earlier, however, using creativity and a variety of sources to find a relatively hidden portion of a population.[3] For example, monster studies has been used to make sense of the historical position of the disabled.[4] These scholars are careful to emphasise that using this lens is not intended to conflate the categories of 'disabled' and 'monster'. Rather, they contend that disability can be found encoded in descriptions of the monstrous in pre-modern Western Europe.

In Scotland, there are at present two major strands of early modern disability history.[5] One is the care of those with disabilities. Christopher Langley

---

[1] Arguably, this is because Henri-Jacques Stiker's work was translated into English for the first time: H. Stiker, *A History of Disability*, trans. W. Sayers (Ann Arbor, MI, 1999).
[2] See for example, I. Hutchison, *A History of Disability in Nineteenth-Century Scotland* (Lewiston, NY, 2007). For a recent example using the Industrial Revolution as a timeframe, see K. Bohata et al. (eds), *Disability in Industrial Britain: A Cultural and Literary History of Impairment in the Coal Industry, 1880–1948* (Manchester, 2020).
[3] There is an interesting line of inquiry in asking why people with disabilities are relatively hidden in historical sources. One of the explanations includes the idea of 'masking', whereby a person with disabilities appears as non-disabled because they develop coping mechanisms to operate within society. See T.A. Siebers, *Disability Theory* (Ann Arbor, MI, 2008), p. 101.
[4] R.H. Godden and A.S. Mittman (eds), *Embodied Difference: Monstrosity, Disability, and the Posthuman in the Medieval and Early Modern World* (Cham, 2019).
[5] It should also be noted that some work has been done on the Renaissance: J.

devotes a chapter to disability in his *Cultures of Care*, exploring the interactions between ecclesiastical institutions and parishioners with disabilities during the seventeenth century.[6] Langley looks at informal networks of care, but the construction of devoted sick hospitals and institutions in the late eighteenth century encouraged more formal care of those with disabilities. In his seminal book on madness, Rab Houston discusses this development, but also notes that studying disability helps scholars to understand how early modern Scottish people defined their own mental world in relation to those they deemed mentally incapable.[7] This argument points to the second strand within Scottish disability studies, which highlights early modern and Enlightenment philosophical writing and its use of disability to help define what it is to be human. Esme Cleall and Onni Gust have been the most recent scholars to explore this deployment of disability in Enlightenment thought, establishing that it helped philosophers question the boundaries of humanity and, as a result, constructed a 'hierarchy of embodiment'.[8]

This previous scholarship has tended, however, to look at external engagements with disability. This chapter, by contrast, uses the domestic sphere to explore internal and more intimate experiences. As the building block of society, the domestic sphere as a framework allows basic but important questions to be asked. Using domestic papers from elite households and ecclesiastical and secular court documents, this chapter argues that people with disabilities were present within early modern Scottish society and navigated social and spatial relationships. These negotiations reveal their dichotomous and emotional experiences. Mining the sources, as well as working to a broad definition of 'disability', this chapter also seeks to demonstrate the range of avenues available to scholars for finding disability in early modern Scotland. Instead of providing the definitive answer, I hope to encourage further discussion on the topic. The chapter will begin by discussing the evidence of a variety of impairments and disabilities in early modern Scotland. Then, it will explore how people with disabilities navigated the domestic sphere. Finally, it will discuss how kinship networks, the Church, and the community cared for people with disabilities. Through this, it is hoped that the experience of disability will emerge, along with a clearer picture of how households managed the care of those with disabilities in a society that was certainly not set up for them.[9]

Secmezsoy-Urquhart, '"Off evere full that in this regeone duellis": The Neurodiverse Natural Court Fool's Vital Relationship with Scottish Stewart and British Stuart Rulers, 1488–1649' (unpublished MSc thesis, University of Edinburgh, 2019).

[6] C.R. Langley, *Cultures of Care: Domestic Welfare, Discipline and the Church of Scotland, c. 1600–1689* (Leiden, 2020), chapter 5.

[7] R.A. Houston, *Madness and Society in Eighteenth-Century Scotland* (Oxford, 2000), p. 8.

[8] E. Cleall and O. Gust, 'Disability as a Problem of Humanity in Scottish Enlightenment Thought', *The Historical Journal*, 65 (2022), 328–48, at p. 348.

[9] It is worth noting that the discipline of the history of medicine informs this chapter's analysis. Some scholars may see this as contributing to a medicalisation of disability,

Early Modern Disability

While the discussion around disability is complex, it is important quickly to sketch some of the sociological theory and its implications for the study of disability in history scholarship. Some scholars follow the social model of disability – sometimes called the British model – which distinguishes between 'disability' and 'impairment': disability is socially constructed, while impairment describes the bodily difference.[10] Others have viewed this separation as unhelpful. They have called for a collapsing of this dichotomy to acknowledge the embodied *and* lived experience of individuals.[11] But, some separation of the body and society allows scholars to discuss how these concepts cooperate and clash in ways that further and spark discourse.

As indicated above, scholarship increasingly has demonstrated the presence of impairment throughout history even without a large body of overt evidence: the silence in sources does not indicate absence, and careful reading of sources can be highly revealing. For example, early modern housewives kept recipe books, containing culinary, household, and medical recipes. The medical portion of these collections indicate the presence of debilitating diseases, which could lead to impairment and disability. Jean Wemyss, countess of Angus and then Sutherland, noted two recipes from different physicians to make a 'salve for the Rickets in Childeren', demonstrating both the presence of this condition, and the fact that she sought at least two different opinions regarding its treatment.[12] Recipe books also imply instances of accidents within a house, which could cause impairments. In one anonymous collection, Lucatella's (or Locatelli's) balsam is noted as good for 'any burning or scalding [by] anointing the place with a feather'.[13] Householders could have used this balsam for servants and cooks who worked closely with fire, either in preparing food or building fires for their masters, who would have been particularly susceptible to such injuries. But more generally, open fires posed a threat to all householders as sources of impairment. Rather than highlighting specific examples, recipe collections imply the possibility of disability in every day early modern life and the fear of it.

---

something I do not want to do. By using the framework of disease, medical historians often treat disability as something to be cured and the person as a 'victim' of their disability. Additionally, I have made every effort to avoid the victimisation of disability in the following analysis, but the source material may use such language. When quoting sources, I have maintained this language for accuracy, but otherwise I have attempted to use more nuanced terminology.

[10] First proposed by M. Oliver in his *Social Work with Disabled People* (London, 1983).
[11] See B. Hughes and K. Paterson, 'The Social Model of Disability and the Disappearing Body: Towards a Sociology of Impairment', *Disability & Society*, 12:3 (1997), 325–40, particularly at p. 326; T. Shakespeare, *Disability Rights and Wrongs Revisited*, 2nd edn (London, 2014), p. 2 and p. 5; R. Garland-Thomson, 'Feminist Disability Studies', *Journal of Women in Culture and Society*, 30:2 (2005), 1557–87, at p. 1559.
[12] NLS, MS 3031, Book of Recipes started by Anna, Lady Elcho, fol. 59v.
[13] Folger Shakespeare Library, Washington, DC, V.a.697, Recipe Book c.1660s–1680s, pp. 40–1.

In addition, life writing often includes narratives of diseases that could cause impairment and disability. Renowned for her medical expertise, the sick and their families often sought the advice of the autobiographer Anne Halkett (d. 1699). Alongside her autobiography, she created extensive spiritual writings within which scholars can also find information about her medical activities. She wrote that a gentleman brought his young son to her because 'efter the Poxe and Measels, [he] had all most Lost his sight'.[14] Complete blindness, therefore, could be the result of surviving otherwise mortal diseases, making the sufferer appear to not fully recover.

Recipe books and life writing are not the only places in which historians can find acquired disability in early modern Scotland. Political and ecclesiastical records indicate the presence and needs of soldiers with acquired impairments returning from wars. Langley has discussed the response of the welfare system to the Civil Wars, concluding that veterans relied on a combination of financial support and practical care in a variety of contexts.[15] In July 1644, parliament created the 'Act in favour of lame soldiers', which provided maintenance for soldiers 'disabled from their ordinary employments and working in their several callings and crafts and have no other means of maintenance for themselves'.[16] Soldiers returning from wars posed financial and social welfare conundrums for government institutions.

Consulting a variety of sources also reveals those who were born with impairments and disabilities. The Edinburgh burgh council minutes noted in January 1690 that Thomas Gowdie became an inmate at Trinity Hospital. It was also indicated that Thomas was 'born blind and hes ane exceiding good memorie bot [he was] unable to doe anything for a mentinance for himself'.[17] Certain examples of fairy changelings – human babies replaced by fairies – could be evidence of congenital disability. Lady Halkett wrote in her meditations of a child who was brought to her, describing it as 'spent' because it looked 'as if itt had beene dead as many months as itt was old, so leane & wrinckled & ill Coulered was itt'.[18] She continued that 'if I did beleeue what ordinary people much affirme of chilldrens beeing changed by fairys that had beene as euident a testimony as any that I euer Saw'.[19] Scholars have attempted to retrospectively diagnose these examples of fairy changelings. Susan Schoon Eberly connected the symptoms to a variety of diseases and impairments, including progeria and cystic fibrosis.[20] The idea that fairy

---

[14] NLS, MS 6501, 'Select and Occationall Obseruations', p. 230.
[15] C.R. Langley, 'Caring for Soldiers, Veterans and Families in Scotland, 1638–1651', *History*, 102:349 (January 2017), 5–23, at p. 9, 23.
[16] Ibid., p. 12.
[17] *Edinburgh Recs.*, vol. 12, p. 27.
[18] Anne, Lady Halkett, *Lady Anne Halkett, Selected Self-Writings*, ed. S. Trill (Farnham, 2007), p. 5.
[19] Ibid.
[20] S.S. Eberly, 'Fairies and the Folklore of Disability: Changelings, Hybrids, and the Solitary Fairy', *Folklore*, 99:1 (1988), 63–7.

changelings might have had congenital or acquired disability is certainly a fruitful avenue and warrants more research and development.

Mental illness, either developed or congenital, was also present in early modern Scotland and disabled sufferers. In Beatrix Leslie's witchcraft trial, the court was told that, in about 1661, Jon Watherston's house in Blackcoat caught fire, causing him to fall 'in that distemper that often he attempted to tak his owne lyfe, bot his wyfe watched him and delyvered him 5 tymes; untill about a year after, his wyfe going out of the house bot a start, she found him hanged in the house'.[21] The contemporary explanation blamed Beatrix Leslie, accusing her of bewitchment, but through a modern lens, Jon clearly suffered from some type of mental health issue brought on by the stressful and socially debilitating experience of a house fire. Therefore, studying witchcraft trials for their purported victims can reveal examples of disability.

Mental illness is fairly visible in sources, but other mental impairments prove tricky. In particular, discerning intellectual disability from sources is difficult because discussions and diagnoses are modern and evolving. But there is no reason to assume that it was not also present. Rab Houston and Uta Frith argue effectively for the presence of autism or autism spectrum disorder in the eighteenth century, using the case study of Hugh Blair of Borgue (1708/9–65).[22] Hugh was at the centre of a lawsuit, which sought to determine if he was capable of being married. In the court records, witnesses remarked on how Hugh interacted with the world, emphasising the codes of behaviour that he broke. For instance, Hugh tended to speak in short utterances consisting of one or two words, which he usually repeated; he also spoke of himself in the third person.[23] Less documented cases also provide evidence of intellectual disability: in 1686, Duncan, eldest son of the 1st earl of Breadalbane and Holland, was passed over in the succession because he was deemed incapable.[24] It is unclear why Breadalbane regarded Duncan as unable to mask his impairment, but certainly skipping the line of succession was not an easy process and thus the earl must have seen Duncan as having some disability. While it might not be possible to be specific, intellectual disability obviously existed in early modern Scotland and secular court documents can be used to find it.

After finding people with disabilities, scholars can begin to understand their experience of living within early modern society. The language used by early modern people to describe impairment encoded difference. In his account book, John Lauder, Lord Fountainhall (d. 1722) noted the provision of six pence to 'criple Robin' in 1673.[25] It is unclear how exactly Robin was

---

[21] NRS, High Court Processes, 1661, JC26/27/9/19.
[22] R. Houston and U. Frith, *Autism in History: The Case of Hugh Blair of Borgue* (Oxford, 2000).
[23] Ibid., 152. For his 'odd' behaviours, see pp. 150–4.
[24] G.E. Cockayne, *The Complete Peerage of England, Scotland, Ireland, Great Britain and the United Kingdom* (7 vols, London, 1887–98), vol. 2, p. 14.
[25] John Lauder, *Journals of Sir John Lauder, Lord Fountainhall*, ed. Donald Crawford (Edinburgh, 1900), p. 270.

impaired, although it can be assumed that he had some form of limb difference. Robin was no longer just himself but rather defined by his difference. In July 1736, the Fordyce kirk session records gave a 'poor man without arms' 8s.[26] In other entries from the same year, the clerk described people who received funds as 'poor man', highlighting that the distinguishing feature was not that the man was poor, but that he had a limb difference. Describing people based on their difference pushes them to the margins of society even if they were able to participate within its structures. Labelling someone by their disability was thus inherently othering.

In addition, when seeking explanations for physical disability in children, early modern people often blamed the parents, focusing attention on the mother. In this way, parents and children shared in the othering of impairments. It was believed in the Highlands, for example, that a harelip occurred when an expectant mother was frightened by a hare.[27] Not explicitly disability, but diseases and poor constitutions could be transferred from parent to child. The physician William Buchan wrote in his *Domestic Medicine: Or, The Family Physician* (1769) that 'diseased parents cannot beget healthy children', adding that 'on the constitution of mothers depends originally that of their offspring'.[28] Buchan does not detail the symptoms, but it is not an incredible conclusion to draw that early modern people believed congenital disability passed in similar ways.

The blaming of parents was rooted, in part, in beliefs about God's providence: God actively governed his creation, and this could be used to explain both favourable and unfavourable circumstances.[29] Pertinent to this chapter, early modern Scottish people saw God's providence in disability as well. George Turnbull, minister of Alloa and Tyninghame, wrote in his diary on the 28 June 1702 of a John Nisbett who was 'formerly a pretty sober lad a merchant in the place [Tyninghame] [who] fell distracted and was possessd with such a spirit of Blasphemy and cursing that it was terrible to hear him and yet he was not furious'. Turnbull described Nisbett's plight as 'a very unusual and sad providence'.[30] In Turnbull's estimation, God had seen fit to punish John for a transgression, but had not yet made him 'furious', or completely insane. He also saw providence in his own son's escape from a potentially fatal or disabling experience: 'My son Will, mett with a very mercifull providence, being in the chamber alone att the fire his cloths tooke

---

[26] NRS, CH2/1114/2, Fordyce Kirk Session Records, p. 418.
[27] James Kirkwood and Edward Lhuyd, *A Collection of Highland Rites and Customes*, ed. J. Lorne Campbell (Cambridge, 1975), p. 77. The English shared this belief: Nicholas Culpeper, the famous English medical writer, mentioned it in his work on midwifery. Nicholas Culpeper, *Directory for Midwives* (London, 1651), p. 109.
[28] William Buchan, *Domestic Medicine: Or, the Family Physician* (London, 1769), p. 9.
[29] M. McGill and A. Raffe, 'The Uses of Providence in Early Modern Scotland', in J. Goodare and M. McGill (eds), *The Supernatural in Early Modern Scotland* (Manchester, 2020), pp. 160–77, at pp. 160–1.
[30] George Turnbull, *The Diary of John [George] Turnbull, Minister of Alloa and Tyninghame 1657–1704*, ed. R. Paul (Edinburgh, 1893), p. 418.

low, and were all burnt, his hair, and very eylids scorcht, and yet his face and wholle body untouched.'[31] In this case, Turnbull understood his son as being divinely saved from difficult circumstances. Providence explained why certain members of society became or were born impaired in a world without many other explanations. It was a powerful explanatory tool for many situations, but it could also lead certain portions of society to be ostracised because, either in behaviour or appearance, they possessed visual embodiments of God's disapproval.

There was also a connection between disability and the supernatural, particularly the 'second sight' or ability to predict the future. The 'blind seer' trope does not appear to have been overly present in early modern Scotland.[32] Other senses, however, could predict future events, including sound and smell.[33] Interestingly, contemporary commentators viewed nonverbal people – sometimes accompanied by deafness – as being particularly susceptible to second sight. John Fraser wrote in his 1754 treatise on the ability that 'it is found that many dumb Persons foretel many Things beforehand'.[34] The anonymous *The History of the Life and Adventures of Mr Duncan Campbell* (1720) was a biography of a Scot who supposedly was born deaf and nonverbal and was gifted with second sight.[35] There is some debate as to whether Duncan truly could not hear or speak, but nonetheless his biography illustrates the connection often drawn between certain impairments and supernatural ability.[36] These last few examples illustrate that impairment could be othering but used to the person's advantage.

The Domestic Sphere

Importantly, space and wealth affected the type of care that could be carried out within the house for those who required it. In the larger houses of the wealthy, and particularly in rural areas, people with disabilities could be enclosed, literally shut off from the rest of society. It is arguable that part of the invisibility of disability in early modern Scotland is due to this enclosure. After being passed over in the line of succession, Duncan Campbell, eldest

---

[31] Ibid., pp. 380–1.
[32] Conversely, scholars have connected the tradition of second sight to eidetic imagery, a clear vision that almost convinces the seer that pictures appearing in the mind are real: S.A. Cohn, 'The Scottish Tradition of Second Sight and other Psychic Experiences in Families' (unpublished PhD thesis, University of Edinburgh, 1996), pp. 244–6.
[33] Ibid., pp. 243–4.
[34] John Fraser, *A Treatise Containing A Description of Deuteroscopia, commonly called the Second Sight* (Edinburgh, 1754), p. 40.
[35] *The History of the Life and Adventures of Mr. Duncan Campbell* (London, 1720). T.F. Henderson and D. Turner in the ODNB credit William Bond with writing the text: 'Campbell, Duncan (c.1680–1730), Soothsayer', ODNB, https://doi.org/10.1093/ref:odnb/4494 [accessed 5 December 2022].
[36] L.J. Davis, *Enforcing Normalcy: Disability, Deafness and the Body* (London, 1995), p. 57.

son of the 1st earl of Breadalbane, was styled Lord Sinclair and later Lord Ormelie. He lived under surveillance and there is not much to suggest any substantial public life.[37] Logically, however, there is little evidence of this practice because the household sought to keep secret the person and their actions. With more space and servants onto whom work could be passed, the wealthy could more easily enclose people with disabilities than could people in lower classes. The space was closed off or impassable, disabling the impaired because they were unable to experience society and their wider world. But perhaps, Breadalbane and his countess understood it as a haven, shielding Duncan from the problems of accessibility.

That is not to imply that those in the lower echelons did not also enclose disabilities to the extent that they could. C.F. Goodey has shown that the early modern English Church discussed disability by questioning whether certain people should participate in the Eucharist.[38] Attending the sermon and taking part in communion were important aspects to early modern Scottish life at every social level, and if someone were excluded from either of these acts, the alternative would be to enclose the person by shutting them off from community and society. After all, since it was forbidden to move around in public during the time of sermon, there was nowhere else to go but the home. The limitations of the source-base, however, make it more difficult to find concrete evidence of such practices among the lower echelons of society, even if we can strongly suspect that they took place.

Some people with disabilities were enclosed by those around them, but others chose to remain in the domestic sphere because of their disability. In an undated petition to the countess of Breadalbane, Christian Macfarlane, or her representative, wrote:

> that the petitioner who is the daughter of very poor people in Fernan has been disabled from her infancy, [cannot] earn her livelyhood by any other means except at her needle, and as she cannot get werk into the house and being unable to travel out, she humbly hopes that your Ladyship may be pleased to consider her case[39]

This petition probably dates to the late eighteenth century, but there is no reason to suspect that such a predicament did not exist in earlier periods.[40] While Christian supposedly could not move outside of the house, she prob-

---

[37] P. Hopkins, 'Campbell, John [called Iain Glas], First Earl of Breadalbane and Holland (1634–1717), Magnate and Politician', *ODNB*, https://doi.org/10.1093/ref:odnb/4512 [accessed 12 December 2022].

[38] C.F. Goodey, 'Exclusion from the Eucharist: The Re-shaping of Idiocy in the Seventeenth-Century Church', in Patrick McDonagh et al. (eds), *Intellectual Disability: A Conceptual History, 1200–1900* (Manchester, 2018), pp. 53–74, at pp. 80–101.

[39] NRS, Breadalbane Muniments, GD112/11/9/3/62.

[40] The land in and around Fearnan was given to the earls of Breadalbane in the 1760s. The use of 'disabled' also points to this being a later petition because the term was not usually used in this way during the period in question for this chapter.

ably navigated the space within the domestic sphere. Because Fearnan was a small rural settlement, the houses would have been the longhouse style, which consisted of either one long rectangular room, or one that was divided in two.[41] Christian would have benefited from the lack of stairs, but it is possible that the floor of the house was earthen and thus uneven. Christian's disability enclosed her because society did not have the proper accommodation for her movement, but also, she dealt with the limitations of her domestic space.

Christian lived within a rural settlement, but people with disabilities living in urban centres also dealt with irregular terrain, and also with stairs. In March 1687, the dean of guild reported to the Edinburgh burgh council about a recently demolished timber tenement building. The land belonged to a merchant and two writers, indicating that multiple people lived within the building, which must have had at least one level for each person. In his report, the dean also mentioned an 'entrie or stair of the celler' connected to the shop on the lowest level.[42] It is not new to argue that Edinburgh buildings were tall but navigating these spaces for someone like Christian, who was unable to move outside of a single storey building, would have been difficult if not impossible. Therefore, it is understandable why many early modern people with disabilities were unhoused, as indicated by the help received by the burgh councils and kirk sessions. The basis of society, the domestic sphere, was unavailable to them because of inaccessibility.

Beyond the physical structure, the domestic sphere consisted of actors: householders and animals negotiated the space either inside the house or in the area around it. In the language referring to households, there was an acceptance of dependence; clerks for example often noted the female householder simply as the wife of her husband. Records indicate that other householders were similarly defined by bodily difference through association. On 6 July 1669, the clerk of the Canongate kirk session noted that 'the crippell boyis mother' was to be warned. The next meeting, on 13 July, she was to be warned for a second time.[43] Unfortunately, the cause of the warning is not clear, but this example remains important. The othering language referred to earlier alienated both those with impairments and the other inhabitants of the household, locking them together socially and perhaps even physically. The domestic sphere, therefore, could become either a haven or a prison. The emotional consequences of this have yet to be fully studied in the early modern Scottish context.

---

[41] For an archaeologist's description of these types of houses, see J.H. Stewart and M.B. Stewart, 'A Highland Longhouse – Lianach, Balquhidder, Perthshire', *Proceedings of the Society of Antiquaries of Scotland*, 118 (1988), 301–17.
[42] *Edinburgh Recs.*, vol. 12, pp. 200–1.
[43] NRS, CH2/122/5, Canongate Kirk Session, 1668–71, pp. 38, 40.

Care in the Domestic Sphere

Care within the house is the meeting point of medical, disability, and domestic history. Each member of the household contributed to providing sustenance, medical treatments, and financial assistance, and the domestic space thus became the accustomed setting for the care of those with disabilities. Indeed, the domestic sphere was considered so vital to the care of impaired people that the authorities tried to recreate the space and social networks that comprised that framework. In May 1698, the minutes for the barony court of Urie noted 'Robert Barclay and his said balzie appoints and ordans ane peck and ane halfe peck of meal to be given weekly to Riachel [sic] Lightoune, in Glithno, blind woman, and ane servant to attend her'.[44] Instead of expelling people from the community, authorities took steps to provide care in a way that would help them preserve their domestic environment.

In other cases, the community cared for a person with disabilities by providing physical shelter where none existed before. Prior to the widespread availability of institutions like poor hospitals, Scottish authorities 'boarded out', placing people within an already established domestic space, with the householder being paid for their services. Even during the rise of institutions in the nineteenth and twentieth centuries, boarding out continued, illustrating that it was viewed positively or at least as an effective measure. Rab Houston has traced this practice to the mid-eighteenth century, but there is evidence that it was occurring still earlier.[45] On 28 June 1653, an elder of Canongate parish was asked to visit a 'Leprose boy' in his quarter and to enquire how much money the woman who currently housed him required for his upkeep.[46] There are two curious aspects to this case. Firstly, it was understood in the early modern period that leprosy was contagious; and secondly, the records do not indicate the relationship between the boy and the woman. For the former, it can be argued that instead of leprosy, the child perhaps suffered from an unsightly skin condition that proved as disabling as leprosy. For the latter, the session records usually noted relationships between subjects, and as none exists in this record, the woman most likely took the child in as a form of charitable care and was not related to him. The woman, therefore, provided an alternative domestic sphere for the child, allowing him to participate in a vital aspect of early modern Scottish society while gaining shelter and sustenance. But there must have been an adjustment period as strangers became accustomed to each other in a relationship with an inherent power imbalance.

If the opportunity to board out was not available, people with disabilities could live within a penal institution as a quasi-lodger, essentially accessing a

---

[44] D.G. Barron (ed.), *The Court Book of the Barony of Urie in Kincardineshire, 1604–1747* (Edinburgh, 1892), p. 103.
[45] R.A. Houston, '"Not simple boarding": Care of the Mentally Incapacitated in Scotland during the Eighteenth Century', in P. Bartlett and D. Wright (eds), *Outside the Walls of the Asylum: The History of Care in the Community, 1750–2000* (London, 1999), pp. 19–44.
[46] NRS, CH2/122/4, Canongate Kirk Session, 1649–68, p. 111.

surrogate domestic sphere. In such cases, the provision remained beneficial but was perhaps not quite as desirable. In 1684, the Edinburgh burgh council gave the tack (lease) of the correction house to Robert Mowbray, a silk-weaver. They tasked him with maintaining 'these that are criple or blind for two shilling Scots dayly And these that are able and sturdie begars to mentain them for Twelve pennies scots dayly'.[47] The distinction between the lodgers underlines how far disability could act as a defining feature. But this example also illustrates the complicating factors of providing for people institutionally in this period. For one, there needed to be a big enough space in which many people could live. For another, the motivations of the person in charge become questionable: why was a silk-weaver taking charge of the correction house? Such practical difficulties, however, did not alter the underlying desire of local authorities to provide care for people with disabilities in a quasi-domestic sphere wherever possible.

When this was not possible, the alternative was not especially desirable: people with disabilities were sometimes forced to beg and become vagrants. The minutes of the general assembly in May 1728 illustrate that early modern people understood this possibility. When the Royal College of Physicians of Edinburgh came before them asking for voluntary contributions to the 'Infirmary or Hospital for Diseased Poor at Edinburgh', the representatives argued for the necessity of the institutions by highlighting that:

> many poor tradesmen, servants, apprentices, journeymen, and labourers, who casually meet with fractures, bruises, wounds, dislocations, or do fall into sickness, may, by the blessing of God, and the timeous application of proper medicines, be recovered and restored to health and strength, who, through the want of such help, become beggars, or a burden upon their friends or the public[48]

The authorities were therefore willing to explore providing purely financial support for people with disabilities, but it nonetheless remained the case that creating a surrogate domestic sphere was generally regarded as the best response.

Importantly, any help from the community placed a burden of responsibility on the person to help themselves as much as possible. There was an expectation with most people with disabilities that the kirk session treasury bolstered their income rather than providing their sole source of revenue. In July 1681, the clerk for Edinburgh's burgh council noted:

> Upon petition given in be James Keith a blind boy whoe inclynes to learning and hes com some lenth by the ear appoynts John Murray present kirk thesaurer to put him to some school master and pay his quarter payment

---

[47] *Edinburgh Recs.*, vol. 11, p. 106.
[48] *Acts of the General Assembly of the Church of Scotland 1638–1842* (Edinburgh, 1843), pp. 601–2.

And to aggree with some person for his mentinance quarterly and pay the same during the Councells pleasure.[49]

While not strictly earning a wage, as a student James would have learned skills to enable him to earn an income for himself later in life. The council clearly believed in his ability enough to warrant payment towards his schooling. This type of payment aligns with studies on the 'deserving' poor in Scotland, but also shows that people with disabilities could both benefit from financial help from community sources and adapt to society to live a more independent life.[50]

Much early modern medical care occurred in the domestic sphere, sometimes under the guidance of medical professionals trying to offer advice on when disability might be cured. William Buchan wrote in his *Domestic Medicine* that 'persons who are born deaf are seldom cured. When deafness is the effect of wounds or ulcers in the ear, or of old age, it is not easily removed.' But he then listed several causes of deafness, such as fever and coldness of the head, in which cases the deafness could be cured.[51] Archibald Campbell, bishop of Aberdeen's collection, compiled largely between 1709 and 1732, contains a recipe entitled 'To Cure Deafness if Cureable', indicating that the efficacy of the recipe was related to the permanency of the hearing loss.[52] George Hume of Kimmerghame, conversely, wrote in his diary that George Baillie of Jerviswood 'has been at Prestonpans sweating in a saltpans returned to toune yesterday, and is very much the better of it, and is better of his deafness that troubled him'.[53] George Baillie was only thirty-three, therefore his difficulty with hearing was perhaps not due to age.

Mental illness appears often to have been considered short-term and thus curable. In the witchcraft accusation of Jean Thomson (Borg, 1658), James Thomson – seemingly no relation – suffered a madness twelve years earlier that:

> continued for the space of 20 dayes, sometymes beating all that came nigh him, sometymes hanging and climbing upon the bed posts, sometymes excessively laughing, sometymes running out naked: till upon the menaceing of a young woman Agnes Sprot (who then was servant unto his father) Jean came and clapped and said God mak thee well my boy and at that very instant he setled (though when she came in he was in his mad fitt beating a woman with a staff) and from that tyme recovered day by day and shortly after he came to his perfect health and wits.[54]

[49] *Edinburgh Recs.*, vol. 11, p. 22.
[50] J. McCallum, *Poor Relief and the Church in Scotland, 1560–1650* (Edinburgh, 2018), chapter 7.
[51] Bucan, *Domestic Medicine*, pp. 550–1.
[52] NLS, MS 3773, Recipe Book of Archibald Campbell, p. 91.
[53] NRS, Miscellaneous Collections, GD1/649/2, p. 56.
[54] NRS, High Court Processes, 1659, JC26/26/4/8.

This instance illustrates that insanity could be relatively temporary – twenty days – but still leave a legacy, in this case being vividly remembered and conditioning the way the community responded to the individual for the space of twelve years. It is difficult to know how 'perfect' James's wits were, particularly because of the circumstances in which his impairment came to light. The courts certainly had a vested interest in illustrating James's tenuous health.

As discussed above, disability could be enclosed within the domestic sphere, but some of the treatments involved travelling some distance from the household. Many water sources were associated with healing mental illness, including, for example, St Fillan's Well and Loch Maree. The bell of St Fillan would be placed on the sufferer's head in a ritual meant to cure the ailment.[55] But, as Langley has highlighted, it was often not the sufferer who was punished by the kirk and community, but the carer. He cites an example from Perth Presbytery, which in 1664 sought advice from the archbishop for a punishment befitting the crime of taking a mentally ill boy to a well for a cure.[56] Thus, a mentally ill person was deemed incapable of decision and movement for treatment – a form of enclosure – and the carer was subjected to more social scrutiny as they left the relative safety of the domestic sphere. The fact that carers and others sought such treatments also indicates the belief that domestic medical treatment was insufficient in some cases.

Medical treatment beyond the domestic sphere could be perilous for people with disabilities as the early modern medical marketplace grew. There appears to have been many medical practitioners who touted knowledge in curing disabilities. For one of his recipes for deafness, Archibald Campbell noted that 'My Author gott it of the famous woman In Chelsey who Lived by Cureing Ears of Deafness for many years, he cur'd her of Lameness and she gave him her receipt [recipe] with which he Cur'd him selfe when as deaf as a stone'.[57] This woman was not perhaps Scottish, but this example certainly illustrates the renown of people claiming to cure impairments. In the 1690 edition of *Edinburgh's True Almanack*, John Sart advertised his healing 'To all blind People, or others troubled by Distemper in their eyes'.[58] Gaining any sort of notoriety or attempting to advertise cures for certain disabilities indicates that many people sought or needed their help. Unfortunately, in these two sources, only John Sart's methods are clear and perhaps unsettling. He claimed to be able to perform surgery on cataracts 'with so much dexterity and ease, that there is not one in twenty Cries, oh, in the Operation'.[59] Of

---

[55] E. Donoho, 'The Madman amongst the Ruins: The Oral History and Folklore of Traditional Insanity Cures in the Scottish Highlands', *Folklore*, 125:1 (April 2014), 22–39, at pp. 23, 28.
[56] Langley, *Cultures of Care*, p. 147.
[57] NLS, MS 3773, p. 91.
[58] James Paterson, *Edinburgh's True Almanack or a New Prognostication* (Edinburgh, 1690), fol. 7v.
[59] Ibid.

course, people tend to avoid painful and invasive surgeries if possible, and it was a desperate person indeed who sought the help of someone like Sart.[60]

Alternatively, all the above examples can be viewed as a wish for impairment to be temporary: even if the impairment did not last for long, the person and their kinship network felt the effects. The primary impact was financial. Fundamentally, the maintenance of health and provision of medical care could be a difficult challenge for an early modern family. The financial strain from lost labour or increased medical costs disproportionately affected the poorer classes. This was especially the case with chronic illness or disability among children, which deprived the family of the potential for child labour as well as the work of the parent because of the duty to provide the necessary care. Such pressures would certainly have strained relationships between other householders and the person with disabilities.

In addition, documents discussing the care of people with disabilities highlight fears over the potential permanence of the impairment and subsequent disability. In the earlier example of Anne, Lady Halkett and the boy who suffered sight impairment after illness, the father had already brought his son to 'the best Phisitians And found noe good'.[61] In addition, the father brought a letter from Sir Patrick Murray, recommending the child to Anne's care along with another letter written by Murray recommending the minister, Simon Cooper, to pray for the child. The prospect of disability induced enough anxiety for the father to pursue multiple avenues of care, consulting medical practitioners, friends, and a minister. It is not unreasonable to assume that the child felt these parental anxieties. Even if unwell, exploring all options would have been physically and mentally exhausting for the child and would further a sense of othering. There were many concerns regarding the health of a child and there were many ways in which relationships and finances had to be negotiated if a child was sick. There was, therefore, an emotional cost to caring for those with disabilities.

Conclusions

It is perhaps obvious, but it is still important to emphasise that people with disabilities existed in early modern Scotland. If historians read sources 'against the grain', such individuals become very apparent. It is important to reiterate this because much more work could be done on this section of society.

This chapter has looked at disability through the framework of the domestic. As the basis of early modern Scottish society, the domestic sphere shaped the experience of all people and especially people with disabilities. The space and look of the domestic sphere were created by socio-economic circum-

---

[60] L. Whaley, *Women and the Practice of Medical Care in Early Modern Europe, 1400–1800* (Basingstoke, 2011), p. 176.
[61] NLS, MS 6501, p. 230.

stance and living within the space created social bonds between householders. These two aspects of society – the social and the spatial – are arguably the most difficult for people with disabilities to negotiate because these aspects *caused* the disability. The relationship between people with disabilities and the domestic sphere, as well as the care provided within, illuminates many dichotomies about how people with disabilities experienced early modern Scottish society. Their kinship networks, households, and communities enclosed them, but many carers sought treatments far from the domestic sphere. People with disabilities could be cared for within a domestic sphere, or a quasi-domestic sphere, or cast out entirely, forced to become beggars and vagrants. Early modern people also conceived of disability as medical and non-medical depending on severity and type of impairment. This implies people with disabilities and those around them felt hope for a cure and fear of social ostracisation caused by an inability to navigate a world meant for able-bodied people. These dichotomies should not encourage black and white thinking, rather, they illustrate the polarising experience of impaired people in early modern Scottish society. It was possible to live a fulfilled life as defined by the period. But of course, a great deal of struggle and negotiation was required, both socially and physically, to accomplish this. Studying these dynamics can help historians understand the experience of this otherwise silenced portion of society.

2

Relieving the Poor in Mid-Seventeenth-Century East Fife

Samantha Hunter and Allan Kennedy

In the *First Book of Discipline* (1561), Scotland's Protestant reformers committed themselves to caring for the poor. While insisting that the Kirk would not be 'patronis for stubburne and idill beggaris', the *First Book* was clear that offering succour to 'the wedow and fatherless, the aiged, impotent, or laymed' was a special commandment of God , and that therefore the new Protestant Church must make it a priority to offer 'such provisioun' that 'of oure aboundance should [the poor's] indigence be releaved'.[1] Despite such high-flown rhetoric, the conventional historiographical assessment was that the poor relief system Scotland eventually developed, administered wholly by the Kirk and almost completely reliant for its funding on voluntary giving at the church door, was essentially a failure. For T.C. Smout, it was 'weak and mean', and indeed 'the very opposite from what had been intended by the reformers'.[2] Larry Patriquin is still more dismissive, arguing that there was effectively no poor law in early modern Scotland. This he attributes to the country's social, economic, and political under-development, and it meant that no reliable assistance was offered to the poor until the nineteenth century.[3] Much of the most important articulation of these ideas has come, however, from Rosalind Mitchison. For her, the inadequacy of the poor laws meant that Scotland was left with a chaotic, disjointed system, marked by chronic under-funding and inefficiency and consequently unable to offer proper care for the needy. This structure, Mitchison suggests, looks even worse when Scotland is compared to England, which over the same period was developing exactly the kind of statutory, secular poor-relief system to which Scotland unsuccessfully aspired.[4]

These pessimistic conclusions were, however, unduly influenced by the rhetoric of poor-relief legislation. It is certainly the case that Scotland's formal poor laws, especially as embodied in the key 1579 'Act for the

---

[1] D. Laing (ed.), *The Works of John Knox* (6 vols, Edinburgh, 1895), vol. 2, pp. 200–01.
[2] T.C. Smout, *A History of the Scottish People, 1560–1830* (London, 1969), p. 94.
[3] L. Patriquin, 'Why Was There No "Old Poor Law" in Scotland and Ireland?', *Journal of Peasant Studies*, 33:2 (2006), 219–47.
[4] R. Mitchison, *The Old Poor Law in Scotland: The Experience of Poverty, 1574–1845* (Edinburgh, 2000).

Punishment of Strong and Idle Beggars', were notably harsh, focusing largely on the punishment of beggars and making only vague and minimalistic provision for the genuinely needy.[5] It is also undeniable that Scotland, lacking the relative centralisation or bureaucratisation of England, was never able to build a secular or statutory system. Yet more recent scholarship, in focusing on the real-life mechanics of poor relief rather than the theoretical or legislative framework, has presented a less gloomy picture. John McCallum, in particular, argues persuasively that, at least outside periods of subsistence crisis, the Scottish system was in fact broadly effective in relieving the poor, precisely because its decentralised, largely uncodified nature made it nimble and locally responsive.[6] This revisionist impulse has been reinforced by a number of local case studies, which between them have underlined the point that Scotland's voluntary, Church-based poor relief system generally performed better than the conventional account allowed, with its great advantage being its ability to respond quickly to highly specific circumstances.[7]

Most of this revisionism, however, is based upon either high-level surveys of poor relief practice, or on urban case studies. We currently know little about how poor relief worked in more rural areas, and it is this gap which the present chapter seeks to address. Focusing in-depth on how kirk sessions responded to the poor in rural East Fife between 1640 and 1680, it will underline the recent trend towards rehabilitating Scottish poor relief.[8] It demonstrates that, while never in a position to draw upon lavish funding, sessions were nonetheless able to care consistently for the local poor, and to do so in a manner that was far more flexible, forward-looking, and often generous than either conventional accounts or the letter of the law would allow. In doing so, the chapter not only underlines the disconnect between (harsh) rhetoric and (compassionate) reality in terms of poor relief, but also speaks to the ambivalence of marginality: the poor, while clearly a 'marginalised' social group, were certainly not cut off from wider society, and were instead able to draw upon the mechanisms of poor relief to maintain their social presence and position.

---

[5] *RPS*, 1579/10/27.
[6] J. McCallum, *Poor Relief and the Church in Scotland, 1560–1650* (Edinburgh, 2018).
[7] R.E. Tyson, 'Poverty and Poor Relief in Aberdeen, 1680–1705', *Scottish Archives*, 8 (2002), 33–42; K. Wilbraham and C. Lodge, 'Responses to Poverty in Ayrshire, 1574–1845', *Scottish Archives*, 8 (2002), 57–70; L. Stewart, 'Poor Relief in Edinburgh and the Famine in 1621–24', *International Review of Scottish Studies*, 30 (2007), 5–41; J. McCallum, 'Charity and Conflict: Poor Relief in Mid-Seventeenth-Century Dundee', *SHR*, 95:1 (2016), 30–56.
[8] The parishes considered in this study, determined largely by record survival, are: Anstruther Easter; Auchtermuchty; Crail; Dairsie; Dunbog; Dunino; Elie; Ferryport; Kemback; Kilconquhar; Leuchars; Pittenweem; St Leonards; and St Monans.

Ordinary Relief

In theory, poor relief in Scotland was available only to the 'impotent' poor – that is, people physically or mentally unable to work for their sustenance. All other kinds of supplicant were classed as 'idle' poor and not technically entitled to assistance under any circumstances.[9] As we will see shortly, the divide between 'impotent' and 'idle' poor – an enduring component of the Scottish approach that would carry over into the New Poor Law after 1845 – was not as stark as the letter of the law implied.[10] But there was also a fundamental division in early modern thinking between what McCallum has characterised as the 'ordinary' poor, meaning those entered on the poor roll and receiving continuous relief, and the 'extraordinary' poor, who were not regular pensioners but were nonetheless given relief on a one-off or emergency basis.[11] In the parishes of East Fife, it is possible to reconstruct some general patterns as to the composition of the 'ordinary' poor. Collectively across all parishes, for example, it is clear that – notwithstanding the familiar stereotype of the widowed female poor-relief recipient – numbers of male and female pensioners were broadly similar throughout the period.[12] The figures diverged occasionally: for instance, there was a spike in male pensioner-payments in the late mid- to late-1660s, presumably serving a population of ex-soldiers following the Civil Wars and Restoration, while the number of female pensioners was slightly higher in the mid-1670s, likely a consequence of the Second Anglo-Dutch War creating more abandoned wives and war widows. But these were temporary aberrations, and seen in the round, there is nothing to suggest any particular gender bias in the admission of parishioners to the poor rolls.

[9] Smout, *History of the Scottish People*, p. 90.
[10] B. Harris, 'Parsimony and Pauperism: Poor Relief in England, Scotland and Wales in the Nineteenth and Early Twentieth Centuries', *Journal of Scottish Historical Studies*, 39:1 (2019), 40–74.
[11] McCallum, *Poor Relief and the Church*, p. 168.
[12] All analysis in this chapter is based on the following sources: NRS, CH2/625/1, Anstruther Easter Kirk Session Minutes, 1654–69; NRS, CH2/625/2, Anstruther Easter Kirk Session Minutes, 1668–1710; NRS, CH2/24/1, Auchtermuchty Kirk Session Minutes, 1649–58, NRS, CH2/1543/1, Crail Kirk Session Minutes, 1648–84; NRS, CH2/427/1, Dairsie Kirk Session Minutes, 1648–1704; NRS, CH2/102/1, Dunbog Kirk Session Minutes, 1666–1730; NRS, CH2/405/1, Dunino Kirk Session Minutes, 1647–97; NRS, CH2/1581/1/1, Elie Kirk Session Minutes, 1639–53; NRS, CH2/1581/1/2, Elie Kirk Session Minutes, 1653–85; NRS, CH2/150/1, Ferryport Kirk Session Minutes, 1640–74; NRS, CH2/204/1, Kenback Kirk Session Minutes, 1657–65; NRS, CH2/210/1, Kilconquhar Kirk Session Minutes, 1637–53; NRS, CH2/210/2, Kilconquhar Kirk Session Minutes, 1653–66; NRS, CH2/210/3, Kilconquhar Kirk Session Minutes, 1673–79; NRS, CH2/1209/1, Leuchars Kirk Session Minutes, 1665–77; NRS, CH2/833/2, Pittenweem Kirk Session Minutes, 1653–5; NRS, CH2/1561/1, St Leonards Kirk Session Minutes, 1663–95; NRS, CH2/1056/2, St Monans Kirk Session Minutes, 1641–60; NRS, CH2/1056/3, St Monans Kirk Session Minutes, 1665–82.

The age range of 'ordinary' pensioners is more difficult to establish, largely because kirk session minutes only made a specific effort to record individuals' ages when they were either very old or very young. For example, in 1678 Anstruther Easter stated that £1 10s had been given to 'a distrest old man' named John Wood, while Dunino and Kemback both gave 12s to a poor child who was being cared for in Carnbee in 1650.[13] Such age-specific references account for only around 4 per cent of cases, however. It is possible that any recipients whose ages were not specified were considered of 'working' age – broadly from age 16 to around 60 – but this must remain largely conjecture.

Kirk sessions were little more forthcoming in recording why individuals were 'impotent' enough to require regular relief. In many cases, presumably, the reason was old age, but there was also one particular form of long-term disability that seems to have been generally accepted as a legitimate reason for admission to the poor roll: blindness. David Clerk, 'the blind lad', received a recurring payment of 6s from Ferryport between May 1667 and November 1670.[14] Between 1672 and 1676, Isobel Pryd, a blind woman, received a 6s 'top up' to her regular pension from Leuchars specifically because of her impairment. Aside from these examples, there is nothing to suggest that other forms of infirmity or disability were present among formal pensioners, and it may well be that people with such infirmities were regarded more as objects of 'extraordinary', rather than regular, relief. On care for people with disabilities more generally, see Chapter 1 of this volume.

It is also frustratingly difficult to discern very much about the mechanics of the relief offered to 'ordinary' pensioners. While there were several ways in which the kirk sessions received income – such as personal donations, fines, and specific contributions – the primary source of poor-roll money was the weekly collections taken during church services. A session's weekly collection would be distributed to their poor either partially or in its entirety (depending on the amount that was collected and the number of pensioners registered), unless an emergency case was presented.[15] Distribution practice is, however, often obscured by approaches to record-keeping. Some parishes, such as Crail, specifically named their pensioners on a weekly basis – eighteen of them in September 1662, for example.[16] Others, among them Kilconquhar, only recorded the area of the parish in which the money was being distributed, so that, for example, alms went to 'the pensionars of the ferrie' or 'the pensionars in the barnyards'.[17] Finally, there were those parishes like Anstruther Easter that simply recorded the fact that the weekly distribution to 'the ordinarie poor' had taken place.[18] In all of these cases, the existence of a regular roll of pensioners is clear, but record-keeping inconsistencies make it difficult to be

[13] NRS, CH2/625/2, p. 76; NRS, CH2/405/1, p. 32; NRS, CH2/204/1, p. 120.
[14] NRS, CH2/150/1, p. 260, p. 287.
[15] Mitchison, *Old Poor Law*, chapter 4.
[16] NRS, CH2/1543/1, p. 190.
[17] NRS, CH2/210/3, p. 15.
[18] NRS, CH2/625/1, p. 28.

more specific about how poor relief obligations were met, or how much relief was typically given to individual recipients.

However inconsistently they recorded their activities, kirk sessions clearly saw the weekly provision of poor relief as a priority activity. Notes continued to be taken of it and the practice remained largely unaffected by external circumstances. As a consequence, it is possible to see that, across all parishes, the amount of money gathered at weekly collections slowly and steadily declined over the mid- to later seventeenth century. By way of an example, the weekly collections in Anstruther Easter sank from an average of around £7 per week in 1654 to less than £4 a week in 1680, albeit with week-by-week income fluctuating wildly.[19] This experience was replicated in every other East Fife parish – a reflection, presumably, of the pressures of conflict, civil unrest, and economic malaise that marked this period.[20] Yet the decline in poor relief collections was not rapid enough to have caused serious concern. Indeed, the sessions seem but rarely to have even noticed. In December 1675, Anstruther Easter noted that 'the poor was dayly multiplying [and] that the weekly contribution was decreasing', yet they made no further mention of the issue.[21] Sessions made occasional efforts to reduce their outgoings, and sometimes this was allied to rhetorical anxiety about a lack of funds. In Crail in June 1660, 'the sessione finding that the weekly collection could scearsly affourd the portione allotted to the pentioners' appointed a panel of four elders to investigate whether any of the pensioners could 'subsist (especially now in the summer tyme) without ther ordinarre pensions'.[22] In the winter of the following year, 1661, the session noted that they could not afford to clothe all of those in need with the funds currently in their possession. In this case, James Sharp, the minister (and later archbishop of St Andrews), gifted £66 13s 4d to the session to help overcome the immediate shortfall.[23] This kind of financial discomfort was relatively unusual, however, and in general East Fife parishes seem to have received sufficient donations to cover their ordinary poor relief expenses, notwithstanding the gradual dropping off of this income over the decades.

Due to the differences in recording practice, it is difficult to determine how long a 'typical' pensioner remained on the poor roll. What is clear is that, in some cases, the time periods in question could be very substantial. Agnes Creich, for example, was a recurring pensioner in Kilconquhar between May 1651 and November 1653, while Agnes Dishington, who generally received monthly payments of 12s–16s in St Monans, was another long-term

[19] NRS, CH2/625/1-2.
[20] For a succinct survey of social and political conditions, see L.A.M. Stewart and J. Nugent, *Union and Revolution: Scotland and Beyond 1626–1745* (Edinburgh, 2021). On the economy, see T.C. Smout, *Scottish Trade on the Eve of Union, 1660–1707* (Edinburgh and London, 1963).
[21] NRS, CH2/625/2, p. 57.
[22] NRS, CH2/1543/1, p. 76.
[23] Ibid., p. 82.

recipient, drawing her pension between July 1669 and July 1673.[24] Some individuals had experiences of being on the pensioner roll for a time before being removed, and then reappearing at a later date. Margaret Latae in Elie was an example of this phenomenon. She received fortnightly assistance of roughly 4s between January 1640 and April 1645. She then disappeared from the session minutes until January 1654, when she once again began receiving aid, generally 2s–4s per week until October 1658.[25]

None of the pensioners, however, came close to the record of Isobel Grube in Elie.[26] In total, she received regular relief from the kirk session for thirteen-and-a-half years uninterrupted. Starting in April 1640, Isobel chiefly got monthly assistance of between 2s and 6s up to February 1645, when her relief switched to weekly until November 1653. It became more generous, rising to around 8s a week in 1649–52, and as high was 10s–12s from May 1652 onwards. The precise reasons for the changes to Isobel's pension are impossible to ascertain, although we might hypothesise that growing need on her part – perhaps on account of simple ageing – lay at the heart of the affair. Regardless, her case is testament to the fact that, in some cases, being part of the 'ordinary' poor could be a long-term experience, and one that could see pensioners' needs being continually reassessed in an active and responsive way.

Despite sensational cases like Isobel Grube's, having pensioners on the roll for significant periods of time appears to have been quite uncommon. Across East Fife parishes, there were only about two dozen individuals who can be said for certain to have received long-term care lasting for two years or more. What this demonstrates is that while, as we have already seen, no 'typical' situation can be described, it does in general appear that membership of the poor roll was usually a short-term experience in the parishes of East Fife.

In the vast majority of cases, the recipients of ordinary poor relief were given aid in the form of money. Sometimes, though, this money was for specified things. For example, one of Isobel Grube's early payments – 3s in 1640 – was earmarked for purchasing meal.[27] In St Monans in February 1642, Elspeth Paterson was given 13s 4d 'to buy coals'.[28] In May 1670, Dunino kirk session gave £1 to Katherine Flooker 'our ordinary pensioner for her shoes'.[29] If restrictions could be placed on how pensioners used their money, there was also an expectation that, once entered onto the poor roll, individuals should expect some scrutiny of their behaviour. Nans Kay, for example, was 'denudit of her pensione' from the kirk session of Crail in 1649 after repeated citations

---

[24] NRS, CH2/210/1, p. 203; NRS, CH2/210/2, p. 18; NRS, CH2/1056/3, p. 58, p. 96.
[25] NRS, CH2/1581/1/1, p.15, p. 118; NRS, CH2/1581/1/2, p. 4, p. 112. There are no records surviving for 1659–64, so it is possible that Margaret's relief payments continued for some time after.
[26] Her surname is sometimes rendered 'Grub'.
[27] NRS, CH2/1581/1/1, p. 25.
[28] NRS, CH2/1056/2, p. 17.
[29] NRS, CH2/405/1, p. 202.

for 'her oft swearing and profanation of the Lords name, [and] for flytting and scalding' and was summoned to appear before the kirk session.[30] For those on the ordinary poor roll, relief invariably came in the form of cash, but this money could come with certain strings attached.

In summary, the provision of ordinary relief in the parishes of East Fife was restrictive, but operational. It could be called upon by those in need regardless of whether they were male or female, young or old, able-bodied or disabled (at least if the disability in question was blindness). While generally a short-term expedient, it was also possible to subsist as a pensioner for more extended time periods – although in so doing, recipients sometimes had to be prepared to accept a degree of behavioural direction from kirk sessions. The level of support offered, insofar as it is possible to judge, was far from extravagant, but sessions seem to have taken seriously their responsibility to provide a basic level of care to those in need. For those relying upon them, therefore, the pension rolls in East Fife apparently did an adequate job of relieving the poor.

Extraordinary Relief

Formal poor rolls only ever contained a small, select group of the parish poor. A far greater number of people received 'extraordinary' relief, and for a huge variety of reasons. Relief of this kind was intended to alleviate an unexpected or emergency need; it was a quick, time-limited helping hand to see people through unforeseen difficulties, and did not in any way imply a right to regular or long-term relief. Often, indeed, emergency relief was strictly one-off. For example, Isobel Stirk received 6s from the session of Ferryport on 1666 as she was suffering from an illness.[31] In Dunino in 1674, a gentlewoman in distress received 4s 4d to aid her after 'all she had was [burnt]'.[32] One further example again comes from Ferryport, this time for Thomas Rymer, who received £2 4s in 1647 for 'his exspences whill his finger was mending'.[33] In cases like these, relief was not only tied to a specific emergency circumstance, but was clearly envisioned as a one-time affair.

Cases like Isobel Stirk's, involving poor-relief recipients suffering from disease or disability, were very common.[34] Often, little detail is given about the conditions in question. For example, Archibald Stirling of Dunino was simply reported as 'being sick' in 1648, while Grisel Fleming was described as a 'poor sick woman' when she received relief from the session of Crail in

---

[30] NRS, CH2/1543/1, p. 24.
[31] NRS, CH2/150/1, p. 254.
[32] NRS, CH2/405/1, p. 218.
[33] NRS, CH2/150/1, p. 29.
[34] C. Langley, *Cultures of Care: Domestic Welfare, Discipline and the Church of Scotland, c.1600–1689* (Leiden, 2020), chapter 5; McCallum, *Poor Relief and the Church*, pp. 178–81

1676.[35] In many cases, however, information is recorded, and this allows us to build up a general picture as to the sorts of ailments likely to attract 'extraordinary' relief. The most common such condition was, once again, blindness. In Dunino, for instance, a blind student received £2 in 1653, while St Monans gave 12s to 'a blind lad' in 1667 and 2s to 'a blind child' in 1668.[36] St Leonards granted 18s to 'a blind minister in the west country' in 1672, while Anstruther Easter gave 6d to 'a blind boy' on two occasions in 1679.[37] After blindness, generalised lameness was the next most common reason for providing extraordinary relief, followed by a range of other ailments – including deafness, being 'crippled', palsy, leprosy, and cancer – which appeared much less regularly.[38] Strikingly, however, relief could also be given for mental illness. Ferryport gave 4s to 'a poor dumb lad' in 1668, while St Monans aided a father 'with a dumb child' in both March 1666 and January 1667 with 4s and 2s respectively.[39] In Dunino, one woman described as 'dimit' received 4s in 1676.[40] In 1641, £2 5s was given to a woman in Kilconquhar who regularly attended Betty Edison, known for 'not being well in [her] mynd'.[41] A wide range of physical and mental impairments could therefore receive extraordinary relief, a testament, as we saw in Chapter 1 of this volume, to the willingness and ability of the early modern poor relief system to respond to both short-term and permanent disability.

Another group in frequent receipt of extraordinary relief was military personnel. While the records underpinning this study are not entirely unbroken, it is nonetheless clear that a significant spike in the number of soldiers or military prisoners receiving relief occurred in the 1650s – more than fifty in 1652 alone, for example – clearly as a consequence of the Civil Wars. But wounded soldiers continued to secure relief in smaller numbers (typically fewer than fifteen per year) right up until 1680. The vast majority of these recipients were soldiers and veterans returning home or passing through on their journey, often injured or maimed in the course of their service. Their payments were strict one-offs. Kilconquhar kirk session gave William Duncan, 'ane hurtt sojor in this parish', £3 in September 1650.[42] In 1653, Dunino aided a man named John Alexander, who was described as a lame soldier, by giving him 7s 8d, and in 1655 the same session gave James

---

[35] NRS, CH2/405/1, p. 17; NRS, CH2/1543/1, p. 213.
[36] NRS, CH2/405/1, p. 58; NRS, CH2/1056/3, p. 30, p. 43.
[37] NRS, CH2/1561/1, p. 87; NRS, CH2/625/2, p. 81, p. 84.
[38] See, for example, Joan Paterson in Dunino, 1655 (lameness), NRS, CH2/405/1, p. 85; an unnamed deaf man in Anstruther Easter, 1678, NRS, CH2/625/2, 74; John Craig in Ferryport, 1659 (crippled), NRS, CH2/150/1, p. 194; Peter Ramsay in Kilconquhar, 1645 (palsy), CH2/210/1; David Ireland in Leuchars, 1676 (leprosy), NRS, CH2/1209/1, p. 302; John Walker in Dairsie, 1650 (cancer), NRS, CH2/427/1, p. 19.
[39] NRS, CH2/150/1, p. 266; NRS, CH2/1056/3, p. 16, p. 30.
[40] NRS, CH2/405/1, p. 229.
[41] NRS, CH2/210/1, p. 72.
[42] NRS, CH2/210/1, p. 218.

Brown, 'a lame souldiour… recommended by the presbyterie', 18s.[43] Dunbog gave to David Gordon, 'ane indegent old soger', 6s in June 1667, while in December 1678 Anstruther Easter gave 4s to 'Hew Kennedie a lame souldier with his familie'.[44] All these recipients were named, but that was in fact quite unusual. The overwhelming majority of soldiers in receipt of relief were anonymous; people like the 'lame sojoure' given 12s in Dairsie in 1650, or the distressed soldier who received 8s from Anstruther Easter thirty years later.[45] While relief for soldiers typically involved single payments, it was sometimes possible to subsist in this way over the longer term. One recipient, a 'Captain Houston', secured relief several times across three different parishes: £2 from Kilconquhar in September 1652; £2 12s 4d and 10s from the same parish in May and July 1653 respectively; 12s from Dunino in 1657; and £1 10s from Anstruther Easter in the same year.[46] Houston's case underlines the highly mobile lifestyle of many wounded ex-soldiers, but it is also testament to the opportunities available to such people in terms of securing relief.

Alongside these individualised payments, the parishes of East Fife also occasionally sought to offer more generalised relief to soldiers. The most important example of this was the drive to collect money for Scottish troops held prisoner in England following their capture after the battle of Dunbar (1650). As early as November 1650, only around two months after the battle, both Dairsie and Kilconquhar intimated collections to be gathered for 'our prisoners in Ingland'.[47] In just one week, Dairsie raised £14.[48] Kilconquhar, on the other hand, was much slower. It was 8 February 1652 before they sent £17 6s to the prisoners.[49] In December 1651, Auchtermuchty sent 29 merks 8d 'for supply of the prisoners in England'.[50] On 22 February 1652, Dairsie, Kilconquhar, and St Monans all noted a collection was to be raised for 'the prisonners at Tinmouth Shills', with Kilconquhar raising £18.[51] In May 1652, Dunino contributed 'nyne pounds collected for the prisoners in Ingland'.[52] Pittenweem and Ferryport followed in September 1653, the former raising £20.[53] The last mass collection for the Dunbar prisoners came from Kilconquhar in February 1652, which sent £18.[54] By the end of September 1653, St Andrews presbytery as a whole had collected £229 6s 8d

---

[43] NRS, CH2/405/1, p. 59, p. 83; NRS, CH2/102/1, p. 11
[44] NRS, CH2/625/2, p. 78.
[45] NRS, CH2/427/1, p. 27; NRS, CH2/1543/1, p. 229.
[46] NRS, CH2/210/1, p. 240; NRS, CH2/210/2, p. 11, p. 14; NRS, CH2/405/1, p. 106; NRS, CH2/625/1, p. 63.
[47] NRS, CH2/210/1, p. 219; NRS, CH2/427/1, p. 29.
[48] NRS, CH2/427/1, p. 29.
[49] NRS, CH2/210/1, p. 232.
[50] NRS, CH2/24/1, p. 35.
[51] NRS, CH2/427/1, p. 42; NRS, CH2/210/2, p. 233; NRS, CH2/1056/2, p. 106. This refers to Tynemouth, North Shields in Newcastle.
[52] NRS, CH2/405/1, p. 45.
[53] NRS, CH2/150/1, p.86; NRS, CH2/833/2, p. 26.
[54] NRS, CH2/210/2, p. 18.

for the Dunbar prisoners – a testament to the willingness of the poor relief system to invest significant sums of money in assisting veterans, either singly or as a group.[55]

As one of the most vulnerable groups in society, children frequently became the subjects of poor relief supplications, typically made on their behalf by parents or other adult carers.[56] Often, such youths were suffering from some injury or ailment. Elie kirk session gave £3 to 'ane youth that wants his arme' by recommendation of the presbytery in 1641.[57] Anstruther Easter gave £4 4s to John Peatt, 'a distracted lad', in October 1656.[58] Dunino kirk session paid 3s 4d to 'a poor boy lying seek of a fever' in November 1676.[59] Slightly more sustained relief was given in the case of John Craig, 'a criple boy' who received 12s from Ferryport kirk session in June 1659, with a further 3s 4d and 12s in October and November respectively.[60]

As well as being given to sick children, relief was often provided for orphans and foundlings. In Kilconquhar in March 1649, for example, the kirk session gave £20 'for the relieffe of ane motherless chyld'.[61] They gave assistance to another motherless child (possibly the same one) in October and November 1649, and again in January 1650 – £5 12s, £5, and £2 12s respectively.[62] Even wider, and longer-term, collaboration was evident in the case of one unnamed orphan living in Leuchars, who seems to have been under the care of the presbytery. The child's primary benefactor was the kirk session of Ferryport, which sent payments in 1651 (£2), 1652 (£1 10s), 1658 (£1 19s, then £2 13s 4d), 1662 (£2), and 1666 (£2), but money was also promised or forthcoming at various points from Pittenweem, Anstruther Easter, and Dunino. Receiving sustained support over a period of at least fifteen years, the Leuchars orphan is a striking demonstration of the capacity of the poor relief system to care for parentless children, even beyond the confines of a single parish.[63]

Challenging conventional assumptions, recent research has demonstrated that itinerants and 'strangers' often secured support through the Scottish poor relief system, and this certainly held true in East Fife.[64] In the period under review, more than 1,000 outsiders presented testimonials to the various kirk

---

[55] NRS, CH2/1132/18, p. 278.
[56] The study of children and childhood in early modern Scotland remains fairly limited, but for the most important work, see E. Ewan and J. Nugent (eds), *Finding the Family in Medieval and Early Modern Scotland* (Aldershot, 2008), and J. Nugent and E. Ewan (eds), *Children and Youth in Premodern Scotland* (Woodbridge, 2015).
[57] NRS, CH2/1581/1/1, p. 40.
[58] NRS, CH2/625/1, p. 39.
[59] NRS, CH2/405/1, p. 229.
[60] NRS, CH2/150/1, p. 194.
[61] NRS, CH2/210/1, p. 194.
[62] NRS, CH2/210/1, p. 205, p. 209.
[63] NRS, CH2/150/1, p. 49, p. 65, p. 174, p. 180, p. 184; NRS, CH2/833/2, p. 31; NRS, CH2/405/1, p. 121; NRS, CH2/625/1, p. 89
[64] Langley, *Cultures of Care*, pp. 29–30; K. Barclay, *Caritas: Neighbourly Love and the Early Modern Self* (Oxford, 2021), pp. 150–8.

session, and many of these incomers secured some poor relief. Often, such people still came from the local area. For example, in July 1669 St Monans received a supplicant with a testimonial from Anstruther who was given 4s.[65] Others came from slightly further afield, such as the skipper's wife who presented a testimonial from Burntisland to Dunino in 1658 and got 12s.[66] Another St Monans supplicant, Robert Frazer, who was eventually given 16s in 1670, had travelled a bit further, since he presented a testimonial from the presbytery of Inverness, while George Gibson, received at Leuchars and awarded 2s in 1676, brought paperwork from London.[67]

In cases like these, the rationale for providing relief is not clear. In other instances, though, reasons were specified, and these could vary greatly. In August 1648, Elie received a poor man from Portpatrick who had suffered a house fire. He was given £2 14s.[68] Dunfermline kirk session aided '12 distrest frenche men robbed by sea' with £4 in April 1650.[69] In July 1658 in Ferryport, two Englishmen sought aid after their horses received burn injuries, and they were accordingly given £1.[70] Anstruther in particular aided many supplicants who had faced difficulties at sea, such as the three shipwrecked men from Orkney who were given 6s in December 1678.[71] One particularly interesting example of relief-provision for a stranger concerned a poor Jewish man named Paul Shallit. On 11 May 1670, he made an appearance before the presbytery of St Andrews to request 'the charity of the Brethren in regard he was in mean condition and minded fortwith to go into Ingland if he had aney thing to bear his expense'.[72] The presbytery agreed to give him some assistance. Over the course of the following few weeks, Dunbog, Anstruther Easter, Leuchars, and Crail all gave collections to him. On 8 and 16 May, Dunbog presented £1.[73] On 29 May, Leuchars gave him half a crown.[74] Crail raised £2 8s in June.[75] Anstruther Easter also gathered a significant collection over the course of a two-week period before handing it over on 22 May, although, for unknown reasons, only around two-thirds of the money raised (£6 13s 4d out of £10 5s 8d) was actually given to Shallit.[76] This is the only reference in East Fife's records to a Jewish person – intriguingly claimed to have been a convert to Christianity – and although it might be presumed that Shallit was a refugee escaping from contemporaneous pogroms

---

[65] NRS, CH2/1056/3, p. 57.
[66] NRS, CH2/405/1, p. 119.
[67] NRS, CH2/1056/3, p. 68; NRS, CH2/625/2, p. 70.
[68] NRS, CH2/1581/1/1, p. 69; NRS, CH2/592/1/1, Dunfermline Abbey Kirk Session Minutes, 1640-fo. 89, fo. 109.
[69] NRS, CH2/592/1/1, fo. 109.
[70] NRS, CH2/150/1, p. 175.
[71] NRS, CH2/625/2, p. 78.
[72] NRS, CH2/1132/19, St Andrews Presbytery Minutes, 1656–87, p. 244.
[73] NRS, CH2/102/1, p. 29.
[74] NRS, CH2/1209/1, p. 107.
[75] NRS, CH2/1543/1, p. 161.
[76] NRS, CH2/625/2, p. 21.

on the Continent, this must remain speculation. What his presence does demonstrate, however, is that a diverse range of 'strangers' could, and did, win support from the parishes of eastern Fife.

If 'strangers' inside the parish regularly received relief, aid could also be given to needy strangers elsewhere, typically through special collections.[77] As we have already seen, the Dunbar fundraising campaign lasted for some time; however, there was another such drive that lasted even longer. This related to sailors and ministers captured and taken to Algiers, where they were held as 'prisoners and slaves' by those referred to as 'the Turks'.[78] From its first mention in May 1643 through to August 1680, this was a long-standing cause. Initially, collections were initiated every few years, targeting individuals or a small group. Then, in 1673, Anstruther Easter took note of a collection that was to be intimated by order of the privy council for some men from Glasgow who had been captured and taken prisoner.[79] While it took nearly eighteen months for anything to come of this, Leuchars recorded that an order had been sent for this purpose from the 'secret counsel for a generall collection throw all Scotland'.[80] Over the following five years, numerous collections and contributions were raised in an effort to save the men. In 1678 alone, Dunino raised £5 14s 8d, Kilconquhar £27, Leuchars £15, and Kemback £14 13s 8d.[81] In June 1679, Anstruther Easter observed another order from the privy council, this time to organise a collection for 'the Ransome of John Atchisone younger in Pittenweem and his company detained under Turkish captivitie', raising £66 13s 4d.[82] Just as Christian compassion could move the sessions of eastern Fife to provide relief to 'strangers' on their doorstep, so too did it motivate them to provide charity for needy groups or individuals far away from home.

In most of the cases discussed thus far, kirk sessions were making their own decisions about relief distribution. Sometimes, however, extraordinary relief was instigated by external forces. Recommendations by presbyteries were, by far, the most common sources of such referral. St Monans received 'an hurt man called Walter Grahame' who had a testimonial from the presbytery of Kirkcaldy in May 1641.[83] In 1651 in Auchtermuchty, Margaret Duncan received 12s, having presented a recommendation from the presbytery.[84] In May 1655, Elie answered the calls of one distressed man and a gentleman with a presbytery recommendations, giving them 18s and £3 12s respectively.[85] In

---

[77] J. McCallum, 'Charity Doesn't Begin at Home: Ecclesiastical Poor Relief beyond the Parish, 1560–1650', *Journal of Scottish Historical Studies*, 32:2 (2012), 107–26.
[78] NRS, CH2/1543/1, p. 207.
[79] NRS, CH2/625/2, p. 40, p. 44, p. 50; *RPCS*, 3rd Series, vol. 3, pp. 573–4.
[80] NRS, CH2/1209/1, p. 232.
[81] NRS, CH2/405/1, p. 235; NRS, CH2/210/3, p. 103; NRS, CH2/1209/2, p. 31; NRS, CH2/204/1, p. 112.
[82] NRS, CH2/625/2, p. 81; *RPCS*, 3rd Series, vol. 6, pp. 116–17.
[83] NRS, CH2/1056/2, p, 10.
[84] NRS, CH2/24/1, p. 27.
[85] NRS, CH2/1581/1/1, p. 34.

1680, Anstruther Easter gave £2 18s to 'a grecian priest by the appointment of the presbitrie'.[86] The next level up in the ecclesiastical hierarchy was the synod, and while synodal recommendations were rarer than presbyterial ones, they did still happen. Both Leuchars in November 1670 and St Monans in January 1671 answered the request of Mrs Jean Currier, 'recommended unto our charity by an act of the synod', from which she received £1 10s and 8s respectively.[87] In most cases like these, it is not clear why presbyteries and synods decided to engineer relief payments, but clearly such recommendations could be an effective way for those in need to secure support.

While the hierarchy of Church courts accounted for the bulk of external poor relief recommendations, similar requests occasionally came from other bodies. In Dunino in May 1647, a man named Alexander Henton was 'recommended by the generall assemblie', and he received £1.[88] In the same year, Ferryport received a distressed woman who had also been recommended by the general assembly.[89] The unnamed 'captaine' given £2 10s in Kilconquhar in 1650 was 'recommendit by the commity of estats'.[90] John Morison secured 6s 8d from Dunbog kirk session in 1674 after showing a recommendation from the king.[91] George Abernethie had to rely on a slightly less eminent sponsor in 1680; his 15s payment from Anstruther Easter came after recommendation 'be the ministers and magistrats of Aberdeen'.[92] In a few cases, recommendations were even accepted from non-Scottish authorities. Arthur Whit, for example, was given £1 10s by Crail kirk session in December 1667 upon 'a recommendation from London of his loss by the fire' – most likely referring to the previous year's Great Fire.[93] People seeking extraordinary relief could therefore come armed with recommendations from a wide array of ecclesiastical and secular authorities, and it was not at all unusual for such sponsorship to yield positive results.

As we have seen, the most common form of 'extraordinary' poor relief was dispensing a cash payment. Amounts awarded varied hugely. For example, in Elie Margaret Latae received an 'extraordinary' payment of 40d, while Elspeth Adamson received 6s 8d on the same day.[94] The reasons for this difference in payment are unclear, but presumably Adamson's circumstances were judged the more serious. Cash payments were not always given no strings attached, however; sometimes money was provided only for specified purposes. In 1648 in Dunino, £2 16s was given to Andrew Walker for purchasing new clothes.[95] In Kilconquhar in 1663, £2 7s was similarly granted

---

[86] NRS, CH2/625/2, p. 85.
[87] NRS, CH2/1209/1, p. 119; NRS, CH2/1056/3, p. 75.
[88] NRS, CH2/405/1, p. 3.
[89] NRS, CH2/150/1, p. 32.
[90] NRS, CH2/210/1, p. 214.
[91] NRS, CH2/102/1, p. 63.
[92] NRS, CH2/625/2, p. 91.
[93] NRS, CH2/1543/1, p. 135.
[94] NRS, CH2/1581/1/1, p. 24.
[95] NRS, CH2/405/1, p. 14.

to George Davidson for clothing, while the 16s given to Andrew Wide by Anstruther Easter in 1664 was meant to buy him shoes.[96] Efforts were also made to assist with burying the dead. In August 1645, Ferryport gave £1 to Andrew Walker to pay for his wife's winding sheet, with a further £2 9s 4d in September to help him bury his wife.[97] In June 1650, Kilconquhar kirk session paid £3 'for ane burial kist for ane poor woman'.[98]

Crail, in particular, demonstrates the more creative way in which kirk sessions were able to support the poor. Although the cash payments were often awarded, the authorities also utilised a range of other approaches. In 1668, for example, David Fairfull requested a recommendation from the session to allow him to 'goe through the countrie seing he was infirme and not able to work for his livlyhood and... desired not [to] be burthensome to the poors box'.[99] This request for, in essence, a licence to beg elsewhere was readily granted. A different approach was used in the case of William Logan, the son of a poor widow, in 1648; he was put 'to the tailyours craft', likely meaning he was matched with a local master who would provide him with the professional skills to support himself.[100] In June 1649, George Dewar's children were similarly ordained to be put to trade, and the session provided £8 towards the necessary expenses – but only with 'this special provision that he nor they sall not be chargeable to the session heerafter'.[101] In cases like these, we see the kirk session responding to need in creative ways, often with the intention not only of providing relief, but of offering a route out of alms-dependence. 'Extraordinary' relief, then, could be rather more far-sighted than might be expected.

Conclusion

The Reformation made it clear that aiding the poor was one of the central duties of all Scots. By the mid-seventeenth century, this was an obligation that was clearly recognised by the kirk sessions of rural East Fife. While the operation of their regular poor rolls remains quite opaque, they seem generally to have performed the expected role of providing reliable relief to a small number of 'impotent' poor. This usually continued for a relatively short time, but occasionally sessions would support individuals for longer periods. Yet it was in the provision of 'extraordinary' relief that the principles and approaches underpinning poor relief practice are laid bare most clearly. A wide range of people, including many not technically entitled to relief such as 'strangers' or the working poor, could call upon kirk session resources in their

---

[96] NRS, CH2/210/2, p. 131; NRS, CH2/625/1, p. 186
[97] NRS, CH2/150/1, p. 10, p. 11.
[98] NRS, CH2/210/1, p. 215.
[99] NRS, CH2/1543/1, p. 136.
[100] Ibid., p.18.
[101] Ibid., p. 23.

hour of need, and the authorities very often proved themselves willing to provide some degree of support. Usually, they did so through cash payments, but there was room for more creative approaches if circumstances called for it. All of this speaks to a system of poor relief governed ultimately by local feeling and Christian charity, its very lack of strong central regulation becoming, from this perspective, something of an asset.[102] This chapter has looked only at one part of the country over a restricted time period, but its conclusions tie in with a broader revisionist trend towards rehabilitating early modern poor relief in Scotland. The rhetorical harshness and technical stringency of poor law legislation notwithstanding, historians are now increasingly aware of the flexible, creative, compassionate, and often surprisingly generous ways in which the Kirk discharged its duty of care towards the poverty stricken. The system remained ramshackle and inconsistent, and it provided little more than subsistence-level support, but it was generally able to meet its obligations. In doing so it demonstrated – in East Fife as elsewhere – that the poor were not cut off from the community around them, but continued to be regarded as an integral part of it, worthy of having their position shored up with communal resources where this was deemed necessary and appropriate. Poverty may have been a marginalising force, but one key function of Scotland's poor relief system was to confront this marginalisation and provide a mechanism for sustaining social position.

---

[102] On charity and 'neighbourly love' more broadly, see Barclay, *Caritas*.

3

The Marginalisation of Gypsies in Scotland, 1573–c. 1625

Thomas M. Tyson

In November 1609, the privy council responded to an unusual request: a petition to recognise Moses Faw and his family as ex-Gypsies. Six months previously, parliament had passed the 'Act anent the Egiptians', a law permanently banishing all Gypsies from the realm under pain of death.[1] Petitioning the council, Faw praised the act as 'worthelie set doun' against the 'infamous thevis' who, 'undir the counterfute name of Egiptianis', had committed 'sa mony villanyis in the cuntrey'. He suggested that the act was not intended to be used against 'honnest, lauchfull, and trew personis' such as himself, whose 'birth, educatioun, and residence' had been in Scotland, and who had withdrawn from the 'infamous societie' of Gypsies and disdained their 'thevishe forme of doing'. Rather, Faw declared his wish to 'spend the rest of his dayis' in Scotland as 'a quiet, modest, trew, and humble subject'. The council assented to the request, and granted a licence exempting Moses Faw and his family from the act.[2]

Less than three years later, Moses Faw and three of his kinsmen – David, Robert, and John Faw – had been arrested, tried, and executed. They became the first individuals to be prosecuted under the 'Act anent the Egiptians' by a justiciary court, their crime that of being 'known' Gypsies. According to the privy council, Faw and other 'counterfoote lymmaris callit the Egiptianis' had found shelter in Selkirkshire, where they were suspected of committing robbery and other crimes, unchecked by local magistrates. Following his arrest, Moses Faw once again petitioned the council, arguing that he and his family were the only Gypsies licensed to live and travel in Scotland, and complaining that he had been apprehended at the instigation 'of the Egiptianis that callis them selvis Bailzeis [Baillies]'.[3] In fact, the king's advocate and privy council had been attempting to arrest Faw and his kinsmen for at least three months, and over the course of their trial in Edinburgh Moses Faw was found to have been 'in companie and societie with the Egiptianis', breaking the terms of his licence. All four men were sentenced to death by hanging.[4]

[1] *RPS*, 1609/4/32.
[2] *RPCS*, vol. 8, p. 372, p. 712; vol. 9, p. 555.
[3] Ibid., vol. 9, p. 171, p. 205; vol. 14, p. 563, p. 652.
[4] NRS, JC2/5, High Court Books of Adjournal, 1611–1619, fos 5v–6r; *Criminal Trials*, vol. 2, p. 201.

The case of Moses Faw encapsulates the paradoxical position of Gypsies in Scotland under James VI. From 1573 onwards, they were subjected to a slew of repressive legislation and proclamations that sought to stigmatise and curtail their way of life, culminating in the 1609 'Act anent the Egiptians'. Thereafter, Gypsies were not just a marginalised group, but also a criminalised one whose extirpation was both sanctioned and regularly encouraged by governing authorities. Yet Moses Faw was one of many Gypsies to be tolerated, even supported, by magistrates throughout Scotland, ranging from constables and kirk elders to the monarch himself. The following chapter explores this paradox. It considers how and why Gypsies were stigmatised and condemned, and shows the ways anti-Gypsy measures were enforced, adapted, and neglected. The desire of Scotland's governing authorities to extirpate Gypsies, together with their failure to achieve such an aim, sheds light on the ambitions and purpose of early modern government, as well as the limits of governmental reach during Scotland's 'long Reformation'. It also shows how the processes of marginalisation could be shaped and intensified by governmental action, and how a marginalised group was able to survive and resist persecution.

Gypsies have received very limited attention from historians of early modern Scotland, or indeed of the early modern period more generally.[5] Like scholars of other marginalised groups, historians of early modern Gypsies face the challenge of studying a group whose archival presence is slight.[6] The surviving traces of Gypsies in early modern Scotland are overwhelmingly confined to the records of authorities hostile to their very existence. The archival bias is such that it is not only difficult to recover the culture and way of life of early modern Gypsies in the British Isles, but even to identify who early modern writers meant by 'Gypsies' or 'Egyptians'. These terms may refer to an ethnic group whose distinct cultural identity was obvious to outsiders, members of the Roma diaspora with genetic and linguistic origins in India; or 'the Gypsy' may be a discursive category or literary trope, constructed by early modern writers and used to describe and stigmatise a diverse range of itinerant people.[7]

The various methodological and archival difficulties in defining early modern Gypsies also creates terminological challenges for historians. The terms Gypsy, gypsy, 'Gypsy', 'Egyptian', Roma, and Romani have all been

---

[5] See D. MacRitchie, *Scottish Gypsies under the Stuarts* (Edinburgh, 1894); J. McCallum, *Poor Relief and the Church in Scotland, 1560–1650* (Edinburgh, 2018), especially chapter 6; M. Todd, *The Culture of Protestantism in Early Modern Scotland* (New Haven, CT and London, 2002). For a concise recent survey of the wider historiography of Gypsies, Roma, and Travellers, see B. Taylor and J. Hinks, 'What Field? Where? Bringing Gypsy, Roma and Traveller History into View', *Cultural and Social History*, 18:5 (2021), 629–50.

[6] D. Cressy, 'Trouble with Gypsies in Early Modern England', *The Historical Journal*, 59 (2016), 45–70.

[7] The subject has generated some debate that is beyond the scope of this chapter. For an overview, see D. Cressy, *Gypsies: An English History* (Oxford, 2018), especially the introduction and epilogue.

used by historians to describe the same early modern group. In early modern Scottish records, 'Egiptian' and 'gipsy' (both spelled various ways) are the most commonly used terms. They appear to be exonyms, labels applied by outsiders to identify a group with presumed origins in Egypt. There are no first-hand accounts of what those labelled as such called themselves. However, from the late sixteenth century onwards Scottish authorities often used the phrase 'people calling themselves Egyptians' or 'counterfeit Egyptians', at once suggesting that 'Egyptian' was how the group presented themselves and also expressing doubt as to their presumed origins.[8] 'Gypsy', widely used in England from the sixteenth century onward, was less commonly used in early modern Scottish records: it was almost never used in legislation and proclamations, though it had currency as early as 1597 and had become widespread by 1700.[9]

Following the practice of Becky Taylor and David Cressy, this chapter uses the term Gypsy: capitalised and without quotation marks, it refers both to a legal category constructed by early modern authorities and to an ethnic group, culturally and linguistically distinct from other Scots.[10] While 'Egyptian' may be more historically precise, the term Gypsy gestures towards the wider archipelagic context in which they should be understood. Gypsies were subject to comparable repressive legislation in Scotland, England, and Ireland, and regularly crossed the borders between the three kingdoms.[11] Although this chapter is not concerned with establishing the ethnicity of early modern Gypsies, there is no reason to doubt that many of the Gypsies described in the source material were the ancestors of today's Romanichal Gypsies and Nawken. However historically or ethnologically imprecise the term Gypsy may be, it invites instructive historical and geographical comparisons that are, on balance, worth preserving.

Criminalisation

Throughout the early modern period, Gypsies occupied an economically and socially marginal position in Scotland.[12] The first record of Gypsies in Scotland dates to 1505, when the crown gave support to an 'afflicted and miserable tribe' who were taken to be impoverished pilgrims from 'little Egypt'. Over the following decades, magistrates came to see Gypsies as troublesome

---

[8] *RPS*, A1575/3/5; A1593/9/14.
[9] For the earliest Scottish use of Gypsy ('gipseis'), see NRS, CH2/171/32, Glasgow Presbytery Transcripts, 1595–98, p. 128. The preference for 'Egyptian' over 'Gypsy' in Scottish records may be a result of archival bias, skewed by the preponderance of legal over literary evidence.
[10] B. Taylor, *Another Darkness, Another Dawn: A History of Gypsies, Roma and Travellers* (London, 2014), p. 19; Cressy, *Gypsies*, pp. x–xi.
[11] G. Power, 'Gypsies and Sixteenth-century Ireland', *Romani Studies*, 24:2 (2014), 203–09.
[12] See Cressy, *Gypsies*, pp. 18–26.

foreigners with a reputation for theft and disorder, resulting in an order of expulsion in 1541 that proved to be ineffectual. The early treatment of Gypsies by Scottish authorities is similar to that of other European states in the fifteenth and early sixteenth centuries. Under James VI, however, Scottish lawmakers undertook an intense and sustained persecution of Gypsies with few parallels. Between 1573 and 1625, four acts of parliament and seven proclamations were enacted that aimed to extirpate Gypsies' way of life and criminalise interactions between Gypsies and non-Gypsies.[13] These measures also stigmatised Gypsies by painting them as foreign vagrants, counterfeits, witches, and thieves: a 'criminal identity' anathema to the ideals of crown and Kirk.[14]

Gypsies and Roma suffered comparable criminalisation and persecution across early modern Europe, a phenomenon historians have generally understood as part of a broader trend of state formation. As early modern polities consolidated authority under a single sovereign and centralised the exercise of military and fiscal power, groups perceived to pose a threat to the social order and the crown's sovereignty were stigmatised and persecuted, ranging from religious dissenters and unruly magnates to vagrants and Gypsies.[15] Other scholars have pointed to economic upheaval and a growth in the number of landless poor as a factor driving governmental persecution of Gypsies, Roma, and other travelling groups during the period, even as grand explanatory narratives of the 'decline of feudalism' and the 'proletarianisation of labour' have lost much of their former relevance.[16] Looking at Scotland, Julian Goodare has situated the persecution of Gypsies as part of an 'expansion of the public sphere' and 'the scope of government' during the reign of James VI, which taken together laid the foundations of an 'absolutist state', though this view has not gone unchallenged.[17]

---

[13] This counts only general acts and proclamations that were explicitly concerned with Gypsies covering the whole of Scotland. There were many more privy council proclamations dealing with specific groups or individuals, as well as further anti-Gypsy measures taken by lower civil and ecclesiastical jurisdictions.

[14] See J. Morgan, '"Counterfeit Egyptians": The Construction and Implementation of a Criminal Identity in Early Modern England', *Romani Studies*, 26 (2016), 105–28.

[15] Although the literature on early modern state formation is vast and beyond the scope of this chapter, the following works touch on the intersection of state formation and the persecution of Gypsies, Roma, and other travelling groups: L. Mróz, *Roma-Gypsy Presence in the Polish-Lithuanian Commonwealth* (Budapest, 2016); R.J. Pym, *The Gypsies of Early Modern Spain, 1425–1783* (Basingstoke, 2007); Taylor, *Another Darkness, Another Dawn*, especially chapters 1 and 2.

[16] See A.L. Beier, *Masterless Men: The Vagrancy Problem in England, 1560–1640* (London, 1985); K. Michael-Bogdal, *Europe and the Roma* (London, 2023), especially chapter 2; L. Lucassen, 'Between Hobbes and Locke. Gypsies and the Limits of the Modernization Paradigm', *Social History*, 33 (2008), 423–41; and D. Mayall, *Gypsy Identities 1500–2000: From Egipcyans and Moon-Men to the Ethnic Romany* (Abingdon, 2004).

[17] J. Goodare, *State and Society in Early Modern Scotland* (Oxford, 1999), p. 262, pp. 293–4; J. Goodare, *The Government of Scotland, 1560–1625* (Oxford, 2004), p. 216, p. 264. For a concise account of the scholarship challenging Goodare's position, see L.A.M.

While Scotland's laws and proclamations against Gypsies should undoubtedly be understood alongside broader developments in early modern governance unfolding across the continent, the impetus, tenor, and timing of these measures were deeply influenced by the country's Protestant Reformation. The criminalisation of Gypsies was a significant, if little-recognised, part of what has been called Scotland's 'long Reformation', a political and social project that sought the establishment of a well-ordered and 'godly' Scotland built on Calvinist principles, spearheaded by central authorities from 1560 until the late seventeenth century.[18] Often rancorous disagreements during James VI's reign over the nature of the Church polity, the relative authority of the Kirk and crown, and the spiritual role of each have understandably attracted scholarly attention. In this context, the prosecution of Gypsies has been seen as part of the crown's efforts to exert and extend its power over the Kirk during the period. There was, however, also some consensus amongst leading Protestants regarding 'sinful' behaviour: authorities across the ideological spectrum agreed that the new theological orthodoxy must be established and maintained throughout the kingdom, and threats to the envisioned social and spiritual order should be suppressed.[19] In 1587, for instance, the privy council ordered that a court of justiciary be held to try various 'heich offenssis' in the king's presence, including both violent crimes and spiritual misdemeanours such as incest, adultery, witchcraft, harbouring Jesuits, and hearing Catholic Mass. The list concluded with a call for the execution of justice upon 'the wicked and counterfute theveis and lymmaris calling thame selffs Egiptianis'. The list of offences gives a sense of the shared judicial priorities of the crown and Kirk, treating spiritual disorder as an urgent threat alongside unlawful violence.[20] Tackling Gypsies, who were perceived to embody a range of sinful and anti-social behaviours, attracted consensus and agreement amongst central authorities, regardless of their differing positions on bishops and presbyteries.

The first post-1560 measure against Gypsies was a privy council proclamation of 1573, the 'charge upoun the Egiptianis', which accused the 'people of diverse nationis falslie namyt Egiptianis' of living by theft and other unlawful means, having 'bene lang permittit to wander up and doun this realme unpuneist'. All Gypsies were ordered to leave Scotland or settle themselves under a master and learn a trade; failure to do so within a month of the proclamation would result in their being scourged from parish to parish until 'utterlie remo-

---

Stewart, 'The "Rise" of the State?', in T.M. Devine and J. Wormald (eds), *The Oxford Handbook of Modern Scottish History* (Oxford, 2012).

[18] See K.M. Brown, 'In Search of the Godly Magistrate in Reformation Scotland', *Journal of Ecclesiastical History*, 40:4 (1989), 553–81; J. McCallum (ed.), *Scotland's Long Reformation: New Perspectives on Scottish Religion, c.1560–c.1660* (Leiden, 2016).

[19] For a narrative summary of the disagreements between Church and state during the period, see A.R. Macdonald, *The Jacobean Kirk, 1567–1625: Sovereignty, Polity and Liturgy* (London, 1998).

[20] *RPCS, 1st Series*, vol. 4, p. 218.

vit' from the realm.[21] As in the reigns of James IV and James V, the privy council in 1573 continued to see Gypsies as foreign itinerants, but now classified as 'vagabonds', a group that governing elites were finding increasingly intolerable. Vagrancy, begging, and the regulation of poor relief periodically occupied lawmakers in the half century following 1560, resulting in a series of acts in which Gypsies were often explicitly named among those deemed the 'undeserving poor'. Like other vagrants, Gypsies were seen as parasites oppressing the king's settled, law-abiding, and church-attending subjects. Though a distinction between the 'deserving' and 'undeserving' poor had been made by Scottish authorities since the fifteenth century if not earlier, it assumed new theological resonance following the Reformation.[22] Two poor laws passed in 1575 and 1579 restricted eligibility for charitable relief only to those deemed unable to work and resident in a particular parish, and sought to punish 'masterfull idyll beggaris' whose 'wiked and ungodlie forme of leving… without mariage or baptizing' attracted 'the wraith and displesar of God' (for discussion of poor relief in practice, see Chapter 2 of this volume). Punishment involved being scourged and burnt through the ear. The two laws attempted to streamline the 'confusioun' of various anti-vagrancy laws by outlining the types of people unworthy of charitable relief and deserving arrest. They grouped Gypsies with tricksters, conjurers, and fortune-tellers.[23] Anti-vagrancy legislation of 1592 and 1597 also mentioned Gypsies, and stressed the duty of local civil and ecclesiastical magistrates to apprehend them alongside other vagrants.[24] Repetition of anti-vagrancy laws, as well as innovations in enforcement and punishment, imply the perceived failure of authorities to suppress vagrancy. Central authorities were nevertheless more ambitious about tackling vagrancy after 1560, leaving little doubt that many local authorities took very seriously their responsibility to exclude and punish able-bodied vagrants, including Gypsies.[25]

The late sixteenth century also saw Gypsies come to be associated with the crime of witchcraft, which had been made a capital offence in 1563. A parliamentary statute of 1575 bracketed Gypsies with fortune-tellers and those who have 'knawlege in physnomie, palmestre or utheris abused sciencis', and the following year, the privy council claimed that Gypsies had recourse to 'sorcery and devinatioun'.[26] Both measures suggested a degree of official scepticism regarding the practice of magic by Gypsies and itinerant fortune-tellers, implying conjuring and deception rather than *maleficium*.[27] In

[21] RPCS, 1st Series, vol. 2, p. 210.
[22] RPS, 1425/3/22 and A1493/5/21. See also L.A.M. Stewart, 'Poor Relief in Edinburgh and the Famine of 1621–24', *International Review of Scottish Studies*, 30 (2005), 5–41, at pp. 7–8.
[23] RPS, A1575/3/5; 1579/10/27.
[24] RPS, 1592/4/46; 1597/11/46.
[25] McCallum, *Poor Relief and the Church in Scotland*, p. 190.
[26] RPS, A1575/3/5; RPCS, 1st Series, vol. 2, pp. 555–6.
[27] P.G. Maxwell-Stuart, *Satan's Conspiracy: Magic and Witchcraft in Sixteenth-Century Scotland* (East Linton, 2001), pp. 39–40.

a witchcraft trial of 1590 held before the justice general's court in Edinburgh, Katherine Ross was charged with sending a servant to 'the Egyptians' to find out how to poison a relative, alongside other acts of witchcraft.[28] She was acquitted, and the Gypsies themselves never faced trial. Gypsies were more explicitly described as 'thevis, witcheis and abusaris' in an act of 1593, and in the early seventeenth century there were a number of cases seen by church courts in which Gypsies were associated with witchcraft and charming.[29] In 1621, a tailor named Patrick Bodie was censured by the presbytery of Aberdeen for 'consultatioun of witches' after 'he maid inquirie at Egiptianes' regarding a gown stolen from his shop, and in the late 1620s, a number of poor parishioners of Dundonald were censured for soliciting Gypsies for charms and fortune-tellings.[30] Gypsies were associated with charming and might, on occasion, be suspected of witchcraft, but were never central to a witch hunt: indeed, no instances survive of Gypsies being tried under the 1563 Witchcraft Act, and accusations of magic and sorcery do not feature in any criminal trials under the 'Act anent the Egyptians'. The equation of Gypsies with witchcraft was largely confined to the rhetoric of lawmakers, and appears to have found little purchase amongst local magistrates or the wider population.

By contrast, perceptions that Gypsies were violent thieves had greater traction. Groups of Gypsies had been accused of theft by burgh authorities since 1527 and the crown since 1541, and by James VI's reign, theft was seen as Gypsies' primary means of livelihood. The 1573 'charge upoun the Egiptianis' stated that Gypsies made a living by 'stowth [theft] and utheris unlauchfull meanys', and the 1576 proclamation against Gypsies stated that any magistrates who failed to arrest Gypsies should be held 'as favouraris and sustenaris of thevis and murtheraris'.[31] Subsequent anti-Gypsy legislation and proclamations under James VI consistently referred to Gypsies as thieves, and, following the 1609 'Act anent the Egiptians', the privy council formulaically labelled Gypsies 'the counterfoote theeves and lymmars callit the Egyptians'.[32] The term 'lymmar' meant rogue or lawless person, and was usually applied to vagrants, Gaels, and Borderers by central government. Whereas earlier acts and proclamations had ordered that Gypsies be prosecuted as vagrants or for specific criminal acts, the 1609 act mandated that Gypsies be punished as thieves. After 1 August 1609,

---

[28] NRS, JC2/2, High Court Books of Adjournal, 1584–91, fos 169v–175r; *Criminal Trials*, vol. 1, p. 195.
[29] *RPS*, A1593/9/14.
[30] NRS, CH2/448/3, Aberdeen St Nicholas Kirk Session Minutes, 1609–20, pp. 313–14; H. Paton (ed.), *Dundonald Parish Records. The Session Book of Dundonald, 1602–1731* (Edinburgh, 1936), pp. 277–8, p. 280, p. 284.
[31] *RPCS, 1st Series*, vol. 2, p. 210 and at pp. 555–6.
[32] Ibid., vol. 10, p. 556, p. 655; ibid., vol. 12, pp. 2–5, p. 151, p. 251, p. 253, p. 292, p. 472; ibid., vol. 13, pp. 295–6, p. 392, p. 406, pp. 410–11, 415; *RPCS, 2nd Series*, vol. 1, pp. 542–3; ibid., vol. 2, p. 444; ibid., vol. 3, pp. 533–4; ibid., vol. 4, pp. 85–6; ibid., vol. 4, p. 15, p. 325, p. 333.

all his majesteis subjectis… [may] tak, apprehend, imprisone and execute to death the saidis Egiptianis, aither men or wemen, as commoun, notorious and condemned theiffis, by ane assyse onlie, to be tryed that they ar callit, knawin, repute and haldin Egiptianis.[33]

The 1609 act did not so much create a new offence as make the status of being a 'known Egyptian' sufficient evidence of theft, without requiring proof of a specific criminal act. It allowed any subject to arrest a suspected Gypsy and act as pursuer (prosecutor). Later seventeenth- and eighteenth-century jurists such as Sir George Mackenzie of Rosehaugh, Sir John Lauder of Fountainhall, and Baron David Hume of Ninewells would comment on the irregularity of these provisions, Hume deeming it 'so unusual and so dangerous a form of process' in permitting a criminal charge to be brought 'without any specification of particulars'.[34] This legal innovation worked on the assumption that Gypsies were an easily identifiable group of people and widely accepted as irredeemably criminal. To be recognised as a Gypsy was sufficient proof to secure a conviction.

The 1609 act also confirmed that Gypsies should not be supported or tolerated by any law-abiding subject. Under the act, anyone could act as a complainant against Gypsies and initiate a prosecution, the implication being that all law-abiding subjects were 'oppressed' by Gypsies' continued presence in Scotland. In the same vein, the act made it an offence to 'resett [harbour], receave, supplie or intertein' Gypsies, punishable by the forfeiture of all the offender's property. Prior to the act, responsibility for censuring resetters – not just of Gypsies but of Jesuits, rebels, and others suspected of criminality – fell primarily on the lowest church courts.[35] By contrast, during the late 1610s and 1620s, the privy council repeatedly stressed the role of civil magistrates in enforcing this aspect of the act, creating commissions of justiciary to apprehend and try resetters of Gypsies in local areas where it was believed Gypsies had found sanctuary. Every provision made in the 1609 act sought to ease the process of prosecution and remove any ambiguity regarding the legal status of Gypsies in Scotland.

---

[33] RPS, 1609/4/32.
[34] B.D. Hume, *Commentaries on the Law of Scotland, Respecting the Description and Punishment of Crimes* (2 vols, Edinburgh, 1797), vol. 2, p. 348; John Lauder, *Historical Notices of Scottish Affairs* (2 vols, Edinburgh, 1848), vol. 2, p. 188; George Mackenzie, *Observations on the Acts of Parliament* (Edinburgh, 1687), pp. 333–4.
[35] See, for instance, NRS, CH2/1/1, Presbytery of Aberdeen Minutes, 1598–1610, p. 463; CH2/171/31, Presbytery of Glasgow Minutes, 1592–1595, pp. 41–5; CH2/171/32, p. 128.

Enforcement and Moderation

By 1 August 1609, Gypsies may have been the most proscribed people in Scotland. Over the following decade, however, the privy council became aware that while the law had initially pushed Gypsies to the geographical and social margins of Scotland, it was not effectively enforced, and had certainly not resulted in their extirpation. Reiterating the need to prosecute Gypsies and their resetters in 1616, the privy council noted that 'for some shorte space after' the passing of the 1609 act, Gypsies had 'dispersit thame selfis in certane derne [hidden] and obscure placeis in the countrey' and stopped the practice of travelling 'in troupis and companies to thair accustomed maner'. Thereafter, however, they had regrouped 'in infamous companies and societies under commanderis' and were committing the same crimes of which they had been accused: theft, robbery, fortune-telling, charming, and conjuring. To make matters worse, the proclamation identified that many of the king's subjects, including some who 'outwardlie pretendis to be famous and unspotted gentilmen', continued to harbour Gypsies and offered them patronage without suffering any legal or social penalties.[36]

The descriptions of criminality and the state of Scotland in privy council proclamations during the period should not necessarily be taken at face value. The language deployed tended towards the paranoid, hyperbolic, and formulaic, better reflecting the anxieties and preoccupations of the central executive than actual social problems.[37] The council's assessment of the 1609 act is nevertheless revealing, and borne out by other evidence. As the case of Moses Faw showed, the aspirations of James VI and his lawmakers were checked by the messiness of reality. Governing authorities were inconsistent in applying the law, on numerous occasions displaying leniency to Gypsies and their resetters. People from across the social spectrum continued to tolerate and actively support Gypsies, and there are also instances suggesting that the enforcement of anti-Gypsy legislation attracted hostility and open opposition. The 1609 act was the last piece of parliamentary legislation explicitly targeting Gypsies, but the privy council continued to spearhead the persecution of Gypsies and improve the enforcement of anti-Gypsy laws until 1630, and individuals were sporadically prosecuted under the act throughout the seventeenth century and well into the eighteenth century.

Although the passing of the 'Act anent the Egiptians' had a significant and immediate impact on Gypsies, obtaining a full picture of how many Gypsies were prosecuted under the act, and by whom, remains challenging. The act empowered 'all his majesteis subjectis, or ony ane of them' to pursue Gypsies and have them tried by an assize, meaning Gypsies could be prosecuted in justiciary courts as well as in inferior jurisdictions such as sheriff courts. In the late seventeenth century, Mackenzie of Rosehaugh noted that 'immediatly

---

[36] *RPCS, 1st Series*, vol. 10, pp. 655–7.
[37] Goodare, *Government of Scotland*, pp. 119–20.

after this Act [of 1609,] Sheriffs and others did Hang very many [Gypsies], by warrand thereof'.[38] Early modern court records dating to the period survive from sheriffdoms across Lowland Scotland, albeit often unindexed and untranscribed, potentially offering further insights into Gypsy prosecution in the localities. Though a detailed investigation of the sheriff court records is beyond the scope of this chapter, records of justiciary courts and privy council action in the decade following 1609 yield some sense of the act's effectiveness in marginalising Gypsies, even if it remains impossible to estimate the number of individuals prosecuted under the act to the same extent as that achieved by historians of Scottish witchcraft persecution.[39]

The first justiciary trial implicating Gypsies after the act did not even use the new legislation. In 1610, Elizabeth Warrock was indicted by the justice general's court at Edinburgh for theft and being 'ane cowmone Vagabund and follower of the Gipseis'. While Warrock was sentenced to be scourged and banished from Edinburgh as a thief and vagabond, neither her indictment nor the verdict referred to the 'Act anent the Egiptians'.[40] Moses Faw and his kinsmen were the first to be convicted by the central criminal court in accordance with the 1609 act, in a trial made possible only by the concerted efforts of the privy council, lord advocate, and local authorities. The initial failure of Selkirkshire magistrates to arrest Moses Faw prior to the council's direct intervention may well have been the catalyst for a proclamation in July 1611 outlining the duties of justices of the peace (JPs) and constables in arresting 'vagabundis, sturdie beggaris, and Egiptianis'.[41] Nevertheless, two months later, the council issued a commission of justiciary to Sir James Erskin for the arrest and trial of one Captain Harry Faw and his kin, 'falslie calling thameselffis Egiptianis'.[42] In 1613, a similar commission was issued to the provost and bailies of Stirling for the trial of Elspeth Maxwell and her sons, James and Alexander Faw.[43] Despite privy council expectations that Gypsies would be pursued vigorously, local magistrates often fell short.

It was not until 1616 that Gypsies once again faced trial at the central criminal court in Edinburgh. In the first half of that year, JPs in Angus apprehended an unknown number of Gypsies who were detained in the tolbooth at Dundee. Lacking authority to bring them to an assize, the JPs passed the prisoners to the sheriff of Forfar, Andrew Gray, 7th Lord Gray, for trial. Gray dragged his feet, for in early July the privy council accused him of delaying the Gypsies' trial with 'frivolous… excuisis'. Echoing cases earlier in the decade, the council commissioned Gray to try the Gypsies for contravening the 1609 act; and if found guilty by an assize, to execute the four leading men and women and banish the rest. The council also threatened to declare Gray

---

[38] Mackenzie, *Observations*, p. 333.
[39] These questions are explored further in the author's forthcoming PhD thesis.
[40] *RPCS, 1st Series*, vol. 3, p. 99.
[41] Ibid., p. 221, p. 224, p. 226.
[42] Ibid., vol. 9, p. 256.
[43] Ibid., vol. 10, p. 132.

a rebel should he delay proceedings any longer.[44] For reasons that remain unclear, Gray did not try the Gypsies in Dundee, but transported them to Edinburgh and presented four individuals to the privy council, who ordered their trial before an assize.

Gray's failure to move swiftly concerned the privy council, and it was from 1616 to 1624 that it paid most attention to the enforcement of the 1609 act. During this period, the council was also pacifying 'idill and insolent persones' of the Scottish Borders with renewed vigour, and beggars and vagrants were perceived to be increasing in numbers and disruptiveness, particularly during the famine of 1623.[45] The growth of vagrancy was not blamed on material want or lack of employment, but the laziness of magistrates and 'the preposterous pitie of the countrey people' who supported vagrants 'without reassoun or discretioun'.[46] Resetters of Gypsies attracted particular alarm, since they included not only those the privy council deemed 'simple and ignorant' but also landowners – the outwardly 'famous and unspotted gentilmen' – who were denounced as 'patronis to theivis and lymmaris' for resetting Gypsies on their estates, and threatened with censure and punishment as an example to others.[47]

After 1616, Scottish authorities introduced several innovations to streamline the prosecution of Gypsies and their resetters. In 1617, parliament ratified a 1611 privy council proclamation outlining the duties of JPs and constables. Among their duties outlined in the proclamation was the enforcement of laws 'against maisterfull beggaris and vagaboundis', and to 'punische and fyne thair resettaris accordinglie'. The parliamentary statute echoed this language, but with two additions: the role of JPs in enforcing legislation against Gypsies was explicitly stated, and constables were directed to arrest all Gypsies and bring them before the relevant JPs for 'punischment according to the statute of parliament'.[48] A new way to incentivise the punishment of resetters of Gypsies was adopted in 1619, when James VI received a petition from three minor courtiers offering to apprehend and try resetters of Gypsies on condition that they received half the value of all fines levied from offenders. The king referred the petitioners to the council, which granted their request.[49] The new approach yielded results. In 1620, the leading petitioner, Alexander Forbes, was granted commission-in-chief and sent to the sheriffdom of Moray, where reset was 'maist frequent and commoun'. Forbes appointed the powerful Moray landowner John Grant of Freuchie to assist him, and was evidently successful in levying fines, albeit less willing to surrender to

---

[44] Ibid., p. 556, p. 559.
[45] Ibid., vol. 10, pp. 470–1; vol. 11, pp. 33–4, p. 443; vol. 12, pp. 2–5, pp. 92–3, pp. 149–50; vol. 13, p. 257, pp. 288–90.
[46] Ibid., vol. 12, p. 2.
[47] Ibid., vol. 10, pp. 655–7; RPS, 1609/4/32.
[48] Ibid., 1617/5/22.
[49] RPCS, 1st Series, vol. 10, pp. 151–2.

the crown its proportion of the revenue.[50] Forbes oversaw the appointment of commissioners across north and north-east Scotland from Sutherland to Aberdeenshire, and the king's advocate pursued at least seventeen named individuals from Perthshire for reset of Gypsies.[51]

In the Highlands and north-east, Gypsies seem to have found places sufficiently 'derne and obscure' to avoid prosecution after 1609. In the Highlands, as in the Borders, kinship ties remained politically significant and many feuds were still settled privately, and Gypsies may have developed ties of obligation with powerful landowners and heads of kinship groups. Clan chiefs and surname leaders offered patronage to Gypsies and protected them from hostile magistrates, though the services that Gypsies rendered in return remain obscure. But it should not be assumed that the reset of Gypsies by landowners only occurred at the periphery of crown authority. In Roslin, less than half a day's walk from Edinburgh, Gypsies found protection under Sir William Sinclair, 16th baron of Roslin. According to Richard Augustine Hay, writing in 1700, the Sinclairs had a long connection with Gypsies; he claimed that the 14th baron of Roslin (also named Sir William Sinclair) had 'delivered ane Egyptian from the gibbet' in 1559, possibly in his capacity as lord justice general of Scotland. Thereafter, Hay explained, 'the whole body of gypsies were of old accustomed to gather in the stanks [marshes] of Roslin every year, where they acted severall plays, dureing the moneth of May and June'.[52] It is a tantalising anecdote, if unverifiable. Gypsies had been associated with performance since their first arrival in Scotland, and remained so in the seventeenth century.[53] In 1623, the privy council described Roslin as a safe haven for Gypsies, a place where they were treated like 'laughfull subjectis', despite the efforts of the local kirk session to discourage reset.[54] Sinclair was both owner of the Roslin estate and sheriff of Edinburghshire, so the council ordered that he apprehend all Gypsies within his jurisdiction and transport them to Edinburgh for trial. If need be, Sinclair was to arm Roslin's inhabitants to assist him in making arrests.[55] It is likely that Sinclair complied with the order: by January, twenty adults suspected of being Gypsies had been transported to Edinburgh to await trial.[56]

A fortnight before the imprisoned Gypsies were tried, the privy council issued what would be its last general proclamation against Gypsies residing

---

[50] W. Fraser, *The Chiefs of Grant* (3 vols, Edinburgh, 1883), vol. 3, pp. 216–17; *RPCS, 1st Series*, vol. 12, p. 433.
[51] Ibid., vol. 10, pp. 312–14.
[52] R.A. Hay, *Genealogie of the Sainteclaires of Rosslyn* (Edinburgh, 1835), p. 136.
[53] In 1634, for instance, the kirk session of Stow punished Bessie Scott for joining 'the egiptianis' in guising and singing. NRS, CH2/338/1, Stowe Kirk Session Minutes, 1626–53, fo. 34v.
[54] NRS, CH2/471/1, Lasswade Kirk Session Minutes, 1615–1637, fo. 3r.
[55] *RPCS, 1st Series*, vol. 13, pp. 295–6.
[56] The connection between the Sinclair's 1623 commission and the 1624 trial is made by David MacRitchie, though evidence of the connection is circumstantial. See MacRitchie, *Scottish Gypsies under the Stuarts*, p. 99; *Criminal Trials*, vol. 3, pp. 560–62.

in Scotland. Once again, the council complained that many Gypsies who 'had abandonit and left the cuntrey' following the 1609 act had 'returnit agane... as yf the lawis maid aganis thame wer become voyde and deade, without lyffe or executioun'. Repeating earlier statutes and proclamations, Gypsies were accused of travelling throughout the realm, openly armed and committing acts of violence. They took advantage of 'the simple and ignorant with thair jugling trikkis' and oppressed those of 'soundar judgement' with theft and robbery. Sheriffs throughout the Lowlands and Borders were ordered to apprehend, try, and execute any Gypsies in their jurisdictions, and all sheriffs were given the authority to arm local inhabitants to assist in arresting Gypsies.[57] The twenty adult Gypsies imprisoned in Edinburgh's tolbooth were indicted and put to an assize at the end of the month, in two trials that proved to be a test for the new proclamation. In the first trial, the eight male prisoners were indicted by the lord advocate as 'callit, knawin, repute, and haldin egiptianes', in contempt of the 1609 act. They were found guilty by an assize and the justice, Sir George Erskine of Innerteill, sentenced them to death by hanging.[58]

But the executions, to be carried out within days of sentencing, did not go to plan. As the prisoners were led to the gallows, the bailies received a warrant from the privy council delaying the hanging. This caused uproar amongst the gathered spectators, to the Gypsies' benefit: the crowd attempted to free the Gypsies and succeeded in unfettering one prisoner, Gavin Trotter, who 'wes cunninglie and craftelie convoyed away'. The council absolved the Edinburgh bailies of Trotter's escape, and commended their 'cair and foirsight' in securing the others from being liberated.[59] The councillors then voted on whether to allow the executions of the remaining male prisoners to proceed, and on whether to try the female prisoners. A plurality of councillors voted in favour of both motions. The twelve adult women were also tried for contravening the 1609 act, found guilty, and sentenced to death by drowning.[60] The privy council then issued a warrant staying their execution as well, and wrote to James VI seeking direction. In the letter, the council justified execution of the male prisoners, described as 'chiftanis and leadaris', because it was 'the best expedient to gif a terrour to the whole companyis' of Gypsies. Though the women had also been sentenced to death, the councillors explained, it had been found that some were pregnant, others breastfeeding, and many had children under the age of ten. Three women were also described as 'young damosellis' less than sixteen years old, who had probably 'not bene grite offendaris'.[61] In response, the king commended the execution of the Gypsy men, but remarked that the women and children had been imprisoned for so long that 'We can not bot inclyne to pittie and

---

[57] RPCS, 1st Series, vol. 13, pp. 392–3.
[58] Criminal Trials, vol. 3, pp. 560–2.
[59] RPCS, 1st Series, vol. 13, pp. 410–11.
[60] Criminal Trials, vol. 3, pp. 560–1.
[61] RPCS, 1st Series, vol. 13, pp. 415.

compassion of them'. Moved by their plight, he commuted their sentence to banishment, under pain of death should they return.[62]

The clemency shown by the privy council and king on this occasion complicates the story of central authorities determined to extirpate Gypsies. But it was one of several instances in which the same individuals who promulgated anti-Gypsy measures also demonstrated lenience and clemency in practice. Individuals who could technically be prosecuted under the 1609 act might be tried for other, lesser crimes, as was the case with Elizabeth Warrock mentioned above.[63] In a 1612 trial in Shetland, five Gypsies were tried on charges of slaughter, incest, adultery, theft, and sorcery. But they were not indicted under the 1609 act, and only one was convicted – Katherine Faw for the slaughter of her husband. The rest were acquitted, despite being recognised as 'Egyptians' and their indictment for crimes stereotypically associated with Gypsies. During the trial, the defence counsel even argued that it was 'the practique of this realm Egiptianis have never been judged to the death for slauchter amongis thame selffis'.[64] When Lord Gray reluctantly brought four Gypsies before the privy council in 1616, the councillors sought the advice of the king as 'no vther cryme was layed to thair charge' beyond that of being Gypsies. As in 1624, the king ordered that the prisoners be banished, even though they had already been convicted and sentenced to death by a justiciary court.[65]

Resetters also received considerable leniency. No instances survive of resetters of Gypsies having their property escheat, and it seems that it was more common for resetters to be tried by the kirk session and presbyteries rather than criminal courts.[66] When resetters did appear before civil magistrates, they often got off lightly, with a censure or small fine. Even when the privy council was most dedicated to tackling reset, between 1616 and 1620, remissions were granted to provosts, bailies, and prominent landowners who had supported and protected Gypsies.[67] Despite the best efforts of those who drafted anti-Gypsy measures, the punishment of Gypsies and their resetters remained inconsistent and haphazard throughout James VI's reign. From the king down, magistrates found that compromise and discretion were required; both in dealing with the (sometimes powerful) individuals who protected Gypsies, and with Gypsies themselves, whom magistrates found to be human, not the crude caricatures of statute and proclamation. It is tempting to speculate that the riot that saved Gavin Trotter from execution in 1624 was a popular revolt against a harsh law

---

[62] NRS, JC2/6, High Court Books of Adjournal, 1619–31, fos 140r–141v.
[63] *RPCS, 1st Series*, vol. 3, p. 99.
[64] *Miscellany of the Maitland Club*, Volume 2 (Edinburgh, 1840), pp. 164–6.
[65] *Criminal Trials*, vol. 3, pp. 397–9; NRS, PC9/1, Privy Council Inventories, 1611–23, fo. 14v, fo. 15r.
[66] M. Todd, 'Fairies, Egyptians and Elders: Multiple Cosmologies in Post-Reformation Scotland', in B. Heal and O.P. Grell (eds), *The Impact of the European Reformation: Princes, Clergy, and People* (Aldershot, 2008), pp. 189–208, at p. 205.
[67] *RPCS, 1st Series*, vol. 12, pp. 243–4; 'Notices Concerning Scottish Gypsies', *Blackwood's Edinburgh Magazine*, 1 (1817), pp. 43–58, at p. 47; NRS, E2/33, 'Remissiones for recept of Egiptianes'.

under which Gypsies were sentenced to death for no other crime than being Gypsies. But setting such speculations aside, it is clear that anti-Gypsy measures encountered resistance. Magistrates had to compromise, reset remained commonplace, and Gypsies continued to live in Scotland despite the threat of prosecution. All of this points to Gypsies' widespread acceptance in Scottish society, an integral part of the realm and not foreign 'strangers', easily removed.

Conclusion

In the half century or so following the Reformation of 1560, Scotland's Gypsies were subjected to a series of laws and proclamations that sought to criminalise their identity and way of life. Gypsies were believed to embody qualities and engage in activities considered anathema to Scotland's central authorities, intent on forging a godly and law-abiding realm. Their criminalisation left them at risk of prosecution and execution by zealous magistrates; anyone who supported them risked fines and censure. But proscription did not lead to extirpation: despite the risk of penalties, individuals from across the social scale and throughout Scotland protected Gypsies from prosecution, whether actively by giving them trade, shelter, food, and drink, or passively by accepting their presence or failing to arrest them. In detailing these developments, this chapter goes some way to showing how Gypsies were prosecuted in Scotland, and how they avoided prosecution.

In marked contrast with England, the criminal prosecution of Gypsies under Scottish anti-Gypsy laws did not end with the death of James VI, but continued sporadically in justiciary courts throughout the rest of the seventeenth century.[68] Criminal processes continued to evolve, and new punishments came to be favoured, particularly transportation. The interpretation of anti-Gypsy measures also changed, if anything becoming more strict and inflexible over the 1670s. Even after the Acts of Union, and as other criminal offences with their roots in Scotland's long Reformation had fallen by the wayside – for instance, witchcraft, adultery, and blasphemy – prosecutors continued to try individuals as 'Egyptians'. The 1609 act's draconian prescription that anyone 'callit, knawin, repute and haldin Egiptianis' should be executed, and the low threshold of evidence required for conviction, continued to attract comment, even admiration, well into the eighteenth century.[69] The last trial that made use of the 1609 act was in 1771, and it was not until the 1790s that this 'long succession of severe and anxious statutes' passed under James VI finally fell into desuetude.[70]

---

[68] The last execution under English anti-Gypsy laws appears to have been in 1627. See Cressy, *Gypsies*, p. 100.
[69] The act's harshness was commented on approvingly by Sir John Clerk of Penicuik as late as 1742. See NRS, Penicuik Papers, GD18/5447.
[70] Hume, *Commentaries on the Law of Scotland*, p. 351.

4

Burgesses on the Edge

Kevin Hall

> I have little hopes of success unless some Respectable Characters who have had an oportunity of knowing some thing of those I have come of, and of my former life, interest themselves on my behalf.[1]

These words were part of a letter sent in an unsuccessful attempt to avoid the gallows and the 'Ignominious death' he so feared by the infamous eighteenth-century Edinburgh housebreaker and thief, William Brodie. Brodie wrote two such letters from the confines of Edinburgh's tolbooth prison, where he was kept 'in the Iron Room and in Chains', with both letters aiming to use his social connections and former standing in Edinburgh's burgess community to have his sentence commuted to life transportation to Botany Bay.[2] Born the son of the well-connected burgess Francis Brodie, young William benefited from an enviable start in life.[3] He would go on to be elected deacon of the wrights' guild in Edinburgh, a prestigious position affording him status, connections, respectability, and the ability to afford commodious accommodation in a 'tenement in Horse Wynd … a substantial building, well furnished'.[4] Brodie, it would seem, had almost everything one would need to enjoy a comfortable lifestyle in eighteenth-century Edinburgh, but, driven by the excesses of his own behaviour, he suffered the miserable end of a common thief. Brodie's duality in being a respectable burgess by day and common thief by night so shocked society that the proceedings of his trial were in print even before he went to the gallows.[5]

As Deacon Brodie, William was a powerful and influential figure, the head of an incorporated guild, benefiting from economic, social, and political privileges afforded him by his title. Prior to his discovery, the then unknown night-time housebreaker and thief was the scourge of Edinburgh's society.

---

[1] EUL, Laing Collection II, fo.131, Letters of Deacon Brodie, 1788.
[2] Ibid.
[3] NRS, OPR 685/1, Edinburgh Old Parish Registers – Baptism, p. 115. One of the witnesses to Brodie's baptism was his uncle, Ludovic, a writer to the signet.
[4] W. Roughead, *Trial of Deacon Brodie* (Glasgow, 1906), p. 158. See also NLS Maps, EMS.s.786, Plan of the City and Castle of Edinburgh, William Edgar, 1765. Horse Wynd was fashionable residential area near to 'Society Hall'.
[5] EUL, Laing Collection II, fo.131. 'As my trial is printed it would ill suit me to make any reflections.'

Brodie, then, was operating on two levels, making him simultaneously both central and peripheral to society. Some authors have argued that Brodie's story was the inspiration for Robert Louis Stevenson's *Strange Case of Dr Jekyll and Mr Hyde*, although that case cannot be proven.[6] His story continues to fascinate to this day, and the modern-day tavern on Edinburgh's Lawnmarket which bears his name is a regular stopping point for many tour guides and visitors.

Brodie of course is an example of extremities, an individual at the top of his profession yet given over to a secret criminality to support his excessive lifestyle. But we ought not to be too surprised by Brodie's actions; he was not even the first Edinburgh craftsman to hit on the idea of fashioning housekeys for both his clients and himself to enable him to break in when he knew the occupants would be away. Over a century before Brodie's birth, the burgesses Alexander Smith (1601) and William Kerr (1604) were both hanged for housebreaking in similar fashion.[7] And in the nearby burgh of Haddington, the burgess John Dickson was similarly a convicted shop-breaker, who upon his sentence of lifetime banishment was told 'the sentence [was] more favourable than he deserved'.[8] Brodie, Smith, Kerr, Dickson, and no doubt others in Edinburgh and other Scottish burghs stepped way over and beyond the boundaries of acceptability. For contemporaries, their actions placed them across sharply defined social boundaries, between that of 'citizen and criminal'.[9] Their cases demonstrate the ability of a lone individual to operate simultaneously in opposite spheres of society, and that is perhaps why we find the stories of people like Brodie so compelling. Certainly, studies of such human deviance draw scholarly attention from a broad range of disciplines, including social psychology, criminology, sociology, and of course history.[10]

The twentieth-century criminologist Frank Tannenbaum argued that the 'young delinquent becomes bad because he is defined as bad and because he is not believed if he is good … The community cannot deal with people whom it cannot define.'[11] In labelling youths as delinquents, Tannenbaum suggests we are then collectively unable or unwilling to accept them as being capable of good too. If Tannenbaum is correct, then we must be able to turn at least this part of his theories upside down and suggest that, equally, we are unable or at least initially unwilling to believe someone bad when they are

---

[6] J.S. Gibson, *Deacon Brodie, Father to Jekyll and Hyde* (Edinburgh, 1977); R. Wilson, *The Man Who was Jekyll and Hyde: The Lives and Crimes of Deacon Brodie* (Stroud, 2015).
[7] NLS, Adv. Mss. 33.7.28, Copy by Sir James Balfour of the Diary of Robert Birrell, Burgess of Edinburgh, p. 54, p. 62.
[8] NRS, RH9/11/13, Haddington Burgh Court Books, 1723.
[9] P. Griffiths, 'Overlapping Circles: Imagining Criminal Communities in London, 1545–1645', in A. Shepard and P. Withington (eds), *Communities in Early Modern England: Networks, Place, and Rhetoric* (Manchester, 2000), pp. 115–33, at p. 115.
[10] See F. Heidensohn, 'Changing Perspectives on Crime: From Interactionism to Critical Criminology', in F. Heidensohn (ed.), *Crime and Society* (London, 1989), pp. 63–84.
[11] F. Tannenbaum, *Crime and Community* (New York, 1951), pp. 19–20.

commonly or universally accepted as good. Intersections between accepted and non-acceptable forms of conduct can be crossed back and forth, either by knowingly manipulative operators, or through a sudden loss of control.

In her recent thesis, Charlotte Berry notes that marginality is 'not so much a category intrinsic to certain people and places but a relative and mutable quality'.[12] Inclusion and exclusion, both being fluid in nature, are constructs created 'through a dialectic between the individual (and their behaviour) and society'.[13] By being neither fixed to an individual, a group, or indeed a location or space, marginality may be an ephemeral experience or long-standing, depending on wide-ranging variable factors. The fluid nature of marginality is as true for space and location as it is for people. A successful tradesman might have sought parish alms in times of economic crisis before trade flourished again, while an urban area can over time be transformed from possessing 'grand and commodious housing' to be a 'workman's quarter among breweries and gasworks'.[14] That being the case, anyone or any place is vulnerable to, or capable of, being marginalised at any point in time.

Erik Spindler argues that marginality can exist at any level in society, offering wide-ranging examples such as a young apprentice whose master had died and left the boy homeless and masterless, and a wealthy merchant who found himself imprisoned in a foreign city as he lacked the social networks there to help him avoid imprisonment.[15] Having the security of social connections was imperative in medieval and early modern urban society. Social networks and connections can alter over time through the course of one's life, either temporarily or irreversibly. Change can be triggered by 'structurally forceful conditions' beyond one's control and through 'a dialectic of definition and self-definition'.[16] Definitions of acceptable behaviour can thus be a fulcrum in temporarily shifting social connections and networks.

In this chapter, I will argue that it is possible to move from the very centre of society to the margins and back again, supporting Berry's position of perceived marginality having a fluidic nature. I will present two case studies which focus on the behaviour of two male burgesses, both resident in the burgh of Canongate at the same time, in the first quarter of the seventeenth century, and both facing economic vicissitudes. Significantly, both men were engaged in the same craft, and at a time when the burgess cordiners of Canongate were suffering economically, not least because of the often fierce

---

[12] C.E. Berry, 'Margins and Marginality in Fifteenth-Century London' (unpublished PhD thesis, University of London, 2018), p. 13.
[13] Ibid., p. 221.
[14] E.P. Dennison, *Holyrood and Canongate: A Thousand Years of History* (Edinburgh, 2005), p. 70, p. 134.
[15] E. Spindler, 'Marginality and Social Relations in London and the Bruges Area, 1370–1440' (unpublished DPhil thesis, University of Oxford, 2008), pp. 104–07.
[16] R.W. Scribner, 'Wie Wird Man Aubenseiter? Ein Und Ausgrenzung In Freuzeitlichen Deutschland', in N. Fischer and M. Kobelt-Grosch (eds), *Aussenseiter Zwischen Mittelalter Und Neuzeit: Festschrift fur Hans Jurgen Goertz Zum 60. Geburtstag* (Leiden, 1997), pp. 21–46, at pp. 41–2 [English translation courtesy of Uta Rosenbrock, Edinburgh, 2023].

local resistance against their access rights to markets.[17] Both men responded to external pressure through expressing varying degrees of disorderly, violent, and socially unacceptable behaviour. Their outbursts almost always corresponded with times when they each faced serious social or economic problems, triggering their departure from the norm.

John Riddle

John Riddle was a cordiner or shoemaker burgess of the Canongate. He would most likely still have been quite a young man in the early 1620s when the economic impact of a devastating nationwide famine hit Scotland and several English regions.[18] He married Isobel White on 6 January 1618, in the parish church of the Canongate.[19] Isobel, just sixteen years of age at the time of the marriage, had been born in Edinburgh, the daughter of a brewster, William White.[20] The couple had been together for at least the best part of a year before marriage, having both been charged by the kirk session for their illicit 'carnal copulation' committed in 1617.[21] Until the point of a sudden violent outburst by John inside the parish church in 1626, the young couple had no other interactions with either civil or kirk courts for any form of antisocial behaviour; they were an ordinary young couple trying to make a living for themselves.

Although not directly referred to in the kirk proceedings against Riddle, it is likely that his frustration at their economic precarity was weighing heavily on his mind. Additionally, it may or may not be purely coincidental that Riddle was charged with riotous behaviour by the session on the couple's eighth wedding anniversary. On Friday 6 January 1626, he was alleged to have entered the church in an angry state of mind the previous Sunday whereupon he began 'obbraiding and molesting his Deacon and sum utheris master friemen of his craft'. It is possible that the couple's discussion of their approaching wedding anniversary and their financial precarity were tipping points for the overstressed Riddle. The charge against him goes on to say that he had been 'straiking his hand on the seit of the cordiners loft in tyme of divyne service', and that he had declared himself to be as 'worthie to sit in the foir seat as ony of his craft'.[22] In saying that, Riddle was clearly demonstrating his frustration at not having the status, and presumably economic success, of

---

[17] A. Allen, 'Conquering the Suburbs: Politics and Work in Early Modern Edinburgh', *Journal of Urban History*, 37:3 (2011), 423–43, at p. 432.
[18] K. Hall, 'The Famine of 1622–23 in Scotland', in H. Cornell, J. Goodare and A. MacDonald (eds), *Agriculture, Economy and Society in Early Modern Scotland* (Woodbridge, 2024).
[19] NRS, OPR 685/3, Canongate Old Parish Registers, p. 107.
[20] NRS, OPR 685/1, Canongate Old Parish Registers, p. 253.
[21] NRS, CH2/122/1, Canongate Kirk Session Minutes, 1613–19, p. 427.
[22] NRS, CH2/122/2, Canongate Kirk Session Minutes, 1619–29, p. 309.

those master craftsmen and their deacon who did sit in the fore lofts.

The kirk records suggest shock and astonishment from the entire congregation at Riddle's behaviour. Considering his 'offence [was] Done so publictlie befoir the haill congregatioun', he was to find caution for himself to appear the next Sunday 'befoir the pulpit thair to be oppenlie rebuikit for committing sick a ryot in tyme of divyne service'.[23] Riddle duly appeared the following week, whereupon he 'humbled himselff befoir the haill congregation, craving Gods mercie and the peoples forgivenes'.[24] Riddle's contrition – whether genuine or not – would have been a humiliating climbdown for a young man who had argued that he was the equal of anyone in his craft, but he would have known that his 'public sin required public reform'.[25] His participation in the ritualised punishment demonstrated an acceptance that his actions had crossed the boundary between permissible and unacceptable behaviour. He did not, unlike so many others facing kirk discipline, put forward mitigating circumstances explaining his outburst, although he could have justifiably argued that certain factors ought to have been considered.

Thus, the kirk session was most likely unaware that at the time Riddle and his young wife were enduring severe financial difficulties, difficulties which would see their standard of living plummet and their social networks shrink in just two years. Just a few months after his contrition before the pulpit, Riddle and Isobel were forced to move to a new house, evicted by their landlord for non-payment of their annual rent.[26] Their landlord, Jon Veitch, instructed them to 'flit and remove thameselffis' from his upper storey or 'heich' property on the north side of Canongate (technically a separate burgh from Edinburgh located on the eastern stretches of what is now the Royal Mile). But Veitch immediately offered them a lower rental value 'laich' or lower storey property in the less desirable Leith Wynd area.[27] Twelve months later and Veitch was evicting the couple yet again, but this time the tenant/landlord relationship had been soured beyond recovery, as Riddle obstinately refused to leave the property and was fined for his 'violent possession' of the house. He was further instructed to settle the outstanding rent and ordered to pay 20s court costs.[28] This time, Veitch did not offer to accommodate the couple and they moved to another 'laich' property of low rental value on the north side of the burgh, from which they were subsequently evicted just two years later in 1629. And their troubles did not end there either, as they were evicted once

---

[23] Ibid.
[24] Ibid., p. 311.
[25] J.R.D. Falconer, *Crime and Community in Reformation Scotland: Negotiating Power in a Burgh Society* (London, 2013).
[26] ECA, SL150/1/13, Canongate Burgh Court Books, 1623–6, no pagination.
[27] Ibid. See also NRS, CH2/122/2, p. 309. 'Many of thair people wer hindered from keiping thair awin paroch kirk be reason of the grit multitude of beggeris that sitest in Leith Wynd of Canogait.'
[28] ECA, SL150/1/13, no pagination.

more in 1632, this time from another 'laich' property in Leith Wynd, with annual rental value of just £5.[29].

In just six short years, the young burgess and his wife had been evicted from their family home no fewer than four times, twice by the same landlord, and had seen the standard of accommodation they lived in plummet. From a respectable higher storey property with 'pertinents', they had moved to several lower value properties, the last of which equalled some of the lowest property values in Canongate at that time.[30] Riddle's actions had broken a connection with a wealthy Edinburgh property owner who had previously stood by him and offered his family alternative accommodation. He had incurred the wrath of the kirk session and alienated himself from the elected and master craftsmen of his guild, forcing his very public and humiliating display of contrition, inflicting damage on his own reputation in the process. Riddle's story, therefore, had been one of slippage from a central to a marginal social position. However, the scale of his movement between centre and periphery is negligible in comparison to the following case study.

William Cuthbertson

My second case study focuses on the tumult and vicissitudes that made up the life of William Cuthbertson, another Canongate burgess cordiner. Cuthbertson first appears in kirk records in March 1619, when he and his wife were key witnesses in the adultery conviction of Charles Fortoun and Helen Wilson. Katherine Kells – Cuthbertson's wife – gave damning evidence to the session's inquiry with her meticulously detailed statement. Kells told the session that she 'perceived hir selff be hir cullors and seikness that sche [Wilson] was with bairne and that infant had come to perfectioun, it had bene borne at Lambes' and that 'Agnes Pearson quha dwells at the border in the south country told hir that Helen Wilson was with bairne And that sche sould go to hir house to bere it'. Kells had convinced Wilson that a safe house was awaiting her for the birth of her illegitimate child, and then promptly stood as a key witness against Wilson in her prosecution – assisted by her husband, William Cuthbertson.[31] Kells' duplicitous nature would not have troubled Cuthbertson in the slightest, for the two were a quarrelsome – often violent – couple who thought nothing of exposing their neighbours to kirk discipline and yet were often called before both kirk and civil courts themselves. Katherine Kells (or Kellows) was called to answer charges of misbehaviour or misconduct before the Canongate bailies on no fewer than four occasions

---

[29] ECA, SL150/1/14, Canongate Burgh Court Diet Book, 1626–1631, no pagination; SL150/1/15, Canongate Burgh Court Diet Book, 1631–1634, no pagination.
[30] For Canongate rental values, see ECA, SL150/1.
[31] NRS, CH2/122/1, pp. 468–71.

between 1620 and 1630. She features prominently in a recent thesis, where she is described as 'a disorderly, grudge-bearing woman'.[32] In 1620, for example, both she and her husband were ordered by the bailies 'not to truble nor molest in ony tyme comeing' John Osnall and his family. The couple were threatened with a sizeable fine of £40 should they not comply, and their cautioner, William Lowrie, was also threatened with a £10 fine if they failed to keep the peace in future.[33] Lowrie's presence as their cautioner or guarantor is significant, as we shall later see, and he must have been a friend of theirs to undertake such a commitment, especially given their disputatious reputation. However, the couple's quarrelsome nature did not prevent them from offering others hospitality, most likely for reward, as Kells supplemented the household income by selling ale.

Resetting and Sabbath Breaking

Cuthbertson and his wife were both convicted in March 1623 of 'resetting' Elspeth McNair, described as 'ane scandalous persone orray [unattached, unmarried] and out of service'.[34] The session enquired of Cuthbertson 'how oft sche resortit to his hous', to which Cuthbertson personally responded that she 'had lodgit with him for twa nichts'. Cuthbertson and Kells were jointly fined £5 and confined to ward until they paid in full.[35] A local woman called Elspeth Pool was also charged with harbouring McNair, where the session claims that McNair was not only single and not engaged in lawful employment but was also 'ane alledgit fornicatrix'.[36] As it was her first offence, and considering her perceived penitence, the session admonished her 'to carie hir selff honestlie and keip hir hous frie of all sclanderous persones' in the future. McNair had also been lodging with John Scobie, listed in proceedings as a burgh officer, who admitted that she had stayed with him eight days, for which he was fined £10 and ordered to bring the money on the next session day. The following week neither he nor Cuthbertson had paid their fines but neither received any further punishment. This may have been for a few related reasons, the first of which is that from the spring to autumn of 1623 Scotland was in the grip of a severe nationwide famine which had first emerged in 1622, a famine which caused instances of resetting or harbouring people moving into the urban areas in search of food to rise across the country.[37] By the spring of 1623, many parishes across Scotland found their poor

---

[32] A. Glaze, 'Women's Networks of Family, Work, Support and Slander in Canongate, 1600–1660' (unpublished PhD thesis, University of Guelph, 2017), p. 176.
[33] ECA, SL150/1/12, Canongate Burgh Court Diet Books, 1620–2, p. 261.
[34] NRS, CH2/122/2, p. 157.
[35] Ibid.
[36] Ibid.
[37] See Hall, 'Famine of 1623'. Evidence exists for resetting cases rising in Canongate, Aberdeen, Stirling, Belhelvie, Dysart, Kirkcaldy, Burntisland, Perth, Ayr, Kelso, Dunfermline, and Dumfries.

relief structures facing 'unsustainable pressure'.[38] Secondly, Cuthbertson was a burgess cordiner, and members of his craft guild were suffering more than some through the economic impact of the famine, as people struggled with higher food prices and most likely cut back on clothing and other expenses.[39] The plight of some cordiners in the burgh can be judged from the plea for temporary assistance from Charles Fortoun, who 'gave in his bill desyring the support of the session now in his grit extremitie', for which they agreed to give him 'ane ten merk gold coin' on the proviso that he ask for no more after that, to which he agreed.[40] For Charles to have asked the session in the first place for help in this way suggests that he felt any assistance given through other available networks such as his craft guild may have been insufficient and needed supplementing.[41]

Cuthbertson was called before the session again in 1624 to answer a charge of 'haveing [his] common servants working upon the Lordis Saboth ... quhilk challengis he simply denyit'.[42] The session could prove that his servants were working on the Sabbath, but without witness evidence against him, they could not prove that Cuthbertson had instructed them to do so – although there could have been little doubt that he had. He was admonished for not taking better care of his household and instructed to do so in future. Sabbath breaches by craftsmen during and immediately after a nationwide 1623 famine were commonplace as prices rose and incomes dropped. At one point during the peak of the famine almost every baker in the Fife burgh of Dysart was imprisoned for baking bread on the Sabbath.[43]

Cuthbertson transgressed again a few years later, although in slightly different fashion, when he appeared before the session charged with another Sabbath breach offence just months before his first witchcraft accusation against Bessie Purcell. In May 1628, he was ordered not to allow 'personis of ony degrie quhatsumever to drink in tyme of divyne preaching'.[44] Katherine Kells, was well known to the local magistrates for her swiftness in bringing her debtors to court in pursuance of full settlement and she mainly did this for debts relating to purchases of ale.[45] Kells sold considerable quantities of ale, with debtors owing her anywhere between £2 and £8.[46] Kells' selling of

---

[38] Ibid., p. 8.
[39] On rising food prices during this famine, see T.C. Smout and A.J.S. Gibson, *Prices, Food and Wages in Scotland, 1550–1780* (Cambridge, 1994).
[40] NRS, CH2/122/2, p. 167.
[41] For analysis of informal care networks across early modern Scotland, see C.R. Langley, *Cultures of Care: Domestic Welfare, Discipline and the Church of Scotland, c.1600–1689* (Leiden, 2020).
[42] Ibid., p. 201.
[43] NRS, CH2/390/1, Dysart Kirk Session Minutes, 1619–43, p. 27.
[44] Ibid., p. 495.
[45] Glaze, 'Women's Networks', pp. 79, 178.
[46] Ibid.

ale and their both being convicted for harbouring suggest that hospitality was an additional source of income for the couple at a time when the entire cordiner's craft membership were under economic strain. The strain brought on initially by the famine of 1623 may have encouraged William to take additional work too.

Burgh Constable

On 8 April 1625, a young woman called Helen Ramsay was ordered to appear before the kirk session of the Canongate charged with 'keiping scandalous companie with Laurence Skene'. Her charge said she had been 'deprehendit' with Skene 'be ane of the constables' between 11 pm and midnight the previous evening. Whilst the session acknowledged the pair were promised to each other in marriage, they were not permitted to 'be fund together in ane scandalous maner untill that purpous of marriage was completit'.[47] They were both instructed to return the following session day whereupon they would 'heir futher of the kirks deliberatiouns'.[48] That same day, the session also requested that the 'bailyie Adam Bothwell put William Cuthbertson in ward … to compeir this day, aucht dayis to answer to sick thingis as the session hes to lay at his charg'. It seemed that Cuthbertson was in trouble again. The following week's entry makes it clear that these two incidents were related, as Cuthbertson was 'demandit at quhat tyme he apprehendit Heleine Ramsay quhen he put her in the Tolbuith'.[49] Cuthbertson declared that he came across Ramsay and Skene walking down the High Street 'at ane efter midnight', which was later than the session had been previously told by Ramsay, so the session asked Cuthbertson for verification, which he provided in the shape of witnesses John Sweet and the burgh's jailer, Thomas Robinson. Robinson confirmed that he had received Ramsay as a prisoner at around 1 am and further added that she 'ves sa extraordinair that skairsch sche [knew] quhat sche wes doing', suggesting that Ramsay was severely inebriated when arrested by Cuthbertson. Cuthbertson's other witness, John Sweet, likewise confirmed that she had been apprehended around 1 am but he added the significant detail to his testimony that Cuthbertson had seized her by the throat. It was probably this overly zealous, heavy-handed approach which led to Cuthbertson's arrest and warding pending the session's examinations.

The very next case to be heard by the session that day again involved Cuthbertson in his role as a burgh constable. Giving evidence against John Fleming, Cuthbertson told the session that Fleming 'keipit ane oppin scandalous hous and ves ane common resaitter of evill personis', and further added that they would arrive at 'dyvers tymes efter ten hours at evin by [in contra-

[47] NRS, CH2/122/2, p. 259.
[48] Ibid.
[49] Ibid.

vention of] the ordinances of kirk and counsall'.[50] In a remarkable display of hypocrisy and duplicity, Cuthbertson savaged a neighbour for committing a similar offence to the one of which he and his wife Katherine were guilty just two years earlier, resetting scandalous or undesirable people. As this was not Fleming's first offence of this nature, the consequences for him and his family were considerably more severe than for Cuthbertson in 1623. The session recommended that Fleming be put to trial at the burgh court, and, on the presumption of a guilty verdict fuelled by Cuthbertson's extensive testimony, that 'he [be] removit frome this toun', that is, banished.[51] The burgh court duly banished him under pain of public scourging should he return, in keeping with the session's wishes.[52] Fleming was one of ten individuals banished from Canongate that year, but his was the only banishment for resetting.[53] Fleming would have been shamefully 'conveyed out at the Water Yett with the foure officers' in a publicly humiliating ritualised procession, witnessed by his friends and neighbours.[54] The impact of banishment on Fleming and his family would have been profound and life-changing, and all stemming from Cuthbertson's testimony as a burgh constable.

By the spring of 1628, Cuthbertson was no longer serving as a burgh officer, so would no longer have been in receipt of the officer's annual 'pension' or salary. He may have withdrawn from the part-time role following the introduction of additional duties, agreed upon 'be universall consent of the session'.[55] These duties required the officers to accompany the kirk elders known as 'searchers' twice each Sunday, as they went from house to house looking for Sabbath breakers. The irony of his disappearance from burgh records as an officer at a time when they were engaged in looking for Sabbath breakers would most likely not have been lost on those who knew Cuthbertson, himself a regular Sabbath breaker, as we have seen.

Cuthbertson does, however, reappear quite quickly in the kirk records, and it relates to neighbourly conflict involving his quarrelsome family. His wife, Katherine Kells, was called before the kirk session in March 1628 following a bill of complaint given in against her by Alison Baillie, the wife of a Canongate litster (dyer) burgess, John Gray. Baillie and her husband claimed that Kells had called Baillie 'ane common hure, fals tinker', and furthermore said that if Alison had spent any more time in Edinburgh than she had done then she would have been publicly scourged. They also alleged that Kells had taken to standing outside Gray's workshop telling prospective customers that Gray 'wald steall [from] thame'.[56] Kells countered Baillie's claim by insisting that Baillie had called her a harlot. Based on the testimony

---

[50] Ibid.
[51] Ibid.
[52] ECA, SL150/1/15, p. 311.
[53] Ibid.
[54] NRS, CH2/122/2, p. 385.
[55] Ibid., p. 465.
[56] Ibid., p. 471.

of several witnesses, the session decided that 'baith the said personis had done wrang' and so warded both Gray and Cuthbertson until they found caution for their wives. Most interestingly of all, both parties called the same witnesses to verify their claims against one another: Alexander Miller, Michael Dryburgh, John Porteous, Findlay Williamson, Alexander Sleich, and, most significantly, Thomas Lowrie, a burgess cordiner and friend of William Cuthbertson. Lowrie supported Kells as he had been asked and gave evidence on her behalf, but crucially he also gave evidence *against* her too, verifying at least part of Baillie's claim.[57] Lowrie's actions surely cannot have been well received by Cuthbertson and Kells, and as much as Kells was noted as a 'grudge-bearing woman', her spouse was equally capable of holding onto enmity for prolonged periods.[58] Future trouble between the Lowrie and Cuthbertson households was assured.

Witchcraft Accusations

William Lowrie, who stood as cautioner for William Cuthbertson in 1620, was the son of Canongate cordiner Thomas Lowrie and his wife Bessie Purcell. Appointing a cautioner was a way of ensuring an offender's future good behaviour and 'ensuring the maintenance and stability of order in the burgh'.[59] By placing themselves at risk of financial loss should the offender reoffend, the cautioner then would not take up the role without having some leverage over the defendant; they were someone that they knew well. Clearly then, prior to the events of 1628, the relationship between the Cuthbertson and Lowrie households was at the very least cooperative and cordial. However, the peaceful relationship was shattered shortly thereafter. Within a few months of Lowrie's testimony against Katherine Kells, Bessie would be accused of witchcraft by William Cuthbertson, and the accusation was repeated in 1631. Purcell had appeared before the session in 1625 when slandered with the first of her many witchcraft accusations, then by her daughter-in-law, Katherine Bryson, and Bryson's mother, Agnes Clark.[60] John Craig, a 'servitor to Archibald Lowrie cordiner', was presented as a key witness by Thomas Lowrie in defence of his wife before the session, where he 'deponit that quhat was alledgit was trew' and Bryson had slandered her mother-in-law.[61] Although not mentioned in the deposition, Craig was in fact in service to the couple's son, Archibald, who, like his father, was a burgess cordiner. Familial and craft guild connections were not the only weapons in Thomas Lowrie's arsenal, as testamentary records show that he acted as a 'sumtyme baillie' or

---

[57] Ibid.
[58] Glaze, 'Women's Networks', p. 176.
[59] Falconer, *Crime and Community*, pp. 62–3.
[60] NRS, CH2/122/2, p. 251.
[61] Ibid.

magistrate too.[62] Ironically, in a fateful twist for Lowrie, Craig was called as a witness by Clark's husband, Alexander Bryson, in a counter claim which resulted in Lowrie and Purcell being held responsible for the family fallout and Lowrie was threatened with 'heichest censure' if the matter arose again. But Lowrie's ability to quickly organise a defence based on his networks, connections, and status as a magistrate ought to have forewarned Cuthbertson that here was a formidable adversary who would not take slanderous accusations lightly and also had the means and knowledge to take matters to higher levels. Cuthbertson, though, possessed an insatiable desire for revenge, an insatiable urge that would rise to the fore in December that year. And from his time as a burgh constable, Cuthbertson would have known that defending a slander of witchcraft could be a risky strategy for the offended party. For, in July 1627, whilst Cuthbertson was still a burgh official, Margaret Cowan and her husband Henry Fenton raised a bill of complaint before Canongate session against Bessie Robertson and her father James Robertson.[63] Initially in that case, the session found in favour of Margaret and her husband and ordered Bessie to 'publictlie in the streit befoir the said Margaret hir dure, ask forgiveness for hir offence befoir Adam Bothwell, bailyie'.[64] A humiliating backdown for Bessie, but yet she and her father had set a chain in motion, for sufficient levels of suspicion were aroused around Margaret to encourage others to level accusations at her. Just a few months later, an application was sent to the privy council seeking and gaining a commission for her to be tried for witchcraft.[65]

On Tuesday 2 December 1628, Cuthbertson and Henry Futhie made a formal accusation of witchcraft against Bessie Purcell to the kirk session of the Canongate 'and desyret the session to tak tryall thairanent'.[66] The session instructed Cuthbertson and Futhie to appear again the following week, and ordered them to bring John Meggat, a burgess cordiner, and William Smith, a litster, whom they had both named as fellow 'complainers in thair bill'.[67] The following week, Futhie appeared before the session along with Meggat, but neither Cuthbertson or Smith were in attendance. Futhie explained Smith's absence by stating that he, Cuthbertson, and Meggat were 'at the penning of the complaint againes Bessie Purcell ... and that William Smith wes not thair bot thay put in his name with his knawledge' and Futhie added that Smith would – in his opinion – 'abyde be this complaint and bill in all points'.[68] The session were clearly dismayed by Cuthbertson's

---

[62] NRS, CC8/8/57, Edinburgh Commissary Court: Register of Testaments, 1634–6, p. 489.
[63] NRS, CH2/122/2, pp. 421, 425, 427.
[64] Ibid., p. 427.
[65] RPCS, 2nd Series, Vol. 2, p. 470.
[66] NRS, CH2/122/2, p. 531.
[67] Ibid.
[68] Ibid., p. 533.

absence and requested the civil magistrates to 'incarcerat him quhill he find caution' to appear before them.[69] They also referred the case to the higher Kirk court of the presbytery. On 20 December, Cuthbertson appeared before the session 'accusit for not insisting upon the complaint given in be him againes Bessie Purcell', whereupon he immediately claimed that Purcell 'and utheris in hir name' had in fact implored him not to proceed with the case and if he dropped the bill against her that 'sche promeist ... also to be as guid to him as hir sones William and Archibald'.[70] Cuthbertson then declared that he had given in the bill of his own accord and that 'he wald insist till the finisching ... and that he sall compeer the morne befoir the Presbitrie'.[71] Unfortunately, Edinburgh presbytery records for the time have not survived, so Cuthbertson's full testimony is possibly beyond recovery. What can be known is that further accusations, most likely inspired by Cuthbertson, forced both Thomas Lowrie and his son William to conduct a rigorous defence of Bessie. Cuthbertson and his co-accusers had clearly made the case against Purcell a very public point of discussion within the confines of a small urban community where the population would have numbered no more than 4,000.[72] The slur on Bessie's character surfaced again in October 1630, forcing Thomas into defending his wife once more, this time giving in a bill of complaint against Agnes Robeson and her husband, Henry Livingston.[73] Robeson's slander against Purcell was nothing if not colourful, as Lowrie's complaint made claims of liaisons with Satan, Robeson allegedly saying of Purcell that 'the Devil read upon quhen he lykit and the said Bessie danced with him in ane bak chalmer and more callit hir common rinkle facet witch'.[74] The session heard from Henry Livingston that his wife was not able to answer the charges against her due to 'hir seikness' and so he was ordered to present her before them the following week or pay a £40 fine. When they next appeared before the session, Henry and Agnes presented their own bill of complaint against Bessie and Thomas, saying that Bessie had called Agnes 'ane pypperis whore' and that she had challenged the masculinity of Henry, saying that 'he wore ane yellow bonnet and with many uther filthie speiches'. Further lurid details of slanderous accusations against Agnes were given too, as she was said to have called Thomas Lowrie 'Incestuous adulterous doge' and claimed Bessie had 'givin hir soull to the Divil'.[75] Agnes denied calling Thomas an adulterous dog, but several witnesses called by Lowrie verified his claim. As for the witch accusations against his wife, the session sympathised that 'the said Bessie Purcell is daylie upbraided by sundrie of hir nichbouris with the odious name of a witch'. The session further added that they would

[69] Ibid.
[70] Ibid., p. 535.
[71] Ibid.
[72] Hall, 'Famine of 1623', at p. 17.
[73] NRS, CH2/122/3, Canongate Kirk Session Minutes, 1629–49, p. 77.
[74] Ibid.
[75] Ibid.

postpone disciplining Agnes until such time as Bessie and Thomas 'obtain ane absolvitour for sick ane odious and vyld imputation befoir the competent judge'.[76] Unable to absolve his wife before the session, Lowrie took his case to the privy council in January 1631, seeking to 'obtain a discharge to the Commissaries of Edinburgh of any further proceedings in respect of the alleged slandering of Bessie Pursell'.[77] The privy council contacted the archbishop of St Andrews, who was in possession of the 1628 depositions given in by Cuthbertson, Futhie, and Meggat. Upon hearing that the archbishop had dismissed the depositions as 'meere fantasies', the privy councillors discharged the commissaries 'of all further procedure … unless upon new and other grounds than those submitted to the said Archbishop'.[78] Cuthbertson and his co-accusers had been dismissed as malicious fantasists by one of the highest courts in Scotland. The outcome must have come as a huge relief for Purcell, as many women, including four burgess' wives, were convicted of witchcraft during a nationwide panic between 1628 to 1631.[79]

That ought to have been the end of the matter, but Cuthbertson was such an incorrigible character that he simply would not let it rest, and so it was that he again slandered Purcell in December 1631. This time, Cuthbertson did not present a bill to the session; rather, he was named in a complaint given in by Thomas Lowrie, Purcell's husband. Interestingly, Lowrie named Agnes Robeson and her husband Henry Livingston in the bill of complaint too, strongly suggesting that their earlier slander was indeed at least partly fuelled by Cuthbertson. At the first hearing before the session for this case on 13 December 1631, Cuthbertson was accused of calling Purcell 'ane witche, hir sones witches whelpis'. On examination by the session, Cuthbertson said that he would partly deny the allegations and partly not but asked for a further week to arrange a defence, which was granted. He was ordered to ensure that Livingston and his wife appeared the following week too.[80] On 20 December, Thomas Lowrie dropped his complaint against Livingston, but retained the complaint against his wife, Agnes Robeson, and Cuthbertson.[81] Cuthbertson, when questioned by the session, 'declarit that he wes fynned already for calling hir bairnes witches whelpis be the baillies and counsall and that ane of hir bairnes and he wes agreit and that scandal wes takin away and thairfor suld no more be heard'.[82] Furthermore, he added that he had not slandered Purcell anytime at all after the privy council ruling of 11 January that year. The session, possibly sensing an end to this epic saga, absolved him of all slander preceding the privy council ruling but warned

---

[76] Ibid., p. 79.
[77] *RPCS*, 2nd Series, Vol. 4, p. 111.
[78] Ibid., p. 112.
[79] L. Yeoman, 'Hunting the Rich Witch in Scotland: High-Status Witchcraft Suspects and their Prosecutors, 1590–1650', in J. Goodare (ed.), *The Scottish Witch-Hunt in Context* (Manchester, 2002), pp. 106–21, at p. 109.
[80] NRS, CH2/122/3, p. 153.
[81] Ibid.
[82] Ibid., p. 155.

him that any future slanderous accusations would result in his being 'censurit … accordinglie'.[83] Cuthbertson was never called again for slandering either Purcell or Lowrie. It cannot be said for certain whether the stress of repeatedly defending themselves against witchcraft accusations played any part in his declining health, but Thomas died not long after in 1635.

Multiple Evictions and an Acquittal for Wounding

Both Cuthbertson and Riddle repeatedly endured one of the most stressful situations that a family can face – they were each evicted several times (1624, 1626, 1627, 1630, 1632, 1634, and 1640 for Cuthbertson, and 1626, 1627, and 1629 for Riddle). This may partly explain their belligerence and hostility to others, particularly other cordiners and their families. It is evident that internal divisions existed within the craft at the time, and they may have been heightened by a period of a downturn in trade. Another cordiner to have suffered eviction in the 1620s was one of Cuthbertson's co-accusers in the Purcell witchcraft case, John Moggat. Interestingly too, another of Purcell's accusers, the litster William Smyth, had been evicted in 1624 from the same area of Canongate as Cuthbertson was evicted from that year.[84] It will probably never be known if Cuthbertson had persuaded his co-accusers that Purcell was responsible for their earlier evictions, as neither appeared in front of the session before the case was referred to the presbytery.[85] Purcell, as we have seen, had been called a witch during a heated family dispute in 1625.[86] As we have a proven link between Cuthbertson's family and Purcell's through her son standing as his cautioner, he probably knew of this prior accusation, and it is worth noting that it was Cuthbertson who presented the bill of accusation to the kirk in 1628.[87] Cuthbertson was evicted again in 1630, and in 1631 he again accused Purcell of witchcraft, this time extending his slur to other members of her family, as he called her sons 'witches whelpis'.[88] Cuthbertson would go on to be evicted again in 1632, 1634, and 1640, but no further records exist to suggest that he troubled Purcell or her husband Thomas Lowrie again.[89] However, in May 1634, just weeks after being informed he was to be evicted again, he was accused of attacking the burgh's jailor, James Davidson, in Davidson's own house on the High Street. In the dittay or bill presented against him to the barony court, Cuthbertson was said to have taken Davidson's sword from him and struck him upon the hand. Cuthbertson denied the charge and was acquitted by a fifteen-man

[83] Ibid.
[84] ECA, SL150/1/13, no pagination.
[85] NRS, CH2/122/2, p. 531.
[86] Glaze, 'Women's Networks', p. 184.
[87] NRS, CH2/122/2, p. 531
[88] NRS, CH2/122/3, p. 153.
[89] ECA, SL150/1/14-5, no pagination; ECA, SL150/1/18, Canongate Burgh Court Diet Books, 1640–2, no pagination.

assize.[90] That thirteen of the fifteen men on the assize were fellow burgesses like Cuthbertson speaks for itself.

Cuthbertson did not appear before the burgh court anymore after the 1634 sword incident and must have accepted his final 1640 eviction without lashing out at either his neighbours or colleagues. Interestingly though, on 21 December 1641, a mass altercation erupted in the Canongate between the schoolboys of that burgh and nearby Edinburgh. Canongate session called the schoolmasters before them the following week, instructing them to take order with the boys whom they described as 'thair insolent knaves who did violat the Lords day by thair abhominabill bikkering'.[91] After making enquiries relating to the incident, the session determined that the 'Edinburgh youthis were the provokers of the Cannogait boyes to bikkering' and called upon Edinburgh presbytery and ministers to take order with the boys there 'for suppressing of such'.[92] However, on 4 January 1642 the session, acknowledging that Canongate boys had responded violently to the provocation, called before them 'twa of the ringleaders to the bikkerings' and ordered that the boys be kept in ward until their fathers find cautioners for them. Furthermore, the session intimated that a 'diligent search for uther notorious villans' such as the two apprehended ringleaders would continue. The captured ringleader's names were 'Findlayson ... and Cuthbertson'.[93] William's progeny was following in his father's footsteps.

Conclusions

William Cuthbertson and John Riddle are both examples of people failing to cope when suffering severe repeated economic and social upheaval. They were of the same trade or profession at a time when competition was particularly fierce, and the local market was deflated by the impact of severe demographic crises associated with famine. Structural forces beyond their control plunged both men and their families into unsettling periods of economic precarity. Unable to cope emotionally with the trauma that economic misfortune and forced relocation bring, both men responded violently, Riddle on just one occasion, whilst Cuthbertson embarked on a series of disputes, altercations, and accusations: a man raging against the world and his seemingly unending predicaments.

Both men knew that their disruptive behaviour would take them up to, and sometimes beyond, boundaries of acceptability, and they were equally aware of the social and community forces that would be deployed against them to ensure their future conformity. Riddle played his part in a theatrical

---

[90] ECA, SL150/1/16, Canongate Burgh Court Diet Book, 1634–6, no pagination.
[91] NRS, CH2/122/3, p. 459.
[92] Ibid., p. 461.
[93] Ibid.

display of contrition, thereby returning to expected social norms, and only once offended again, when most likely exasperated at yet another eviction for his young family. Cuthbertson, on the other hand, denied allegations made against him, and seems to have known instinctively how far to push and usually whom to push; it must be said that despite his many confrontations with neighbours and colleagues, he never once challenged or insulted a figure of authority, suggesting he was gameplaying, constantly testing boundaries all along. When he did finally step too far into the margins and engage in a campaign of slander against a former magistrate's wife, in the end he backed down completely, knowing that he was no longer a burgess on the edge of acceptability, but beyond it. In the end he survived, aided by his burgess status – and he handed on a tradition of troublemaking to the next generation.

5

Enslaved and Formerly Enslaved Young People in Eighteenth- and Nineteenth-Century Scotland

Matthew Lee

Enslaved and free people of colour lived in Scotland during the early modern period. The enslaved in Scotland were put to work, sold as property, and, in some cases, fled from their enslavers. Children born in the Americas to Scottish fathers – some born enslaved and then manumitted, others born free – were sent to Scotland for education or work purposes. They occupied the same spaces as the people with whom they lived, learned, and laboured. Their wider community would have been aware of their existence. Yet, as Dolly MacKinnon has argued in her work on enslaved children, they have been a 'visible yet invisible presence' in Scotland.[1] Until recently, Scots forgot, ignored, or disavowed the historic presence of enslaved and free people of colour in Scottish society. Historians have begun to reverse that process by paying closer attention to enslaved and free people's lives in Scotland.[2] New evidence about these people continues to emerge through individual case studies and larger repositories of information like the *Runaway Slaves in Britain* database.[3] These studies highlight the historic Black presence in Scotland. Early modern Scottish society was not racially homogenous. Centring this idea provides a basis for a more diverse and nuanced account of Scottish history.

This chapter contributes to this growing historiography by examining enslaved and formerly enslaved young people in eighteenth- and early nineteenth-century Scotland. It reconstructs aspects of the lives of these

---

[1] D. MacKinnon, 'Slave Children: Scotland's Children as Chattels at Home and Abroad in the Eighteenth Century', in J. Nugent and E. Ewan (eds), *Children and Youth in Premodern Scotland* (Woodbridge, 2015), pp. 120–35, at pp. 120–1.
[2] See, for example, I. Whyte, *Scotland and the Abolition of Black Slavery, 1756–1838* (Edinburgh, 2006), pp. 9–36; J.W. Cairns, 'Freeing from Slavery in Eighteenth-Century Scotland', in A. Burrows et al. (eds), *Judge and Jurist: Essays in Memory of Lord Rodger of Earlsferry* (Oxford, 2013), pp. 366–81; S. Newman, 'Freedom-Seeking Slaves in England and Scotland, 1700–1780', *English Historical Review*, 134:570 (2019), pp. 1136–68; L. Williams, 'African Caribbean Residents of Edinburgh in the Eighteenth and Nineteenth Centuries', *Kalfou*, 7 (2020), 42–9; D. Alston, *Slaves and Highlanders: Silenced Histories of Scotland and the Caribbean* (Edinburgh, 2021), pp. 257–99.
[3] *Runaway Slaves in Britain*, www.runaways.gla.ac.uk/.

young people through adverts in the *Runaway Slaves* database and hitherto under-examined archival material. The second half of the chapter details the early life of James Innes, a formerly enslaved child who spent time in Jamaica and Shetland. A determination to 'give voice' to the marginalised has spurred attempts to produce histories of childhood.[4] The interaction of age, race, gender, class, or sexual orientation can compound a young person's social marginality.[5] The youths this chapter discusses were marginal because of their age, race, and enslaved or formerly enslaved status. This acute marginalisation provides the rationale for examining this cohort.

However, examining the history of the marginalised through a study of children and young people has its limits. A dilemma inherent to the history of childhood is the relative dearth of source material produced by children. A further issue is whether historians can ascribe to children the agency possessed by adults. Sara Maza has noted that individual children have exerted their desire for autonomy throughout history. Nevertheless, Maza has questioned whether these actions represent coordinated attempts to subvert structures of oppression.[6] These problems become more difficult when one considers the lives of enslaved children. Their age and the power relationships that undergirded enslavement limited their agency to a far greater extent than other children. Moreover, the sources concerning their lives are fragmentary and written from the enslaver's perspective. As Saidiya Hartman has observed, the search for enslaved people's voices may well be a fruitless one. Historians must, in Hartman's words, 'imagine what cannot be verified' when writing the history of enslaved people.[7] By examining enslaved and formerly enslaved youths, this chapter attends to questions of agency. While accepting the narrow scope for action open to the enslaved, it shows that they tried to exert their autonomy and shape their world with the tools available to them. Through its focus on James Innes, whose life appears to have been controlled by people older than him, the chapter underscores the complex nature of the agency – or lack thereof – possessed by young people in early modern Scotland.

From the Plantation to Scotland

Children contributed significantly to the plantation economy through their forced labour. Despite this importance, historians have overlooked enslaved children's roles in the functioning of plantations until recently.[8] Enslaved

---

[4] N. Musgrove, C.P. Leahy, and K. Moruzi, 'Hearing Children's Voices: Conceptual and Methodological Challenges', in K. Moruzi et al. (eds), *Children's Voices from the Past: New Historical and Interdisciplinary Perspectives* (London, 2019), pp. 1–25, at p. 2.
[5] Ibid., p. 11.
[6] S. Maza, 'The Kids Aren't All Right: Historians and the Problem of Childhood', *American Historical Review*, 125:4 (2020), pp. 1268–9.
[7] S. Hartman, 'Venus in Two Acts', *Small Axe*, 26 (2008), pp. 1–14.
[8] J. Teelucksingh, 'The "Invisible Child" in British West Indian Slavery', *Slavery and*

children inhabited a violent and unhealthy world. Infant mortality rates in the Caribbean were high. The Scottish plantation doctor and poet James Grainger observed that white children were 'less liable to perish within the month than those of the Blacks'.[9] Care for enslaved infants and the supervision of children's labour were the purview of older enslaved women, thus disrupting the connection between enslaved children and their mothers.[10]

Enslavers considered enslaved people as children until fifteen years old. They entered the labour force aged six or seven.[11] A series of gangs organised by age carried out enslaved labour on plantations. Tasks became increasingly strenuous as enslaved youths grew older. The youngest members of the gangs carried out basic agricultural work. Grainger stated that 'at eight years of age, they are made to pick grass, carry a small basket with dung, and under the direction of those of riper years, to pull up weeds in the cane-piece'.[12] Once they were around seventeen or eighteen years old, enslaved people took on the arduous tasks associated with planting, cultivating, and harvesting sugar.[13] From an enslaver's perspective, this increasing productive capacity meant that children became a more valuable commodity as they matured.[14]

This gradual introduction to harsher forms of labour had various purposes and consequences. Particularly from the late eighteenth century, enslavers considered enslaved children's characters as pliable. On this basis, they hoped to inculcate a sense of loyalty among the younger members of their enslaved labour force.[15] By moving children through different gangs, enslavers aimed to acclimatise enslaved people to the idea they were property with no other function than to perform labour.[16] Putting children to work and coercing increasingly demanding tasks from them – from field work to reproductive labour – unsettled the definitions of childhood. Plantation overseers devised terms like 'men-boys' and 'women-girls' to describe the blurred boundaries between childhood, adolescence, and adulthood engendered by enslavement.[17] However, enslaved children did not accept their enslaved status without challenge. They resisted enslavement through actions including slow work and running away.[18]

Abolition, 27 (2006), pp. 237–50, at p. 237.
[9] J. Grainger, *An Essay on the More Common West-India Diseases* (London, 1764), p. 16.
[10] D. Paton, 'The Driveress and the Nurse: Childcare, Working Children and Other Work Under Caribbean Slavery', *Past & Present*, 246: Suppl. 15 (2020), pp. 27–53.
[11] C.A. Vasconcellos, *Slavery, Childhood, and Abolition in Jamaica, 1788–1838* (Athens, GA, 2015), p. 9.
[12] Grainger, *Essay*, p. 18.
[13] Teelucksignh, 'Invisible Child', at p. 243.
[14] S. Turner, *Contested Bodies: Pregnancy, Childrearing, and Slavery in Jamaica* (Philadelphia, PA, 2017), p. 214.
[15] Ibid., p. 223.
[16] C. Jones, 'Youthful Rebels: Young People, Agency and Resistance against Colonial Slavery in the British Caribbean Plantation World', in G. Campbell et al. (eds), *Child Slaves in the Modern World* (Athens, OH, 2011), pp. 64–83, at p. 65.
[17] Turner, *Contested*, p. 214; Vasconcellos, *Slavery*, p. 31.
[18] Jones, 'Youthful', at pp. 70–80.

Enslaved people came to Scotland through various mechanisms. One route was directly from the coast of West Africa. For example, an African-born enslaved person known as Scipio Kennedy was captured by a Scottish mariner and lived at Culzean Castle in Ayrshire.[19] Other enslaved children were conveyed from the Americas to Scotland by a middleman. A pertinent example of this practice occurred in 1762 when James Watt and his brother John were involved in importing an enslaved boy named Frederick.[20] In other cases, enslavers travelling back to Scotland from the Americas brought enslaved people with them. Being taken on this kind of journey was the means by which most enslaved people arrived in Scotland.[21] The advertisements in British newspapers offering enslaved people for sale show that they were almost always children or youths. They were also overwhelmingly male. Once in Scotland, they attended to an enslaver's personal needs or they performed other domestic duties.[22] Furthermore, enslaved people represented the (often newfound) wealth and status an enslaver had built up thanks to their involvement with slavery in the Americas.[23]

Enslavers tended to bring 'favourites' or those with experience of domestic labour. Theoretically, taking an enslaved youth to Scotland meant removing them from the harsh plantation regime. Enslavers may have perceived the decision to bring an enslaved person to Scotland as a benevolent act.[24] Yet, there is evidence that enslaved people endured difficult conditions during their time in Scotland. Aberdeen Infirmary records show that its doctors treated at least two young people in the 1760s who were likely to have been enslaved. The infirmary admitted a boy named Cato on 14 October 1766. The admission notes refer to him as a 'Negro' – a racial descriptor that appears in relation to only one other person in these records. At the time of his admission, Cato was eleven years old and 'from Rain' (likely present-day Old Rayne in Aberdeenshire).[25] The admission record does not make Cato's enslaved status explicit but its description of him as a 'Negro' hints strongly at this possibility. It is unclear who took Cato to the infirmary and his enslaver's identity is uncertain. Cato was suffering from 'Scorbut[ic] Eruptions universally over his body', a complaint that had lasted for a year prior to his admission. The record states that Cato believed that 'cold' caused his

---

[19] MacKinnon, 'Slave Children', at pp. 128–9.
[20] S. Mullen, 'The Rise of James Watt', in M. Dick and C. Arche- Parré (eds), *James Watt (1736–1819): Culture, Innovation and Enlightenment* (Liverpool, 2020), pp. 39–60, at pp. 44–5.
[21] Whyte, *Abolition*, p. 13.
[22] S. Mullen, N. Mundell, and S.P. Newman, 'Black Runaways in Eighteenth-Century Britain', in G.H. Gerzine (ed.), *Britain's Black Past* (Liverpool, 2020), pp. 81–98, at pp. 83–5.
[23] MacKinnon, 'Slave Children', at p. 121.
[24] Newman, 'Freedom-seeking', at p. 1153.
[25] NHS Grampian Archives, Aberdeen Royal Infirmary: Daily Journal, GRHB 1/4/14, p. 307.

condition.[26] These 'Scorbut[ic] Eruptions' were a symptom of scurvy. Rather than cold weather, the cause of his condition was a poor diet. It is possible that Cato arrived in Scotland with scurvy, given that enslaved people in the Caribbean had nutritionally deficient diets, including a lack of vitamin C.[27] Alternatively, his illness may point to a lack of access to nutritious food during his time in Aberdeenshire. The infirmary discharged him as 'cured' on 3 December 1766.[28]

Cato was not the only enslaved person admitted for treatment for scurvy around this time. Fanny, 'a Negro from Town aged 15 years', entered the infirmary on 22 October 1766 suffering from 'Scorbut[ic] Eruptions on her Arms' and gonorrhoea 'of 6 Weeks standing'.[29] It is unclear how long Fanny had lived in Scotland before she went into the infirmary. Therefore, it is difficult to determine whether she caught gonorrhoea before or after she reached Aberdeen. Given the power imbalances inherent to enslavement, it is doubtful whether Fanny consented to the sexual intercourse that caused her infection. Fanny was 'Cured' and discharged on 24 December 1766.[30] She was readmitted to the infirmary in January 1767 because of a recurrence of her scurvy symptoms (but 'perfectly cured' of her gonorrhoea at the point of her readmission). Like Cato, she ascribed her ailment to 'Cold'.[31] She was discharged again on 17 February 1767.[32] Her illnesses serve as a reminder of the poor conditions and threats of violence experienced – and resisted – by enslaved people in Scotland.

Fugitives from Enslavement in Eighteenth-Century Scotland

The examples of Cato and Fanny show that enslaved people had no guarantee of good treatment in Scotland. It is unsurprising, therefore, that enslaved people sought freedom by leaving their enslavers' homes. The advertisements concerning freedom-seeking enslaved people placed in Scottish newspapers provide useful information about this group. Sixty-six adverts concerning forty-seven enslaved people appeared between 1719 and 1779 (sometimes one person appeared in multiple adverts). In line with the more general demographic trends within Scotland's enslaved population, these adverts suggest that fugitives from enslavement were mostly younger males. Forty-five adverts state a freedom-seeker's exact or approximate age. Taking duplicate or multiple adverts into account, there were thirteen fugitives younger than

---

[26] Ibid.
[27] K.F. Kiple, *The Caribbean Slave: A Biological History* (Cambridge, 1981), pp. 84–5.
[28] NHS Grampian Archives, Aberdeen Royal Infirmary: Daily Journal, GRHB 1/4/15, p. 38.
[29] Ibid., p. 317.
[30] Ibid., p. 66.
[31] Ibid., p. 99.
[32] Ibid., p. 123.

eighteen years old. A further eight were eighteen or nineteen years old. Seven were between twenty-two and twenty-five years old. A final two were in their thirties. The youngest age stated in the adverts is thirteen. The oldest is thirty-seven. A further sixteen adverts provide no age but include an age-based descriptor like 'boy', 'lad', or 'man'. A single advert refers to a 'woman'. Only five advertisements offer neither an age nor an age-based descriptor.[33]

Given these facts, enslavers appear to have perceived making reference to age as a useful tactic in their efforts to capture fugitives. However, the adverts point to practical problems associated with specifying an enslaved person's age. Many of the adverts state a person was 'about', 'around', 'between', or 'betwixt' a particular age. Sometimes two adverts provide different ages for the same person. For example, the 21 November 1769 edition of the *Edinburgh Advertiser* describes an enslaved person from America named James as 'about 15 years of age'. Nine days later, there was an advert for 'an American Black boy, name James, about sixteen years of age' in the *Glasgow Journal*.[34] James may have had a birthday between the publication of these notices. Equally, James' enslaver may have had only a rough idea of his age.

The adverts affirm the difficulties in distinguishing the point at which a person moved between childhood, adolescence, and adulthood. In August 1758, 'A BLACK BOY, about 14 years of age' fled from a Mrs Campbell in Inveraray.[35] Another descriptor for adolescents was 'lad'. This term appears in a 1779 advert for Neptune: a fifteen-year-old with experience as a sailor.[36] However, the eighteen-year-old Peter appears as a 'boy' in the advert about his escape.[37] Despite being nineteen or twenty years old, the advert seeking information about Hamlet – who sometimes called himself O'Dow – describes him as a 'boy'.[38] An unnamed nineteen-year-old freedom-seeker was a 'man'.[39] This insistence on describing young adults as children provides an insight into an intellectual justification for enslavement. By casting them as childlike and requiring adult supervision, enslavers asserted their right to control enslaved people.[40] Meanwhile, the only advert discussing a

---

[33] Based on an analysis of the Runaway Slaves in Britain database, filtered for newspapers published in Scotland.
[34] *Edinburgh Advertiser*, 21 November 1769, www.runaways.gla.ac.uk/database/display/?rid=33 [accessed 13 October 2022]; *Glasgow Journal*, 30 November 1769, www.runaways.gla.ac.uk/database/display/?rid=58 [accessed 13 October 1769].
[35] *Glasgow Courant*, 4 September 1758, www.runaways.gla.ac.uk/database/display/?rid=49 [accessed 11 October 2022].
[36] *Edinburgh Advertiser*, 24 December 1779, www.runaways.gla.ac.uk/database/display/?rid=35 [accessed 13 October 2022].
[37] *Edinburgh Evening Courant*, 28 May 1757, www.runaways.gla.ac.uk/database/display/?rid=6 [accessed 13 October 2022].
[38] *Edinburgh Advertiser*, 1 December 1769, www.runaways.gla.ac.uk/database/display/?rid=34 [accessed 13 October 2022].
[39] *Glasgow Journal*, 11 December 1766, www.runaways.gla.ac.uk/database/display/?rid=57 [accessed 13 October 2022].
[40] T. Rollo, 'The Color of Childhood: The Role of the Child/Human Binary in the Production of Anti-Black Racism', *Journal of Black Studies*, 49 (2018), 307–29, at p. 312.

female fugitive calls eighteen-year-old Ann a 'Woman'.[41] It is possible that Ann was a 'woman' rather than a 'girl' because enslavers viewed females as young as twelve years old as prospective mothers. This potential for reproductive labour hastened the onset of adulthood.[42] Taken together, these sources underline the extent to which childhood is an unstable and historically contingent analytical category – particularly in the context of enslavement.[43]

Over the almost sixty years covered by runaway advertisements, enslaved youths evinced an ongoing determination to flee enslavement. Yet, freedom-seeking actions carried risks. One hazard was the potential for recapture. In April 1720, the Glasgow merchant Andrew Ramsay had 'TAken [sic] up a Strolling Negro'. He gave the unnamed person's enslaver two weeks to reclaim their legal property. Ramsay planned to 'dispose of him at his Pleasure' if no one came forward.[44] A 'MULATTO or INDIAN BOY who calls himself *Essex Peter*' was in Glasgow's prison in 1744. Essex Peter was due to be 'Indented for a certain Term of Years as a Servant to Jamaica' unless anyone came forward to assert their legal ownership over him.[45] These instances demonstrate that captured freedom-seekers faced the prospect of being sold or sent abroad without their consent.

Fugitives devised tactics to mitigate the risks associated with running away. Taking valuable items and money was one such approach. In Muirton, Perthshire, an enslaved seventeen-year-old who answered to the name London fled from Oliphant Kinloch. Prior to leaving, London took a silver watch with the likely intention of selling it.[46] On 10 March 1773, an unnamed 'East-India Negro lad' of around sixteen or seventeen 'eloped from a family of distinction' in the Canongate area of Edinburgh. According to the advert regarding his escape, he was heading toward Newcastle. The unnamed freedom-seeker had 'carried off sundry articles of value'.[47] This detail suggests he planned to fund his escape by selling the items. On an unspecified date in 1775, an 'EAST INDIA BOY' who answered to the name Campbell fled from his enslaver. The advert requesting his capture states that Campbell was 'suspected to have carried with him some Bank Notes, particularly one

---

[41] *Edinburgh Evening Courant*, 13 February 1727, www.runaways.gla.ac.uk/database/display/?rid=2 [accessed 13 October 2022].
[42] Turner, *Contested*, pp. 50–1.
[43] S. Mintz, 'Why History Matters: Placing Infant and Child Development in Historical Perspective', *European Journal of Developmental Psychology*, 14 (2017), pp. 647–58, at p. 650.
[44] *Edinburgh Evening Courant*, 28 April 1720, www.runaways.gla.ac.uk/database/display/?rid=30 [accessed 11 October 2022].
[45] *Caledonian Mercury*, 12 January 1744, www.runaways.gla.ac.uk/database/display/?rid=55 [accessed 11 October 2022].
[46] *Edinburgh Advertiser*, 7 June 1768, www.runaways.gla.ac.uk/database/display/?rid=32 [accessed 20 October 2022].
[47] *Edinburgh Evening Courant*, 15 March 1773, www.runaways.gla.ac.uk/database/display/?rid=26 [accessed 6 October 2022].

Ten pound Note'.[48] £10 in 1775 is worth around £1,300 at 2021 prices.[49] Taking so much money suggests that Campbell did not intend to return to his enslaver. He seems to have realised that he required money to pay for a journey to his desired destination. By implication, Campbell developed and executed a detailed escape plan.

Heading to ports was another survival tactic freedom-seekers employed. This approach would have relied on geographical knowledge of Scotland and Great Britain, and perhaps help from other people. Both Tont (sometimes known as Simmons) in October 1739 and Peter in May 1757 were reportedly 'lurking' in Leith.[50] Peter's enslaver, Neil MacNeil of Bristol, was worried that Peter would escape by sea. The advert regarding his escape warns 'no shipmaster or private family' to 'give him countenance'.[51] The 3 January 1773 edition of the *Edinburgh Evening Advertiser* publicised that an eighteen-year-old joiner named Sylvester was making for a port so he could travel to London. An alternative to making for a port was to head for a place of perceived safety. The aforementioned Neptune told his friends 'that he was going to Dalkeith'.[52] The significance of this destination is unclear. A potential reason that Neptune headed to Dalkeith is that he knew people there who he believed would give him protection. Indeed, hiding in plain sight seems to have been Neptune's method for evading his enslaver. The advert detailing his flight from enslavement asserts that Neptune was 'an artful fellow' who 'will give himself out for a free man'.[53]

Enslaved youths accepted serious risks when they made bids for freedom. They crafted escape plans and undertook measures designed to lessen their chances of recapture. Not all of them would have been successful. Nevertheless, these efforts underline their desire to break free from the confines of enslavement. That people as young as thirteen engaged in this behaviour points to the harsh conditions they experienced and hoped to escape. It would be a mistake to interpret individual examples of freedom-seeking as a coordinated bid to destroy enslavement altogether. However, these actions show that young enslaved people understood ways they could assert their agency and bid for autonomy. In these cases – perhaps only for short periods of time – young freedom-seekers grasped the right to determine the outcome of their own lives.

---

[48] *Edinburgh Advertiser*, 26 May 1775, www.runaways.gla.ac.uk/database/display/?rid=820 [accessed 6 October 2022].
[49] Estimate based on the Measuring Worth online relative values calculator, www.measuringworth.com/.
[50] *Caledonian Mercury*, 15 October 1739, www.runaways.gla.ac.uk/database/display/?rid=36 [accessed 13 October 2022].
[51] *Edinburgh Evening Courant*, 28 May 1757, www.runaways.gla.ac.uk/database/display/?rid=6 [accessed 13 October 2022].
[52] *Caledonian Mercury*, 22 December 1779, www.runaways.gla.ac.uk/database/display/?rid=42 [accessed 20 October 2022].
[53] Ibid.

James Innes: A Manumitted Child in Shetland

James Innes was born in Jamaica in July 1794. His father, also James Innes, was from Shetland (I have designated him James Innes Sr for ease of understanding).[54] His mother, whose name is unknown, was an enslaved woman. After his death, James Innes Sr's associates sent his son 'home' to Shetland. The relevant sources shed light on James Innes' early life, but they also reflect one of the fundamental problems inherent to histories of childhood. It was the adults in James Innes' life, rather than James himself, who produced this source material. None of the letters that deal with the decision to send James 'home' convey his thoughts about being sent across the Atlantic. The history of this child is 'mediated through the perceptions of the adult'.[55] James' age and enslaved status allowed the adults in his life to silence his voice. The manner in which these men recorded James' story highlights the power imbalances built into the archives of enslavement.[56]

The known details of James Innes' life begin and end in Shetland. By February 1772, James Innes Sr had left Shetland for Edinburgh to serve an apprenticeship in the linen trade.[57] In August 1772, he travelled to Greenock to prepare for his departure to the Caribbean.[58] By 1774, he worked at Monteagle estate in Jamaica's Westmoreland parish.[59] His primary task was to supervise the labour of 200 enslaved people. Innes Sr complained he was 'continually in motion' from Monday morning until Saturday evening. He had to be in the fields by 'break of day' to ensure that the enslaved people 'turn out in good time'. Innes worked until it was 'pitch dark'. His letters home show no reflections on the fact that Monteagle's enslaved population laboured from morning to night in conditions far more arduous than he experienced.

By 1792, Innes Sr lived at Anchovy Valley. This estate was on Jamaica's northern coast in Portland parish, some eighty miles from Kingston.[60] He purchased land and a 'considerable number' of enslaved people by November 1793.[61] His landholding was 'betwixt 5 and 6 Hundred Acres' according to a letter he sent to his friend and brother-in-law Robert Scollay.[62] Innes Sr was

---

[54] James Innes' month and year of birth are confirmed in his father's will. See TNA, Will of James Innes, Planter of Portland Island of Jamaica, West Indies, PROB 11/1413/153.
[55] H. Cunningham, *Children and Childhood in Western Society Since 1500*, 2nd edn (Harlow, 2005), p. 2.
[56] M. Trouillot, *Silencing the Past: Power and the Production of History* (Boston, MA, 1995), pp. 44–58.
[57] SA, Letter of James Innes to James Hay, 11 February 1772, D40/12/5.
[58] SA, Letter of James Innes to James Hay, 11 August 1772, D40/12/36.
[59] SA, Letter of James Innes to James Hay, 29 July 1774, D40/13/14; 'Mount Eagle [Jamaica | Westmoreland]', *Legacies of British Slavery Database*, www.ucl.ac.uk/lbs/estate/view/256 [accessed 25 October 2022].
[60] SA, Letter by James Innes, Anchovy Valley Estate, Jamaica, to Arthur Nicolson of Lochend, June 1792, D24/57/8.
[61] NLS, Letter of James Innes to Robert Scollay, MS.50277, fol. 42r.
[62] SA, Letter by James Innes, Jamaica, to Mr Robert Scollay, merchant in Garth in

'Anxious to settle the Land' he had purchased. He intended to use the forty 'young and old' enslaved people to cultivate it.[63] Enslaved labour was essential to Innes Sr's project. However, he insisted his landholding represented the 'fruits of [his] own industry'.[64]

For all his boasts about his apparent affluence, Innes was not as prosperous as he implied. Financial pressures meant he rented out the enslaved people he had purchased to a nearby estate. Hiring out enslaved people was known as 'jobbing'. It was one of the most pernicious forms of enslavement in the Caribbean.[65] Beyond financial pressures, Innes Sr was eager to cultivate the land he bought because he was unwell. Due to his 'indifferent state of health', Innes wrote a will around June 1795.[66] This document refers to his 'reputed son' James. It describes him as 'belonging to Anchovy Valley estate' as the 'property' of Thomas Gregory Johnston and his heirs. The will calls him a 'Quadroon', meaning one of James' grandparents was African and the other three were racialised as white.[67] Therefore, his mother was of mixed heritage. She passed her enslaved status down to him. None of the documents regarding James Innes include his mother's name. She too occupies a position at the margins of the archival record.

James Innes Sr died in April 1798. At the time of his death, his legal property included thirty-six enslaved people.[68] The letter relaying this information from Jamaica, written by Archibald Anderson, mentions Innes Sr's 'fine stout healthy' son.[69] The news of Innes Sr's demise reached Shetland in November 1798. Replying the next month, Scollay and Thomas Bolt – another of Innes Sr's friends and brothers-in-law – instructed Anderson and Charles Bryan to sell their friend's property, including enslaved people and land. They requested Anderson to 'procure an adequate price' for this property to pay off Innes Sr's debts in Jamaica. Scollay and Bolt left their 'Dear friends [sic] Son' to the 'care and attention' of Anderson and Bryan and expressed a hope that the latter had paid for James' manumission.

Shetland, with news of his life in Jamaica, D/139/2. Robert Scollay and Thomas Bolt identified themselves as Innes Sr's brothers-in-law in a letter they sent to Archibald Anderson in December 1798. See SA, Letter Book of Thomas Bolt (Lordship Estate) December 1798–February 1799, D24 Box 28 No 9.

[63] SA, Letter by James Innes to Mr Robert Scollay, D1/139/3. This letter appears to have been sent to Bolt rather than Scollay.
[64] SA, D/139/2.
[65] NLS, Letter of Archibald Anderson and Charles Bryan to Thomas Bolt and Robert Scollay, MS.50277, fol. 12r. For more on 'jobbing', see N. Radburn and J. Robert, 'Gold versus Life: Jobbing Gangs and British Caribbean Slavery', *William and Mary Quarterly*, 76:2 (2019), pp. 223–56.
[66] SA, D1/139/3.
[67] TNA, PROB 11/1413/153.
[68] NLS, Copy of the inventory of James Innes, with a list of enslaved people, MS.50277, fol. 56r.
[69] NLS, Letter of Archibald Anderson to Thomas Bolt and Robert Scollay, MS.50277, fol. 10r–v.

Scollay and Bolt stated they were 'anxiously interested for the Child James [sic] welfare' and that they wanted him to be sent to Britain when he was an appropriate age. They insisted he would be 'carefully attended to' upon his arrival.[70] This assertion reflects a contemporary shift in attitudes towards children, including a closer focus on their intellectual development.[71] However, it is unclear from their letter whether they were surprised by the news of James' existence. As Daniel Livesay has noted, requests for family members in Britain to care for children of colour came as a shock to some but 'reinforced and confirmed well-known relationships' for others.[72] Scollay and Bolt's request to Anderson accorded with Innes Sr's instructions to his executors. He asked them to purchase his son's freedom after his death and then send him to Britain at a 'sufficient age'. Innes Sr wanted his son to be 'properly brought up and instructed' then 'put to some trade or business' when he became older.[73] The strictures Innes Sr laid down express the eighteenth-century notion that childhood was a vital period during which boys needed to acquire an education.[74] These instructions had serious repercussions for James Innes. To comply with the will, his father's friends removed him from Jamaica and sent him 'home' to a place he had never visited before.

According to Anderson, writing in March 1800, 'Mr Innes's reputed Son James is well and lives with his Mother on Anchovy V. Estate'. Anderson stated he had expected James' 'freedom would have been got this year and He sent home for Education'. The failure to sell James Innes Sr's property stymied this plan.[75] James' fate became the central question pertaining to his father's affairs. Resolving this situation created tensions between Anderson, Scollay, and Bolt. In June 1800, Anderson complained that Scollay and Bolt had 'contradicted' themselves and, for reasons that are unclear, imposed 'restrictions' on the sale of the property. This delay coincided with a fall in the price of land and enslaved people in Jamaica, which made any potential sale harder. Anderson impressed upon his correspondents that James' manumission hinged on the sale of the rest of his father's property. He warned them James was 'yet at Anchovy Valley Estate and cannot be removed from there without Mr Bryan's consent, which I hope me [sic] be obtained

---

[70] SA, Letter Book of Thomas Bolt (Lordship Estate) December 1798–February 1799, D24 Box 28 No 9.
[71] Cunningham, Children, p. 59.
[72] D. Livesay, *Children of Uncertain Fortune: Mixed-Race Jamaicans in Britain and the Atlantic Family, 1733–1833* (Williamsburg and Chapel Hill, NC, 2018), p. 310.
[73] TNA, PROB 11/1413/153. The names of the executors are mentioned in SA, Probate document concerning deceased James Innes, formerly of the parish of Portland, Jamaica, planter (died 1798), D24/56/69.
[74] C. Heywood, *A History of Childhood: Children and Childhood in the West from Medieval to Modern Times* (Cambridge, 2001), p. 24.
[75] NLS, Letter of Archibald Anderson to Robert Scollay and Thomas Bolt, MS.50277, fol. 14v.

next year, provided we are able to dispose of his Fathers [sic] Property'.[76] Therefore, James' manumission could be triggered only if Anderson sold other enslaved people.

In July 1801, Anderson informed Scollay and Bolt of his intention to sell these enslaved people by public auction. This action would generate funds to send James 'home' – in Anderson's words – the next year. He asked where in Scotland Scollay and Bolt wanted him to send James.[77] This comment reflects three noteworthy points about James' story. First, it suggests that Anderson decided to rid himself of the inconvenience associated with James' situation. He tried to do so by presenting Scollay and Bolt with a *fait accompli* about sending James to Scotland. Moreover, it shows that as a child and an enslaved person, James had no say about where he lived. Additionally, Anderson's declaration that he wanted to send James 'home' suggests that he considered the boy a Scot whose proper place was in Scotland.

Despite this threat to send James 'home' quickly, he remained in Jamaica until July 1803. Anderson 'at last got the opportunity of sending home Master James Innes' to Glasgow on the *Alford*. He intended to send James to a merchant in John Street named David Lamb. Anderson had only two days' notice to get James ready to leave Jamaica.[78] This speedy process suggests that James would have had virtually no time to process the idea of his impending departure. The letter containing this information makes no reference to his reaction to this news. Nor does it refer to his mother's feelings. It is unclear whether she knew about the plan. Their preferences appear to have been unimportant to Anderson's considerations. With the letter confirming James' voyage to Glasgow, Anderson enclosed a 'Bill of Exchange for £100 from Mr Bryan in part payment of the Negroes to answer the immediate Expenses of Master J. Innes'.[79] This evidence confirms that the sale of enslaved people funded James' manumission and passage to Scotland.

The journey from Anchovy Valley to Glasgow would have exposed James to new environments and experiences. It is probable that he embarked on his journey from the bustling port of Kingston. Then he would have spent weeks crossing the Atlantic under the care – or surveillance – of a young man named William Houston. Upon his arrival in Glasgow, James would have encountered yet another busy maritime hub. After disembarking, he and Houston visited David Lamb. James presented Lamb with a letter from Anderson, which explained that Anderson sent James to Lamb at Scollay and Bolt's behest.[80]

---

[76] NLS, Letter of Archibald Anderson to Robert Scollay and Thomas Bolt, MS.50277, fol. 18r.
[77] NLS, Letter of Archibald Anderson to Robert Scollay and Thomas Bolt, MS.50277, fol. 21v.
[78] NLS, Letter of Archibald Anderson to Robert Scollay and Thomas Bolt, MS.50277, fol. 24r.
[79] Ibid.
[80] NLS, Letter of Archibald Anderson to David Lamb, MS.50277, fol. 26r. This letter confirms that William Houston accompanied James Innes on the voyage from Jamaica to Glasgow.

It is unclear how James Innes travelled from Glasgow to Shetland. He lived with Thomas Bolt – either in his home in Lerwick or the Haa of Cruister in Bressay. Beyond this fact, little information about his life there has emerged.[81] However, it is possible to raise questions or offer speculations about his time in Shetland. For example, how did Bolt, Scollay, and their family members explain the sudden arrival of a child from Jamaica? His background as a formerly enslaved child born out of wedlock seems like a subject that may have sparked conversation in his new community. James' introduction into a new household points to contemporary ideas regarding kinship and childhood. According to Philippe Ariès, the eighteenth century was the period in which the family unit became increasingly private and separated from the wider community.[82] Tighter definitions of family and a narrower range of potential marriage partners reflected anxieties associated with colonial expansion. Returnees from Britain's colonies imperilled established patterns of land ownership. Marriage between elite families consolidated landholding, with a view to stymieing newly wealthy arrivistes. Similarly, children born out of wedlock in the Caribbean became rival heirs to legitimate children. In this way, colonialism encouraged a closing of ranks among British families.[83] Yet, James' entry into his relatives' household(s) suggests that understandings of family in Scotland remained loose enough to accommodate kin from outside the nuclear family.[84]

However, it is important to acknowledge that James' life in Shetland would not necessarily have been easy. His illegitimacy is a factor that could have shaped his relationship with his relatives. Families in Scotland were not unaccustomed to dealing with illegitimate children.[85] Yet, as a 'reputed son', James occupied a place on the legal margins of family life. By extension, it is possible that he was also on its emotional periphery.[86] Race is another factor that would have influenced James' relationship with his family members. His background, which included a Scottish father and a mixed-heritage mother, may have allowed James to pass as white. However, it remains certain that

---

[81] A. Johnson, 'Shetland's First Jamaican', *Unkans*, November 2007, p. 4, www.shetland-museumandarchives.org.uk/site/assets/files/1689/unkans_no5.pdf [accessed 27 September 2022].
[82] P. Ariès, *Centuries of Childhood*, trans. Robert Baldick (London, 1962), pp. 398–9. More recent scholarship has pointed to more capacious definitions of family and kinship than Ariès presented. See, for example, N. Tadmor, *Family and Friends in Eighteenth-Century England: Household, Kinship and Patronage* (Cambridge, 2001) and K. Barclay, 'Family and Household', in S. Broomhall (ed.), *Early Modern Emotions: An Introduction* (London, 2017), pp. 244–7.
[83] Livesay, *Children*, pp. 55–8.
[84] E. Gordon, 'The Family', in L. Abrams et al. (eds), *Gender in Scottish History Since 1700* (Edinburgh, 2006), pp. 235–68, at p. 245.
[85] Livesay, *Children*, p. 13; A. Blaikie, 'A Kind of Loving: Illegitimacy, Grandparents, and the Rural Economy of North East Scotland, 1750–1900', *Journal of Scottish Historical Studies*, 14:1 (1994), pp. 41–57.
[86] K. Barclay, 'Natural Affection, Children, and Family Inheritance Practices in the Long Eighteenth Century', in Nugent and Ewan, *Children and Youth*, pp. 136–52, at p. 143.

a person of colour would have been conspicuous in nineteenth-century Shetland. While Bolt promised James a warm welcome upon his arrival to Shetland, there was no guarantee that his relatives would accept him fully into their circle. Perceptions of racial difference and a feeling that children of colour came from a different lineage made nineteenth-century British families less willing than previous generations to accept people like James into their fold.[87] The emotional landscape of James' life in Shetland is impossible to chart. Nevertheless, his example elucidates wider changes in and ambivalences around early modern notions of family.

The last archival trace of James suggests the possibility of tension between him and Bolt. Dated 2 July 1808, the final letter that mentions James shows that Bolt sent him to a David Smith in London. Bolt thanked Smith for offering to find James employment aboard a ship. Bolt described James as a 'Smart clever Boy' possessed of 'good Natural Parts'. However, he was not as 'attentive' as Bolt would have liked. He recommended that James' master kept him 'Strictly' to his duties. Bolt's assessment of James' character point to friction between them. In turn, their relationship was emblematic of the difficulties associated with attempts by children of colour to assimilate into kinship groups in Britain.[88] By securing employment for James, Bolt had complied with Innes Sr's wishes. He had taken in James, ensured he was educated, and set him on the path to adulthood. A less generous reading of Bolt's actions implies he sent James to sea at the earliest possible opportunity and divested himself of any further obligations. Whatever Bolt's motivations, James had reached the appropriate age by contemporary standards to begin working.[89] His entry into the labour force as a fourteen-year-old – and his forced move from Jamaica to Shetland – bears out Steven Mintz's observation that the notion of a 'carefree childhood' is a deeply 'modern' concept.[90]

This final archival record has deteriorated and some of it is illegible. The information concerning James becomes increasingly faint as the letter progresses. This fading symbolises his disappearance from the historical record. It is unclear what happened to James Innes after he left for London aboard the *Venus*. It is likely that he became one of the many people of African descent who served on British ships in the eighteenth and nineteenth centuries.[91] A further possibility is that he settled in London or another port city, which would have allowed James to build a life in a maritime community that included people from a similar background to him.[92] Pursuing this employment path may have facilitated a return to his homeland. Perhaps he was lost at sea. Whatever the precise outcome of James Innes' life, there is no clear evidence that he came back to Shetland. The possibility that he did

---

[87] Livesay, *Children*, p. 314.
[88] Ibid., pp. 301–23.
[89] Heywood, *Childhood*, p. 37.
[90] Mintz, 'Why History Matters', at pp. 648–51.
[91] R. Costello, *Black Salt: Seafarers of African Descent on British Ships* (Liverpool, 2012).
[92] Ibid., pp. 70–94.

not return suggests that he had reached an age where he had more autonomy about important life decisions. His possible decision to leave Shetland forever implies his time there was not necessarily happy. No kinship bonds seem to have drawn him back. This permanent departure from Shetland is significant given that James had been buffeted between locations by adults until this point in his life. The possibility of his deliberate refusal to return to Shetland could be understood as a young person's attempt to gain agency over a life previously controlled by adults.

Conclusion

The evidence presented in this chapter shows the enduring presence of enslaved and formerly enslaved people in eighteenth- and nineteenth-century Scotland. These young people had experienced arduous agricultural or domestic toil in the Americas before they arrived in Scotland. Beginning in their youth, enslaved people were subject to their enslavers' attempts to inure them to the idea that they were chattels with the primary purpose of performing labour. This exposure to labour during their early years disrupted kinship ties and destabilised the very notion of childhood. Enslavers may have considered their decision to bring enslaved people to Scotland an act of apparent compassion. However, as the examples of Cato and Fanny show, enslaved youths experienced privation and ill health in Scotland.

Enslaved youths would have played an essential role in their enslavers' households, not least through domestic labour. Given their relatively small numbers, however, enslaved people occupied a position on the periphery of Scottish society. This marginality signals the broader challenges related to histories of childhood and enslavement. Most children did not produce historical records on which present-day scholars can rely. This problem is heightened in the context of enslavement. Enslavers, not enslaved people, wrote the first draft of slavery's history. The historical record's fraught and inchoate nature looms over the history of enslavement. Certainties about enslaved lives, particularly of enslaved children, are challenging to find. Nevertheless, opportunities remain to glean inferences about enslaved people's lives, offer careful speculations about their actions, and upend enslavers' narratives. Efforts to produce the history of enslaved and formerly enslaved youths provide the possibility to reconstruct – however falteringly – the lives of an especially marginalised group.

Enslaved youths fled their enslavers repeatedly. The evidence in newspaper adverts confirms these young people's determined efforts to escape enslavement. However, this freedom-seeking activity came with the prospect of recapture and punishment. Despite this possibility, some enslaved youths made multiple escape attempts. Moreover, their tactics to evade capture demonstrate these young enslaved people's ingenuity and resilience. They took money or valuable objects to finance their escapes, headed to ports and places of safety, and sometimes hid in plain sight. These acts do not necessarily constitute a premeditated collective attempt to undermine the system of enslavement. However, they reflect enslaved people's persistent refusal to adhere to slavery's strictures and signal their efforts to gain control over their lives.

James Innes' status as an enslaved child allowed adults to control his life. People executing his father's wishes dispatched him from Jamaica to Shetland without consideration for James' view on the matter. This aspect of Innes' story indicates the limits on enslaved children's agency. The absence of material that outlines Innes' feelings about being sent to Shetland underlines his marginality. What is evident, however, is the complexity of Innes' story. His passage to freedom in Shetland – at least in a legal sense – relied on the sale of people his father enslaved. Furthermore, the evidence about Innes' time in Shetland points to possible antagonism between him and his relatives. His departure from Shetland – seemingly never to return – may have been when a formerly enslaved youth wrested control of his life from the adults around him. This case study exemplifies the interplay between independence and control that enslaved and formerly enslaved children had to navigate.

Part II

Occupational Margins

6

Working on the Margins: Freemen, Unfreemen, and Stallangers in Early Modern Scotland

Aaron M. Allen

In the National Museum of Scotland is a sculptured stone which once belonged to an Edinburgh baxter at the Netherbow (Figure 1). The stone, with its gothic script and male and female figures in classical dress, is quite striking, not least because of the messages it conveys. The figures are of Adam and Eve, and the message carved on the stone is a reminder of a curse. After the Fall, Adam and Eve were cast out of the Garden of Eden, and one consequence of their sin was that, from that point forward, mankind would have to work for their living. The stone from the Netherbow therefore achieved several things at one time. It was a marker, telling passers-by where to get their bread; it was a status symbol, illustrating the cultural pretensions of the tradesman; and – most importantly – it was a pious *aide-mémoire*. 'With sweat on your brow shall you eat your bread' was the Genesis curse. In this one carving customers were reminded not only of their own sinfulness and need for Christ, but also of the hard work which had gone into baking their bread. While customers might not have to sweat in front of the oven, it was certainly in the baxters' interest to remind them of those who did.

That said, the baxters did not actually want anyone else to sweat in the baking of bread. They sought to exclude all others from this work, as there were supposedly two kinds of people in the early modern corporate system: free and unfree. To be a baxter meant joining the privileged and chartered Incorporation of Baxters. In this context of 'corporatism', there were the privileged few and the excluded majority. There were those inside, and the rest who must remain outside. While this meant different things in different contexts, as with political estates, houses of the great families, or religious confessions, in the world of work it meant actively defending one's right to work by denying those outside the corporate body. Of course, the ideal and the reality were not necessarily the same thing, and despite expensive court cases and appeals to councils to enforce charters, many unfreemen continued to work free trades. Monopoly may have been the goal, but it was not always achievable.

Still, the system was intended to maintain privilege. Towns, full of people, had few citizens. To be a burgess was to be free of a burgh, but one study of the

Figure 1   Sculptured stone panel showing Adam and Eve, with a paraphrase of Genesis 3:19: 'In sudore vultus tui vesceris pane tuo'. From the Netherbow, Edinburgh, sixteenth century. NMS, H.KG 41.
Image © National Museums Scotland.

capital has suggested that only about 30 per cent of householders were actually burgesses.[1] Other studies have suggested this was somewhere between 7 and 14 per cent of the whole population of a town.[2] Exclusivity was the hallmark of corporatism, and corporatism was how early modern Scotland was structured. The majority were unfree.

Of course, the unfree still worked. Many occupations and professions were not governed by an incorporated trade, as with cooks, taverners, or teachers. Others, such as the vast labour force of apprentices, journeymen, clubs, and servants, worked *for* freemen or freemen's widows.[3] They were closer to the privileges of the freemen, but restricted numbers of free masters meant that many skilled craftsmen worked their whole lives as journeymen, unable to progress. Others lived without hope of freedom, such as the enserfed salters, colliers, and coal bearers.[4] Still others worked clandestinely, only showing up in the records when caught. Others, known as 'stallangers', were allowed stalls in the market for set periods for a fee.[5]

---

[1]   M. Lynch, *Edinburgh and the Reformation* (Edinburgh, 1981), p. 10.
[2]   H.M. Dingwall, *Late Seventeenth-Century Edinburgh: A Demographic Study* (Aldershot, 1994), p. 181; E.P. Dennison, *The Evolution of Scotland's Towns: Creation, Growth and Fragmentation* (Edinburgh, 2018), pp. 37–8.
[3]   'Clubs' were apparently less-skilled servants. *DSL*, 'Club'; DAC, EGD47/5/2, Shoemakers: Minutes 1658–1762, fols 55v, 77v, 78v; W.E. Watson, *The Convenery of the Six Incorporated Trades of Elgin* (Elgin, 1960), Chapter VI: 'Shoemakers', pp. 6–9.
[4]   T. Johnston, *The History of the Working Classes in Scotland* (Glasgow, 1946), pp. 73–84; C.A. Whatley, 'The Dark Side of the Enlightenment? Sorting Out Serfdom', in T.M. Devine and J. Young (eds), *Eighteenth Century Scotland: New Perspectives* (East Linton, 1999), pp. 259–74.
[5]   Turners and wheelwrights were tolerated in Edinburgh so long as they paid stallanger fees to the wrights (woodworkers) but were not included in the ten trades which made up the composite Incorporation. A. Allen, *Building Early Modern Edinburgh: A Social History of Craftwork and Incorporation* (Edinburgh, 2018), pp. 40–7.

So, in the context of corporatism, what kinds of people worked on the margins, and why were they tolerated? Clearly, there were many working beneath the corporate system – many more than can be covered here – and not all of their work was clandestine. Looking at the available sources for them gives important glimpses of their lived experiences, which in turn gives us a fuller and richer picture of everyday life in early modern Scotland. Aside from not always fitting neatly into the free–unfree dichotomy, there were also certain tensions cutting across such corporate divisions, such as differences in station, gender, or residency. Such factors complicated decisions about work privileges, but might also occasionally enable access to work. All of this will be explored below, through three broad categories of such marginal workers: those who contributed labour; those who contributed provisions; and those who repaired goods. Many were tolerated to a greater or lesser degree, but none were esteemed as fully equal to the free burgesses. Instead, they worked on the margins.

Labour

One group which was not only tolerated, but indispensable, was the vast array of men and women who provided labour. Not everyone had the right to labour, though some were forced into the role of labourer. As space is limited, two groups will be considered: the women associated with freemen, and the feed labour on short-term contracts.

Despite common perceptions which have more to do with middle-class Victorian ideals than the lived reality, women were indeed found in the workplace. While they certainly laboured in domestic spaces, they also worked in family businesses, undertook hard agricultural labour, and were even found on building sites. While there were restrictions on female work, it is inaccurate to think that women stayed in the home.[6] Indeed, there is evidence that wives could be considered partners in their husbands' businesses. At Torphichen, in West Lothian, the mill was set in 1540 to both Thomas Boyd *and* his wife, Margaret Forrat, in a tack (lease) of nineteen years.[7] The fact that Margaret was named on a legal document demonstrates her involvement in the family business. Similarly, in Edinburgh's shoe market, it was the cordiners' wives who ran the stalls and retailed the shoes. According

---

[6] C. Spence, *Women, Credit, and Debt in Early Modern Scotland* (Manchester, 2016), pp. 3–4, chapters 2 and 3; T.C. Smout, *A History of the Scottish People, 1560–1830* (London, 1985), p. 136; W. Howatson, 'The Scottish Hairst and Seasonal Labour 1600–1870', *Scottish Studies*, 26 (1982), 13–36; E. Ewan, '"For Whatever Ales Ye": Women as Consumers and Producers in Late Medieval Scottish Towns', in E. Ewan and M.M. Meikle (eds), *Women in Scotland, c.1100–c.1750* (Edinburgh, 1999), pp. 125–35 at p. 130; Allen, *Building Early Modern Edinburgh*, pp. 71–6, 97–101.

[7] 'The Rental of 1539–1540', in I.B. Cowan, P.H.R. Mackay, and A. Macquarrie (eds), *The Knights of St John of Jerusalem in Scotland* (Edinburgh, 1983), p. 3.

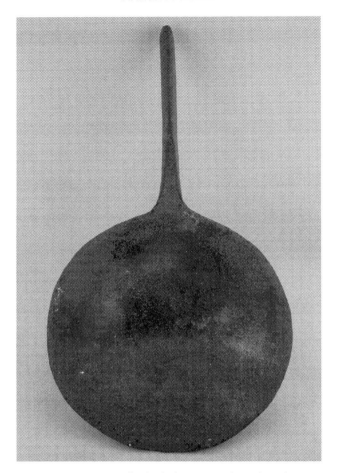

Figure 2   Iron girdle for baking oatcakes, thought to be of the Culross type. National Trust for Scotland, 2017.2422. Reproduced by kind permission of the National Trust for Scotland.

to one historian, the cordiner trade's toast was 'a fou purse – the guidwife to the booth, and the guidman to the cutting knife'.[8] In a market economy, production meant little without sales, and again we find wives as integral to family businesses.[9]

---

[8]   A.H. Dunlop, *Anent Old Edinburgh and Some of the Worthies who Walked its Streets with Other Papers* (Edinburgh, 1890), p. 118.
[9]   In 1742 Old Aberdeen sought to limit female shopkeepers to unmarried daughters and widows only. *Old Aberdeen Recs.*, vol. 1, p. 188; Colston noted that Newhaven's fishwives were the 'bargain-makers' and therefore 'conjoint breadwinners'. J. Colston, *The Town and Port of Leith; Its Historical Connection with the City of Edinburgh* (Edinburgh, 1892), p. 75.

While women laboured outside the home, this does not mean that there were no restrictions or challenges. Several trades which were traditionally female domestic tasks were later commercialised and taken out of women's hands. Both brewing and candle-making were originally done within the home by women. In the capital, however, by the sixteenth century corporate bodies such as the Society of Brewers or the Incorporation of Candlemakers sought to exclude women from commercial production.[10] For example, while domestic production of candles was still allowed, they were no longer allowed to sell the surplus for a profit, unless they were producing as part of their husband's or late husband's business. For others, even a connection to the craft aristocracy might not be enough. For example, in 1738 in Jedburgh, the ex-deacon of the tailors, John Porteous, was arrested for 'employing his daughter to work in his trade as a journeyman'.[11]

Not all decisions about who could work implied an outright exclusion of women, though. We find women working in and alongside the building trades.[12] We find women labouring as shore porters.[13] We find women bearing coal out of mines (for which, see Chapter 9 of this volume),[14] and we find them in heavy industries, such as the 'girdlemakers' of Culross.[15] Widow Anderson's smithy produced 646 girdles between January 1674 and May 1675, but it was not her skill which allowed her to work 'in hyr forge'.[16] Instead, it was her relationship to a deceased freeman, and in her particular case, there was much resistance from the Incorporation.

For some, the right to labour was through association, as with wives and widows of freemen, but for others it was through a formal business contract. Many were short-term, offering little stability. Agriculture relied on seasonal labour, as with the annual harvest, which brought about a 'hiring-market structure' of bi-annual hiring fairs.[17] Even professions held exploitatively short-term arrangements, as with the pensionary clergy and the perpetual clergy. At the Cistercian nunnery of St Mary's, Haddington, perpetual vicars had tenure, whilst the pensionary vicars employed as the actual parochial

---

[10] Ewan, 'For Whatever Ales Ye', at p. 132; A. Allen, 'Production and the Missing Artefacts: Candles, Oil and the Material Culture of Urban Lighting in Early Modern Scotland', *Review of Scottish Culture*, 23 (2011), 20–53, at 26–8.
[11] W.W. Mabon, 'The Tyranny of the Old "Trades": Some Jedburgh Examples', *Transactions of the Hawick Archaeological Society* (1934), 7.
[12] Allen, *Building Early Modern Edinburgh*, pp. 71–6 and at pp. 97–101.
[13] G. Gordon, *The Shore Porters' Society of Aberdeen, 1498–1969* (Aberdeen, 1970), pp. 15–16 and at pp. 14–25.
[14] B.F. Duckham, *A History of the Scottish Coal Industry, Vol. I 1700–1815* (Newton Abbot, 1970), p. 49 and at pp. 94–112; P. M'Neill, *Tranent and its Surroundings: Historical, Ecclesiastical, & Traditional* (Edinburgh, 1884), pp. 29–48.
[15] D. Beveridge, *Culross and Tulliallan or Perthshire on Forth: Its History and Antiquities* (2 vols, Edinburgh, 1885), vol. 2, pp. 172–8.
[16] Ibid., pp. 164–5 and at p. 174.
[17] Howatson, 'Scottish Hairst', p. 13 and at pp. 15–16; T.M. Devine, *The Scottish Clearances: A History of the Dispossessed, 1600–1900* (London, 2018), pp. 189–90 and at p. 24.

chaplains were 'mere hirelings' employed from year to year.[18]

Short-term labour was certainly a feature of corporate trades, which all relied on the feed work of journeymen. The word journeyman comes from the French, *journée*, or 'day', indicating their role as day labourers. Indeed, in Glasgow in 1626, journeymen hammermen appear to have moved between masters frequently, as booking fees were only to be kept by the Incorporation if the journeyman stayed with the master more than eight days.[19] Booking fees to the Incorporation were of course expensive, but a good working relationship might make it worth the expense. This trial period before booking could lead to abuse, as journeymen could be bounced around without stability. At Culross in 1670, one girdlesmith who owed money was forced to pay off his debt to the Incorporation by serving each master week about.[20] While this was an exceptional case due to the debt, still it demonstrates a culture in which journeymen could be moved between masters on a short-term basis.

Though short-term contracts might be a source of anxiety, they also meant being less obliged to one's master. Indeed, such anxieties could cut both ways, as demonstrated by the many acts in burgh records against feeing another master's servant. To mention but a few cases, this problem is found with the bonnet-makers in Kilmarnock; with the tailors in Kirkwall; and with the cordiners in Aberdeen.[21] While short-term contracts were less than stable, labour could always be taken elsewhere.

Provisions

Another tolerated group were those who provisioned the marketplaces with necessities. Here we see important limitations to corporate privileges, as there was a constant tension between corporate privilege and the 'common weal'. The former limited competition, but supposedly ensured quality and social stability, while the latter required adequate provision for *all* of society and not just the privileged few. Both were intrinsic to the organisation of early modern society, despite the obvious tension between them.

Corporate privileges were about limiting competition. Taking burghs as an example, if only freemen could produce goods, then supplies were kept artificially low, ensuring enough demand to sustain the livelihoods of the

---

[18] J.H. Jamieson, D.E. Easson, and G. Donaldson, 'The Cistercian Nunnery of St. Mary, Haddington', *Transactions of the East Lothian Antiquarian and Field Naturalists' Society*, 5 (1952), 1–24, at 10.

[19] This time increased to fourteen days by 1700, and by 1713 written agreements were required. H. Lumsden and P.H. Aitken, *History of the Hammermen of Glasgow* (Paisley, 1912), pp. 31–2.

[20] Beveridge, *Culross and Tulliallan*, vol. 2, pp. 169–72.

[21] A. M'Kay, *The History of Kilmarnock* (Kilmarnock, 1858), pp. 36–7; J. Flett, 'Kirkwall Incorporated Trades', *Proceedings of the Orkney Antiquarian Society*, 7 (1928–9), 45–56, at 54; E. Bain, *Merchant and Craft Guilds: A History of the Aberdeen Incorporated Trades* (Aberdeen, 1887), p. 276.

freemen. While this system was certainly in the burgesses' interest, it did not always coincide with the common weal of the rest of society, and therefore the magistrates had a problem. It was in their interest to protect corporate privileges, as they brought order, both socially and economically, but they also needed to ensure adequate provision. In relation to necessities like victuals or shoes, this often meant curtailing corporate privileges when demand outstripped supply.

To fully understand the tension between privilege and the common weal, we must consider *where* work happened, as a fundamental concept in the regulation of corporate privilege was residency.[22] Originally, to be a burgess was to own property in a burgh, but over time this qualification lapsed.[23] While ownership of property ceased to be a requirement, abiding within the town walls remained crucial, as with the growth of many burgh populations, it became more difficult to regulate just who had privileges and who did not. Residency within burgh boundaries helped in regulating the national, local, and domestic economies which were interwoven through the urban fabric.

The significance of residency can be seen in the great efforts made to demarcate burgh from landward with town walls or ditches. There were natural boundaries, as with the rivers separating Dumfries from Bridgend, or Glasgow from Gorbals, but others were manmade, as with the moat around Perth, or the Flodden Wall at Edinburgh.[24] While St Andrews' West Port is extant, many such boundaries survive only in name, as with 'World's End Close' at Edinburgh's former eastern boundary. To be inside meant access, but if one lived outside, then they might as well have fallen off the face of the earth, because residency once *mattered*.

For the burgesses of the capital, the idea that the world somehow ended beyond the walls was important for the constant battle to defend their privileged status, but the reality was, of course, far more complex. Burghs – even royal ones – were much more integrated with and dependent on their hinterlands for victuals, raw materials, and labour. Those to the landward were also reliant on the towns for access to markets, and to legal and educational institutions. Town and country were therefore intrinsically linked, though

---

[22] M. Lynch, 'Continuity and Change in Urban Society, 1500–1700', in R.A. Houston and I.D. Whyte (eds), *Scottish Society 1500–1800* (Cambridge, 1989), pp. 85–117, at pp. 109–13; W. Dickie, 'Incorporated Trades of Dumfries: With Special Reference to the Weavers', *Transactions and Journal of Proceedings of the Dumfriesshire and Galloway Natural History and Antiquarian Society*, 17 (1906), 411–21, at p. 420; Allen, *Building Early Modern Edinburgh*, pp. 154–63.

[23] J.D. Marwick, 'The Municipal Institutions of Scotland: A Historical Survey', *SHR*, 1:2 (1904), pp. 123–35, at pp. 125–6; W.M. Mackenzie, *The Scottish Burghs* (Edinburgh, 1949), p. 134.

[24] W.A. Dodd, 'The Medieval Town Plan at Dumfries' (unpublished MPhil dissertation, University of Edinburgh, 1979), pp. 158, 181; Lumsden and Aitken, *Hammermen of Glasgow*, pp. 61–9; M. Verschuur, *Politics or Religion? The Reformation in Perth 1540–1570* (Edinburgh, 2006), pp. 2–3, 5; G. Guidicini, *Triumphal Entries and Festivals in Early Modern Scotland: Performing Spaces* (Turnhout, 2020); Allen, *Building Early Modern Edinburgh*, pp. 154–63, 201–13.

access was not freely given. Instead, it was heavily regulated, with zones of exclusion known as 'liberties' surrounding royal burghs. Even if the world did not end at the burgh boundaries, there were still the few privileged insiders and the great majority of outsiders, both metaphorically and literally.

With control of liberties in mind, some burghs allowed a second class of freemen with reduced privileges. Various labels existed for these non-resident burgesses, such as 'rustic', 'calsay', 'churl', or 'outland' burgesses.[25] In Dumfries, the Shoemakers' Incorporation referred to such second-class freemen as either 'country' or 'outtintown' freemen.[26] In 1667, one such shoemaker in Lochfoot, to the west of Dumfries, was given 'full libertie' to work and exercise the trade as fully and freely as any other 'outtintowne friemen'. This included buying leather upon the market day in Dumfries from 2 pm until evening; booking and discharging apprentices; and selling shoes or other work, except from 9 am to noon on the market day only.[27] As with other towns, the economy of Dumfries did not stop at the edges of the town. Instead, there was often an element of fluidity to burgh boundaries, due in part to the interconnectedness of urban and rural economies.[28]

This can be seen again with Dumfries's shoemakers. In 1657, the Incorporation included thirty-nine freemen, of whom twenty-seven were in the town and twelve were in the suburb of Bridgend (Maxweltown).[29] Of the twenty-seven town freemen meeting at the Chrystal Chapel, two were noted as being either 'at Goatherd' or 'at Porthole', likely indicating residence is extra-urban locales and therefore suggesting that, by the mid-seventeenth century, there were both suburban freemen and 'country' or 'outtintown' freemen within the ranks of the 'haill body of the shoemaker trade'. Exactly what the difference was between being free of the town, of Bridgend, or of the country is not wholly clear, though through the seventeenth century certain shoemakers continued to be admitted as freemen to work in the country *only*, with limitations apparently set on their access to Dumfries' markets.[30] Still, even with more limited freedoms, they were able to work their trades in the countryside and sell their goods within the town.[31]

---

[25] Marwick, 'Municipal Institutions', at p. 126; Mackenzie, *Scottish Burghs*, pp. 132–4.
[26] DAC, EGD47/5/2, Shoemakers: Minutes 1658–1762, fols 9r, 29v–35v, 36v.
[27] Ibid., fol. 17v.
[28] A. Allen, 'Conquering the Suburbs: Politics and Work in Early Modern Edinburgh', *Journal of Urban History*, 37:3 (2011), 423–43, at pp. 423–5.
[29] DAC, EGD47/5/2, fol. 9r.
[30] Ibid. fols 9r, 17v, 29r–30v, 35v, 36v, 40v, 42v, 45v, 47r–47v and passim. Dickie found similar 'country only' circumstances for some weavers. Dickie, 'Incorporated Trades of Dumfries', at pp. 419–20.
[31] In 1691 the Dumfries shoemakers were 'egregiouslie damnified hurt and prejudiced by out landit & newtrall men comeing in', so their entry fees were increased. Country shoemakers could still buy access, providing they had the £60 Scots, with a dollar of earnest money, 'by and attouer the former dewes and causualities' for their admission. DAC, EGD47/5/2, fol. 36v.

While town and country were heavily dependent on each other, occasionally, the lines between them became even more blurred by the development of other towns outside the town walls. The dominant settlements, usually royal burghs, viewed these lesser towns as beneath them, and often insisted that they were suburbs, whether legally burghs or not.[32] While Aberdeen had several suburbs, such as the Green, its Incorporation of Cordiners complained about two in particular: Spithill, with its 'Spitalmen', and the baronial burgh of Old Aberdeen – a legal burgh in its own right.[33] Lines were easily blurred between town and town, just as they were between town and country.

It is thought that Perth was the first Scottish burgh to develop suburbs, though by the sixteenth century, the perceived problem was to be found across Scotland.[34] Perth, Jedburgh, and Haddington each had two suburbs to worry about, while St Andrews, Dundee, Coupar Angus, and Kirkcaldy each had one.[35] Edinburgh, however, had nine suburbs competing with the capital's burgesses, though one study of the suburb of West Port has suggested that they were more focused on producing for the landward markets than on undercutting Edinburgh's markets.[36]

The issue was unfair advantage, as suburbs offered proximity to urban markets without the same burdens of taxation. Lynch notes an 'unchecked flight to the suburbs' for certain trades from sixteenth-century Edinburgh.[37] Burgesses with particular freedoms from tolls were still expected to pay taxes and undertake burgess duties, known as 'scot and lot'. By pursuing their trades

---

[32] Allen, 'Conquering the Suburbs', at pp. 425–7.

[33] Bain, *Merchant and Craft Guilds*, p. 283 and at pp. 286–7. Bain listed outlying districts whose shoemakers paid fees to Aberdeen's Incorporation, including Well o' Spa, Futtie, Garden Nook, Hardweird, Loanhead, Rubislaw, Hazelhead, Couparstoun, Ruthrieston, Hardgate, Pitmuxton, and Bridge of Dee. See also J. Gordon, 'A Topographical Description of Both Towns of Aberdeen', in A. Mitchell (ed.), *Geographical Collections Relating to Scotland made by Walter Macfarlane* (2 vols, Edinburgh, 1907), vol. 2, p. 495; E.P. Dennison, D. Ditchburn, and M. Lynch (eds), *Aberdeen Before 1800: A New History* (East Linton, 2002), p. 35.

[34] M. Lynch, *Scotland: A New History* (London, 2000), p. 64.

[35] Perth: R.M. Spearman, 'The Medieval Townscape of Perth', in M. Lynch, M. Spearman, and G. Stell (eds), *The Scottish Medieval Town* (Edinburgh, 1988), pp. 42–59, at pp. 52–5; Jedburgh: F.H. Groome, *Ordnance Gazetteer of Scotland: A Survey of Scottish Topography, Statistical, Biographical, and Historical*, vol. 4 (Edinburgh, 1885), pp. 329–33, at p. 329; Haddington: W.F. Gray and J.H. Jamieson, *A Short History of Haddington* (Stevenage, (1944) 1995), p. 83; St Andrews: E. Ewan, 'Living in the Late Medieval Town of St Andrews', in M. Brown and K. Stevenson (eds), *Medieval St Andrews: Church, Cult, City* (Woodbridge, 2021), pp. 117–40, at pp. 117, 126; Dundee: W.C. Skinner, *The Baronie of Hilltowne Dundee: Its Industrial, Social and Religious Life* (Dundee, 1927), pp. 3–10, 31–44; Elizabeth P. (Dennison) Torrie, *Medieval Dundee: A Town and its People* (Dundee, 1990), pp. 35–6, 55; Coupar Angus: Dennison, *Evolution of Scotland's Towns*, p. 99; Kirkcaldy: J.T. Davidson, *The Linktown of Abbotshall* (Kirkcaldy, 1951), pp. 19–20.

[36] Allen, 'Conquering the Suburbs', at p. 436, n. 12; Dunlop, *Anent Old Edinburgh*, pp. 117–18.

[37] M. Lynch, 'Social and Economic Structure of the Larger Towns, 1450–1600', in Lynch, Spearman and Stell, *Scottish Medieval Town*, at p. 276.

outside the walls, they were able to get away 'scot free', to the detriment of those who remained within the town.[38] It was not long before national legislation was put in place to tackle the problem.[39]

Despite attempts to stamp out suburbs, they were, in fact, heavily integrated into the urban economies. For some, it proved more practical to seek control over suburbs rather than to eliminate them, as has been demonstrated for the capital.[40] Edinburgh was not alone in such policies. Other burghs also sought to control craftwork within their suburbs rather than eliminate it; especially when the craftwork provided for a critical need, such as shoes. Haddington's Incorporation of Cordiners in 1654 allowed Alexander Carmichael, an indweller of the Nungate, to import and export his shoes so long as he paid a quarterly fee.[41]

Dumfries's Incorporation of Shoemakers certainly allowed suburban craftsmen by 1657, but when exactly they gained control over shoemaking in their suburb of Bridgend is not clear.[42] What is clear is that through the last half of the seventeenth century their meetings included 'the haill body of the shoemaker traid both in towne & Brigend'.[43] For Bridgend shoemakers this meant paying entry fees to the Dumfries Incorporation. If they took an apprentice, they were obliged to book them with the Incorporation. When they feed a servant, again the Incorporation had to be notified and paid. To what extent they were able to enforce this is not clear, but the minutes show that at least some suburban craftsmen submitted to the corporate body across the river.[44]

Through the famine of the 1690s, we see the relationship breaking down as lines hardened and additional fees were demanded of incoming suburban shoemakers.[45] In September 1695, the Dumfries Incorporation enacted that a Bridgend shoemaker was *only* free in Bridgend and not within the town.[46] Whilst previously the minutes described the trade as being 'both in towne & Bridgend', following the 1695 act we find 'oprobrious indiscreet and baser' speeches being hurled against the Incorporation by a suburban shoemaker named John Marson, and for the rest of the decade the minutes remain silent about Bridgend men.[47] Though relations were strained through the economic

---

[38] Allen, 'Conquering the Suburbs', at p. 430.
[39] RPS, 1592/4/98; Mackenzie, *Scottish Burghs*, p. 83.
[40] Lynch, 'Social and Economic Structure', at p. 275; Allen, 'Conquering the Suburbs', at p. 431; Allen, *Building Early Modern Edinburgh*, pp. 154–63.
[41] ELCALHS, HAD/13/2/2, 'Cordiners' Minute Book, 1605–1755', fol. 4v. He was to pay six shillings eight pence quarterly on top of his quarter compts.
[42] DAC, EGD47/5/2, fol. 9r. Earlier volumes are not extant; records also show glovers and weavers in the suburb of Dumfries. H. McArthur (ed.), 'Acts of the Glovers' Trade of Dumfries 1650–1846', Unpublished Typescript Notes from the Original Manuscript, Db151 (67), fol. 20; Dickie, 'Incorporated Trades of Dumfries', at pp. 418–19.
[43] DAC, EGD47/5/2, fol. 17v.
[44] Ibid. fols 1v, 37v, 40v, 55v, 78v.
[45] Ibid. fol. 37v.
[46] Ibid. fol. 38v.
[47] Ibid., fol. 39r.

hardship of the later 1690s, by 1701 we find Bridgend men in the records again, and through the eighteenth century they continued to book entries, apprentices, and servants, suggesting that the 1695 intolerance of the Dumfries trade was more reactionary than strategic.[48] On the whole, Bridgend men were tolerated, so long as they paid their dues and put up with inequalities.

Toleration did not, however, mean complete freedom. Instead, judicious use of restrictions regulated suburban and country work, ensuring provision by allowing controlled access to urban markets. In eighteenth-century Perth, we find legislation against unfreemen taking measurements in the town or selling shoes *outside* the marketplace, while another act reminded freemen not to 'pack and peel' with unfreemen by buying their shoes and selling them as their own.[49] Such decrees demonstrate attempts to control labour, but they also show the utility of country and suburban shoemakers, as freemen were clearly turning to them to meet demand. But such reliance on marginal labour was clearly perceived as a threat. As such, a decision was taken by the Perth Incorporation in 1683 that extra fees were needed for 'outlander' shoemakers who presumed to marry freeman shoemakers' daughters.[50] Their provision might have been necessary, but competition was still carefully regulated.

Whether external or internal, provisioning often meant toleration. Lynch sees this phenomenon as leading the capital towards an 'open door policy', though there were times when that open door was judiciously shut.[51] Still, generally speaking, boundaries were permeable, allowing for an ebb and flow to meet the needs of the community. This might mean the adoption of 'land-markets', where special space was given over to country producers,[52] or the admission of country freemen when demand outstripped the production capacity of privileged insiders, but such toleration was not a right. Instead, it was an expediency, predicated on necessity, and many unfree workers were able to gain access through the need for provisions.

Repairs

One last tolerated group were repairers, or 'clouters'. A 'clout' was a patch in Scots.[53] It is frequently found in place names, such as 'Castle o' Clouts' or 'Souterclutes', speaking to the importance of repairs to the wider economy, but therein lies the problem. Repairs delayed sales of new items, and in the

---

[48] Ibid. fols. 40v, 55v, 78v.
[49] P. Baxter, *The Shoemaker Incorporation of Perth, 1545 to 1927* (Perth, 1927), pp. 72–3, 90.
[50] Ibid., p. 13.
[51] Lynch, 'Continuity and Change', at p. 93.
[52] A. Allen, 'Governance, Regulation and the State', in T. Reinke-Williams (ed.), *A Cultural History of Shopping in the Early Modern Age* (London, 2022), pp. 191–212, at p. 206.
[53] *DSL*, 'Clout'.

Figure 3   Howie's depiction of a cobbler working under a stair. ECA, Howie Prints, 'A Cobbler in his Stall, John Knox's corner, the last of the race in Edinburgh', vol. 2 (c. 1850), 17. By kind permission of City of Edinburgh Council.

context of corporatism, with its emphasis on protecting the privileged few producers, such clouters could be ill regarded.

One example of the clouter has become so established that many consider it synonymous with the trade which once sought to exclude them. This is the humble cobbler, which is not a shoe *maker*, as many understand the word today, but instead a shoe *repairer*. Repairing worn-out soles cut into the market for new shoes. As such, the established incorporations of 'cordiners', or shoemakers, sought to either stop or at least control such work.[54]

Instances abound. Aberdeen's cordiners often had legal wranglings with cobblers, and several statutes forbade the employment of cobblers by brethren of the craft.[55] Occasionally it was an outsider cobbling shoes, but it also might be journeymen already working for the trade, as with James Simpson in 1619 Edinburgh, who was found working in a cobbler shop only five years before he

---

[54] The word 'cordiner', which differentiated freemen from common 'soutars', originates from a type of leather associated with Cordoba, which was favoured for shoes.
[55] Bain, *Merchant and Craft Guilds*, pp. 275, 283.

himself would join the ranks of the capital's burgesses.[56] Others were found acting as merchants, as with the Kirkwall cobbler who was admitted by the town to his trade, but was then found in 1682 'buying and selling hazell and uther commodities which he wes not privildged to doe'.[57]

As with Kirkwall, many town councils saw utility in allowing people to pay for repairs, highlighting the divergent agendas of council and craft. Still, not all incorporations of cordiners were opposed to cobbling. In Stirling, we find booking fees being charged for cobblers by the seventeenth century.[58] Perth allowed cobblers so long as they did not sell any *new* work.[59] Indeed, disputes between cordiner and cobbler usually focused on the age of the leather. Cordiners made new shoes from new leather, which was a precious material in limited supply. Cobblers were supposed to recycle *old* leather, which restricted them to work such as turning old boots into shoe parts.

Of course, many of the skills of the cordiner were also seen in the cobbler. The height of skill was in cutting, as it involved careful planning so as not to waste valuable leather. The core skill, seen in all apprentices and journeymen, was sewing. Neither of these skills were beyond the cobbler, which is part of the reason 'clouters' were a threat. If carefully regulated, however, then even cobblers could be a useful addition to the pool of labour.

Hence, in Haddington, in 1654, for 20s quarterly, the cobbler William Baird was granted liberty to 'mend old boots and schon' within the burgh, but there were certain stipulations. Firstly, it was only during the Incorporation's pleasure, but more importantly, there were provisions against: cutting up old boots to make shoes or pattens; using new leather in any shoes, boots, or mules he mended; and making any kind of new work.[60] So long as he observed these restrictions, his work was tolerated.

In Edinburgh from 1406 to 1760, only two cobblers appear in the burgess rolls, demonstrating limitations on their access to freedom.[61] While they were clearly not encouraged to join the ranks of the burgess class, they were still very much part of the capital's economy. A 1655 list included the names of forty-three cobblers, but this was in the back of an entry book for suburban shoemakers, highlighting their second-class status.[62]

---

[56] NRS, GD348/104, 'xxvij Julij [c.1619]', regarding, inter alia, cobblers' shops, fol. 1r; C.B.B. Watson (ed.), *Roll of Edinburgh Burgesses and Guild-Brethren, 1406–1700* (Edinburgh, 1929), p. 481
[57] J. Mooney and W.D. Simpson (eds), *Charters and Other Records of the City and Royal Burgh of Kirkwall* (Aberdeen, 1952), pp. 216, 222, 358–9.
[58] SCA, PD7/6/1, Stirling Incorporation of Cordiners, Account Books, 1694–1824, unpaginated, 'Compt of Receets since Mayday till Lambiss 1696'.
[59] Baxter, *Shoemaker Incorporation of Perth*, pp. i–ii.
[60] ELCALHS, HAD/13/2/2, Cordiners Minute Book, 1605–1755, fols 4v–5r.
[61] C.B.B. Watson (ed.), *Roll of Edinburgh Burgesses and Guild-Brethren, 1701–1760* (Edinburgh, 1930–3), pp. 146 and 217.
[62] 'The names of the cobbleris within the Libertie of Edinburgh upone the 20 of November 1655', in NRS, GD348/211, Roll Books of the Incorporation of Cordiners of

While the 1655 list gives only names, subsequent entries for the early 1660s give short explanations, giving important insights into the group. One tells us that entry was 'upone supplication', provided that they kept an unspecified 'generall act' made about cobblers.[63] One mentions payment of quarter compts, while another generously allowed the cobbler to 'give satisfactioun to the calling quhen he sall become abills', suggesting the economic challenges faced by many cobblers.[64] Indeed, many of the entries denote 'old journeymen', highlighting that length of service did not mean access to freedom.[65]

These last two elements, of being journeymen and being aged, are particularly telling, as earlier legislation from the sixteenth century sought to impose limits on who could work as a cobbler. Due to alleged years of negligence, in late 1586 the cordiners petitioned the town council for a ratification of their rules, which led to a negotiated set of statutes regarding the production and sale of shoes in the capital.[66] One item relating to cobblers is of particular importance here, as it betrays the Incorporation's strategy in relation to repairers of shoes. While their original petition requested that no able young men be allowed to keep a cobbler's booth 'except he be fourtie yeirs or mair', the council's ratification lowered the age to thirty.[67] The Incorporation wanted a greater limitation on their competition, but the council wanted to ensure supply. Importantly, though, both saw the utility of allowing *some* repairers in the marketplace, and both agreed there needed to be controls on who was allowed to undertake such work. It was not the youth, who were already difficult to control, but instead cobbling was to be reserved for more mature craftsmen less likely to cause problems.

Some flouted the rules, as when the Incorporation's searcher found a servant 'cobling auld shone' in James Symson's shop.[68] There were crackdowns, as when two cobblers were hauled before the deacon for soling boots and

---

Edinburgh, 1657–1727, no pagination [back of volume]. Despite the title this is actually a roll of suburban cordiners in Leith.

[63] Ibid., no pagination, entry of Mathow Reidheid [back of volume, 9 July 1662].

[64] Ibid., no pagination, entries for James Fairly [3 March 1663] and Johne Gibsone [2 September 1662].

[65] Ibid., no pagination, entries for Johnne Mcilhois [6 December 1660], Johnne Grier [2 September 1662], and Johnne Smith (journeyman) [29 November 1660].

[66] *Edinburgh Recs.*, vol. 4, pp. 480–4.

[67] Compare *Edinburgh Recs.*, vol. 4, p. 483, with NRS, GD348/104, 'Certaine heids desyrit be the cordineris to be ratified be the counsall of Edinburgh for the Weill of the craft' (c.1586), fol. 1v: 'Item that na habill young maen be sufferrit to keip ane cobularis buyth except he be fourtie yeirs or mair, that fremen may haif servands to serve thame, and that the numer of the saids cobularis exceed nocht xvj personis becaus tha Numer thairof is presentlie overgrit bayth of fremen & unfremen, that seducis our servands to steill our stuf and sell to thame, and that the saids cobularis sell thair auld wark in the Cowgait on the Monundayis and nocht at the croce nor on the Hie Streit in dishonour of the gude toun under the pane of escheiting thairof to be employit as said is.'

[68] NRS, GD348/104, Unnumbered bundle of vouchers and legal papers, 1589–1630, fol. 1r. The same document shows Symsone himself was found working in a cobbling shop on 13 July, and gives a list of nine men who were complained against as being 'cobillers seuwing'.

shoes with new leather and making 'bairnis schone'.[69] Such transgressions were bad enough when the economy was good, but the problem became distinctly acute during times of hardship, as cheaper alternatives to new shoes were no doubt attractive to customers, and the cobblers themselves were also under pressure to find more income.

The 'ill years' of the 1690s demonstrate this well, as we find a clamping down on the cobbler trade in the minutes of the Edinburgh cordiners. In 1695 they made an 'Act Discharginge fremen to Countinance Coblers', where no freeman was to keep a servant for cobbler work unless they lived in the master's house; the master cut the leather; and the master alone reaped any benefit from the relationship.[70] Two years later they went further, banning any cobblers that had not been a servant or journeyman to the masters within the town.[71] Importantly, they also raised the age requirement from thirty to fifty years, intending that cobbling was to be the preserve of old journeymen alone.

As the century turned, and the economic crisis after Darien became acute, the Incorporation also sought to offset their burdens caring for the poor by 'augmenting' the quarter compts and fees of cobblers in both city and suburbs.[72] Such changes were no doubt difficult to bear, and it is unsurprising that tempers flared. One cobbler, Alexander Hutcheson, was incarcerated for 'abusen and callummatting' the deacon of the cordiners, and had to sign a petition that neither he nor his wife would say or do anything to harm any of the brethren of the Incorporation upon the pain of losing his 'freedom as ane Cobler in Edinburgh and suburbs'.[73] What is noteworthy here is not the imprisonment or even the involvement of the courts, but instead the rehabilitation of the cobbler. As long as he abided by the rules, he was allowed to keep repairing shoes. As such, we see that cobblers continued to work on the margins of the capital, as corporate privileges were offset to some degree by market demand.

Conclusion

Work in the early modern period was heavily regulated, but much negotiation also went into deciding who could work and who could not. In the corporate system, those fortunate enough to obtain freedoms had access denied

---

[69] NRS, GD348/206, Minutes of the Incorporation of Cordiners of Edinburgh, 1613–1708, fols 24v–25r.
[70] Ibid., fol. 206v.
[71] 'The Deakon & masters enacts statuts & ordaines that In all tyme comeing noe cobler sall be admitted within the Liberties of Edinburgh upon quhatsoever pretext except such as hes bein servants & jorneymen within the citty & above 50 yers of adge'. Ibid., fol. 210r.
[72] Ibid., fols 221v–222r.
[73] NRS, GD348/117/5, Petition by Alexander Hutcheson, October 1704.

to others. Still, despite the privileges of the corporate system, those who were free could not always exclude the unfree majority. Indeed, they did not always want to, as many of the unfree proved themselves to be quite useful. Hence, many were allowed to work on the margins, either due to their connections or their utility. Some managed to secure stallanger privileges, usually for a set period of time and dependent on payments to the relevant authorities. Many such workers found toleration in an intolerant corporate system.

This chapter started by asking what kinds of people worked on the margins and why they were tolerated. As has been shown, decisions about who could work and when were rarely straightforward, with competing interests and politics abounding, not to mention the many tensions due to the workers' rank or station, their gender, or their place of residency. While many have been left out due to space constrictions, three groups have been explored here whose work proved too useful to disallow. These were the men and women who offered labour, provisions, and repairs. Some were highly skilled, while others were mere 'clubs'. Some were close to freemen, some were not. Some were in the town, and some were outsiders, whether in suburb or country, but all were able to fill a need in early modern society. None appear to have had autonomy, and only rarely do we see them exercising agency. Nonetheless, we find them working on the margins.

So, why were they tolerated? Because the corporate privileges of the few still needed to be balanced with the needs of the community, or the common weal. This may not have extended to an individual's need to work, but it might have allowed for that work if it served the interests of the wider community. Often it was the magistrates who were arbiters of such interests, though external influences, such as the crown or the nobility, could certainly wield influence.[74]

Despite their lack of privileges, many managed to straddle the line between free and unfree. Some had links to privileges, as with the widows of freemen who were usually allowed to carry on their late husband's trade, though even these could face resistance from the corporate bodies which sought to control work. Others found access based on their age and length of service, while others yet found toleration through markets which simply demanded more supply. In all of these, skill level was rarely the crucial factor. Cobblers certainly *could* make shoes, but freemen did not want them making shoes. The freemen did not always have the final say, though. They might resist suburban or outland craftwork, but would the magistrates prioritise corporate privileges over the needs of the community? Land-markets restricting places and times of sales might offer a compromise, but as with all the other decisions about who could work, access was often contested.

There were in fact many types of people, male and female, young and old, who found toleration working for or alongside the freemen, despite the tensions that such dichotomies could bring. While much clandestine work also

---

[74] Allen, 'Governance, Regulation and the State', pp. 207–8.

happened, there were laws which sought to stop it. This can be contrasted with the experiences of those below the corporate system who were *allowed* to work under specific circumstances, offering us intriguing insights into an understudied group of early modern Scots. Whether for a stallanger's fee for a set period of time, or due to their connections, many workers were not quite free or unfree. Instead, they lived their working lives on the margins.

7

The Life of the Lockman

Laura I. Doak

EPITAPH
The Man who liv'd by choaking Breath,
Ly's here, at Length o'recome by Death.[1]

The 'lockman', or public executioner, forms a shadowy figure in histories of early modern Scotland. He stands namelessly on the scaffold alongside the noted rebels, accused 'witches', and others so often written about by historians as he enacted the penalties dealt by well-studied systems and regimes. Most often, he is nameless in both primary and secondary literature alike: 'the lockman'; 'the hangman'; 'the executer'. It is even easy to overlook the lockman's existence as a real person or, rather, a series of individuals whose lives were united by employment in a grisly role that their contemporaries deemed brutally undesirable,[2] yet simultaneously imperative for maintenance of law and order.[3] Considering their existence in the context of these contradictory social demands, this essay uses three core case studies to explore the lockman's role and his relationship to the community he served, underscoring the need to appreciate such marginal characters in order to better understand early modern Scottish society as a whole.

Named after the 'lock', or small measure, of meal he was conventionally entitled to from each sack in the local marketplace, the lockman was responsible for a variety of grim, arduous roles.[4] Contemporary records note lockmen clearing latrines and recovering corpses, as well as constructing gallows, pillories, and other apparatus of public punishment.[5] Precise duties often varied, but one common task was driving 'uncouth beggars' from burgh or parish bounds.[6] At Edinburgh, Dumfries, and many other towns, lockmen

---

[1] *Elegy on the Death of Hary Ormiston, late Hangman in Edinburgh* (Edinburgh, 1720). I would like to thank staff at the local archives of Shetland, Orkney, and Perth for their assistance and advice whilst preparing this chapter.
[2] L. Paterson, 'Executing Scottish Witches', in J. Goodare (ed.), *Scottish Witches and Witch-Hunters* (Basingstoke, 2013), pp. 196–214, at p. 198.
[3] D. Nash and A.-M. Kilday, *Cultures of Shame: Exploring Crime and Morality in Britain 1600–1900* (London, 2010), p. 48.
[4] DSL, 'lokman'.
[5] 'Haddington Records: Books of the Common Good', *Transactions of the East Lothian Antiquarian Society*, 7 (1958), 46–80, at 66, 69; *Edinburgh Recs.*, vol. 4, p. 484.
[6] *Dumbarton Recs.*, p. 37; Margo Todd (ed.), *The Perth Kirk Session Books 1577–1590* (Woodbridge, 2008), p. 15n.

were also commonly responsible for cleaning the blood of slaughtered animals spilt in marketplaces,[7] and killing nuisance stray dogs, cats, and swine.[8] On occasion, therefore, the role may have overlapped with that of skinner, as was far more common elsewhere in Europe.[9] As in Germany, Scottish lockmen also occupied the pseudo-legal role of torturer,[10] an apparent contradiction only further entrenched with time since, by the end of the eighteenth century, the position of executioner often became merged with the court office of dempster.[11]

It was the enacting of corporal and capital punishment, however, for which the executioner was best known and by which, indeed, he continues to be defined. Scholarship on early modern Europe has drawn out the intricate messages communicated by public punishment, which – rather than aiming simply to shock and awe spectators into fearful subservience – functioned within what James Sharpe has termed a complex 'context of ceremony and ritual'.[12] The aim was to provide theatrical demonstration of the criminal subversion embodied by an individual's actions[13] and, at times, even to offer elements of reconciliation between them and their community.[14] A common form of physical punishment performed by Scottish lockmen was scourging (whipping) men and women convicted of petty crimes like forni-

---

[7] *Edinburgh Recs.*, vol. 4, p. 134.
[8] A. Truckell, 'Extracts from Dumfries Burgh Court Records', *Transactions of the Dumfriesshire and Galloway Natural History Society*, 72 (1997), 112–15.
[9] Nella Lonza, 'The Figure of the Executioner in Dubrovnik between Social Acceptance and Rejection', *Dubrovnik Annals*, 20 (2016), 93–108, p. 100.
[10] K. Stuart, *Defiled Trades and Social Outcasts: Honor and Ritual Pollution in Early Modern Germany* (Cambridge, 2000), p. 140.
[11] R. Bennett, *Capital Punishment and the Criminal Corpse in Scotland, 1740–1834* (Basingstoke, 2018), p. 126.
[12] James Sharpe, "Last Dying Speeches': Religion, Ideology and Public Execution in Seventeenth-Century England', *Past & Present*, 107:1 (1985), 144–67, pp. 146–7.
[13] P. Friedland, 'Beyond Deterrence: Cadavers, Effigies, Animals and the Logic of Executions in Premodern France', *Historical Reflections*, 29:2 (2003), 295–317, pp. 297–8; P. Friedland, *Seeing Justice Done: The Age of Spectacular Capital Punishment in France* (Oxford, 2012), pp. 10–11, 15; L. Doak, 'On Street and Scaffold: The People and Political Culture in Restoration Scotland, c.1678–1686' (unpublished PhD thesis, University of Glasgow, 2020), pp. 175, 178; K. Royer, *The English Execution Narrative, 1200–1700* (London, 2014), pp. 16–17, 43, 95–6; K. Royer, 'The Body in Parts: Reading the Execution Ritual in Late Medieval England', *Historical Reflections*, 29:2 (2003), 319–39, at pp. 320, 322–3.
[14] L. Doak, 'Militant Women and "National" Community: The Execution of Isabel Alison and Marion Harvie, 1681', *Journal of the Northern Renaissance*, 12 (2020); N. Terpstra, 'Body Politics: The Criminal Body between Public and Private', *Journal of Medieval and Early Modern Studies*, 45:1 (2015), 7–52, at 34.

cation.[15] This often took place on a burgh's high street at the mercat cross,[16] but at Aberdeen, Ayr, Inveraray, and many other towns it was also usual to scourge 'throw the haill toune',[17] rendering it an even more exhausting physical task. Scottish executioners were also responsible for branding the cheeks or palms of repeat offenders.[18] Bodily punishments might even be embellished to further elaborate intended meanings. In addition to scourging and branding, a woman named Marion McCaul had her tongue bored by Alexander Cockburn, lockman of Edinburgh, in 1671 for toasting the devil's health out loud and in public.[19] A man named Donald MacClerich was tried for murder at Inveraray in June 1708 but when the jury found him guilty only of manslaughter by a narrow margin, the court instructed the local hangman to issue forty 'stripes' of the whip, brand him on the palm, and then cut off his right ear, nailing it to the gibbet as a longer-term reminder about just how close he had come to ultimate condemnation.[20]

When it came to the death penalty, the most common means of execution throughout the early modern period in Scotland was hanging, which led to the interchangeability of lockman, hangman, and executioner as common terms. Until the late seventeenth century, women could also be executed by drowning[21] and those considered guilty of witchcraft, bestiality, and other 'unnatural' crimes were often burnt at the stake.[22] Additionally, executioners at Edinburgh made routine use of 'the Maiden', an early form of guillotine. Originally engineered for the murderers of David Rizzio in 1566, the Maiden was chiefly used to execute traitors, murderers, and other serious criminals of higher rank.[23] Yet although the Scots, in common with the English, did not generally share the same impetus for more 'spectacular' capital punishments as regularly witnessed in early modern France and Germany, Edinburgh

---

[15] NRS, Leven and Melville Papers, GD26/4/1022; *Aberdeen Recs.*, vol. 2, p. 207. In his study of crime and punishment in Restoration Argyllshire, Allan Kennedy calculates around 2 per cent of 1489 relevant indictments resulted in scourging sentences. However, burgh records across the kingdom reference whipping more frequently than executions. As Kennedy notes, much more work is required to understand crime and punishment in Restoration Scotland. A. Kennedy, 'Crime and Punishment in Early-Modern Scotland: The Secular Courts of Restoration Argyllshire, 1660–1688', *International Review of Scottish Studies*, 41 (2016), 1–36, at pp. 1, 8–9, 22–3.

[16] *PJC*, vol. 1, p. 87.

[17] *Old Aberdeen Recs.*, p. 83; NRS, Argyll Justiciary Court, SC54/17/2/8/1; G. Pryde (ed.), *Ayr Burgh Accounts 1534–1624* (Edinburgh, 1937), p. 248; Robert Barclay (ed.), *The Court Books of Orkney and Shetland 1614–1615* (Edinburgh, 1967), pp. 55–6, 116–17.

[18] NRS, SC54/17/2/33/3.

[19] J. Maidment (ed.), *Analecta Scotica: Collections Illustrative of the Civil, Ecclesiastical, and Literary History of Scotland* (Edinburgh, 1837), p. 167.

[20] NRS, SC54/17/2/33/3.

[21] E.J. Burford and S. Shulman, *Of Bridles and Burning: The Punishment of Women* (London, 1992), pp. 31–2.

[22] Paterson, 'Executing Scottish Witches', at pp. 203–5. For the execution of 'heretics' during the Scottish Reformation see J. Dawson, 'The Scottish Reformation and the Theatre of Martyrdom', *Studies in Church History*, 30 (1995), 259–70.

[23] Doak, 'On Street and Scaffold', p. 182.

lockmen were on rare occasions called upon to enact more theatrical demonstrations of destruction. In 1591, Borders heritor John Dickson of Bellchester was 'broke upon the wheel' for parricide, a sentencing anomaly left mysterious by a lack of surviving evidence.[24] In 1685, the execution of captured Hertfordshire man Colonel Richard Rumbold occasioned an English-style traitors' death of being 'hanged, drawn, and quartered' for his reputed participation in Charles I's regicide in 1649, all carried out on command by lockman Harry Ormistoun, discussed in more detail below.[25] Even as late as the 1820 'Radical Rising', convicted traitors' heads – or even hearts – were held up to spectating crowds, a bloody, theatrical, yet legally ordained task that fell to the executioner on the scaffold.[26]

The executioner's role as primary performer within this 'theatre of death' has been explored for other areas of pre-modern Europe and the British Isles, but this chapter provides the first specific analysis of Scottish lockmen and their unique experience.[27] Reconstructing this role and the men who filled it requires careful scrutiny of manuscript and printed sources. Incomplete judicial records, together with their anonymising tendency to refer to executioners by title rather than name, make the kingdom's lockmen difficult to trace, except where they themselves were in trouble with the law. No known autobiographical material survives comparable to Franz Schmidt's famous Nuremberg journal[28] and no Scottish executioner is known to have produced their own public-facing address, such as Englishman Jack Ketch's *Apologie ... in vindication of himself* (1683).[29] But they were often the subject of popular print themselves, particularly from the late seventeenth century onward. Source material from the earlier part of the period is particularly patchy, meaning that the following case studies all date to the seventeenth and eighteenth centuries. But burgh records do offer useful glimpses of executioners' status and activities throughout the early modern era, offering valuable sixteenth-century evidence that can be used to better contextualise later, better documented examples. Likewise, executioners' financial transactions across the early modern period can often be recovered from local government receipts and treasurers' accounts. The explicitly public nature of pre-modern

---

[24] H. Arnot, *A Collection and Abridgement of Celebrated Criminal Trials in Scotland* (Glasgow, 1812), p. 145.
[25] Rumbold was captured after joining the 1685 Argyll Rising but had already outlawed and sentenced to death in absentia. To be 'hanged, drawn, and quartered' was a far rarer punishment in Scotland than England. Additionally, although English 'quartering' meant to quite literally quarter the condemned's torso, in Scotland the term referred only to removal of limbs and – with the exception of assassin David Hackston of Rathillet in 1680 – did not usually involve additional mutilations. See Royer, *English Execution Narrative*, pp. 39–40.
[26] A. Young, *The Encyclopaedia of Scottish Executions 1750–1963* (Orpington, 1998), pp. 86–8; Bennett, *Capital Punishment*, p. 130.
[27] See Doak, 'On Street and Scaffold', p. 169.
[28] H. Erik (ed.), *The Executioner's Journal: Meister Franz Schmidt of the Imperial City of Nuremberg* (Charlottesville, NC, 2016).
[29] Jack Ketch, *The Apologie of John Ketch Esq; The Executioner of London* (London, 1683).

penal punishment also occasioned comment in letters, diaries, and other witness accounts, as drawn on throughout ensuing analysis. Investigation of primary records for the marginal figure of the Scottish lockman reveals that he was not so detached from mainstream society as might be assumed, but lived an ambiguous existence among his community.

John Mouat, Shetland

In December 1791, John Mouat humbly petitioned Patrick Graeme, sheriff-depute of Orkney and Shetland, and his local deputy James Malcolmson, as 'an old weak and infirm man' who was 'no longer fit to perform his office as hangman'. Mouat had served in the post for a decade, also acting as dempster to announce individuals' sentences at local trials, but he was now unable to fulfil the position's physical demands. He also stated that his annual £10 salary was 'not adequate' to cover the expenses he incurred through travelling to the court and punishment site at Kirkwall, Orkney, which lay a considerable distance from his family home at Skaw, on the most northern part of Unst, Shetland. The aging executioner requested that Graeme and Malcolmson accept his resignation and also 'liberate him from any sentence that was or might have been pronounced against him at the Commencement of his office'.[30]

Mouat was typical of most pre-modern Scottish executioners in that he was first appointed to the post in lieu of his own capital conviction. In 1781 Mouat himself had been scourged and banished from Shetland on pain of death after being found guilty of stealing cattle,[31] returning three years later after petitioning and offering his services as hangman to ensure residence at home with his family.[32] Commutation of a death sentence to individuals willing to act in this capacity was widespread in pre-modern Scotland. At Glasgow in September 1605, local magistrates 'acceptit admitit and reseaveit' one John McClelland as the burgh's 'executour' after he was caught within its bounds despite a prior sentence of banishment.[33] Returning to Orkney, Mouat was clearly the latest in a long line of convict hangmen. On 7 October 1614, a group of men were found guilty of rebellion but one, William Donaldsone, was offered his life should he agree to hang the rest of his erstwhile comrades and then continue to act as local executioner.[34] Donaldsone's tenure was short and he was succeeded the fol-

[30] SA, Lerwick Sheriff Court, SC12/6/1791/53, fol. 1r–v.
[31] SA, SC12/6/1781/17.
[32] SA, SC12/6/1783/17.
[33] *Glasgow Recs.*, vol. 1, p. 233.
[34] NRS, Miscellaneous Papers, RH9/15/150. A similar offer was accepted by Ayrshire man Cornelius Anderson in 1666, when he executed nine of his fellow rebels active in the Pentland Rising. Robert Wodrow, *The History of the Sufferings of the Church of Scotland, from the Restauration to the Revolution* (4 vols, Edinburgh, 1721), vol. 2, p. 260.

lowing November by sheep thief Olaw Smyth.[35] Then came Robert Flawt in 1635, another 'notorious theif' who agreed 'of his oune consent' to 's[e]rve as Lockman all tyme comming' to evade his own condemnation.[36] Given the post's responsibilities, this was a brutal bargain but some requested it on their own initiative, such as soldier John Finnison, arrested for theft in 1736 and subsequently appointed executioner of Forfar.[37] Condemned for rape and infanticide, innkeeper Alexander Barrie had earlier pleaded with Forfar magistrates in November 1694 for a commutation of his sentence on similar terms, but was refused on the grounds he was 'ane old cunning wicked mane'.[38] In some cases, particularly for those already considered marginalised within society, the appointment could even stand for minor offences. Writing to a deputy on 16 February 1751, for example, James Erskine, Perthshire's sheriff-depute, suggested that their present 'difficulty' in lacking an executioner for a condemned highwayman might be resolved by 'the Common Beggar you have in custody for the Highland Dress' who 'might easily purchase his liberty by performing in that capacity'.[39] There are also instances where appointment to the post of executioner seems to have been a judicial sentence in itself. On 14 December 1746, for instance, serial livestock rustler Dugald Leitch was 'Doomed to be Hangman' for the sheriffdom of Inveraray, following the personal intervention of the Lord Justice General, Archibald Campbell, duke of Argyll.[40] There were, of course, some exceptions. John Hamilton, archbishop of St Andrews attempted to establish the Wann family as hereditary hangmen at St Andrews during the 1560s by providing them with a living at Guardbridge.[41] The unnamed lockman brought to Peebles in 1630 to burn two witches travelled and worked with his son,[42] and Laura Paterson has used this example to presuppose European-style hereditary appointments throughout the kingdom.[43] However, with no further information about this unnamed son's subsequent employment and a dearth of additional examples, it is difficult to further confirm this suggestion. The weight of evidence shows that – like Mouat – the vast majority of Scottish lockmen were individuals condemned by their own crimes to act in that capacity.

Scotland's continued use of criminal lockmen diverged significantly from most European states, where the trade of executioner evolved into a professional heritable position.[44] Paul Friedland has demonstrated how those in

---

[35] Barclay, *Orkney and Shetland*, p. 38 and at p. 43.
[36] NRS, RH9/15/153.
[37] PKA, Perth Burgh Records, B59/24/11/153.
[38] NRS, PC1/50, Privy Council Acta, 1694–6, p. 43.
[39] NRS, Campbell of Barcaldine Papers, GD170/1213.
[40] NRS, SC54/17/2/40/4.
[41] C. Rogers, *Scotland: Social and Domestic* (London, 1869), p. 312.
[42] W. Chambers (ed.), *Charters and Documents relating to the Burgh of Peebles* (Edinburgh, 1872), p. 416.
[43] Paterson, 'Executing Scottish Witches', at p. 198.
[44] H. Klemettilä, *Epitomes of Evil: Representation of Executioners in Northern France and*

early modern France existed as 'a caste of untouchables'; 'an entire outcast race of people' who 'inherited rather than earned' their position but were still trained to a high standard.[45] Parallel situations have been identified in Italy and Croatia, as well as among the *unehrliche Leute* (dishonourable people) of German-speaking regions.[46] Lacking the professional skillset of their European counterparts,[47] it is tempting to suggest that Scottish executioners would have been less successful at fulfilling this demanding role. Certainly, the distinction explains the comparative rarity of more elaborate punishments in Scotland. Mouat himself was often accused of being unwilling and sometimes proved unreachable when called for to carry out his work. On at least one occasion in 1785, a local judge deliberately passed a lenient sentence because Mouat twice 'refused, as was alleged' to answer warrants summoning him to Kirkwall.[48] The decision Orkney's sheriff scrawled on the bottom of Mouat's petition, mentioned above, certainly hints at ongoing tensions, noting that he had already previously ordered the hangman to move his residence to the more accessible location of Lerwick or lose his annual salary. Furthermore, he noted Mouat's lack of enthusiasm had meant 'public justice has been often delayed and sometimes escaped'.[49] Executioners were no doubt reluctant to punish old associates and many convict hangmen certainly appear to have continued participating in criminal activity. In October 1576, an unnamed Edinburgh lockman was discharged by the burgh council for 'monyfald offenssis' in extraction of his emoluments.[50] His replacement, a petty vagrant recorded only as 'Smythie', was not only dismissed but laid in irons and bound to his own gibbet for stealing clothes and jewellery from plague victims in 1585.[51] A century later in 1682, Alexander Cockburn, another of the capital's hangmen, was even himself publicly executed for robbery and murder.[52]

A sense emerges that the lockman lived as a walking margin between their community and the criminally condemned, likened by Friedland to 'a kind of metaphysical as well as literal border guard'.[53] The terms of their appointment certainly implied this to be true. Hangmen in Scotland were technically appointed 'to the death', even if that meant their own execution

---

the *Low Countries in the Late Middle Ages* (Turnhout, 2006), p. 44; Lonza, 'Figure of the Executioner', at p. 97; Stuart, *Defiled Trades*, at pp. 27, 78–9.

[45] Friedland, *Seeing Justice Done*, pp. 72–3.
[46] Stuart, *Defiled Trades*, at pp. 1, 12–13; Lonza, 'Figure of the Executioner', p. 97. England appears to have been the other exception to this trend, see G. Robin, 'The Executioner: His Place in English Society', *British Journal of Sociology*, 15:3 (1964), 234–53, 238.
[47] Lonza, 'Figure of the Executioner', at p. 96.
[48] P.N. Sutherland Graeme, 'Sheriff Patrick Graeme and his Substitute in Shetland', *Orkney Miscellany*, 3 (1956), 40.
[49] SA, SC12/6/1791/53, fol. 2r.
[50] *Edinburgh Recs.*, vol. 4, p. 53.
[51] Ibid., p. 432.
[52] John Lauder, *Historical Observes* (Edinburgh, 1837), p. 58.
[53] Friedland, *Seeing Justice Done*, p. 78.

in final resolution of the law.[54] Should McClelland at Glasgow, noted above, have deserted his post, for example, it was expressly stated that he would be 'hangit to the dead'.[55] Likewise, Leitch at Inveraray was sentenced to serve the post 'during all the days of his Life time and never to run away or leave his office under the pain of death'.[56] Mouat's plea for immunity in 1791, therefore, was not simply a formulaic courtesy but can actually be read as a nervous test that he would not have to pay the ultimate price for tendering his resignation. Yet there is little evidence that this was put into practice. The troublesome sixteenth-century Edinburgh hangmen noted above were released alive, although shamed, after conviction of yet further criminal activity. And, in spite of complaints laid against his conduct in office, Mouat was also released unscathed when the sheriff-depute signed the permission for him 'to Return to Unst or to any other place he pleases' with no outstanding criminal charges or punishments.[57] Superficially, at least, this might read as Mouat's readmission to mainstream society, but, for him and other lockmen, the reality was far more complex.

John McEwen, Perth

On 18 February 1713, the provost of Perth, Robert Robertson, wrote to John Campbell, 1st earl of Breadalbane to thank them for his 'gift' of a lockman named John McEwen. Robertson and his fellow councillors also took the opportunity to compile a detailed list of 'the Dues and emolluments thats wer allowed to his predecessors in that office'.[58] This included a basic weekly wage of 20s as well as 10 merks for every person that he was required to hang and a crown for each that he was asked to either scourge or brand. Local convention also permitted him to seek additional work as a gravedigger or to undertake other unpleasant and menial employment like slaughtering animals, meaning that McEwen could also expect to receive 'accedent casualities at the church Doors and att Burials, and may gaine sixpence a day for comon work if he Incline'. More profitably, however, McEwen was also to receive payment from every coal bark passing along the river, as well as dues on fish, kale, and potted herbs. Particular attention was paid to rules about lending the hangman to other burghs. For every execution carried out elsewhere McEwen was to receive 10 crowns (rather than merks) as well as any incurred expenses. He was also to be escorted there and back under armed guard, with the town or laird borrowing his services agreeing to a cautionary penalty of

---

[54] Robin, 'The Executioner', at p. 236.
[55] *Glasgow Recs.*, vol. 1, p. 233.
[56] NRS, SC54/17/2/40/4.
[57] SA, SC12/6/1791/53, fol. 2v.
[58] NRS, Breadalbane Muniments, GD112/41/3, p. 177.

1,000 merks.[59] McEwen was a treasured asset and Perth's councillors knew his services were required far and wide. Whilst Mouat drew criticism for his perceived lack of enthusiasm, extant correspondence reveals authorities' frustrations that McEwen could be too difficult to procure and keep in one place. Preceding years had seen McEwen carry out executions at Elgin and Thurso,[60] and his permanent placement at Perth was still referenced in local magistrates' letters as he was moving through surrounding areas on loan to Inverness and Pitlochry.[61] Indeed, although interpreted by the town as a generous gift, McEwen's residence at Perth may well have been a primarily practical decision, placing the executioner at a town where he could be conveniently reached and dispatched as required.[62]

McEwen's experience and circumstances show that, despite cries of poverty from Mouat in Shetland, executioners could be keenly sought and well compensated. The unsavoury yet indispensable nature of their daily work often meant that they were comparatively well paid, particularly in busier areas, and although primary evidence remains inconsistent it can be suggested that McEwen's salary and perks were not unusual. In the 1550s, Haddington burgh council paid their executioner, William Brown, 40s per annum,[63] a respectable income above that of an average labourer in the face of rising inflation.[64] By the late 1650s, Linlithgow burgh council paid their lockman 12s a week.[65] In March 1632, Dumbarton recorded an annual salary of £8 for hangman David Glen's 'thankfull services'.[66] By 1677 they were reimbursing Donald McKenzie to the sum of £10 4s 8d, again demonstrating a real wage increase.[67] As representative as he was of most Scottish lockmen's background circumstances, then, Mouat's limited earnings of £10 a year in Orkney and Shetland in 1791 appear to have been caused by ongoing local issues.[68] Complaints by James Sinclair, one of Mouat's predecessors, certainly suggests the same, since he became embroiled in a lengthy legal dispute during the early 1770s when he attempted to claim against the burgh for benefits promised on entering office, which had included 'a free house', peats, and an annual pair of shoes.[69]

---

[59] Ibid., p. 178.
[60] NRS, GD112/39/244/18.
[61] PKA, B59/24/11/89.
[62] NRS, GD112/41/3, p. 177.
[63] 'Haddington Records', at pp. 53–6.
[64] A. Gibson and T. C. Smout, *Prices, Food, and Wages in Scotland 1550–1780* (Cambridge, 1995), pp. 274, 278; A. Blakeway, 'The Sixteenth-Century Price Rise: New Evidence from Scotland, 1500–85', *Economic History Review*, 68:1 (2015), 167–90, at 176–7, 179.
[65] Maidment, *Analecta Scotica*, p. 204.
[66] *Dumbarton Recs.*, p. 37.
[67] Ibid., p. 88.
[68] Gibson and Smout, *Prices, Food, and Wages*, p. 279.
[69] OLA, Kirkwall Sheriff Court, SC11/5/1772/76.

A burgh lockman was a significant outlay, but for towns reliant on borrowing executioners the cost of public justice could be even higher. Treasurer's accounts from Ayr between 1593 and 1618 show that permanently appointed lockmen like Archibald Banquhill were paid an annual salary of £5 with an additional £1 payment for every hanging, but in years when the burgh did not have a resident executioner, local authorities were forced to pay well over £6 for each single public condemnation.[70] Although previously employing their own executioner, with no suitable local criminal to press into the position Dumbarton became reliant on borrowed lockmen throughout the 1680s, paying well over £6 to those of Crieff or Stirling each time one was required.[71] Prior to the appointment of McEwen, Perth also borrowed frequently from Crieff, paying for the services of a man named Donald McCarie in 1706.[72] Even larger burghs did not always possess their own executioner. Glasgow appears to have lacked one for most of the seventeenth century. In July 1634, burgh records note payment to the hangman of Irvine for scourging two petty thieves.[73] Irvine's executioner was borrowed again in November 1645 at a cost of £20 plus expenses,[74] as was as Edinburgh's throughout the 1680s and 1690s.[75] In the early 1750s Walter Ranken, executioner at Perth, lodged in Glasgow on long-term loan.[76] As late as 2 November 1813, Provost Kirkman Finlay urged appointment of a Glasgow lockman on a suggested and substantial annual salary of £50.[77]

The need for executioners to travel was also exacerbated by the custom of hanging and 'gibbeting' convicted murderers at the scene of their crime, a practice particularly common from the late seventeenth century.[78] After being condemned at Stirling in 1718, John McNiccoll was sent thirty miles away to Mugdock for execution at the scene of his crime, leaving local laird James Graham of Kilmannan to pay £20 8s to the executioner of Hamilton 'per aggriement', as well as an additional £14 14s travel expenses, including an armed guard to prevent interruption by McNiccoll's friends.[79] A similar situation at Thurso in May 1711 threw local landowner Duncan Toshach of Monzievaird into a palpable flap, dispatching multiple letters in 'all heast' to the earl of Breadalbane and his deputies to urgently request John McEwen's services after one Robert Munro was sentenced to be hanged on the town's

---

[70] Pryde, *Ayr Burgh Accounts*, pp. 176, 188, 204, 209, 214, 223, 231, 267.
[71] NRS, GD1/755/9; *Dumbarton Recs.*, pp. 94–5; SCA, Stirling Burgh Records, B66/25/457.
[72] NRS, GD1/479/10. See also PKA, B59/24/11/88.
[73] *Glasgow Recs.*, vol. 2, p. 22.
[74] Ibid., vol. 2, p. 87.
[75] Ibid., vol 3, p. 358; NRS, PC2/24, Privy Council Decreta, 1692–4, fol. 258r.
[76] PKA, B59/24/11/95 and B59/24/11/95.
[77] *Glasgow Recs.*, vol. 7, p. 200.
[78] Z. Dyndor, 'The Gibbet in the Landscape: Locating the Criminal Corpse in Mid-Eighteenth-Century England', in R. Ward (ed.), *Global History of Execution and the Criminal Corpse* (London, 2015), pp. 102–25, at pp. 103, 106–7.
[79] NRS, Montrose Muniments, GD220/6/716.

high street for the murder of local bailie Laurence Calder.[80] 'If McEwen come not,' Monzievaird begged, 'I know not what may be the event or Consequence of this mater', adding that he could 'get non here to undertake that trade [of hangman]' even after he had 'offered ten Crouns to any that wold undertake it tho In disguise'.[81] Fearing that the task might even fall to him, Monzievaird inserted this same telling phrase into each of his letters: 'nor do I think that any will supose that I will undertake that trade, lest what it will *officium nemini debet esse damnosum* [an office ought to be injurious to no-one]'.[82]

The role of lockman, then, although unwillingly filled, could be lucrative, and was made even more so by their conventional entitlement to the 'lock' of marketplace goods (see above), as well as contractual stipulations for clothes and housing.[83] The 'benefit of the ladle at the mercat', a ladle-full of each sack of goods that was brought there for sale, was gifted to George Gray, lockman of Dunbar, at his appointment in 1698, and at Inverness the hangman was entitled to one haddock from every creel and a handful of meal out of every sack in the market until the post lapsed at the end of the eighteenth century.[84] Elsewhere, however, the amount this extended to could cause tension. At Edinburgh, for example, the lockman's sixteenth-century entitlements to part of every boll sold within the marketplace was gradually eroded after 1660, although given the city's role as Scotland's commercial capital the value of goods claimed by later hangmen must still have been substantial.[85] A handful of men were even known to have voluntarily taken up the post of lockman for their own financial gain. Edinburgh's notorious John Dalgleish, who took up the role of hangman in 1722 after an earlier career of money-lending, fraud, and illegal horse trading, was popularly lampooned over stepping up 'For Greed of Geir', even though it caused his children's ruin and social embarrassment.[86] On McEwen's death at Perth in October 1735, Dunfermline's hangman notably petitioned the burgh provost expressing his desire to succeed to the position and the emoluments to which it was entitled.[87]

Harry Ormistoun, Edinburgh

Harry Ormistoun, with whose satirical elegy this chapter began, was lockman of Edinburgh from 1684. The exact nature of Ormistoun's appointment is unclear, but he originally served the burgh alongside his brother, George,

---

[80] NRS, GD112/39/253/4.
[81] NRS, GD112/39/253/6, fol. 1v.
[82] NRS, GD112/39/253/4.
[83] In this, Scotland mirrors France. Friedland, *Seeing Justice Done*, p. 79.
[84] J. Mitchell, *Reminiscences of My Life in the Highlands* (2 vols, Newton Abbot, 1971), vol. 1, p. 52.
[85] *Edinburgh Recs.*, vol. 10, p. 281.
[86] Alexander Pennecuik, *The Last Speech and Dying Words of John Dalgleish, Lock Man alias Hang-man of Edinburgh* (Edinburgh, 1727).
[87] PKA, B59/24/11/92.

with whom he was imprisoned for theft whilst still a boy.[88] Some considered Ormistoun too soft on many of those sentenced to scourging, particularly when bribed by their family or friends, and it was for this 'corruption' that he was banished in late 1720. His dismissal was commemorated in a series of satirical slip ballads and broadsheets that mocked his friendship with 'Thieves, Bauds and Whores' and the fact he could be bribed by 'a Plack' to 'spair their Back'.[89] Both he and George were also remembered for acting mercifully to those experiencing prolonged deaths and expressing compassion – even if reputedly only a 'counterfeit Tear'.[90] Yet, notably, Ormistoun was also responsible for some of the bloodiest and most infamous public executions ever staged in Edinburgh, including Richard Rumbold's for treason in 1685, noted earlier, and that of student Thomas Aikenhead for blasphemy in 1697.[91]

Ormistoun's salutation as the subject of popular discussion was undoubtedly influenced by his lengthy tenure but, as Adam Fox notes, it also demonstrates how hangmen could be considered local 'characters' with a noted presence and role within the bustle and news of the burgh community.[92] The same ephemera also notes him settling traders' disputes in the Fishmarket outside his home.[93] Several of Ormistoun's successors were also the subject of popular caricature. John Dalgleish, for instance, was teased for his gambling losses[94] and placed in satirical dialogue with infamous executees,[95] casting the hangman as something akin to a pantomime villain amidst the theatricality of the scaffold.[96] Whilst their hereditary European counterparts were forbidden from physical contact with mainstream society,[97] many of Scotland's early modern executioners even left marks of their physical interaction. In 1750, John Newall at Kirkcudbright personally marked receipt of his wages with an 'X',[98] as did John Colonel, executioner of Stornoway and

---

[88] *Elegy On the Death of Hary Ormiston*.
[89] *The Sorrowful Lamentation of Herrie Ormistoun late Hang-man in Edinburgh, for the Loss of his Post* (Edinburgh, 1720).
[90] *Elegy On the Death of Hary Ormiston*.
[91] M. Graham, *The Blasphemies of Thomas Aikenhead: Boundaries of Belief on the Eve of the Enlightenment* (Edinburgh, 2008), pp. 2–4, 100.
[92] A. Fox, *The Press and the People: Cheap Print and Society in Scotland 1500–1785* (Oxford, 2020), p. 248.
[93] *Elegy On the Death of Hary Ormiston*.
[94] Alexander Pennecuik, *Huy and Cry for Apprehending George Fachney, Professor of Gaming* (Edinburgh, 1722).
[95] [Alexander Pennecuik], *A Letter from Doctor Dalgleish to his Patient Mrs M'Leod, and her Answer* (Edinburgh, 1727).
[96] U. McIlvenna, *Singing the News of Death: Execution Ballads in Europe 1500–1900* (Oxford, 2022), pp. 445–52.
[97] Friedland, *Seeing Justice Done*, pp. 71–2, 78–9, 82–3. An exception is Croatia where Lonza notes 'archival data from Dubrovnik provides no evidence on any form of heavy stigmatisation of neither the executioner nor his family'. Lonza, 'Dubrovnik', at p. 104.
[98] Dumfries and Galloway Council, 'The Hangman's Receipt 1750', SCRAN [ID: 000-000-580-843-C].

Lewis, in 1791.[99] Likewise, although unable to personally sign his petition, John Mouat 'touched the pen in token of his Consent'.[100] Appointed after stealing chickens in 1778, Edinburgh's Jock Heich even continued work as a cobbler, keeping a shop at his home in Hangman's Close and producing goods purchased and worn by other members of the community.[101]

This cements a key distinction between lockmen in Scotland and executioners elsewhere in early modern Europe in that they were not born apart to fulfil their gruesome role, but had once lived as ordinary people and thus continued, in at least some way, to exist as part of their community. Scotland's hangmen lived as the 'other within' rather than a figure completely apart. However, their criminal past and – however forced – apparent preparedness to act in such a brutal capacity must surely have marked them as individuals to be feared. Throughout the early modern period, Ormistoun and other Edinburgh hangmen were served communion at a separate table in the tolbooth kirk. Sixteenth-century executioners were often recorded in burgh records simply as 'Dustefute', an insulting slang word for travelling vagrant or beggar.[102] They were also excluded from sitting on burgh councils or appearing as court witnesses because of a 'praesumption of crualty', as seventeenth-century lawyer John Lauder observed.[103] Lockmen acted as the conduit of societal 'shame' as much as they functioned as instruments of judicial punishment. Part of a penalty's ignominy was its enaction by 'the hand of the hangman'. Although tolerated and normalised in some social scenarios, within the context of public justice the hangman's touch could transform a being or object into an outcast entity.[104] A clear illustration of this was the Scots' convention of burning treasonous books at the mercat cross 'be the hand of the hangman' as a form of totemic condemnation.[105] And, when it came to the physical destruction or harm of other living people, participation in such acts was clearly considered to leave an irrevocable stain. Returning to the panicked comments of Monzievaird as he tried to ensure James McEwen's services in 1711, fulfilling the role of lockman was as infamous and injurious as it was indispensable.[106]

This ambiguity manifested in lockmen's daily life. At Edinburgh, it was particularly clear in the location of 'Hangie's House', the lockman's home, which was gifted as part of the role and situated at the 'Back of the

[99] NRS, Seaforth Papers, GD46/1/552, no. 33.
[100] SA, SC12/6/1791/53, fol. 1v.
[101] *The Coblers' Tears: An Elegy* (Edinburgh, 1816).
[102] *Edinburgh Recs.*, vol. 4, p. 54.
[103] John Lauder, *Historical Notices of Scottish Affairs* (2 vols, Edinburgh, 1848), vol. 1, p. 159.
[104] Nash and Kilday, *Cultures of Shame*, p. 10; K. Kesselring, 'Law, Status, and the Lash: Judicial Whipping in Early Modern England', *Journal of British Studies*, 60:3 (2021), 511–33.
[105] *Edinburgh Recs.*, vol. 10, pp. 217-18; Doak, 'On Street and Scaffold', pp. 148, 187–8, 200. For an example, see NRS, PC1/50, pp. 473–4.
[106] NRS, GD112/39/253/4.

Fishmarket Close'. Located in this spot from at least the 1590s, an 1820 illustration by James Skene depicts a building not unlike any other in the area and on the corner of two busy streets lined with traders and passers-by.[107] In contrast, Spanish hangmen had their houses painted bright red,[108] and in France, Italy, and the Netherlands executioners' homes were located as far as possible from the main population and significant political spaces, most often being placed outside of city walls.[109] Here, in the Scottish capital, however, the lockman was purposefully lodged just meters from the burgh's civic, spiritual, and political heart of the mercat cross, St Giles' Cathedral, and Parliament House. Housed by the community but placed in a job nobody else wanted to do, the positioning of their dwelling places near the town centre appear to have been usual in pre-modern Scotland, and was replicated at places like Stirling and Linlithgow.[110] An obvious exception appears to have been John Mouat's chosen residence far from his workplace at Kirkwall, for which he was chastised and threatened with dismissal.[111] To live at such at an isolated distance would have been usual for executioners in much of contemporary Europe, but for Scotland, it appears to have subverted usual community expectations.

The lockman's clothing was also provided by their community but, again, marked them as distinct. As hangman of Edinburgh, Ormistoun would have worn grey clothes under a black and white town livery emblazoned with the burgh coat of arms.[112] This uniform was worn by Edinburgh's hangmen from at least the early sixteenth century, when one John Jackson was granted a garment 'of quhyte and blak colouris with the airmis of the towne' in January 1537.[113] Symbolically, this reflected his role within the capital's judicial machinery, but the monolithic grey beneath set him apart as much as it set the tone for his sombre existence. Executioners outside the capital also wore grey, donning a town livery over the top for executions where applicable.[114] A surviving receipt from Linlithgow, dated 26 May 1722, details provision to the lockman of coarse grey linen clothing, a grey linen cravat, and a matching 'bonet'.[115] Again, this marks a notable difference from European 'uniforms', which were most often bright and carried symbols of the trade rather than the town. At Arras in northern France, for example, executioners wore a vivid

---

[107] J. Skene, 'Hangie's House' (1820) Edinburgh Libraries, Museums and Galleries. The house in this image was built by lockman John Whyte in the early 1680s. *Edinburgh Recs.*, vol. 10, p. 11.
[108] Robin, 'The Executioner', at p. 235.
[109] Friedland, *Seeing Justice Done*, p. 81; Klemettilä, *Epitomes of Evil*, p. 74.
[110] NRS, B48/14/181 and RH9/15/153
[111] SA, SC12/6/1791/53, fol. 2r.
[112] *Elegy On the Death of Hary Ormiston*; Pennecuik, *The Last Speech*.
[113] *Edinburgh Recs.*, vol. 2, pp. 80–1. See also *Edinburgh Recs.*, vol. 4, p. 209 and at p. 261. Edinburgh's executioners also carried 'a bandet staf': ibid., p. 378. At Stirling, the executioner was occasionally referred to as 'the Staffman'.
[114] NRS, GD112/41/3, p. 178.
[115] NRS, B48/14/181.

cloak of red, yellow, and blue with the gallows embroidered on the front and a ladder on the back.[116]

Just days after his dismissal in 1720, Ormistoun was mysteriously stabbed to death as he prepared to leave the city.[117] Perhaps his death resulted from criminal connections. It might also have been an act of vengeance. Executioners, as noted by Racheal Bennet, could be targeted by community violence.[118] McEwen, as already stated, travelled with an armed guard and many burghs passed acts outlawing 'abuisis' of their hangman.[119] Alternatively, Ormistoun's ultimate demise may have simply been the product of popular perceptions over what ought to take place as he ended his service. McEwen died in post of natural causes, but Mouat's resignation had included a cautious request for assurance he would now be free. However, left un-investigated at the time by those he had served, Ormistoun's death must remain a mystery. The only certainty was the ambivalence that met his demise, a direct consequence of the life he had lived and a clear reflection of the ambiguity within which it had been spent. Ormistoun's murder became the subject of popular satire, an extension of the scaffold theatrics in which he had been forced to play his part. Although remembered as part of burgh life in ways that could not have happened in contemporary Europe, Ormistoun could not escape the fact that – as his mock elegy at the top of this chapter makes clear – he and all other executioners in early modern Scotland were ultimately despised for and defined by the role they had 'liv'd by choaking Breath'.[120]

Conclusions

The lockman's contradictory existence both within and outwith the communities they served illustrates the need to look beyond the conventional boundaries of academic history and into the perceived margins of historic communities to better understand early modern Scotland. As with the executioners of so many other parts of Europe, each of the case studies and other examples mentioned in this chapter lived within a peculiar and paradoxical 'combination of opprobrium and privilege'.[121] A lockman filled an important role that was deemed necessary and just, but the work was physically demanding and grotesque, leaving these men tarnished in the eyes of those around them. Yet, however undesirable, the post also carried an income and other benefits including, most commonly, commutation of their own sentence of death. Their continued presence in the local community marks Scottish ex-

---

[116] Friedland, *Seeing Justice Done*, p. 79.
[117] *Elegy On the Death of Hary Orimston*.
[118] Bennett, *Capital Punishment*, pp. 136–7, quotation at p. 127.
[119] *Glasgow Recs.*, vol. 1, p. 234.
[120] *Elegy on the Death of Hary Ormiston*; Robin, 'The Executioner', at p. 245.
[121] Friedland, *Seeing Justice Done*, p. 72; Klemettilä, *Epitomes of Evil*, p. 40.

ecutioners as different from those in France, Germany, and many other parts of Europe, rather than existing as an entire caste apart, demonstrating that there was clearly far more room in the daily lives of Scottish towns for marginal characters than we often expect or assume. Layers of ambiguity show that Scotland's lockmen held a uniquely marginal position within their communities and, as a group, are a perfect case study of early modern marginality.

8

'Huirdome and Harlettrie': Female Sex Workers in Early Modern Edinburgh, 1689–1760

Susanne Weston

On 25 January 1759, Margaret Malcolm, the daughter of a shoemaker in Elgin, was admonished before the magistrates of Edinburgh after being found in a bawdy house owned by Janet Dryburgh. The magistrates acknowledged Malcolm's plea that she had no other 'honest and virtuous way of making her bread', and so, to avoid trial and punishment, they instead banished her from the city.[1] The 'bawdy house' from which Malcom was removed was situated in South Gray's Close, also known as Mint Close – part of a narrow street that extended south from the High Street to the Cowgate.[2] The establishment was one of at least four similar premises in Edinburgh operated by Dryburgh from 1756 to 1759, and Margaret Malcolm was her employee. For the most part, when the city constables detected and raided an establishment, both employer and employee relocated, usually within the same area, and continued their trade.[3] Dryburgh and Malcolm were just two of the hundreds of sex workers in early modern Edinburgh, women who, despite facing banishment, imprisonment, public humiliation, and corporal punishment, continued to 'make their bread' through the sale of sex.

In early modern Scotland, social order and moral rectitude were considered essential requisites for any civil society. Accordingly, those who deviated from accepted standards of behaviour were subject to punitive measures and social censure, and this was particularly prevalent after 1700 when moral reformers and clergy railed against the immorality of the people.[4] It is therefore unsurprising that the historical analysis of sex and sexuality has hitherto been considered through an important, yet narrow, framework of deviance

---

[1] ECA, SL232, Edinburgh Burgh Court: Black Books, vol. 4, fol. 55.
[2] S. Harris, *The Place Names of Edinburgh: Their Origins and History* (Edinburgh, 1996), p. 307; A.L. Murray, 'The Scottish Mint after the Recoinage, 1707–1836', *Proceedings of the Society of Antiquaries of Scotland*, 129 (2000), 861–6.
[3] ECA, SL232, vol. 4, fols 21, 33, 50, 55 and 66.
[4] George Rule, *A Discourse of Suppressing Immorality and Promoting Godliness. Being the Substance of Some Sermons* (Edinburgh, 1701); David Williamson, *A sermon preached at Edinburgh in the Parliament House* (Edinburgh, 1700); Francis Grant, *A Brief Account of the Nature, Rise and Progress of the Societies for the Reformation of Manners* (Edinburgh, 1700).

and criminality.[5] Only recently have historians moved beyond the moral and judicial approach to sex and begun to consider sex work in its broader socio-economic context. Susan McDonough, for example, has demonstrated the essential role of sex workers as 'knowledge brokers' in late-medieval Mediterranean port towns. While, she argues, sex workers in city brothels came in contact with a diverse segment of the population, and it was through this broad engagement with travellers, civic officials, and the like, rather than their sexual activities, that sex workers 'accrued, shared and disseminated knowledge about how port cities worked'.[6] In a Scottish context, Leah Leneman's important study of divorce and separation demonstrates the trade in knowledge rather than sex was a key element in several divorce proceeding brought before the courts, many of which relied on the crucial testimony of sex workers against their clients to gain a successful outcome.[7] Recent historiographical developments in contextualising the historical sex trade and its practitioners through a framework of economic marginality, familial connections, and professional networks affords a deeper understanding of the early modern sex trade as experienced by the workers themselves rather than through the moral lens of the authorities who governed them.[8] Accordingly, this chapter will build on these concepts and seek to place sex workers at the centre of their experiences.

A Response to Socio-economic Needs

The revolution of 1688–9 brought about widespread political and religious transformation in Scotland but did little to change the economic status of women. Opportunities outwith the domestic sphere remained limited, and women were often relegated to jobs that offered minimal financial reward

---

[5] See, for example, L. Leneman and R. Mitchison, *Sin in the City: Sexuality and Social Control in Urban Scotland, 1660–1780* (Edinburgh, 1998); R. Mitchison and L. Leneman, *Girls in Trouble: Sexuality and Social Control in Rural Scotland, 1660–1780* (Edinburgh, 1998); J.R.D. Falconer, 'A Family Affair: Households, Misbehaving and the Community in Sixteenth-Century Aberdeen', in E. Ewan and J. Nugent (eds), *Finding the Family in Medieval and Early Modern Scotland* (Aldershot, 2008), pp. 139–50; M.F. Graham, *The Uses of Reform: Godly Discipline and Popular Behaviour in Scotland and Beyond, 1560–1610* (Leiden, 1996); H. Cornell, 'Social Control and Masculinity in Early Modern Scotland: Expectations and Behaviour in a Lowland Parish', in L. Abrams and E. Ewan (eds), *Nine Centuries of Man: Manhood and Masculinity in Scottish History* (Edinburgh, 2017), pp. 183–202.
[6] S. McDonough, 'Moving Beyond Sex: Prostitutes, Migration and Knowledge in Late-Medieval Mediterranean Port Cities', *Gender & History*, 34:2 (2022), 401–19, at 402.
[7] L. Leneman, *Alienated Affections: Divorce and Separation in Scotland, 1684–1830* (Edinburgh: Edinburgh University Press, 1998), p. 161.
[8] H. Barker, 'Women and Work', in H. Barker and E. Challis (eds), *Women's History, Britain 1700-1850: An Introduction* (Oxford, 2005), pp. 124–51; E. Hubbard, *City Women: Money, Sex, and the Social Order in Early Modern London* (Oxford, 2012); G.M. Rodriguez, *Selling Sex in the City: A Global History of Prostitution, 1600s–2000s* (Leiden, 2017).

and little employment security.[9] The markets and streets of Edinburgh, bustling with noise and activity, provided an urban space in which women could make a small profit selling their produce on the market stalls; some had trading licences and set themselves up in the Exchange, while other 'poor women' sat opposite the New Kirk door selling 'old stockings and other small things'.[10] For certain women, their status as the daughters of burgesses offered opportunities in retail, while others accessed the trade by paying entry money and quarterly dues.[11] Demand for domestic servants was also high in the urban centres, and young single women regularly migrated from rural areas towards the larger burghs to seek employment opportunities in service or apprenticeships in sewing or lace-making, which was an expedient method of developing practical skills and potentially generating an income.[12] It is evident that women were active in and made substantial contributions at all levels of the economy in eighteenth-century burghs.[13] However, gaining access to official labour markets was not always possible. Certain professions, such as law or medicine, for example, were still largely inaccessible for women – or lower-status men. Financial capital or produce were required to set up business at the markets, and official licences were needed for specific trades. This is not to suggest that women passively accepted their circumstances. Indeed, in 1736 the Edinburgh burgh council noted the 'great many young women servants' who 'turning wearie have taken up little shops', but complained that this was much to the detriment of the trading burgesses who 'bore the public burden of the place'.[14] For many women, barriers to employment and limited earning power left them with minimal economic choices and the ever-present spectre of financial hardship.

In this respect, the sex market can be understood as a response to socio-economic needs that provided a viable means of employment. The commodification of the female body generated an income that enabled women to support themselves and their extended family and, at times, avoid reliance on external systems of charity or poor relief. Sex work was flexible and thus compatible with female duties in the household. It could be undertaken on a permanent or casual basis, and women occasionally used it to supplement their income from other forms of employment. For instance, in December 1749, Anne Campbell was discovered in her shop at the head of Toddrick's Wynd with a man at 'unseasonable hours' and was warned that any future

---

[9] E.C. Sanderson, *Women and Work in Eighteenth-Century Edinburgh* (Basingstoke, 1996), p. 169; R.A. Houston, 'Women in the Economy and Society of Scotland, 1500–1800', in R.A. Houston and I.D. Whyte (eds), *Scottish Society 1500–1800* (Cambridge, 1989), pp. 118–47.
[10] Sanderson, *Women and Work*, pp. 5–40, quote on p. 39.
[11] Ibid., p. 39.
[12] Sanderson, *Women and Work*, pp. 87–93, and at p. 39; H. Dingwall, *Late Seventeenth-Century Edinburgh: A Demographic Study* (Aldershot, 1994), pp. 144–5.
[13] Ibid., p. 20.
[14] Quoted in Sanderson, *Women and Work*, p. 39.

incidents would see her banished from the city.[15] Margaret Campbell, who also kept a shop in Edinburgh, was removed from the premises in October 1753 after she and another woman were found with a man 'in an indecent way'. Campbell was banished from the city while her accomplice Elizabeth Wemyss was instructed not to frequent houses of bad fame or keep loose and disorderly company.[16] For these women, their professions as shopkeepers provided both an official income and a degree of respectability; however, their place of work also provided a space for them to engage in clandestine activities to supplement their income.

For women employed in domestic service, the work was often low-paid and physically demanding; consequently, some also took on casual sex work to augment their earnings. For example, in July 1745, Janet Hendersone, a servant to Lady Kirkwood, was found in an Edinburgh bawdy house with Jean McPherson, a servant to John Hay, a writer in Forrester's Wynd.[17] Martha Riddle, a 'streetwalker', was the servant of Mr Reich at the head of Peebles Wynd, and Rachel MacKenzie, found in a house of bad fame in November 1752, was employed in service to a street caddie named William Muir.[18] Similarly, other professions came under suspicion of being connected with, or even a facade for, deviant sex work. In January 1694, the town council of Edinburgh targeted female fruit sellers in the city, suspicious that their activities were not altogether reputable:

> Taking to the serious consideration the great profanity that abounds in this City occasioned by several young women who under pretence of selling lemons and oranges and other fruits do go throw this City and become common whores and thieves ... doe therefore statute and ordaine that no women go through the streets to go up to gentlemens chambers carrying the foresaid fruits in baskets under the pain of being prosecute as common whores and to be imprisoned in the correction house.[19]

We cannot know if the council's concerns had foundation. Perhaps this was an elaborate, organised scheme implemented to enable the sex worker and client to avoid detection, or maybe it was simply some enterprising young women finding a means to supplement their income from the sale of fruit with the sale of sex. Nonetheless, the council and magistrates were determined to end the enterprise and prosecute the women – but not the men – involved.

The prevalence of married women working in the commercial sex economy in Edinburgh between 1689 and 1760 contradicts stereotypical views of sex workers as predominantly young and unmarried.[20] Margaret Patterson's

---

[15] ECA, SL232, vol. 3, no pagination [17 December 1749].
[16] Ibid. [5 October 1753].
[17] Ibid. [19 July 1745].
[18] Ibid. [21 April 1749, 15 November 1752].
[19] *Edinburgh Recs.*, vol. 13, p. 140.
[20] K. Barclay, *Love, Intimacy and Power: Marriage and Patriarchy in Scotland, 1650–1850* (Manchester, 2011), p. 191.

husband was a tobacconist in Edinburgh in 1759 while she worked in a bawdy house kept by Miss Robertson in Halkerston's Wynd.[21] Similarly, Janet Cargill kept a disorderly house in 1747 while her husband worked as a journeyman wigmaker.[22] It is impossible to say whether the marital relationship was still intact, and if so, whether husbands supported or at least tolerated their wives' profession. There is evidence, however, that, on occasion, husbands and wives worked together, as in the case of John Court and his wife, who ran a bawdy house together in the Canongate in 1758.[23] Military wives also made up a significant proportion of women trading sex in Edinburgh. Barbara Miller's husband, for instance, was a soldier in Barrel's regiment of foot who fought in the front line at Culloden. In July 1748, she was 'strolling the streets at unseasonable hours' with Anne Willie, whose husband was a gunner in the train of artillery. The two women had previously been working from a house but had since moved their trade to the streets.[24] Similarly, Janet Burns, the wife of Major John Guthrie, was banished from Edinburgh in 1696 for keeping 'a notorious bawdy house' in which she allegedly debased several young women.[25] The period was marked by conflict, both domestically in the form of the Jacobite threat and through international wars, and soldiers, whether quartered within the city or travelling with armies, provided a steady clientele. Women were discouraged from following the army, although many often did.[26] When the Jacobite army retreated north from Carlisle in November 1745, the castle was recaptured by government troops, and at least fifty-six women and girls following the army were also captured, imprisoned, and, in some cases, transported to the plantations in America.[27] Undoubtedly, some were the wives of soldiers; however, it is plausible that some women were unmarried and following the army for their own purposes.

Marriage, however, provided no guarantee of financial, physical or emotional security and for many women, the responsibility of being the sole provider for the family was theirs alone as men abandoned them, left to seek out employment elsewhere, were imprisoned, were banished, or went to fight in the wars abroad – and war left many widows.[28] An absent husband often left a financially distressed wife with very few means to improve her

---

[21] ECA, SL232, vol. 4, fol. 58.
[22] Ibid., vol. 3 [8 April 1747].
[23] Ibid., [14 December 1748].
[24] Ibid., [16 July 1748].
[25] Ibid., vol. 1, fol. 205. Burns was also cautioned in September 1695 for being a 'resetter of whores', ibid., fol. 193.
[26] 'The Orderly Book of Lord Ogilvy's Regiment, with explanatory notes by Sir Bruce Seton', *The Journal of the Society of Army Historical Research*, 2 (1923), 1–52, at 17.
[27] B. Seton and J.G. Arnot (eds), *The Prisoners of the '45 edited from the State Papers* (3 vols, Edinburgh, 1928–9), vol. 1, p. 214; A.P. Rosebery and W. MacLeod, *A List of Persons Concerned in the Rebellion* (Edinburgh, 1890), p. 252.
[28] S. Murdoch and K. Zickermann, '"Bereft of all Human Help?": Scottish Widows during the Thirty Years' War (1618–1648)', *Scottish Society for Northern Studies*, 50 (2019), pp. 114–34.

situation, and in these circumstances, it is not unreasonable to assume that some women looked to sex work for survival. Poor relief was available but restricted (see Chapter 2 of this volume). The kirk session was unlikely to be sympathetic to women like Margaret Langton, who, in 1753, was admonished for entertaining several young gentlemen and having 'carnal dealings' with them while her husband, Matthew Longmuir, was in Jamaica.[29] Likewise, in 1696, Elizabeth Maxwell's husband was a skipper in Glasgow when she was whipped in the House of Correction and banished from Edinburgh for 'notorious whoredom'.[30] In 1758, Margaret Douglas, the widow of a soldier, was also charged with being a 'notorious whore'.[31]

Evidently, a significant number of married women were self-reliant through no fault, or choice, of their own. However, female sexuality that went beyond the boundaries of marriage was considered a serious threat to male authority and women who lived alone, particularly unmarried women, threatened to undermine patriarchal power and the broader social order.[32] The idea that the absence of male influence and protection left females vulnerable to being drawn into crime was rooted in the contemporary belief that women, as moral agents, were inferior to men.[33] Thus, sex workers were broadly defined into one of two sorts – those who had been 'seduc'd to sin', usually by an older woman (a bawd) who, by 'long experience knew the way',[34] or those who were 'vile strumpets' unworthy of even church discipline and should unequivocally be banished from civil society.[35] However, for some women, sex work was potentially self-sustaining, so marriage or a life of service need not have been the only option. In a seventeenth-century cautionary text, written by the poet Edward Ward, the writer takes on the voice of a 'repentant harlot', and forewarns that, in attempting to lure a young prodigy into the business, a persuasive, more experienced sex worker might deplore the shackles of wedlock:

> Marriage, as us'd, is but a woman's yoke
> A knot for life, too stubborn to be broke:
> A prison; which if once you're into cast,
> Makes the sweet fruit but nauseous to taste.
> But if you're married, you're at once undone

---

[29] ECA, SL232, vol. 3 [20 February 1753].
[30] Ibid., vol. 1, fol. 168.
[31] Ibid., vol. 4, fol. 45.
[32] Barclay, *Intimacy and Power*, p. 191.
[33] L. Gowing, *Domestic Dangers: Women, Words and Sex in Early Modern London* (Oxford, 1996), p. 3.
[34] Edward Watt, *The Insinuating Bawd, And The Repenting Harlot. Being A Subject Founded Upon Facts, ... To Which Is Added, The Six Nights Rambles, By A Gentleman, Who Endeavoured To Reclaim Several Of Those Poor Prostitutes* (London, 1753), p. 5; T. Henderson, *Disorderly Women in Eighteenth-Century London: Prostitution and Control in the Metropolis 1730–1830* (London, 1999), p. 4.
[35] NRS, Dundee General Session Minutes, 1716–56, CH2/1218/2; NRS, Canongate Kirk Session Minutes, 1723–7, fol. 16.

>   And made a despicable slave to one.[36]

Undoubtedly, wedlock was not a 'prison' for all women and for some it did provide a degree of respectability and security. However, we cannot presume that women who worked in the sex trade necessarily sought to attain this ideal. As Bernard Capp argued, selling or trading sex was also 'a means of achieving emancipation – with no dependence on the man, they felt able to repudiate his authority'.[37] In this respect, the sex worker threatened the social order, a system sustained by a gendered hierarchy that emphasised perceptions of right and wrong behaviour and institutions that enforced ideas of male and female social responsibilities. In 1694, for example, these ideas were enforced by the privy council, who noted that:

> by the laws of God and nature and by the lawes of this and all other Christian nations, it is the dutie of husbands to love and cherish their wives and to provyde for them and their children… and not suffer them to be brought to miserie.[38]

Men were providers who were responsible for protecting the morality and person of their wives, while women were predominantly regarded as caregivers who ran the household and nurtured the family. The problem with sex workers was that they presented a challenge to this androcentric orthodoxy; they were single women, they were wives, and they were daughters, but they were also often non-conforming, self-sufficient, and opportunistic. This rendered them disdained, yet not entirely disconnected from mainstream society.

Commercial Sex Outlets

Bawdy houses and houses of bad fame or ill repute were a fundamental and surprisingly visible part of urban life in the decades after the revolution of 1688–9. Writing his observations on the city of Edinburgh for the *Old Statistical Account of Scotland*, William Creech, minister of the parish of Newbattle, estimated a sixty-fold increase in brothels and a hundred-fold increase in sex workers between 1763 and 1783. He wrote:

> In 1763 there were five or six brothels, or houses of bad fame, and a very few of the lowest and most ignorant order of females sculked the streets at night. A person might have gone from the Castle to Holyrood-house, [then the length of the city], at any hour in the night, without being accosted by a single street-walker. Street robbery, and pocket picking were unknown. In 1783, the number of brothels had increased twenty fold, and the women

---

[36] Watt, *Repenting Harlot*, p. 15.
[37] Capp, *Gossips*, p. 80.
[38] NRS, PC2/24, Privy Council Decreta, 1692–4, fol. 343r.

of the town more than a hundred fold. Every quarter of the city and suburbs was infested with multitudes of females abandoned to vice.[39]

However, as Rosalind Mitchison notes, this slightly hyperbolic assessment was likely more of an indication of Creech's numeracy skills than the actual state of affairs.[40] The sources for the first seventy years after the revolution tell a very different story to Creech's somewhat nostalgic view of the recent past in which there were no street robberies or 'skulking' females on the streets at night. In the first decade after the revolution, at least 85 per cent of individuals brought before the Edinburgh magistrates for petty crimes were women, 40 per cent of whom were identified as being directly involved in the sex trade. Overall, an estimated 152 women in Edinburgh between 1690 and 1700 were selling, trading, or organising sex, whether as a streetwalker, a bawdy house resident, or a keeper of such a house.[41] By the end of the 1750s, this number had increased by around 6 per cent, and at least 182 women were brought before the magistrates, suggesting a gradual and steady rather than exponential increase in sex for sale.[42] These numbers are, of course, reflective only of the women who came to the attention of the authorities, with the actual numbers likely to have been significantly higher. Men are conspicuously absent from the process in any significant way, although some did own bawdy houses either on their own or as a husband–wife dyad.[43] In December 1747, William Munro, a discharged soldier in Lord John Murray's regiment, had three women removed from his house in Plainstone Close in Edinburgh.[44] Similarly, the constables removed four women from the 'disorderly house' of William Chalmers in March 1753.[45] We know from English evidence that men could also be practitioners in the sex trade. Randolph Trumbach identified at least twenty molly houses in London under the attention of the authorities in 1726,[46] and it would appear that even the monarch was not above suspicion of preferring the company of men. Forced to defend his affection for several of his male courtiers, William II declared 'it seems to me a most extraordinary thing that one may not feel regard and affection for a young man without its being criminal'.[47] The 'molly raids' in the early eighteenth

---

[39] OSA, vol. 6, pp. 612–13.
[40] R. Mitchison, *Sexuality and Social Control: Scotland 1660–1780* (Oxford and New York, 1989), p. 234.
[41] ECA, SL232; ECA, SL150/9/1-3, Canongate Burgh Court Black Books.
[42] Ibid.
[43] John Court and his wife kept 'a bawdy house' in Canongate as previously noted, ECA, SL232, vol. 3 [14 December 1748]. David Ogilvie and Jean Hendersone kept 'an irregular and disorderly house' in Patrick Street Close, ibid. [26 August 1751].
[44] Ibid. [10 December 1747].
[45] Ibid. [5 March 1753].
[46] R. Trumbach, 'London's Sodomites: Homosexual Behavior and Western Culture in the 18th Century', *Journal of Social History*, 11:1 (1977), 1–33, at 15.
[47] N.A. Robb, *William of Orange: A Personal Portrait, Volume Two: 1674–1702* (London, 1966), p. 99; S.B. Baxter, *William III* (London, 1966), p. 352.

century, initiated by the London chapter of the Society for the Reformation of Manners – active between 1690 and 1730 – were instrumental in detecting and prosecuting various degrees of moral crimes.[48] A similar chapter opened in Edinburgh in 1699. However, the society registers reveal no large-scale operations instigated against male sex workers – or indeed female sex workers – as there were in London.[49] This is not to suggest that such establishments did not exist in Scotland, but if they did, they remained under the radar of the magistrates, who focused predominantly on individual female practitioners.

Men of all social classes frequented the bawdy houses and taverns where sex was readily available. Visitors to early Georgian Edinburgh might, for example, visit the houses of Miss Robertson or Miss Bachop in Halkerston's Wynd, then conveniently take their leave in one of the hackney coaches that stood below the wynd.[50] Earlier, in 1694, Elizabeth Cruickshanks stated she had access day and night to a house in Leith Wynd where she 'committed whoredom with the Laird of Bigton' and Bothwell of Glencorse younger, the latter of whom suffered the wrath of his wife when she discovered him with a woman in a drinking house frequented by 'Egyptians' and 'whores'. A witness to the debacle declared, in surprising him there, she 'did take a chopping propp or whatever was closest … and throw it at the woman's face which bashed her and kicked her out of doors and challenge her husband for using such bad company'.[51] Evidently, violence did not always come at the hands of a client and sex workers also ran the risk of encountering an irate wife.

Edinburgh was a city where beggars regularly rubbed shoulders with aristocrats, artisans, and scholars.[52] Sex was readily available and an early visitor to the city commented on the prevalence of 'Bawdy Houses' near the magnificent houses of the nobility, in which the cautious women commonly asked 'if they have got a pair of Canon-Gate Breeches', meaning the venereal disease.[53] In addition to the aforementioned 'bawdy house' kept by Janet Dryburgh in South Gray's Close, another operated in June 1747 in the close

---

[48] See Francis Grant Cullen, *A Brief Account of the Nature, Rise, And Progress of The Societies for the Reformation of Manners* (Edinburgh, 1700); K. Sonnelitter, 'The Reformation of Manners Societies, the Monarchy, and the English State, 1696–1714', *The Historian*, 72:3 (2010), 517–42.

[49] EUL, Laing Collection, Papers of the Society for Endeavouring Reformation of Manners in Edinburgh, 1699–1751; NLS, MS.1954, Register of the Proceedings for the Society of the Reformation of Manners, instituted at Edinburgh, 1700.

[50] Black Book, vol. 4, fols 58 and 59. Since June 1699, Hackney coaches for hire were forbidden to stand in the High Street except on the north side below Halkerston's Wynd due to complaints about robberies; *Edinburgh Recs*, vol. 13, p. 247.

[51] ECA, Canongate Record of Criminal Proceedings, SL150/6, n.p.; NRS, Penicuik Papers, GD18/1756, Copy Declaration by James Wilsone [Wilson], prisoner in the Tolbooth, regarding the robbery at Pennycook [Penicuik] House and other robberies committed by Robert Wach [Waugh] and his associates, c. 1693.

[52] Dingwall, *Edinburgh*, p. 11.

[53] *A Journey Through Part of England and Scotland Along with the Army Under the Command of His Royal Highness the Duke of Cumberland* (London, 1747), p. 84.

of the marquis of Tweeddale.[54] Several establishments were also in plain sight of the authorities. Janet Walls, for instance, kept a 'disorderly house' in May 1755 directly behind the guard house on the High Street.[55] Moreover, in 1694, Elizabeth Kellos kept two establishments, one in Leith Wynd and the other directly above the Canongate tolbooth.[56] Evidently, for these women, the rewards gained from sexual labour outweighed the risks of detection and prosecution. Other outlets were situated in private homes, cellars, and drinking establishments. The retail of food and drink was a customary occupation in Edinburgh for female brewers or innkeepers, and providing additional sexual services was simply an extension of this economy.[57] In 1699, the Edinburgh town council unsuccessfully attempted to control the calibre of women who worked in places of entertainment by introducing an act against woman servants who had been guilty of uncleanliness. They decreed that 'the keeping and employing of women servants for retailing liquors in taverns, cellars, drinking shops and other places where liquors are sold was immediately forbidden as it is a great snare to the youth and occasion of lewdness and debauchery', and any person found to have employed such a person was subject to a fine of £100.[58] The act had little discernible effect on the sex trade, and individuals continued to work from and own various places of entertainment.

Indeed, the experience of women in the post-revolution sex trade was not homogenous. There were various ranks of brothels and sex workers which assuredly impacted upon their marginal status and level of income. Contemporary writers recognised a hierarchy within the sex trade. The 'keeping lady' ranked highest and was assigned the status of a mistress, undesirable but tolerated; the pliers of bawdy houses were middle-ranking and could perhaps be redeemed if they chose a different profession; but the streetwalker was utterly abhorred.[59] However, the women do not seem to have regarded themselves in this way. Women were aware of the pejoratives used against them but, for the most part, designed themselves in the sources as 'daughter of', 'relict of', or 'spouse to' a male relative, thus identifying themselves by family position rather than occupation. The 'hierarchy' was also fluid – streetwalkers sometimes worked in front of bawdy houses, 'keeping ladies' could lose their position if they fell out of favour or their provider died, and pliers of bawdy houses could likewise exercise a degree of mobility by moving from one establishment to another, although assuredly working in an enclosed space like a house or a tavern would have minimised the risks for the practitioner as opposed to working on the streets and being exposed to a greater likelihood of violence.

---

[54] ECA, SL232, vol. 4, fol. 55; ibid., vol. 3 [8 June 1747].
[55] Ibid. [7 May 1755].
[56] NLS, Register of Criminal Proceedings in the Baillie-Court of the Canongate, MS.25.1.4, fols 6–7.
[57] Dingwall, *Edinburgh*, p. 140.
[58] *Edinburgh Recs.*, vol. 13, p. 121.
[59] *The shortest way with whores and rogues: or a new project for reformation* (London, 1703).

Restriction, Risk, and Regulation

The sex trade was an informal economy and thus notoriously difficult to regulate and control. In the first instance, the church courts sharply rebuked men and women accused before the session of engaging in any form of sex work by keeping bawdy houses or entertaining loose and scandalous company, or if the evidence was particularly damning, they were referred to the magistrates for punishment.[60] Several women declined to leave their fates in the hands of the authorities and absconded from the parish when cited to appear, although the kirk sessions did take steps to locate them. Relocating to another parish was made more difficult as a testimonial from the session evidencing good moral conduct was required, and for a woman engaged in the sex trade, these were almost impossible to obtain – except perhaps through a forged certificate.[61] The absence of a testimonial also made it extremely difficult for women engaged in various degrees of sex work to leave the profession or reintegrate into the working poor, especially when we consider the regular punishment imposed by the magistrates for sex workers was banishment from the city. They were simultaneously ejected from one parish and denied the documentation required to settle in another. Obtaining a testimonial was also no guarantee of protection. In February 1693, Janet Anderson was referred to the Canongate kirk session, accused of entertaining scandalous and loose company in her house. She was ordered to produce a testimonial; however, a week later, when she produced a legitimate certificate from a minister, it was rejected on the grounds that it was not from the parish she last resided in.[62]

The paradoxical restrictions on the social mobility of sex workers perhaps account for many instances of women in various parishes being prosecuted and banished from the area or agreeing to voluntary banishment to avoid prosecution, only to be found in the parish again some time later. In January 1753, Janet Fraser undertook before the Edinburgh magistrates to leave the burgh after being found in a house of bad fame. In May the following year, she was found to have returned. Consequently, she remained in prison for a time and was then sent to stand in the pillory from twelve until one in the afternoon, all before being banished again. In April 1758, she was released from the Edinburgh correction house where she had spent the previous six months and swore before the magistrate to once more take voluntary banishment from the city and suburbs. However, in July of the same year, she was again taken from a house of bad fame in Canongate and imprisoned for six months. Fraser was released in January 1759 and ordered to leave the burgh

---

[60] NRS, CH2/1218/2, fol. 31.
[61] A. Glaze, 'Sanctioned and Illicit Support Networks at the Margins of a Scottish Town in the Early Seventeenth-Century', *Social History*, 45:1 (2020), 25–51, at 30–1.
[62] NRS, CH2/122/9, Canongate Kirk Session Minutes, 1690–4, fols 124–5.

for a fourth time.[63] From here, Janet Fraser disappears from the records, but her experience was certainly not unique.

Banishment was implemented periodically to shut down, or at very least curb, the sex trade since at least the mid-sixteenth century.[64] It was a measure intended to exclude miscreants from public and social life and keep them firmly on the very edges of civil society. Using the streets as an arena for public shaming, the magistrates advertised the offender's actions to the wider community. The intention was twofold: firstly, to publicly shame the transgressor, and secondly, to ensure public cooperation in the targeted individual's ostracisation. Barbara Smith worked from several houses of bad fame within the Canongate and was banished four times between 1755 and 1760. Prior to banishment for the second time in June 1755, she was first drummed through the burgh bare-headed (a duty likely performed, as we saw in Chapter 7, by the lockman), with a label on her chest denoting her crimes.[65] Similarly, before being banished in July 1754, Elspeth Marshall was drummed up Leith Wynd, bare-headed with a rope around her neck.[66] Jean McFarlane, described as a 'vagrant' and a 'loose and disorderly person' who 'frequented houses of bad fame', also faced banishment on several occasions from Edinburgh, but seemed to have never left the city. In November 1756, the magistrate sentenced her to be whipped and banished; however, if she agreed to voluntary transportation to the plantations in Jamaica, then the whipping would be suspended. It seems she did agree to the terms, but evidently did not proceed with the transportation, as she was liberated from the house of correction in April 1758, and just three months later was again sentenced to six months imprisonment. Yet in January 1760, she was again found in the burgh 'makin a great disturbance', and was imprisoned for at least a month. On 6 February 1760, she was taken from her cell sometime between 11 am and 12 pm and was then whipped through the streets of Canongate, at each of the 'five public places' receiving 'five stripes on her naked shoulders', and was thereafter banished again.[67]

These experiences indicate not only the relative failure of punitive measures against sex workers, which was in some measure due to a lack of public support from the wider community, but also raise questions as to why some women continued to defy civil censure and prosecution and consistently returned to the place from whence they were banished (or perhaps had never left in the first place), despite facing public humiliation, corporal punishment, and imprisonment. Over the space of years, women in Edinburgh

---

[63] ECA, SL232, vol. 4, fol. 43.
[64] E. Ewan, 'Crossing Borders and Boundaries: The Use of Banishment in Sixteenth-Century Scottish Towns', in S. Butler and K.J. Kesselring (eds), *Crossing Borders: Boundaries and Margins in Medieval and Early Modern Britain* (Leiden and Boston, MA, 2018), pp. 237–57.
[65] ECA, SL150/9/1, fols 18, 22, 34 and 43.
[66] ECA, SL232, vol. 3 [20 July 1754].
[67] ECA, SL150/9/1, fols 11, 27, 29 and 40; ECA, SL232, vol. 4, fols 43–4.

persistently continued to return to familiar neighbourhoods and frequented the same spaces, albeit in various bawdy houses. Perhaps it was the lure of the city as a fruitful source of income. It is just as likely, though, that the women had friends or family members they were returning to. Indeed, when Anna Campbell was found in Edinburgh under a sentence of banishment in December 1750, the town guards faced the wrath of her mother, Lilias Campbell, who was arrested for 'opposing and cursing' the constables 'while in the execution of their duty' in apprehending her daughter. Anna Campbell was again removed from the city, and her mother was released only under the condition that she would keep an orderly house and not entertain her daughter within the city or the suburbs.[68]

Church and state restrictions presented social and economic barriers for individuals working in the sex trade. However, official sanction also presented an ever-present danger of physical risks to their persons. Exclusion from civil society also often meant exemption from social and legal protections, except in the most severe circumstances.[69] The lawyer and twice lord advocate George Mackenzie of Rosehaugh, commenting on the capital crime of rape, opined:

> that to force even a common whore is capitally punishable, though it may seem that they are *infra legum observantiam*, and they ought not to have the protection of the law, who offend against it.[70]

The streets were the workplace, and women were exposed to various risks. They might, for example, encounter some drunk dragoons with malicious intent, or a violent client who refused to pay. Women working from bawdy houses were offered some protections; however, they were still vulnerable to violence by their clients or employer.[71] This fundamental vulnerability was exemplified by the case of Margaret Carnegie, a resident in Dundee, who, in October 1716, was charged before the General Session with scandalous carriage with soldiers. She pleaded not guilty to the charges but was not believed. Male witnesses testified they saw her very drunk, that she fell several times, and soldiers lifted her again. She then fell asleep in a park, and the soldiers left her but returned to her again – at this point, the witness left. The Dundee kirk session ruled Margaret Carnegie was not fit to appear for public repentance, and so she was referred to the magistrate to be permanently banished from the town.[72] Sex workers often took steps to limit the risks they were exposed to by forming loose support networks and working together in groups. The guards in Edinburgh regularly pulled women off the

---

[68] ECA, SL232, vol. 3 [21 December 1750].
[69] K. Barclay, *Love, Intimacy and Power*, p. 183.
[70] George Mackenzie, *The Laws and Customs of Scotland, in Matters Criminal* (Edinburgh, 1699), p. 85.
[71] Janet Walls kept a bawdy house with her innkeeper husband and was charged with beating her employees. ECA, SL232, vol. 3 [7 May 1755].
[72] NRS, CH2/1218/2, fol. 23.

streets in groups of at least two or more.[73] Similarly, when the bawdy houses were raided, there were usually several women working in the establishment in close contact with each other, which would inevitably have facilitated the formation of workplace and personal relationships.

The tenacity of women in defying the authorities and returning to or remaining within a defined geographical space indicates a sense of belonging or, at the very least, loose connections formed from shared experience. Women could work individually but, for the most part, operated collectively with other sex workers. Their marginal status was heightened by a myriad of social and economic pressures, risks, and legislation that contested a women's right to her own body, denied them social protections, and were designed to keep them on the fringes of society. Unlike men who often identified themselves in terms of their occupation or status and operated within the 'communal world' of politics and guilds, women formed informal sub-communities around their daily activities at the marketplaces, washing clothes in the streams, or gathering in the taverns.[74] Historians have often overlooked the importance of informal support networks, but these were likely crucial to women working in the sex trade.[75] The bonds formed through shared experience and exclusion undoubtedly shaped women's lives and were fundamental in forming their perceptions of their own sexuality and femininity.

Conclusions

The marginalisation of female sex workers derived partly from gendered perceptions of acceptable behaviour and ostensibly a lack of adherence to prescribed gendered socio-economic roles. When women stepped beyond the boundaries of the traditional family structure and consequently undermined male authority, they were often considered to be at best immoral and, at worse, criminal. Sex workers not only challenged this orthodoxy but, at times, did so openly, which would not have been possible without networks of support and cooperation. Conversely, women who practised the trade lived with the ever-present threat of sexual and physical violence, shame, and ostracisation. Still, they forged an unconventional place for themselves in the bustling urban life of the city. For some women (and perhaps men) in early modern Scotland, sex work offered a sustainable and tenable livelihood. It

---

[73] In October 1757, for example, three 'whores' who were confined to the guard house for strolling the streets. ECA, SL232, vol. 4, fol. 38. Similarly in August 1760, four women were taken up by the guards for strolling the streets, 'having no honest way of gaining their bread', ibid., fol. 76.
[74] G. Walker and J. Kermode, 'Introduction', in J. Kermode and G. Walker (eds), *Women, Crime, and the Courts in Early Modern England* (London, 1994), pp. 1–24, at p. 7.
[75] Alice Glaze has considered the role of sex workers within these informal communities as part of a broader study on informal support networks. See Glaze, 'Sanctioned and Illicit Support Networks'.

was widespread and diverse, and in addition to personal income, the trade also contributed to the economy in terms of personal and commercial revenue. Moreover, Edinburgh sex workers operated within a profession that transcended social class, and so negotiated and interacted with the world around them through a diverse clientele. Yet they were also part of the wider community – albeit in a marginal capacity – where they paradoxically existed as deviant outsiders who lived, worked, and socialised in the busy city streets of early modern Edinburgh.

9

Navigating Marginality: The Coal Mine Workers of Seventeenth-Century Scotland[1]

Robert D. Tree

'The colliers, in all countries, are generally an unruly set of labourers; and those of this work were like their neighbours.' So declared the minister of Alloa in his 1793 entry into the *Statistical Account of Scotland* when describing the coal mine which had been in operation there since around 1623. The minister recorded that he had recently observed a reformation among the colliers, who had hitherto only been 'remarkable for their ignorance and dissoluteness of manners'.[2] The catalyst for this reformation in the colliers' moral character was the so-called (partial) 'emancipation' of forced or bound labour in 1775, albeit this was not fully abolished until 1799. This concept of miners' wildness has often been accepted in the topic's limited historiography, which tends to focus mainly on the eighteenth century.[3] It can be boiled down to two main schools of thought. The more traditional school has tended to focus on parliamentary statutes on collier serfdom in addition to court cases concerning these. Such scholarship largely takes a high industry approach, rather than focusing on mine workers.[4] Contrarily, the more recent, revisionist school, inspired by both social history and history from below, has focused on manuscript sources.[5] In doing so it has uncovered colliers' independent action and active engagement with the legal system. However, this has been rooted mostly in limited use of account books (largely confined to the Clerks of Penicuik's voluminous records) and reactionary modes of collier agency, tending to exalt the proto-capitalist diversification of the mine own-

---

[1] I would like to thank Dr Neil McIntyre, Dr Andrew Muirhead, and Dr Colin Nicolson for advice and feedback during the writing of this chapter. I also wish to express my appreciation to the editors of this volume and Sir Robert Clerk of Penicuik, 11th Bt for permission to peruse manuscript records from the Loanhead mine.
[2] OSA, vol. 8, pp. 614–15.
[3] See, for example, B.F. Duckham, 'Life and Labour in a Scottish Colliery 1698–1755', *SHR*, 47:2 (1968), at 112–13.
[4] B.F. Duckham, *A History of the Scottish Coal Industry: A Social and Industrial History. Volume 1, 1700–1815* (Newton Abbot, 1970); J.U. Nef, *The Rise of the British Coal Industry* (2 vols, London, 1932).
[5] C.A. Whatley, '"The fettering bonds of brotherhood": Combination and Labour Relations in the Scottish Coalmining Industry c.1690–1775', *Social History*, 12 (1987), 139–54; R. Houston, 'Coal, Class and Culture: Labour Relations in a Scottish Mining Community, 1650–1750', *Social History*, 8 (1983), 1–18.

ers rather than focusing on the influence of the workers in that respect. Also, both schools have concentrated chiefly on male colliers, without sufficient weight being given to those workers, especially coal bearers, who were often women or children.

Scottish coal mine workers of the early modern period can be difficult to trace through primary sources. Civil and church court records are excellent sources for following these people, but by their very nature they rely on actionable offences being carried out or at least suspected. Utilising just this source-base may lead to skewed conclusions which buy into the depictions of coal mine workers as they appear in statute. Coal mine account books, which became increasingly regularised and widespread in the later seventeenth century, offer different perspectives. They are invaluable sources, but are too often tantalisingly laconic, simply recording payments in and out of the mine. Occasionally, though, they give us snapshots into coal mine workers' everyday lives. For example, two rather charming late seventeenth-century love letters from colliers to their wives are preserved in the bindings of an account book from Loanhead mine, which covers the period 1682–99. They are written in the same unrefined hand, but both demonstrate a level of devotion which belies the bleak representation which coal mine workers are often subjected to. One of these letters, from a John Collei to his wife, was structured as a poem:

> My sleeping thoughts ar all imployed on the
> hou sadly I in ters and Discontent
> the tedious nichts of your absence spent
> my Dear you bleve all thes to be trou
> for I canot expers my kend Weshess A nouth to you my
> Dear Who is the only confort of my heart
> O my Dear my heart or yours and all that can mack you happy thes is all from
> Your loving and affectionat housband.[6]

Materials like these remind us that coal mine workers were human beings, with all the hopes, desires, and agency of anybody else.

No author has yet attempted to interrogate coal mine workers' marginality, which has generally been taken as self-evident. This essay endeavours to address that gap, and in so doing it engages with broader historiographical developments. The first of these is the work of Kathy Stuart, who identifies 'dishonourable trades' in seventeenth-century Germany, which either because of or in spite of their ostracisation developed distinct communities.[7] Examples of these kinds of trades were the skinners and public executioners (the latter being discussed in Chapter 7 of this volume), who shared with colliers a black reputation rooted in their proximity to death. In a Scotland permeated with religious division and supernatural belief, colliers' subterranean labour must

---

[6] NRS, Penicuik Papers, GD18/990/1.
[7] K. Stuart, *Defiled Trades and Social Outcasts: Honour and Ritual Pollution in Early Modern Germany* (Cambridge, 1999).

also surely have heightened this, since they were continually digging deeper into the earth and closer to the underworld. Elsewhere, Mary Douglas points out that marginalised groups generally share certain characteristics, such as a stereotype of partiality for immorality, which often combine with metaphors of pollution or disease to 'other' them.[8]

Moreover, Stephen Milner argues that the very idea of a binary distinction between margins and centres can be troublesome, since these are 'porous grey areas'.[9] Part of the focus in Milner's work is on negotiation of marginal status, which involved not only marginalised groups, but governing bodies, courts, and those considered to be at the 'centre' in complex processes of identity formation.[10] This stresses the endogenous and exogenous factors shaping identity which are also pertinent to the subject of coal mine workers. These workers were pioneers in many senses, who were central to industrial and economic development in addition to playing important roles in religion and politics on both a local and national scale. Therefore, they challenged their marginal status but contributed to the emergence of a distinct socio-cultural identity for themselves, which was not purely based in statute.

This essay aims to scrutinise the term 'colliers' and to demonstrate that coal mine workers were proactive in negotiating of their marginality, which was itself complex and multi-faceted. A broader point, with reference to the work of Eric Williams and more recently Stephen Mullen and Andy Wood, is that these Scottish coal mine workers were at the forefront of the development of capitalism, which was a direct result of their codified and institutionalised bound labour, though this was in no way analogous to the chattel slavery which the two former authors study.[11] The essay will begin by outlining the entrenchment of coal mine workers' bondage through parliamentary developments, prior to discussing the stratification of mine work and, finally, investigating how these workers navigated marginal status.

Legislation

In July 1606, the Scottish parliament legislated colliers (or coal hewers), coal bearers, and salters into a system which bound them to both the natural resources they worked and to their masters.[12] These three kinds of industrial

---

[8] M. Douglas, *Purity and Danger: An Analysis of Concepts of Pollution and Taboo* (London, 2003).
[9] S.J. Milner, 'Identity and the Margins of Italian Renaissance Culture', in S.J. Milner (ed.), *At the Margins: Minority Groups in Premodern Italy* (Minneapolis, MN, 2005), pp. 3–20, at p. 4.
[10] See for instance, Samuel K. Cohn Jr, 'The Marginality of Mountaineers in Renaissance Florence', in Milner, *At the Margins*, pp. 236–48.
[11] E. Williams, *Capitalism and Slavery* (Chapel Hill, NC, 1944); S. Mullen, *The Glasgow Sugar Aristocracy: Scotland and Caribbean Slavery, 1775–1838* (London, 2022); A. Wood, *The Politics of Social Conflict: The Peak Country, 1520–1770* (Cambridge, 1999).
[12] RPS, 1605/6/39.

labourers were not allowed to be hired or taken from the service of another master unless a year and a day had passed in between then and their previous service, which was altogether rare. Testimonials had to be obtained from their previous employer, and if they had been poached a fee of £100 was to be paid, or else the worker returned to their erstwhile master within twenty-four hours. This bondage was clearly enforced; for example, in 1723, George Lockhart of Carnwath (c. 1681–1731) reported to his neighbour John Clerk of Penicuik, 2nd baronet (1676–1755) that he had lent a coal bearer to him, but wished her back in his employment as her leave would run out in a matter of days. Lockhart argued that, according to this legislation, 'my title to the girl is unquestionable'.[13]

The Covenanter parliament of 1641 ratified and expanded the legislation on colliers and salters from James VI's reign. Watermen, whose job was to bail and draw water into and out of the mine, plus gatemen, who dealt with the inner workings and passages within the mine, were put into servitude. These workers were considered by the act to be 'als necessar to the owneres and maisteres' as bearers and hewers, with their pay being capped at 20 merks per day, preventing labour-poaching by wily competitors offering more.[14] Finally, the 1641 act enforced a full six-day working week for all 'workmen' (although this included women implicitly). Penalties for withholding labour, since the colliers were often drunken and debauched, read the act, were 'tuentie shillingis for everie day ... and other punishment of ther bodies'.[15]

Legislation in 1661 ratified the 1641 act and again required colliers to work six days per week save for Christmas.[16] This act also explicitly included watermen, windmen, and gatemen as indentured labourers. Alongside this, and like its predecessors, the act introduced penalties – corporal and monetary – for withheld labour. This was partly due to the claim that these workers 'doe ly from their work at Pasch [Easter], Yule Witsunday and certane other times in the yeer, which times they imploy in drinking and debaushrie to the great offence of God and prejudice of thair master'.[17] The wording of the act conforms with John Clerk of Penicuik, 1st baronet's (1649–1722) belief that colliers were inherently deviant, morally repugnant, and drunken, the only remedy for which (he believed) was sustained Presbyterian religious instruction.[18] These two acts fit with the eighteenth-century lawyer John Erskine of Carnock's (1695–1768) dichotomy between 'necessary' and 'voluntary servants'. The former were those 'whom the law obliges to work', such as child labourers, vagrants, beggars, and coal and salt workers.[19] Carnock thus

---

[13] D. Szechi (ed.), *Letters of George Lockhart of Carnwath, 1698–1732* (2 vols, Edinburgh, 1989), vol. 2, p. 191.
[14] RPS, 1641/8/218.
[15] RPS, 1641/8/218.
[16] RPS, 1661/1/418.
[17] RPS, 1661/1/418.
[18] Duckham, 'Life and Labour', at pp. 111–12.
[19] John Erskine, *An Institute of the Law of Scotland in four books in the order of Sir George*

supposes their work to be by its very nature involuntary, since upon entering work in a mine they were bound to serve there indefinitely. Voluntary servants on the other hand were 'those who enter into service without compulsion, by an agreement or covenant, for a determinate time'.[20]

The final piece of late seventeenth-century legislation which intensified the nature of servitude in the coal and salt works came in 1672. This act was part of a series of legislative measures dealing with the poor, which established correction houses for 'idle beggars and vagabonds'.[21] In addition to doing so, the act allowed the owners of coal mines and salt works to seize beggars and vagabonds in order to put them to work in those manufactories. Importantly, the coal owners were 'to have the same power of correcting' those individuals as the masters of correction houses.[22] Furthermore, coal mine workers and salters were exempted from the 1701 'Act for preventing wrongful imprisonment and against undue delays in trials', which was essentially the Scottish version of *habeas corpus*.[23]

While this legislative framework of indentured labour was unique to Scotland, it was part of a wider trend towards the ghettoisation of coal mine workers across the early modern period. Nef argues that even medieval peasants 'were not segregated from their neighbours to anything like the same extent as were the coal miners of the seventeenth century in most colliery districts'.[24] Daniel Defoe remarked that the free miners of Derbyshire were a 'rude, boorish kind of people'.[25] The largely migrant mining communities of Newcastle, which for much of the early modern period was the pre-eminent supplier of coal to the growing metropole of London, were a distinct socio-industrial group, albeit they were (free) wage earners.[26] Miners in the Forest of Dean were more similar in labouring terms to the free miners or 'peakrills' of Derbyshire – themselves fiercely independent and itinerant – while the Mendip miners in Somerset developed disparate communities ('mineries') around their lead mines.[27] Hence, mining in general was a distinct industry which often formed populaces lying at the edge of many wider communities or parishes, in addition to following patterns of endogamous marriage and family ties to the industry. The Scottish colliers existed in a similarly liminal

---

Mackenzie's Institutions of the Law (4 vols, Edinburgh, 1773), vol. 1, pp. 146–7.
[20] Ibid., p. 147.
[21] RPS, 1672/6/52.
[22] RPS, 1672/6/52.
[23] RPS, 1700/10/234.
[24] Nef, *The Rise of the British Coal Industry*, vol. 2, p. 166.
[25] Daniel Defoe, *A Tour Through the Whole Island of Great Britain* (3 vols, London, 1724–7), vol. 3, p. 42.
[26] D. Levine and K. Wrightson, *The Making of an Industrial Society: Whickham 1560–1765* (Oxford, 1991).
[27] S. Sandall, *Custom and Popular Memory in the Forest of Dean, c. 1532–1832* (Cambridge, 2013); Wood, *The Politics of Social Conflict*; John Billingsley, *General View of the Agriculture of the County of Somerset with observations on the means of its improvement drawn up in the year 1795, for the consideration of the board of agriculture and internal improvement* (2nd edn, London, 1798), pp. 24–5.

position as they were neither urban workers nor rural labourers, with the coal fields such as Midlothian lying at the edge of expanding towns.

Strata of Coal Mine Workers

As Duckham notes, the legislation of the later seventeenth-century mentioned above reflects the increasing specialisation of work in a coal mine.[28] The term 'collier' itself is a problematic one since it suggests some sort of homogeneity in the group of individuals working at a coal mine. Yet at the mine there were several strata of worker and collieries in the early modern period were by no means solely staffed by men. Coal hewers were the miners working at the coal face, whose pay was aggregated and divided up individually depending on how much coal each raised. The coal bearers, normally women or children, carried loads of coal from the mine face to another area, often an outbuilding where the coal was checked, counted and recorded by a check, grieve, or oversman, who were not in servitude. A grieve was a kind of middle manager who also conducted a lot of organisational work in the mines and in coordinating with salt works, while oversmen were supervisors who oversaw the whole works.[29] The distinction between the two was blurry at the best of times, and the terms were used interchangeably in some cases. For instance, at the Torry coal and salt works in 1679–80, there were at least four grieves (including one taking coal to the salt pans and occasionally a 'night grieve'), in addition to an oversman and an overseer.[30] Their pay for a regular six-day working week in 1679 was normally £2 for the grieves, £3 for the oversman and £6 for the overseer, although on 5 January that year their wages ranged from £1 6s to £4, since they had worked just four days the previous week.[31]

Hewers were the central workers in the mine, hacking coal from the face. In fact, at the Cassingray mine in Fife, the colliers' pay was recorded in the account book as 'hacking monie'.[32] They had no formal wage *per se*, but were paid by commission according to how much coal was raised, and often by using 'tickets' in lieu of exchanging physical currency. Mining was an extremely dangerous job and we know from the Loanhead account books that lots of people died at work, although there are few specific references to how this happened.[33] It is likely that many died from drowning as well as due to collapsing coal faces. On one occasion, at Sheriffhall, a payment of over £52 Scots was recorded 'for the cure of Robert Wilson Coalzer and

---

[28] Duckham, 'Life and Labour', at p. 111.
[29] Ibid., at pp. 122–5; Houston, 'Coal, Class and Culture'.
[30] NRS, RH9/1/35, Account book of the coal and salt works at Torry, 1679–80, fos 52v, 77r.
[31] Ibid., fol. 2r.
[32] NRS, Leven and Melville Papers, GD26/5/319.
[33] NRS, GD18/990/2.

for his funeral'.[34] And at the Dunfermline coal mine in October 1671, £1 10s was gifted to the mine's remaining colliers after an accident in which an unnamed number of 'huchers dyed'.[35] This demonstrates, again, that these account books can be frustratingly terse, and the exact circumstances of these accidents will probably never be known. The hewers appear to have had some semblance of regimented working hours, although this is rarely clearly defined. We know this because most account books record 'uncost', or supplementary payments. Some mines even had separate 'uncost' account books. This suggests that there was a structure to the working day, with some workers engaging in auxiliary work for extra money. But there was also night work conducted in some mines, evidence of which can be found at Torry and Loanhead.[36]

Bearers were perhaps the most precarious of workers in the coal mine and are certainly under-studied. It is unclear whether this was always their sole job, as they appear to have been seasonal workers. By way of example, in 1698, John Clerk of Penicuik reported that very few or no bearers had come to the works that 'oat seed tyme'.[37] This implies that coal bearing could be supplementary to their other domestic and agricultural labours and would echo the general seasonality of early modern labouring. Bearers were often wives or offspring of coal hewers, but could also be unrelated children. For example, at Loanhead in 1703, two twelve-year-old bearers, Christian Andersone and Thomas Ker, were admitted to the works.[38] The latter had been born at Newbigging and employed there as a bearer to Clerk himself prior to joining the Loanhead mine, though it is unclear from what age. Clerk actually berated coal hewers for withholding their labour, pointing out that when they did so there was no means of earning a living for their bearers. Even more interestingly, Clerk spoke of the hewers as the bearers' 'masters' who held significant power over them, since they were responsible for paying bearers for their labour after they had themselves been remunerated for the coal they mined.[39] This last point implies an internal hierarchy within the mine. Like hewing, bearing could be a dangerous job. For example, in February 1679 a payment of 8 rex dollars was recorded in the Sheriffhall account book for 'cureing Anna Moffet one of the bearers of a broken arme'.[40]

In 1698, John Clerk of Penicuik explicitly spelled out the duties of the grieve, oversman, and other workers at his Loanhead mine. Coal grieves and oversmen at Loanhead were commanded 'to observe Circumspectly all the immoralitys and miscarriages committed by the Coaliers their wives and

---

[34] NRS, Buccleuch Papers, GD224/66/6.
[35] NRS, B20/18/1, Accounts of the coal worked at Dunfermline Muir, fol. 14.
[36] NRS, RH9/1/35, fol. 52v; NRS, GD18/995, p. 30.
[37] NRS, GD18/1003, p. 1.
[38] NRS, GD18/990/2, fol. 1v.
[39] NRS, GD18/1003, pp. 9-10.
[40] NRS, GD224/66/6.

bearers'.[41] They were also to punish drunkenness and generally discourage drinking, swearing and stealing, in addition to fining 'the Coaliers and bearers who shall do any work amiss, either contrary to the said Sir John [or] his acts of baron Court'.[42] The coal grieve at Loanhead also had to 'use all possible means with the Coaliers, their wives, children and bearers ... to wait on divine ordinances and Diets of Catechising'.[43] Clerk himself also occasionally catechised his own colliers, demonstrating that the owner and worker were far from perpetually detached.[44] The grieves' role also required them to monitor the amount of coal being taken by workers to deter illegal sales, which were common, since all hewers and bearers were entitled to coal for personal use in their fires. Whereas at Loanhead the baronial court and kirk session were the means of disciplining and controlling mine workers, at Dunfermline it was the burgh council which was in charge of the mine. There the provost even took an active role in procuring miners for the works.[45]

Despite their comparative legal freedoms, grieves and oversmen were still subjected to the whims of the coal mine owners. Alexander Gibson, 2nd Lord Durie (d. 1656) was the owner of a coal mine in Fife. In July 1655, the minister at Scoonie, Alexander Moncrieff, chose elders for the kirk session there. Amongst his nominations was James Turpie, a coal grieve working for Durie. Moncrieff declared this from the pulpit, following which Turpie publicly declined the invitation, although it transpired that he had privately accepted it the previous night. The minister decried Turpie's retraction as the work of the devil, implying that there had been malicious outside interference to sway his decision. Indeed, Durie proclaimed publicly that he prohibited 'any he had power ouer, or in his grounde' from accepting the call to be an elder, causing Moncrieff to condemn him as an 'opposer and persecutor of the church of Scotland'.[46] Also, Clerk of Penicuik's hewers and bearers were indispensable while his grieves and oversmen were not. In March 1698, Clerk sacked the oversman who had worked at Loanhead since at least 1694 for 'many gross miscarriages & negligences'. His replacement, George Furdie, lasted just over a year before he was also removed 'having abused his trust and walked most profanely & Contrary to his oath'.[47] The supervisors at Loanhead had to swear an oath in front of their workers.

Grieves were often paid more than coal hewers, but this was not always the case. Illustrative of this is the fact that, at the Carden mine in Fife, grieves were paid a flat rate of £2 weekly wages in the 1690s and 1700s, while on 27 May 1704, colliers Thomas Martin and his two sons were paid £10 16s for

---

[41] NRS, GD18/995, p. 11.
[42] NRS, GD18/995, p. 21.
[43] NRS, GD18/995, p. 11.
[44] Duckham, 'Life and Labour', at p. 113.
[45] NRS, B20/18/1, fol. 12.
[46] G.R. Kinloch (ed.), *The Diary of Mr. John Lamont of Newton, 1649–71* (Edinburgh, 1830), pp. 89–90.
[47] NRS, GD18/995, p. 31.

six days work.[48] Similarly, throughout the 1670s the grieve and oversman at Sheriffhall received weekly wages of £3 each, which was often less than that earned by the coal hewers at the mine. At Fawside in the 1670s and 1680s, it was a different story, with the grieve and oversman receiving a consistent sum of £4 per week, while colliers there worked in three companies of two hewers each and seldom earned as much as their superiors.[49]

That being said, colliers sometimes got very little or no payment, and they were not paid a wage as their supervisors were. Employment, though secure, was therefore by no means always financially stable. For instance, 1698 was a particularly bad year at the Loanhead mine. Its owner, Penicuik, noted the dismal production rates and relieved colliers of their duties at Loanhead, allowing them to attach themselves to a different colliery for the time being, until the works were restored.[50] Doing so were nine male coal hewers, and likely the bearers who were attached to them. This level of freedom and mobility complicates the picture of mine workers' unique oppression, but also highlights how precarious their situation could be. Similarly, on 13 November 1703, it was recorded that the Carden coal mine was 'standing 3 days For want off air' the previous week, meaning the hewers working there received no money since they could not mine any coal.[51] Sickness, too, could hit earning potential: Robert Wright, a coal hewer at Carden, was ill from 13 November to 4 December 1703, during which time he received no remuneration from the mine owner.[52] Working at a coal mine could therefore be precarious, and when this is combined with the evidence of workplace stratification outlined above, it underscores the complex and multi-faceted nature of mine workers' marginality.

Navigating Marginality

Although coal mine workers were marginalised, they did not always simply conform to their legal status, nor were they submissive. One of the more overlooked ways in which coal workers expressed agency and, due to this, challenged their marginalisation was through religious nonconformity. For example, a Glasgow collier named Robert Pedy was accused of attending a conventicle at Cathcart in May 1678. With his fellow accused, Pedy was brought before the privy council in June 1678, where he was found guilty and ordered to be imprisoned until appropriate time for his banishment and transportation to the 'Indies'.[53] In another case, William Purdie, a collier, was accused in 1685 alongside numerous other people of attending house con-

---

[48] NRS, GD26/5/320/1.
[49] NRS, Small Collections, GD1/458/1.
[50] NRS, GD18/1003, pp. 1–2.
[51] NRS, GD26/5/320/1.
[52] NRS, GD26/5/320/1.
[53] *RPCS, 3rd Series*, vol. 5, p. 474.

venticles and taking up arms in the 1679 Covenanter rebellion, in addition to refusing the oath of allegiance.[54] Also, a number of colliers such as Peter and Hugh Gold in Newton of Douglas and Alexander Kilpatrick in Dremellan were active members of the radical Presbyterian United Societies in the 1680s, as were two 'coal cutter[s]'.[55] This evidence of religious nonconformity indicates that there may have been some correlation between the social, political, and religious marginality experienced by coal mine workers in the seventeenth century.

Some colliers, however, demonstrated religious commitment to the established Church, but here, too, clear agency can often be traced. After the Williamite revolution, which saw the reinstatement of a Presbyterian system of Church government, a group of coal and salt workers with other parishioners in Tulliallan showed robust religious fervour. In 1704, the minister at Tulliallan, Thomas Buchanan, was proposed as a candidate for the intractable parish of Kilmadock, within the bounds of the presbytery of Dunblane and the synod of Perth and Stirling.[56] Buchanan had been in the ministry at Tulliallan since 1691, and he was very much a product of the revolution Kirk, hence his value to the presbytery to fill in for a colleague who had been hounded out by an oppositional group of heritors and other parishioners.[57] Buchanan and his congregation protested against the decision, however. They complained to the synod in writing, because 'most of us being Coalhewers and Salters to our occupation [we] cannot atend the Reverend Synod for discussing Our Appeal made from the sentence forsaid without Manifest injuring our Master in leaving his work'.[58]

The inhabitants of Tulliallan proclaimed their fondness for their present incumbent. In addition to explaining that Buchanan was a well-respected preacher who lived life with a moral integrity unequalled by many of his contemporaries, concerns were also raised about the size of Kilmadock parish in terms of both geography and population.[59] Furthermore, Buchanan himself complained that the parish was broadly opposed to post-revolution government of both Church and state. The presbytery tried to push the sentence through, clearly trusting Buchanan with the challenge of instilling Presbyterianism upon unwilling locals but choosing to ignore his protestations. When it came before the general assembly in 1705, though, his transfer

---

[54] *RPCS, 3rd Series*, vol. 10, pp. 122–3.
[55] Michael Shields, *Faithful Contendings Displayed: being An historical relation of the State and Actings of the Suffering Remnant in the Church of Scotland, who subsisted in Select Societies, and were united in general correspondencies during the hottest time of the late Persecution, viz. From the year 1681 to 1691*, ed. J. Howie (Glasgow, 1780), pp. 133–4.
[56] NRS, CH1/2/5/1, Church Papers, 1701–5, fos 79–82.
[57] H. Scott, *Fasti Ecclesiae Scoticanae: The Succession of Ministers in the Church of Scotland from the Reformation* (7 vols, Edinburgh, 1915–28), vol. 4, pp. 347, 364.
[58] NRS, CH1/2/5/1, fol. 79; A.T.N. Muirhead, *Scottish Presbyterianism Re-established: The Case of Stirling and Dunblane, 1687–1710* (Edinburgh, 2021), p. 65.
[59] NRS, CH1/2/5/1, fos 80–80A.

to Kilmadock was overruled.[60] It is unclear whether the Tulliallan colliers and salters had any impact on the ultimate decision, but their intervention is nonetheless a powerful example of their devotion to Presbyterianism in addition to demonstrating lay agency in the ministerial call after 1690. Such religiosity also undermines the elite-driven narrative that colliers were uniformly drunken and debauched, which, as we have seen, was reiterated in parliamentary statutes throughout the seventeenth century.

It is difficult to determine exactly how many of the signatories of the 1704 Tulliallan petition to the synod were actually working colliers. Nevertheless, it seems likely that the majority did work in the coal or salt industries. Indeed, two men, James Thomson and Thomas Thomason, identified themselves as coal hewers in their signatures. Both men also signed their names to an address to parliament in 1706.[61] This anti-Union and pro-Presbyterian address – which was incidentally signed by scores of the same people as the 1704 petition to the synod – deplored the commissioners from both kingdoms who were pressing for parliamentary union. An incorporating union like the one being proposed would, they claimed, undermine 'the thrice happy Revolution' of 1689.[62] The petitioners offered a defence of their specific view of the Reformation and its aftermath, as they avowed that:

> Such an Incorporating Union … is contrair to the Honour, Interest, Fundamental Laws, Solemn Oaths and Covenants for Reformation this Nation is lying under, and also contair to the Claim of Right and having a direct Tendency to the subverting of Presbyterian Government.[63]

They also announced that they would defend the kingdom against any 'Pretender', but particularly 'the Pretended K: James the eight'.[64] Such political engagement represents a fundamental expression of agency. Muirhead points out that this anti-union address, signed by 211 people, was one of the earliest, and that through it Tulliallan expressed a form of civic identity which emphasised their community.[65] It also shows colliers defiantly representing their collective opinion in an oppositional address to parliament. These were not passive downtrodden workers, but political actors at the vanguard of the movement opposing parliamentary union.

On a different note, many colliers often joined together to oppose their masters and engage in open resistance. Take for instance the case of John and Robert Pedies in Glasgow in 1667 (Robert Pedies, incidentally, may well be the same collier as Robert Pedy mentioned above). Both men were indicted before the regality court of Glasgow at the instance of Alexander Wardrop of

[60] Scott, *Fasti*, vol. 4, p. 347.
[61] NRS, Supplementary Warrants and Parliamentary Papers, PA7/28/83.
[62] NRS, PA7/28/83.
[63] Ibid.
[64] Ibid.
[65] Muirhead, *Scottish Presbyterianism Re-established*, p. 201.

Carntyne for 'destroying and drowning [his] coal heugh'.[66] This intriguing case was remitted to the justiciary court because of an implication that the havoc wreaked by the two colliers could in fact be classed as treason, due to the stipulations of a 1592 act of parliament.[67] The 1592 act, heard the court initially, stated that 'wilful destroying' of coal mines was treasonous.[68] On the contrary, Sir George Mackenzie of Rosehaugh – who represented the defendants – asserted, correctly, that it was only the burning of a mine which could be classed as treason according to the act. This aspect of the indictment was ultimately dropped but the colliers were nevertheless found guilty of damaging the mine. The case was remitted back to the bailies of Glasgow burgh council for sentencing, despite Mackenzie's remonstrations about the impropriety of such a serious case being adjudicated by a mere local court. The rhetoric in this legal process – especially in Wardrop's and his advocate's accusations – ostracised the colliers and depicted them as workers with a predisposition for violence and recalcitrance. However, the fact that the process was brought before one of the highest courts in the kingdom, where the colliers were represented by arguably the most famous Scottish Restoration legal practitioner, is significant.

Similar, but more pertinent to colliers' collective action is a case in April 1668. Here, a group of seventeen coal hewers was accused of committing a 'ryott and oppression' on Lady Grange's mine the previous July.[69] These workers were accused of throwing stones at and committing violence against Lady Grange's husband after he had damaged the drainage system from one of their mines in protest at the tacksmen of the works taking control unilaterally without his permission. Here we see coal workers – interestingly from both Kinglassie and Grange collieries – taking collective action to protect the source of their livelihoods.

Withholding labour was a common occurrence in the Scottish coal fields of the seventeenth century. Although the 1641 and 1661 acts prescribed six-day working weeks, this was not always the case in practice. At Carden in particular, some people worked as little as three or four days in the early 1700s.[70] Coal hewers had greater freedom in this respect, since they were paid according to how much coal they wrought and could thus conceivably work as much as they wished. As such, it appears from several account books that hewers often brought up enough coal to sustain them for a few days, allowing them to abstain for the remainder of their working week. Bearers on the other hand were in a more precarious position and were often more closely constrained. John Clerk of Penicuik reported in 1703 that his workers were to work 'twelve hour space each day', but in practice this meant that they simply had to provide their bearers with enough coal to work for that

---

[66] *PJC*, vol. 1, pp. 191–5.
[67] *RPS*, 1592/4/90.
[68] *PJC*, vol. 1, p. 192.
[69] *RPCS, 3rd Series*, vol. 2, pp. 429–32.
[70] NRS, GD26/5/320/1.

amount of time.[71] Even if the hewers' work was completed, the bearers were still required to transport the coal from the face. Penicuik himself assailed his workers for 'idle days', including it in his grieve's duties that the hewers and bearers be reminded how 'destructive to the master' it was when they worked half or quarter days.[72]

In a more extreme case of industrial dispute, the workers at Sheriffhall coal mine went on strike for a week in September 1679. The account book recorded that there was 'Noe work this weik because of ane muttinie amongst the coallziars upon changeing of the pryce of the Loads of Coalls'.[73] The colliers nevertheless returned to work the following week. The means of their appeasement on 20 September was a load of ale, costing over £5. Perhaps more important, however, was a payment on that same day of over £4 to a John Prestone for 'setling the workmen'. Delving back to the account books earlier in the 1670s, it becomes clear that Prestone was a former oversman at the Sheriffhall works. Prestone appears to have been a spokesman for the colliers, often liaising with the grieve and oversman and probably acting as a conduit for dialogue concerning industrial relations.[74]

Productivity at Sheriffhall had been dwindling, and profits stagnating, for some time prior to the 'mutiny' of 13 September 1679. Indeed, colliers' pay outstripped profit, so it must surely have been the case that the grieves, overseers, and masters calculated that cost-cutting was unavoidable. The price change at Sheriffhall was likely broached prior to its implementation so this might explain why there was a skeleton workforce for a few weeks before the 'mutiny' itself. Two weeks prior to the industrial action, just three coal hewers worked, gaining the mine a meagre profit of just £3. Preceding this, there had been several weeks when relatively few colliers worked, with some weeks just five or seven colliers, instead of the normal fourteen or so, recorded as raising coal. Seemingly, these workers were consciously withholding labour in protest at the price change, since they were well aware that their labour was directly correlated with the mine's overall profits. After the mutiny, profits increased at a swifter rate than did colliers' pay, but these did not diverge hugely. There followed some of the most productive months for the colliery in the entire late seventeenth-century, with weekly profits in December rising as high as £200.[75] No matter what the specific reason for this, the negotiation of the colliers' labour and their pay was an active process, involving the colliers, their grieves and oversmen, and the coal master.

As mentioned above, another common occurrence was illicit selling of coal by both hewers and bearers, but particularly the latter. Such was Clerk of Penicuik's concern about the regularity of this practice that he flatly pro-

---

[71] NRS, GD18/995, pp. 25–6.
[72] NRS, GD18/995, p. 18.
[73] NRS, GD224/66/8.
[74] NRS, GD224/66/6-8.
[75] NRS, GD224/66/8.

hibited it in his orders to his workers.[76] He used fines, court and kirk session discipline, and the threat of being banished from the works to discourage it. Penicuik's concern reflects the fact that bearers had significant clout in this sense and often had a predilection for illegal selling of coal outwith the mining community, for which they could conceivably earn considerable money on top of their nominal pay.

Interestingly, while we have already seen how mine workers often suffered from a poor reputation, their skills and knowledge could also command respect. This can be traced in two contemporary scientific projects on coal mining, both of which were influential in the late seventeenth century. The first was conducted by George Sinclair (d. c. 1696), who for some time taught mathematics at St Andrews and Glasgow universities before being removed from his post at the latter in 1667 upon his refusal to conform with episcopacy. Sinclair then went on to work as a mine surveyor during the Restoration and published some of his observations, along with some other scientific research (for instance on use of diving bells) as *The hydrostaticks* in 1672.[77] This was republished in 1683 as *Natural philosophy*.[78] Sinclair has been celebrated as one of the first people to suggest a workable means of draining coal mines.[79] However, his observations relied on the expertise of mine workers themselves, who passed on their wisdom and allowed him to conduct his (sometimes rather eccentric) experiments in their place of work, including lowering various animals into a Tranent mine in 1669 to test for natural gas.[80] Sinclair appeared fond of coal miners and recognised that his influential work would not have been possible without their guidance, since they were themselves practitioners of natural philosophy. In the postscript to *The hydrostaticks*, Sinclair dismantled one of his many critics, who had insultingly quipped that he was more of a collier than a natural philosopher due to his observations on mining:

> I must tell this Pedant, that a Coal-hewer is a more useful person in his own station, to the Countrey, than he is; and that the Science of Coal, and other Minerals, is far beyond any knowledge this man hath, or can teach.

---

[76] NRS, GD18/1003, pp. 8–9.

[77] George Sinclair, *The hydrostaticks, or, The weight, force, and pressure of fluid bodies, made evident by physical, and sensible experiments together with some miscellany observations, the last whereof is a short history of coal, and of all the common, and proper accidents thereof, a subject never treated of before* (Edinburgh, 1672).

[78] George Sinclair, *Natural philosophy improven by new experiments touching the mercurial weather-glass, the hygroscope, eclipsis, conjunctions of Saturn and Jupiter, by new experiments, touching the pressure of fluids, the diving-bell, and all the curiosities thereof: to which is added some new observations, and experiments, lately made of several kinds: together with a true relation of an evil spirit, which troubled a mans family for many days: lastly, there is a large discourse anent coal, coal-sinks, dipps, risings, and streeks of coal, levels running of mines, gaes, dykes, damps, and wild-fire* (Edinburgh, 1683).

[79] J. Anderson, rev. A. McConnell, 'Sinclair, George (d. 1696?)', *ODNB*, https://doi.org/10.1093/ref:odnb/25615 [accessed 6 June 2023].

[80] Sinclair, *The hydrostaticks*, pp. 197–9.

But, my Lords and Gentlemen, who are Coal-Masters, mark this: if ye stand to the judgement of this Pedant, though ye had never so much skill in these things, ye may come to gain the repute of being more fit to be Coal-hewers, than Schollars; as if the knowledge of such things were not a part of Natural Philosophy.[81]

Secondly, a late seventeenth-century dissertation on coal mining from the Clerk of Penicuik manuscripts is illuminating for the influence of coal mine workers on intellectuals and mine owners. It is unclear who the author of this dissertation was, but it records that it was 'Anent coale from Mr Plot', so it is reasonable to believe that it was copied from the findings of the naturalist and antiquary Robert Plot (d. 1696).[82] Plot was responsible for the revival of the Royal Society's journal *Philosophical Transactions* in the early 1680s. The dissertation cited Sinclair's work and applauded the workers' observations on natural gases plus their competence in knowing when not to work due to these perils. For instance, it discussed the problems caused by fierce winds and the lack of proper ventilation in the mines. The dissertation commended 'the expert coaliers' for 'noticing dewly [to] take care not to go to the worke quen the wind blows infavourably quich is the only way to avoid this kind of damp'.[83] Without these observations based on coal mine workers' aptitude and experience, Clerk of Penicuik may have not been aware of the risks of mining when natural gases were rife. As shown above, mines were often closed in the later seventeenth century for periods of days or weeks due to this knowledge, including Clerk's Loanhead mine. Mine workers, then, possessed expertise that came to be increasingly valued towards the end of the century. By sharing this knowledge, as well as by demonstrating their agency in the spheres of religion, politics, and labour relations, mine workers challenged the marginal position to which they were nominally confined and exercised a good deal more influence than is often recognised.

In addition to the above, the coal mine workers of the seventeenth century were central to industrial development. For instance, George Bruce's mine in Culross was one of the most productive early in the century and he relied on the labour of his workers for the development of one of Scotland's first dedicated industrialised towns. Despite its closure in 1625, it is testament to the worker's, and the mine's, value that archaeological research has shown that its annual production between 1590 and that year was, on average, 4,000 tons.[84] Moreover, salt brought most people into the market economy since it was the most common commodity used to preserve food. Both industries were intimately connected since the pans needed vast amounts of coal for

---

[81] Ibid., pp. 315–16.
[82] NRS, GD18/1010.
[83] NRS, GD18/1010, p. 2.
[84] D. Adamson, 'A Coal Mine in the Sea: Culross and the Moat Pit', *Scottish Archaeological Journal*, 30:1–2 (2008), 166–99, at p. 184.

heating in the laborious process of producing salt. Indeed, Tranent colliery and Cockenzie salt pans were connected to one another with Scotland's first industrial railway, which was built between the two works in 1722.[85] A consequence of this was that coal mine workers and, by extension, the industry in the macro sense, were imperative to the early development of capitalism in seventeenth- and eighteenth-century Scotland. Coal was undeniably one of the drivers of the industrial revolution. One need look no further than the evidence from Sheriffhall or Loanhead to see that the profitability and capital development which mine owners experienced – and which drove wider national economic advancement – was grounded in the workers' labour and would have, in fact, been impossible without it.

Conclusion

The marginalisation of Scottish coal mine workers in the seventeenth century took different forms. Colliers were subject to increasingly draconian legislative marginalisation in addition to an embedded cultural understanding of them as a 'different breed' or belonging to a 'dishonourable trade'. There were also specific local circumstances and idiosyncrasies at play which makes generalisation of any national experience problematic. The way this marginality was experienced, however, varied depending on one's gender and specific function within the mine, and it was also subject to constant negotiation: through revolts, resistance, religious practice, and labour disputes, workers managed to exercise significant agency despite their bound status.

More broadly, coal mine workers were central to early modern Scottish life. Salt pans could not function without coal, and households relied on it for heating and even cooking. Hence, despite their reputation as marginalised others, these workers were at the core of a developing system of capitalism. They were also capable of direct interaction with their masters and social superiors, and their expertise fed into the development of a growing body of technical knowledge about mining. Despite their layered marginalisation, then, coal mine workers were critical actors in early modern Scotland, who engaged widely in political, religious, social, economic, and intellectual developments in much the same way as many other Scots.

---

[85] C.A. Whately, 'Salt, Coal and the Union of 1707: A Revision Article', *SHR*, 66:1 (1987), 26–45, at p. 32.

Part III

Contemplating Marginality

10

Migrants, Itinerants, and the Marginality of Mobility in Seventeenth-Century Scotland

Allan Kennedy

In August 1636, Henry Ghretsone, a skipper and 'stranger', complained that, while he had previously 'belived that the Scottes had bene gude people', he had now changed his mind. His *volte-face* resulted from an incident that had occurred while he was sailing towards Dumbarton from Glasgow. Another boat, carrying many heavily-armed men, attacked him, shooting multiple holes in his sails before taking him captive. Having dragged him ashore, they demanded customs dues that he could not afford to pay, and he was accordingly held in prison for a number of days until somebody else agreed to pay the fees on his behalf. Such treatment of strangers, Ghretsone protested, 'will do wholl Scotland no gude'.[1] Ghretsone's experience spoke to the fraught and uncertain place of the 'incomer' in early modern society, a society rooted in the ideal that people ought to live in settled, relatively non-porous communities. This theoretical standard, however, did not match reality: early modern people in fact moved around readily and frequently, as a substantial body of scholarship now readily attests.[2] Within a specifically Scottish context, however, migration as a research theme remains unevenly developed. While there is a very considerable stock of work elucidating the experiences of Scots moving to other parts of the globe, we remain surprisingly under-informed about mobility within and to Scotland itself, especially before 1700.[3]

Our lack of detailed knowledge notwithstanding, there is a general recognition within the scholarship that 'strangers', as they were typically termed, whether in the form of vagrants, economic migrants, professional people, or foreign visitors like Henry Ghretsone, were very often marginalised figures, their activities subject to significant restriction and their socio-economic opportunities curtailed – as, indeed, has tended to be the general experience

---

[1] RPCS, 2nd Series, vol. 6, pp. 608–9.
[2] For a still useful primer, see Ian D. Whyte, *Migration and Society in Britain 1550–1830* (Basingstoke and London, 2000).
[3] A good entry point into the substantial literature on Scottish communities overseas is Steve Murdoch and Esther Mijers, 'Migrant Destinations, 1500–1750', in T.M. Devine and J. Wormald (eds), *The Oxford Handbook of Modern Scottish History* (Oxford, 2012), pp. 320–38.

of 'outsiders' in other geographical and temporal contexts.[4] Building on these tentative foundations, this chapter seeks to interrogate the basis and nature of migrants' social marginality in early modern Scotland, focusing especially on seventeenth-century evidence. It begins by discussing the various challenges that migrants and immigrants were thought to pose for their host communities, before moving on to survey the mechanisms – some formal, some not – by which such individuals were confined to the fringes. It then assesses how, and why, this marginal status might be challenged or mitigated. The chapter argues that itinerants had a complex place in early modern society, often provoking suspicion, frequently subject to marginalising pressures, but also capable of becoming valued and important members of their host communities.

The Challenge of Mobility

At its most fundamental, anxiety about migrants and itinerants was based on the conviction that they represented disorder. In part, this was a simple issue of overcrowding and unsightliness, as exemplified by the privy council's complaint in 1616 about 'the large numbers of poor people' who came 'from all pairtes of the countrey to the burgh of Edinburgh':

> They present thame selffis in the day tyme in grite nomberis and companyis ... sua that hardlie can ony man of whatsomever qualitie walk upon the streitis, nor yitt stand and confer upoun the streitis nor under stairs, bot they are impeshit be nomberis of beggaris, to the grite reproche and scandall of this burgh.[5]

There was, however, more to this than mere inconvenience. In a society constructed, at least in theory, around settled communities, an itinerant or mobile lifestyle was problematic by definition.[6] For the magistrates of Inverness, discussing in 1676 the 'sewerall persons strangers' who had recently 'stollen in quyetlie to this burghe', the issue was one of control: by settling clandestinely and without permission, these people had undermined the authority of the burgh council.[7] Given their inherent disorderliness, moreover, migrants might also be feared as vectors for the spread of disorderly conduct. In Dunfermline, for example, the kirk session was greatly exercised in 1650 by the 'enormities on the streets on the Sabbath', a result of many idle 'strangers' who had recently settled in the town after fleeing

---

[4] See, for example, J. Selwood, *Diversity and Difference in Early Modern London* (Farnham, 2010).
[5] *RPCS*, 1st Series, vol. 10, p. 471.
[6] M. Braddick, *State Formation in Early Modern England c.1550–1700* (Cambridge, 2000), pp. 150–2.
[7] *Inverness Recs.*, vol. 2, p. 265.

the Cromwellian armies in the south and who refused to observe the Lord's Day.[8] Even worse, itineracy might go hand-in-hand with crime. Why else, wondered the justiciary court of Argyll in 1691, would the suspected thief Dugald McKiachan have 'withdrawn himself from the company of men' to live peripatetically on the moors except for 'the more easie committing of his villanies'?[9] In a world where orderliness implied settlement, people who moved around would, of necessity, be viewed as potential sources of chaos.

As well as threatening good order, migrants, it was widely feared, could bring with them moral corruption. On one level, the concern was merely about the immoral conduct of the individuals themselves. John Wright, for example, a young man from Torthorwald, was in 1657 rebuked by the nearby kirk session of Dumfries for being 'extraordinarly drunk in this burgh wpon the mercat day'.[10] More worrisome, however, was the possibility that the immoral migrant might drag others down with them, as allegedly happened to Janet Hossak of Elgin, whose moral fibre was questioned in 1650 after she practised a healing charm allegedly taught to her by an outsider from the Highlands.[11] Worst of all, migration might lead to community-wide corruption, a dynamic strikingly – albeit somewhat amusingly – exemplified at Inveraray in 1661. In September that year, the kirk session received reports about 'a filthie, obscean, abominable song sung by severall profane persons in this Toun'. Upon investigation, they discovered that the song had been brought to the town by a local glover who had heard it on a trip to Dumbarton.[12] Mobility, then, had the potential to puncture a community's moral defences, potentially allowing all sorts of corruption to take root.

The dangers posed by mobility were felt particularly acutely in times of pestilence. Despite limited epidemiological knowledge, the role of itinerant individuals in spreading infection was widely intuited, as shown by parliament's reaction in 1645 to the news that 'the plague of pestilence' had broken out in Bo'ness: 'Becaus of the resort of cuntrie people aboute Lithgow, Falkirke and otheres places to that toune this infectione is lyke to spread, to the great hazard of the cuntrie, without remeid be provydit.'[13] For local communities, responding to this danger generally took the form of tightening restrictions on strangers entering the area. Old Aberdeen, for example, announced in 1604 that 'ther salbe na stranger receawit in this towne witout leif of the bailyeis in respect of the present pestilence', adding eighteen months later that unknown beggars were to be ejected wholesale.[14] Neighbouring (New) Aberdeen issued a similar order when it heard in 1645 that 'the plague of pestilence wes rageing in the cuntrey', but allied this to the establishment of

---

[8] *Extracts from the Kirk Session Records of Dunfermline* (Edinburgh, 1865), pp. 35–6.
[9] *Argyll and the Isles*, vol. 1, pp. 135–6.
[10] NRS, Dumfries Kirk Session Minutes, CH2/537/13, p. 165.
[11] *Elgin Recs.*, vol. 2, p. 275.
[12] NRS, CH2/663/1, Inveraray Kirk Session Minutes, 1650–63, fols 65r–66r.
[13] *RPS*, 1645/1/22.
[14] *Old Aberdeen Recs.*, pp. 34–5, 39.

an emergency armed watch, manned by all able-bodied inhabitants, to guard the town against incomers.[15] Concern was not only provoked by local plague outbreaks, however: in obedience to a privy council order, Peebles in 1665 reiterated its long-standing ban on the reset of strangers following reports that plague had broken out in London, simultaneously banning (temporarily) any and all interaction with English merchants.[16] Contemporaneously, Edinburgh, a town with particularly strong international trading networks, went still further, ordering the construction of some temporary accommodation just outside the city in which to quarantine incoming merchants suspected of being potential plague-carriers.[17] This impulse to respond to epidemic disease by heightening controls over population mobility underlined the pervasive sense that the migrant, as well as being a challenge to order and morality, could also threaten a community's health.

Aside from their disordering and befouling potential, itinerants were also feared as sources of resource competition. This was particularly true of poor migrants, vagrants, and beggars, who were often accused of diverting scarce poor-relief resources away from the 'native' poor. This, certainly, was the issue preying on the mind of Dundee's kirk session in 1682:

> It wes given as ane generall grivance by most members of the session that there wes a great number off Stranger poore through all quarters of the town who had there residence in the place and frequented the kirkstyles on the Lords day to the great prejudice of our own poor and the Sabath days Collections.[18]

Such fears about the diversion of resources were not wholly confined to the poor, however: various residents in the Lothians, for example, complained in 1642 that large-scale selling of coal to 'strangers' threatened to denude the area of its coal deposits and thus force the locals to pay 'exorbitant prices'.[19] Another worry, particularly in towns, was that migrants might undercut monopoly rights or other protectionist systems. In Inverness, for example, the council lamented in 1667 that 'diverse of the craftmen dwelling within this burghe' were 'greatunlie prejudiced in ther wocatiounes and callings' by the presence of 'forrenders and strangers' coming to the town daily and siphoning off their business, not only impoverishing the native craftsmen themselves, but also leeching away the burgh's tax-base.[20] A slightly different concern motivated the magistrates of Glasgow when they rebuked William Corse and Frederick Cuninghame in 1691; the two men had sold a boatload of tobacco imported from Liverpool by an unknown stranger 'without makeing ane

---

[15] *Aberdeen Recs.*, vol. 4, pp. 58–9.
[16] *Extracts from the Records of the Burgh of Peebles, 1652-1714: With Appendix, 1367-1665* (Glasgow, 1910), pp. 66–7.
[17] *Edinburgh Recs.*, vol. 5, p. 377.
[18] NRS, CH2/1218/1, Dundee – General Session, Minutes, 1682–1715, p. 9.
[19] *RPCS*, 2nd series, vol. 7, p. 579.
[20] *Inverness Recs.*, vol. 2, pp. 232–3.

tounes offer', thereby threatening civic control over commerce.[21] The protection of resources and economic privileges from the avaricious attentions of outsiders was thus a significant component of anti-migrant feeling throughout the seventeenth century.

Worries about the potentially corrupting and befouling impact of migrants were articulated with particular force – and comprehensiveness – by Edinburgh's town council, which justified a 1646 injunction against harbouring strangers in florid terms:

> The good Toun hath bein and is greatlie abused by suffering strangeris vagaboundis unfrie persones beggeris poor and indigent bodies to plant and have their habitatioun and dwelling within this brugh by the which meanes of the saidis unfrie persones and such as they resett the Toun is defyled with all kynd of vyce, the libertie of friemen usurped by the saidis unfrie persones, the Toun overburdened with sustening of that kynd of people their wyffes children and such as they resett in tyme of pestilence or famine and monethlie contributioun appoynted for their owen poor imployed and consumed upon them.[22]

Whether as a purveyor of vice, a source of uncleanness, a drain on resources, or a challenge to social order, the migrant was regarded as a major and frightening threat to the fabric of seventeenth-century communities.

All of these issues – fears about disorder, concern about resource competition, and 'normative' distaste – help explain why the issue of banditry loomed so large in the seventeenth-century mind. Bandit gangs were associated particularly with the Highlands, and indeed by the second half of the century they had become the primary focus of most government policies towards Highland Scotland. Generally described as 'broken' or 'masterless' men, meaning that they had no fixed abode and recognised no lord, bandits tended to operate in medium-sized gangs, surviving through a range of criminal enterprises including robbery, house-breaking, kidnapping, blackmail, and extortion.[23] While the chief objection to bandits was their violent criminality, the inherent mobility of their lifestyles was also an important component of the particular horror in which they were held. This thinking was made clear in the case of the Callander bandit Calum Oig McGrigor, who was convicted in 1669 of a diverse array of offences. He was, according to his indictment, 'a Lous and broken man and a vagabound' who was 'altogider idle and uithout any land [or] imployment whervpon he might and ought to have Leived', and who instead made his living 'rob[bing] and sorn[ing] through the cuntrey'.

---

[21] *Glasgow Recs.*, vol. 4, p. 7.
[22] *Edinburgh Recs.*, vol. 4, pp. 80–1.
[23] A.I. Macinnes, 'Lochaber – The Last Bandit Country, c.1600–c.1750', *Transactions of the Gaelic Society of Inverness*, xliv (2004–6), 1–21; A. Kennedy, 'State, Community, and the Suppression of Banditry in Seventeenth-Century Scotland', *International Review of Scottish Studies*, 46 (2021), 1–26; A. Kennedy, 'Deviance, Marginality, and the Highland Bandit in Seventeenth-Century Scotland', *Social History*, 43:7 (2022), 239–64.

McGrigor's itinerary, therefore, was understood as core to his crimes, but also as an expression of his deep social marginality – a position apparently rooted, in part, in a scandalous case of incest for which he had previously been disciplined in his home parish.[24] The bandit, then, liberated as he was through his itinerant lifestyle to commit all sorts of heinous outrages, served as a cautionary tale for both the inherent untrustworthiness and the corrupting influence of unrestrained mobility.

Bandits were loathed primarily because of the material consequences following from their lifestyles. As we saw in Chapter 3 of this volume, a slightly different calculus underpinned hostility towards another prominent migrant group: Gypsies. Material concerns were certainly part of anti-Romani hostility; thus, when a number of them were tried before the justiciary court in 1678, the offences laid against them went beyond merely being 'Egyptians' and instead incorporated specific counts of sorning, robbery, assault, and murder.[25] At the same time, Gypsies were habitually castigated for their alleged contempt towards authority – indeed, the fact that they had theoretically been banished from the kingdom in 1609 meant that any Romani living in Scotland thereafter were regarded, *ipso facto*, as criminals.[26] Underlying these concerns, however, was clear ethnic hostility: Romani 'gibbers and Egyptian language' attracted suspicion and contempt; their practices of fortune-telling, juggling, and dream-divination were 'unworthie to be hard of in a cuntrey subject to religioun, law, and justice'; their clothing was denigrated as slovenly and dirty; the large family groups in which they lived were widely reconceptualised as criminal fraternities; and their itinerary itself was claimed to be a cynical cover for law-breaking.[27] The erroneous contemporary association of the Romani with the Egyptians of the Exodus narrative, typically cast in contemporary thinking as archetypes of superstition and wickedness, did not help matters.[28] As obvious outsiders who flouted norms, challenged authority, and allegedly committed all manner of outrages, the Romani were almost perfect distillations of all the fears and anxieties associated with itinerary in the seventeenth-century mind.

Enforcing Marginality

Given the multitude of negative ideas associated with migration, it is little surprise that seventeenth-century society developed a range of tools both for discouraging movement, and for quarantining migrants at the social margins.

---

[24] NRS, JC2/12, High Court Books of Adjournal, 1666–9, fols 334v–356v.
[25] NRS, JC2/14, High Court Book of Adjournal, 1673–8, fols 398r–401r.
[26] *RPS*, 1609/4/32; *RPCS*, 1st Series, vol. 13, pp. 392–3.
[27] Ibid.; *RPCS*, 2nd Series, vol. 10, p. 656; James Kirkwood, *A Short Information of the Plea betwixt the Town Council of Linlithgow, and Mr James Kirkwood School-Master there* (Edinburgh, 1690), p. 12; NRS, JC2/19, High Court Books of Adjournal, 1693–9, fols 430v–437v; George Mackenzie, *The Laws and Customes of Scotland in Matters Criminal* (Edinburgh, 1678), p. 360.
[28] D. Cressy, *Gypsies: An English History* (Oxford, 2020), pp. 2–4, 18–19.

The most amorphous, but also likely the most pervasive, means of doing so was social pressure. This might take the form of simple hostility: in 1670, for instance, English merchant James Stampeild complained to the justiciary court that he had been the victim of vicious Anglophobic slurs from a messenger named James Comrie – this despite the fact that Stampeild had 'lived a considerable pairt of his lyf in this kingdome'.[29] In the worst cases, such hostility towards outsiders could spill over into violence, as it did in 1699, when the two young sons of Irishman Alexander Abercromby were bound and beaten at Kirkliston after allowing their horses to graze on a patch of grass near the local church.[30] But prejudice could also manifest in other, less sensational ways. The Dutch weaver Cornelius Dragge, for instance, complained in 1601 that his abilities were constantly being impugned by native craftsmen who claimed that he could only have won his licence by exaggerating his skill-level.[31] Professional jealousy of this sort was similarly experienced by a group of foreign tanners brought to Scotland near the end of James VI's reign, whose presence was decried by some leather-workers 'as being prejudiciall to the publict goode'.[32] In other cases, unscrupulous individuals could exploit strangers' lack of familiarity with their environment, which was the course taken in 1669 by James Mundy of Malsetter, who tricked a number of German merchants into paying him various fees by pretending to have a commission from the Admiralty.[33]

Social difficulties did not always result from outright hostility, however. Sometimes, they were rooted in the failure, or refusal, of people around the migrant to offer adequate guidance or assistance. This was the crux of John Purdie's defence against the charge of usury in 1666; as a Pole, albeit of Scottish descent, he had simply been unaware that his money-lending practices broke Scottish law.[34] Ignorance of this kind spoke to inadequate support networks, and that was often a significant problem, as demonstrated by the case of one unnamed French woman in 1619. Married in France to a Scotsman, James Hamilton, she was abandoned by him *en route* back to Scotland. She eventually found her way to Glasgow, where she was reduced to great poverty, having 'no meanis heir to leiff be bot such as is bestowit upoun hir of pietie'. Of particular concern was that her faithless husband had fled with two chests full of her clothes, which he stashed out of her reach at Paisley. Lacking any friends or family to support her or to plead her case, she was forced to rely on the good graces of the Church, which interceded on her behalf with the privy council.[35]

---

[29] NRS, JC2/13, High Court Books of Adjournal, 1669–73, fols 35v–36r.
[30] NRS, JC2/19, fols 449v–452r.
[31] *RPCS*, 1st Series, vol. 6, pp. 306–7.
[32] *RPCS*, 2nd Series, vol. 1, pp. 67–8.
[33] *RPCS*, 3rd Series, vol. 3, p. 83.
[34] NRS, JC2/12, fols 23r–24v; *RPCS*, 3rd Series, vol. 2, pp. 174–5.
[35] *RPCS*, 1st Series, vol. 11, pp. 638–41.

The enforcement of migrants' marginality was not, however, left entirely to formless social dynamics, and several rather more tangible tools were also available. The most straightforward was ejection. Local communities, particularly towns, often worked to exile individual migrants whom they regarded as troublesome or problematic.[36] Such was the fate of the horner Robert Fuird and his wife, Jonet Lyndsey, who were thrown out of Glasgow in 1606 for being 'vagaboundis hantand and frequentand with drunkartis, theifis, and vnsuspect persounis night and day'.[37] It was not only individuals who could be targeted in this way, however: a group of Irish beggars were ejected *en masse* from Dumbarton in 1634, and indeed periodic orders for the ejection of all strangers and beggars, such as the one issued by Glasgow's burgh council in 1649, were common in many towns.[38] The most ambitious use of ejection in this way was, as we have seen in Chapter 3 of this volume, the blanket banishment of Gypsies, whom parliament in 1609 ordered expelled from the kingdom under pain of death.[39] The policy proved wholly unenforceable, and Gypsies remained active in Scotland throughout the early modern period, but it can nonetheless be held up as the clearest example of how banishment was used to enforce the marginal, contingent position of migrants and itinerants.

Such activity was haphazard and reactive, but there were examples of local communities taking a more proactive, systematic approach to the ejection of unwanted strangers. Some communities appointed a named official with general responsibility for monitoring incomers and ejecting them if necessary. Old Aberdeen hired Archibald Makgie for this purpose in 1605, and nineteen years later, Banff even went so far as to impose a special stent to pay Thomas Gordoune 'for outhalding of stranger beggaris furthe of this burghe'.[40] An alternative approach was to monitor the hospitality industry, on the assumption that this was the most likely point of contact between itinerants and their host communities. In 1685, for example, Inverness burgh council instructed all innkeepers to notify the town magistrates whenever they gave rooms to strangers. Edinburgh had issued a similar order in 1655 (with notification going to the town guard, rather than the magistrates), but in this case apparently incorporating not just innkeepers, but also any burgh resident letting rooms informally.[41] Probably the most usual form of proactive approach, however, was to take censuses. In order to tackle the 'great number off Stranger poore through all quarters of the town', for example, the ecclesiastical and civil authorities of Dundee in 1682 launched a visitation

---

[36] E. Ewan, 'Crossing Borders and Boundaries: The Use of Banishment in Sixteenth-Century Scottish Towns', in S.M. Butler and K.J. Kesselring (eds), *Crossing Borders: Boundaries and Margins in Medieval and Early Modern Britain* (Leiden, 2018), pp. 237–57.
[37] *Glasgow Recs.*, vol. 1, p. 246.
[38] *Dumbarton Recs.*, p. 45; *Glasgow Recs.*, vol. 2, p. 177.
[39] RPS, 1609/4/32.
[40] *Old Aberdeen Recs.*, p. 36; W. Cramond (ed.), *The Annals of Banff* (2 vols, Aberdeen 1891), vol. 1, p. 53.
[41] *Inverness Recs.*, vol. 2, p. 326; *Edinburgh Recs.*, vol. 4, p. 374.

with the stated aim of identifying and banishing as many poor incomers as possible.[42] Generalised searches of this kind were common, but in some cases, a census was targeted at particular types of stranger. Glasgow was in 1661 particularly focused on incomers who were single women, while the survey initiated by Inverness' kirk session in 1691 was all about migrants seeking employment as servants.[43] Slightly more political in spirit was the investigation ordered by Edinburgh town council in 1648, which aimed to identify and eject anybody who adhered to the recent Engagement with Charles I.[44] Proactive approaches like these ensured that maintaining the marginal status of migrants was not just a result of *ad hoc* decision-making by Scottish communities, but often a positive choice.

As will be apparent from some of the above examples, a key tool in forced-ejection schemes, and indeed arguably the most important weapon available to local communities for the regulation of population mobility, was the testimonial. These were certificates produced on request by local authorities, typically kirk sessions, and they could be presented by migrants to the authorities in their new locale as a kind of character reference. Often, a testimonial would simply attest to the lack of any known 'scandal' against a migrant's reputation, allowing them to be accepted into their new community. They were not always so positive, however, as was discovered by George Mcmollen when he requested a testimonial from the session of Dumfries in 1655:

> George Mcmollen wright now in the parochin of Kirkgrunzeane Is to get ane Testimoniall beiring That tho he hes beene a Louse young man yet there is nothing Iudicially maid out against him, but that he is skandallous for fornication in Sanq[uha]r parosh for which he hes not beene Rebuikit nather is his chyld baptized.[45]

Testimonials thus served both to confirm a migrant's legitimacy and to quantify their desirability, and they could accordingly form the basis of numerous mobility-control efforts. The inhabitants of Elgin were banned in 1618 from employing strangers as servants unless they could produce a satisfactory testimonial.[46] A more general approach was taken by Dunfermline kirk session, which declared in 1649 that an immediate testimonial check be performed on any newly arrived incomer.[47] Similarly, and responding to the 'multitude of strangers [who] hath flocked among the inhabitants', Thurso ordained in 1663 that the minister should lead a general survey of the parish to identify

---

[42] NRS, CH2/1218/1, fol. 9.
[43] *Glasgow Recs.*, vol. 2, p. 457; *Inverness Kirk Session Records, 1661–1800* (Inverness, 1902), pp. 36–7.
[44] *Edinburgh Recs.*, vol. 4, p. 173.
[45] NRS, CH2/537/13, fol. 98.
[46] *Elgin Recs.*, vol. 2, p. 158.
[47] *Records of Dunfermline*, p. 29.

and dismiss anybody lacking 'a testimony of civill deportment'.[48] Testimonials were even part of many communities' plague control toolkit, and it was with this in mind that Aberdonians were warned in 1645 not to welcome any visitors until the magistrates had examined their testimonials.[49] The testimonial system was cumbersome and variable, and could moreover be ignored by both migrants and authorities whenever it was deemed convenient to do so.[50] Nonetheless, testimonials clearly sat at the heart of Scottish communities' efforts to control population mobility.

Another very powerful tool was criminal justice. Gypsies were the most obvious victims of this approach: in 1698, for example, the justiciary court in Edinburgh sentenced four men (John, James, William, and Patrick Baillie) and a woman (Mary Baillie) to death after finding that they had 'for severall yeirs past lived and wandered up and doun within this Kingdome … as Idle vagabonds Under the name and oweneing your selves att least knowen repute and holden for the forsaid wicked people Called the Agyptians'.[51] Such experiences, however, were not entirely unique to 'Egyptians'. John Culter, who travelled to Argyll from Ireland in the 1680s, made his living by wandering around the county claiming to be a healer. Suspicious, the local justices of the peace captured him and put him on trial in 1686, ultimately warding him as a vagrant after concluding that he lacked any skill or training in either medicine or surgery.[52] Still more striking was the fate of John Smith *alias* Donald Macgoun, 'an constant vagabond' who spent several years wandering around Ross and Moray, acquiring an unsavoury reputation as a petty thief (for which he was branded on several occasions) before being finally tried and executed at Nairn in 1670.[53] The law could also be used to punish those deemed to have been encouraging strangers, or offering them inappropriate assistance. Peebles resident Patrick Brotherstanes was fined 20s in 1663 for resetting a 'tinker' within the burgh, a fate that was comparatively mild compared to that of Patrik Wryght's unnamed widow, who was banished from Glasgow in 1655 for allegedly housing stranger vagabonds in her home.[54] Slightly differently, three Elgin men were outlawed in 1652 for selling firs from the protected lands of Mosstowie to outsiders.[55] Criminal prosecution, then, represented a versatile tool for enforcing the marginal position of itinerants, particularly of the poor or vagrant type, either by subjecting them to direct sanctions, or by targeting the informal networks of support upon which they often depended.[56]

---

[48] NRS, CH2/414/1, Thurso Kirk Session, 1647–1706, no pagination.
[49] *Aberdeen Recs.*, vol. 4, pp. 58–9.
[50] R. Houston, 'Geographical Mobility in Scotland, 1652–1881: The Evidence of Testimonials', *Journal of Historical Geography*, 11:4 (1985), pp. 379–94.
[51] NRS, JC2/19, fols 397v–409v.
[52] NRS, Argyllshire Justice of the Peace Court, JP36/5/1/3.
[53] NRS, BN/1/1/1, Nairn Burgh Court and Council Minute Book, 1657–73, fols 94v–96r.
[54] *Records of the Burgh of Peebles*, 56; *Glasgow Recs.*, vol. 2, p. 322.
[55] *Elgin Recs.*, vol. 1, p. 294.
[56] By way of counterpoint, however, work on London's Old Bailey has suggested that

Other legalistic or procedural tools could also be used to both discourage migration and signal migrants' 'otherness'. In 1642, for instance, the ministers of Elie and Kilconquhar were advised not to baptise the children of any strangers until they could prove that they were properly married.[57] In Glasgow, the council decided in the 1690s to impose special fees on all strangers bringing carts into the burgh, ostensibly to offset the costs of any resulting damage.[58] In both Stirling and Elgin, strangers were required to pay additional fees if they wished the church bells to be rung at their interments, while at Inverness's harbour, anchorage charges were higher for outsiders than for residents of the town.[59] Regulations such as these underlined migrants' perceived alienness, and such an approach was especially obvious in the protectionist trade policies adopted by Scotland's burghs, which were designed to limit strangers' ability to profit from, or participate in, the urban economy (as discussed in Chapter 6 of this volume). In Dumbarton, outside hammermen were required to pay a daily fee of 4s or 8d to sell their goods at fairs or markets respectively, a practice that was widely replicated elsewhere and in different industries.[60] In order to protect native practitioners, Stirling banned any stranger from setting up as a wright, cooper, glasswright, litster, barber, or slater unless and until admitted as a burgess, while Inverness in 1667 discharged townsfolk from employing stranger craftsmen of any kind.[61] Even the mere selling of goods to outsiders was often subject to restrictions: brewers in Dysart were banned in 1622 from selling their product to anybody outside the burgh community, while Glaswegian 'fulyie', meaning sewage or waste, could not be sold to strangers under an order from 1656.[62] There were, therefore, a multitude of ways in which local communities could use their regulatory powers to distinguish between natives and migrants, almost always with the goal of privileging the former and confining the latter to the margins.

Mitigating Marginality

The migrant was a threatening figure, and was consequently subject to a wide range of restrictions and handicaps. These marginalising pressures were not, however, insuperable. Indeed, in some cases, clear efforts were made to wel-

---

the criminal justice system – in this case the practice of allowing 'strangers' to be tried by half-English, half-foreign juries – could also work to protect immigrant populations from undue persecution. M. Lockwood, '"Love ye therefore the strangers": Immigration and the Criminal Law in Early Modern England', *Continuity and Change*, 29:3 (2014), 349–71.
[57] J. Kinloch (ed.), *Ecclesiastical Records: Selections from the Minutes of the Presbyteries of St Andrews and Cupar* (Edinburgh, 1837), p. 5.
[58] *Glasgow Recs.*, vol. 3, p. 187, 226.
[59] *Stirling Recs.*, vol. 2, pp. 74–5; *Records of Elgin*, i, p. 357; *Inverness Recs.*, vol. 2, pp. 202–3.
[60] *Dumbarton Recs.*, pp. 91–2.
[61] *Stirling Recs.*, vol. 2, pp. 8–9, 88; *Inverness Recs.*, vol. 2, pp. 232–3.
[62] W. Muir (ed.), *Notices from the Local Records of Dysart* (Glasgow, 1853), 49; *Glasgow Recs.*, vol. 2, pp. 351–2.

come migrants to new areas, or to entice more of them to come in the first place, generally in the hope that their money or august presence would rebound advantageously on the community. In Irvine, for example, the magistrates spent 9s providing wine for 'strangers' in 1670, with later payments of £2 6s (1680) and 12s (1686) for the same purpose. These guests, presumably, were influential people whom the town wished to flatter; this was certainly true in Stirling's case, which outlaid more than £32 in 1700 entertaining various visiting gentlemen.[63] More proactive in its attempts to entice strangers was Aberdeen, which ordered in 1668 that all taverners and vintners must ensure a plentiful supply of space, ale, and wine, so that visitors were not 'disapoyntit of ludgeing and accommodatione', and followed this up in 1670 with instructions to improve and advertise a nearby medicinal well in the hope that 'strangeris knowing of such ane offer of health might make more frequent resort to this brughe'.[64] Glasgow was clearly thinking along similar lines when it proposed to build a new church at Port Glasgow for strangers to use in 1694, as well as a bowling green for both visitors' and townsfolks' enjoyment the following year.[65] Far from seeking to repel strangers, therefore, sometimes positive efforts could be made to attract them.

We do not currently know enough about migrant experiences in early modern Scotland to judge whether, or how far and in what ways, individuals settling in new communities tended to assimilate.[66] There are, nonetheless, scattered indications that both migrants and immigrants could win acceptance in Scottish society.[67] Social interaction, certainly, was not unusual, and, for instance, the English soldiers stationed at Inverness during the 1650s allegedly enjoyed very cordial relations with the native townsfolk, sometimes spending their down-time carousing with them.[68] Romantic entanglements, too, including marriages, were clearly commonplace, serving both to confirm migrants' positions and, in some instances, deepen their integration. Thus, one unnamed vagabond undertook in 1645 to take up permanent residence within the presbytery of St Andrews, and to work there as a horner, upon

---

[63] *Muniments of the Royal Burgh of Irvine* (2 vols, Edinburgh, 1891), vol. 2, pp. 268, 285, 303, 308; *Stirling Recs.*, vol. 2, p. 346.
[64] *Aberdeen Recs.*, vol. 4, p. 249, 263–4.
[65] *Glasgow Recs.*, vol. 4, p. 133, 158–60.
[66] For a case study of the assimilation process, albeit involving a Scottish family in England, see K.M. Brown and A. Kennedy, 'Becoming English: The Monro Family and Scottish Assimilation in Early Modern England', *Cultural & Social History*, 16:2 (2019), 125–44.
[67] In this context, see Michelle Brock's recent work on 1650s Ayr, which demonstrates how adherence to the covenants became both a necessary precondition for being welcomed into the community and a mechanism for winning acceptance. M.D. Brock, 'Keeping the Covenant in Cromwellian Scotland', *SHR*, 99: supplement (2020), 392–411.
[68] James Fraser, *Chronicles of the Frasers*, ed. W. Fraser (Edinburgh, 1905), pp. 413–16, 447; A. Kennedy, 'Cromwell's Highland Stronghold: The Sconce of Inverness', *Scottish Local History*, 106 (2020), 3–7. A. Kennedy, 'The Trial of Isobel Duff for Witchcraft, Inverness, 1662', *SHR*, 101:1 (2022), 109–22.

agreeing to marry a local woman whom he had got pregnant.[69] Less happily, being English did not stop Elizabeth Moor from marrying Thomas Rochead, nor, once settled in Edinburgh in the early 1660s, engaging in a string of adulterous affairs with other Scotsmen, including James Ritchie (a writer), George Duff (a shoemaker), and James Innes (a servant to the earl of Moray).[70]

It is clear as well that a diverse range of employment opportunities were open to outsiders: Alexander Stewart of Clarie was employing a 'French boy' as a servant in 1607; Englishman William Wricht was described as a merchant burgess of Aberdeen in 1661; Zeocham Anneis, Dutch by birth, was naturalised in 1676 after upwards of a decade working as a skipper out of Leith; and Isobel Cuming, a Scot but a stranger in Edinburgh, nonetheless established herself as a tutor to the capital's young ladies in the 1680s.[71] A rather different form of integration was demonstrated by Englishman Thomas Amersone, a litster by trade, who in 1657 answered a summons, and accepted a rebuke, from the kirk session of Dumfries for 'cursing [and] sweiring', suggesting that outsiders could become full communicants of the Scottish Kirk, and indeed may well have been expected to do so.[72] All of this meant that there were real opportunities for successful migrant experiences. Frenchman William Condon, for instance, settled in Cupar in the late 1610s, living in 'ease and contentment' for at least thirteen years and counting among his friends one of the town's bailies, Alexander Jamesone.[73]

Acceptance of this kind was particularly likely in the case of migrants possessing unique or valuable skills. Servants of various stamps typically fell into this category: James Mitchell travelled widely around Fife taking farm service jobs prior to his conviction for bestiality in 1675, while domestic servant Helen Bridges noted in 1694 that her work had seen her move from Balcarras to Kilconquhar, Anstruther Easter, Carnbo, Scotstarvit, Cameron, Perth, and Carnbee.[74] Other professions, such as schoolmaster or minister, similarly entailed frequent and relatively free mobility, as, of course, did apprenticeships.[75] Possession of rare skills was perhaps the surest means by which foreign immigrants could secure their positions in Scotland – something that was encouraged by the government, which consistently promised total liberty of trade to any 'strangers [who] shall come or be brought into

---

[69] Minutes of the Presbyteries of St Andrews and Cupar, p. 25.
[70] NRS, JC2/12, fols 263r–266v.
[71] *RPCS, 1st Series*, vol. 7, pp. 365–6; *RPCS, 3rd Series*, vol. 1, p. 21; ibid., vol. 5, p. 35; ibid., vol. 11, pp. 261–2.
[72] NRS, CH2/537/13, fol. 162.
[73] *RPCS, 2nd Series*, vol. 3, p. 612.
[74] JC2/14, fols 164v–165v; JC2/19, fols 118r–121r.
[75] A. A. Lovett, I. D. Whyte and K. A. Whyte, 'Poisson Regression Analysis and Migration Fields: The Example of the Apprenticeship Records of Edinburgh in the Seventeenth and Eighteenth Centuries', *Transactions of the Institute of British Geographers*, 10:3 (1985), 317–32.

this kingdom by natives to set up work and teach [their] art'.[76] In 1642, John Hunter, originally from England, set himself up as a 'silver and gold laise drawer' at Canongate, and when he died four years later, his work was considered sufficiently valuable that parliament granted licence to his widow, Anna, to carry it on.[77] Frenchman Pierre Chazelon's skills as a fur-trader saw him created a burgess of Edinburgh in 1696.[78] More enterprising still was Peter Bruce, a German engineer initially brought to Scotland in 1680 to build a harbour for the earl of Winton, but who later diversified into paper-making and the specialist importation of playing cards.[79] The extent to which skilled foreigners like these were valued was confirmed, again, by parliament, which, in one of its last acts before the Union of 1707, naturalised forty-four foreigners, mainly soldiers, merchants, and craftsmen, whose contributions to Scotland were judged valuable and whose carriage was thought to have been such 'as becomes the subjection and obedience they owe to her majestie and her government'.[80]

Other skilled foreigners were specifically head-hunted, either to plug skills gaps or build up desirable industries – or, indeed, both. Queen Anna of Denmark brought one unnamed Frenchman to Scotland to serve as royal clockmaker before she departed for England, and he was still in residence, and making clocks, in 1624. Another Frenchman, known only as 'Lues de France', was enticed to Aberdeen in 1675 to teach at the music school.[81] Robert Devinport was brought to Edinburgh from England in 1647 with a brief to manufacture mathematical instruments and repair watches, as well as to teach his trade to others.[82] Philip van der Straton, who was granted naturalisation specifically in order to establish himself as a wool-dresser at Kelso, was a Fleming.[83] This pursuit of foreign expertise sometimes took on a more general character, with the best-studied example probably being the glass industry, which began in East Lothian in 1610 and was entirely dependent on the imported expertise of foreign glassmakers, mostly Venetian.[84] Glass-working was not a unique case, however, and large-scale importation of foreigners was also used to establish or enhance several other industries, including fishing in Lewis (1620s), silk-weaving in Edinburgh (1670s) and

---

[76] *RPS*, 1681/7/36.
[77] Ibid., 1646/11/479.
[78] *Edinburgh Recs.*, vol. 8, p. 198.
[79] *RPCS*, 3rd Series, vol. 6, pp. 383–4; ibid., vol. 7, p. 101; ibid., vol. x, pp. 93–5, 343–5.
[80] *RPS*, 1706/10/457.
[81] *RPCS*, 1st Series, vol. 13, pp. 842–3; *Aberdeen Recs.*, vol. 4, p. 293–4.
[82] *Edinburgh Recs.*, vol. 3, p. 136.
[83] *RPCS*, 3rd Series, vol. 3, p. 472. On Flemish settlement and economic activity in Scotland, see A. Fleming and R. Mason (eds), *Scotland and the Flemish People* (Edinburgh, 2019).
[84] J. Turnbull, *The Scottish Glass Industry 1650–1750* (Edinburgh, 2001); J. Turnbull, 'Venetian Glassmakers in the Prestonpans Area in the Seventeenth Century', *Scottish Archives*, 23 (2017), 103–13.

both sugar and woollen manufacturing in Glasgow (1680s).[85] Such expertise was not always wholly welcome on the ground – leather-workers in Edinburgh strongly resisted the improvements recommended to them by a community of English experts brought in for this purpose in the 1620s and 1630s, for example – but the policy nonetheless spoke to a wider readiness, as we have already seen in Chapter 6 of this volume, to acknowledge and exploit the potential value to the Scottish economy of highly skilled outsiders.[86]

Even when full-blown acceptance or assimilation was not secured – or sought – marginalising attitudes towards itinerants were very often blunted by deep-seated tendencies towards philanthropy.[87] Poor migrants, in particular, attracted widespread generosity. Some of this (despite the theoretical limiting of poor relief to a parish's resident poor) was official, for example the order in 1675 for the treasurer of Kelso kirk session to provide whatever he could spare to 'a sick person a stranger lying in James Craigs house'.[88] In other cases, care was provided more informally.[89] In the winter of 1684–5, James Lanseman in Dundee allowed a 'stranger' and 'vagabound' named Marion Whytt to lodge in his byre – an action he may have come to regret since Whytt gave birth to an illegitimate child while there, causing Lanseman to be rebuked before the kirk session and instructed to 'beware of Lodging any such gwests in tym coming'.[90] This kind of treatment was not limited to poor folk, however; any stranger deemed worthy of assistance might win generous treatment. Two 'Gretians' were awarded five merks by Elgin's kirk session in 1624, part of a wider trend of alms-giving in favour of Greek Orthodox refugees across the seventeenth century. George Lockheart, apparently a refugee from the war in Ireland, was awarded 12s by Livingston kirk session in 1643. An unnamed English woman who had been 'foully wrongit by ane Scottis sojour' received £12 from Glasgow's burgh council in 1653. Edinburgh, meanwhile, granted freedom of the city to the Huguenot refugee Peter Pascall in 1698.[91] Clearly, while routinely cast as dangerous

---

[85] A. MacCoinnich, *Plantation and Civility in the North Atlantic World: The Case of the Northern Hebrides, 1570–1639* (Leiden, 2015), chapter 5; *RPCS*, 3rd Series, vol. 3, pp. 404–5; *RPS*, 1681/7/64, 1681/7/65.
[86] *RPCS*, 2nd Series, vol. 1, pp. 67–8; ibid., vol. 3, pp. 359–60; ibid., vol. 4, pp. 78–9, 162, 281, 443; ibid., vol. 6, pp. 20–1.
[87] C. Langley, *Cultures of Care: Domestic Welfare, Discipline and the Church of Scotland, c.1600–1689* (Leiden, 2020), pp. 29–30; K. Barclay, *Caritas: Neighbourly Love and the Early Modern Self* (Oxford, 2021), pp. 150–8.
[88] NRS, CH2/1173/5, Kelso Kirk Session Minutes, 1668–1676, p. 142; J. McCallum, *Poor Relief and the Church in Scotland, 1560–1650* (Edinburgh, 2018), chapter 7.
[89] A. Glaze, 'Sanctioned and Illicit Support Networks at the Margins of a Scottish Town in the Early Seventeenth Century', *Social History*, 45:1 (2020), 26–51.
[90] NRS, CH2/1218/1, p. 4. Lanseman had been rebuked at least once before for a similar act of charity. Ibid., p. 11.
[91] *Elgin Recs.*, vol. 2, p. 185; NRS, CH2/467/1, Livingston Kirk Session Minutes, 1641–1647, p. 15; *Glasgow Recs.*, vol. 2, p. 269; *Edinburgh Recs.*, vol. 8, pp. 226–7; Langley, *Cultures of Care*, 105; A.C. Grant, 'Scotland's "Vagabonding Greekes", 1453–1688', *Byzantine and Modern Greek Studies*, 46:1 (2022), 81–97.

and threatening figures, on-the-ground responses to migrants could often be considerably more generous than might be expected. Human kindness and Christian charity proved powerful countervailing influences when it came to the marginalisation of the itinerant.

Conclusion

Despite being a lot more widespread than conventionally assumed, mobility represented a significant problem for early modern society. Whatever form they took – vagrants, subsistence migrants, economic migrants, bandits, 'Egyptians', and so on – itinerant people challenged the settled ideals of the age. To this 'normative' threat could be added a range of additional anxieties, principally around order, resource competition, and potential befoulment, that tended to cast the migrant as an inherently dangerous figure. It was for this reason that local communities habitually took (sometimes aggressive) steps to confine outsiders to the socio-economic margins, making use of a diverse array of tools that aimed to protect 'native' individuals from the threat they posed. There were, however, important countervailing tendencies. For all the difficulties, outsiders also presented opportunities – they could boost local economies, plug skills gaps, revitalise communities, and provide objects for the performance of Christian charity. Consequently, there was clearly potential for both migrants and immigrants to carve out successful niches in seventeenth-century Scotland, and if the chances (or desirability) of assimilation remain difficult to assess, social networking, intermarriage, employment, and institutional involvement were all manifestly possible. Itinerants, then, occupied an ambivalent social space. They were, in one sense, quintessentially marginal, regarded with suspicion and forcibly confined to the edges of their communities. On another level, though, they could become valued assets, and this, in turn, could provide them with a route to escape from marginality and become full participants in the society around them.

11

Seeking the Lord, Seeking a Husband: Navigating Marginality in the Diary of Rachel Brown (1736–8)

Martha McGill

Early modern religious institutions were undeniably patriarchal. The Scottish Kirk vested men with religious authority, and expected women to subjugate themselves before both God and their husbands. Visions of John Knox raging about monstrous regiments, or the notion that the witch hunts were primarily a mechanism by which the Kirk policed women's sexuality, have shaped popular conceptions of post-Reformation religion and gender.[1] As Callum G. Brown explores, early waves of scholarship similarly envisaged post-Reformation Scotland as an 'empire of patriarchy' in which both theology and ecclesiastical structures perpetuated the 'demonisation of women'.[2] However, historiography since the 1980s has painted a more nuanced picture. Kirk sessions worked to protect women as well as punishing them, and many ministers – including Knox – had circles of female confidants.[3] In a discussion of the role of women in Scottish divinity between 1590 and 1640, David Mullan highlights women's role in protests, and suggests that women 'had a real impact on other women and on men through their spiritual counsel'.[4] In her analysis of the Covenanting movement, Louise Yeoman similarly underlines how women participated both in prayer groups and in riots, with Presbyterianism promoting 'a brand of female activism and assertion which is rarely seen in other seventeenth century contexts'.[5] Against a backdrop of

---

[1] See C.G. Brown, 'Religion', in L. Abrams et al. (eds), *Gender in Scottish History since 1700* (Edinburgh, 2006), pp. 84–110, at pp. 84–91.
[2] Ibid., at pp. 84, 86.
[3] Ibid., at pp. 93–4; M.F. Graham, 'Women and the Church Courts in Reformation-Era Scotland', in E. Ewan and M.M. Meikle (eds), *Women in Scotland c.1100–c.1750* (East Linton, 1999), pp. 187–98; R. Mitchison and L. Leneman, *Girls in Trouble: Sexuality and Social Control in Rural Scotland 1660–1780* (Edinburgh, 1998), pp. 119–24; S.M. Felch, 'The Rhetoric of Biblical Authority: John Knox and the Question of Women', *The Sixteenth Century Journal*, 26:4 (1995), 805–22.
[4] D.G. Mullan, 'Women in Scottish Divinity, c.1590–c.1640', in *Women in Scotland*, pp. 29–41, at p. 34.
[5] L.A. Yeoman, 'Heart-Work: Emotion, Empowerment and Authority in Covenanting Times' (unpublished PhD thesis, University of St Andrews, 1991), pp. 254–61, quotation at p. 254. See also L. Yeoman, 'A Godly Possession? Margaret Mitchelson and the

conflict, early Covenanters encouraged zealous devotion to the cause, and exalted godliness above all – a democratising approach, for men and women from across the social spectrum might be redeemed by God's grace. The relative stability of the early eighteenth century furnished fewer opportunities for women to take on the mantle of saintliness, but both sexes continued to debate and resist the status quo in prayer societies, as Alasdair Raffe has demonstrated.[6] Thereafter, the evangelical revivals of the 1740s captivated a largely female audience with fresh promises of glorification.[7] Ecclesiastical structures and teachings upheld gendered hierarchies, but religion nevertheless offered some degree of empowerment.

The difficulty of assessing whether religion was a liberating or constraining force is thrown into stark relief when we consider spiritual writing. Before the eighteenth century, Scotswomen's reading and writing almost exclusively focused on religious topics.[8] The project of spiritual growth legitimised – indeed necessitated – the act of self-reflection. In his study of autobiographical writing by Scots born in the early eighteenth century or before, Mullan identifies some fifty works, of which sixteen were produced by women.[9] Recording their lives gave women the opportunity to shape their own identities, and assert their value as members of the godly community. At the same time, Calvinist spiritual progression was an exercise in self-abnegation: humans could reach a state of grace only if their inherently corrupt selves were dissolved and forged anew by the Holy Spirit. Spiritual writing was typically replete with expressions of self-loathing and pleas that the writer might be subsumed by God.[10] In addition, spiritual diarists conformed to recognised templates and couched their sentiments

---

Performance of Covenanted Identity', in C.R. Langley (ed.), *The National Covenant in Scotland, 1638–1689* (Woodbridge, 2020), pp. 105–24.

[6] A. Raffe, 'Female Authority and Lay Activism in Scottish Presbyterianism, 1660–1740', in S. Apetrei and H. Smith (eds), *Religion and Women in Britain, c. 1660–1760* (Farnham, 2014), pp. 61–78.

[7] T.C. Smout, 'Born Again at Cambuslang: New Evidence on Popular Religion and Literacy in Eighteenth-Century Scotland', *Past & Present*, 97 (1982), 114–27, at 116.

[8] J. Stevenson, 'Reading, Writing and Gender in Early Modern Scotland', *The Seventeenth Century*, 27:3 (2012), 335–74, at 353.

[9] D.G. Mullan, *Introduction to Women's Life Writing in Early Modern Scotland: Writing the Evangelical Self c.1670–c.1730*, ed. D.G. Mullan (Aldershot, 2003), pp. 1–22, at p. 1. On the development of life writing in the eighteenth century, see Karina Williamson, 'The Emergence of Privacy: Letters, Journals and Domestic Writing', in I. Brown et al. (eds), *The Edinburgh History of Scottish Literature* (3 vols, Edinburgh, 2007), vol. 2, pp. 57–70.

[10] Mullan, *Introduction to Women's Life Writing*, at p. 17; D.G. Mullan, *Narratives of the Religious Self in Early-Modern Scotland* (Farnham, 2010), pp. 361–3; M. Todd, 'Puritan Self-Fashioning: The Diary of Samuel Ward', *Journal of British Studies*, 31:3 (1992), 236–64, at 262–3; T. Webster, 'Writing to Redundancy: Approaches to Spiritual Journals and Early Modern Spirituality', *Historical Journal*, 39:1 (1996), 33–56, at 42–4. For the spiritual travails of another Scottish woman, in this case a Quaker, see G. DesBrisay, 'Lilias Skene: A Quaker Poet and her "Cursed Self"', in S.M. Dunnigan, C.M. Harker, and E.S. Newlyn (eds), *Woman and the Feminine in Medieval and Early Modern Scottish Writing* (Basingstoke, 2004), pp. 162–77.

in biblical language, often remaining frustratingly unknowable even as they detailed their greatest vulnerabilities and epiphanies.[11] Rarely did they offer any reflection on their own social role or relationships, and Mullan is left to speculate about the practical implications of their godliness: 'these spiritual life-narratives tell a story of women sharing in a common humanity with men ... and they may also have influenced the lives of men, as further research will undoubtedly sustain'.[12]

This chapter looks in more detail at how spiritual writing might have enabled women to negotiate their social positions, using as a case study the diary of a young Edinburgh woman called Rachel Brown (b. 1712). Various factors contributed to Brown's marginalisation. Although her family ranked in society's middle tiers, she lived in poverty. While there were some employment avenues for respectable women in eighteenth-century Edinburgh, Brown's poor health likely rendered work infeasible.[13] She desired to marry, but as a woman, she could not make a direct proposal herself. Her diary was her outlet. Written between June 1736 and November 1738, it extends to more than 300,000 words. It has survived by virtue of being intertwined with the diary of a better-known figure: Brown's friend George Drummond (1687–1766), several times lord provost of Edinburgh, and driving force behind the construction of much of the city's New Town.[14] Brown wrote on loose papers, and Drummond transcribed her work, avowedly preserving her own words.[15] In a discussion of Drummond penned in the 1880s, Alexander Grant dismissed Brown's diary entries as 'very nauseous'. A century later, Jacqueline Cromarty was equally unimpressed by Brown's 'strange religious ramblings'. The diary has received no further scholarly attention, but it is a rich document that deserves to be better known.[16] Brown defied many of the conventions of spiritual writing, detailing a fascinatingly idiosyncratic relationship with the deity, with whom she had extensive conversations.

---

[11] See Mullan, *Introduction to Women's Life Writing*, p. 1; M. Mascuch, *Origins of the Individualist Self: Autobiography and Self-Identity in England, 1591–1791* (Cambridge, 1997), p. 70.

[12] D.G. Mullan, 'Scottish Women's Religious Narrative, 1660–1720: Constructing the Evangelical Self', in Dunnigan, Harker, and Newlyn (eds), *Woman and the Feminine in Medieval and Early Modern Scottish Writing*, pp. 178–91, at p. 188.

[13] On work, see E.C. Sanderson, *Women and Work in Eighteenth-Century Edinburgh* (London, 1996), pp. 74–107.

[14] The diaries span two volumes. They are held in the special collections of Edinburgh University Library, Dc.1.82-83. Hereafter references to the diaries are given in the shortened form of date of entry, volume number, and page number.

[15] 2 May 1737, 1, p. 174.

[16] A. Grant, *The Story of the University of Edinburgh during its First Three Hundred Years* (2 vols, London, 1884), vol. 1, p. 366; J. Cromarty, 'Drummond's Religious Outlook', in *Lord Provost George Drummond, 1687–1766* (Edinburgh, 1987), p. 15. There is mention of R.B. – although only in relation to Drummond – in W. Baird, 'George Drummond: An Eighteenth Century Lord Provost', in *The Book of the Old Edinburgh Club, Fourth Volume* (Edinburgh, 1911), pp. 21, 35, and J. Buchan, *Capital of the Mind: How Edinburgh Changed the World* (London, 2003), pp. 180–3.

Through her writing Brown sought to reforge her social position, underlining her own spiritual eminence and importance to her circle, and making amorous overtures towards Drummond. Her case may be unusual, but it provides an instructive illustration of the power and limitations of religion as a means of navigating marginality.

Relationship with God

The details of Brown's life must be assembled from piecemeal evidence. In the diaries she is identified only as R.B. However, she mentions sisters by the names of Jean Brown and Mary, and brothers called John and Ebenezer. Records of births and christenings lead us to a couple called Patrick Brown and Jane Rowat, who had children named Rachel, Ebenezer, John, Mary, and Jane – as well as Hugh, Gilbert, and another Jane, who perhaps died. Rachel Brown was born on 17 February 1712, which would make R.B. between twenty-four and twenty-six at the time of writing, or about half Drummond's age. The records also reveal that Rachel Brown was christened in St Cuthbert's, Edinburgh; R.B. describes attending services there.[17] At the time of writing, Brown's mother had died. Brown herself regularly vomited blood, had feverish fits, and suffered from 'looseness' (diarrhoea). Her sister Jean was similarly unwell. Their brother John was jailed for his debts, and Brown fretted that he might commit suicide.[18] When it came to Ebenezer, God informed Brown that 'I have set him apart, from the womb, to serve at my altar'.[19] He was later ordained, but was likely too young to offer Brown support at the time of her writing.[20]

Brown was raised in a pious household. Her mother's last words to her were a warning that 'if [Brown] was among the Number of The Unbelievers, she would, with Joy, say, Amen to [her] condemnation'.[21] Although she did not reference texts besides the Bible, Brown may have read works of Covenanting piety. Samuel Rutherford's letters were enduringly popular, and the spiritual autobiographies of Elizabeth West and Katharine Collace were published in 1724 and 1735 respectively.[22] Brown was writing in a period when the

[17] Records of births and baptisms accessed via FamilySearch (The Church of Jesus Christ of Latter-Day Saints), https://familysearch.org [accessed 1 March 2023].
[18] 5 Aug. 1736, 1, pp. 55–6; 21 Jun. 1738, 2, p. 26; 19 Aug. 1736, 1, p. 59; 4 Sep. 1736, 1, p. 62; 20 Sep. 1736, 1, p. 69.
[19] 25 Jul. 1736, 1, p. 27.
[20] H. Scott (ed.), *Fasti Ecclesiae Scoticanae*, new edn (7 vols, Edinburgh, 1915–28), vol. 1, p. 345.
[21] 23 Oct. 1736, 1, p. 103.
[22] Eli[z]abeth [West], *Memoirs, or, Spiritual Exercises of Elisabeth Wast* (Edinburgh, 1724); Katherine Ross [Collace], *Memoirs, or Spiritual Exercises of Mistress Ross* (Edinburgh, 1735); edited version in *Women's Life Writing*, pp. 39–94.

Presbyterian establishment was splintering. In 1733, the Kirk split over the issue of patronage, and the newly formed Secession Church performed renewals of the Solemn League and Covenant and part of the National Covenant. Brown was not a seceder, but she did condemn the Church of Scotland for abandoning the covenants. She recorded conversations with God in which the latter stated that he would rule over Scotland 'with fury', and declared that 'A Gospell ministry is now made contemptible in [Edinburgh] … There are but few faithfull Ministers in it, who speak my mind fully'.[23]

Brown's religious experiences were conventional in some respects. She had undergone the typical Calvinist conversion process, described to her by God as the 'day of Espousals, when I first overcame your heart with love'.[24] Her spiritual journey thereafter was characterised by rapid fluctuation between joy and despair, a pattern memorably described by West as 'up the Brae, and down the Brae'.[25] Her most detailed diary entries focused on communion, the importance of which is signalled by a record at the beginning of Drummond's diary: 'RB.s comunion sabaths in this book. Westkirk … Cannongate … Libbertoun … Leith … Burntisland … Edinburgh … S. Leith'. In line with other spiritual diarists, Brown was haunted by St Paul's warning about the danger of taking communion unworthily (1 Cor. 11:27), and often deliberated painstakingly over whether she ought to attend: 'Dare I go to a comunion table when I see my self altogether void of grace? My going, would be a mocking of God.'[26]

While these elements are typical of spiritual writing, Brown's diary was unorthodox in various ways. She described visionary experiences:

> I saw [Christ] in his agony in the garden, sweating great drops of blood, I saw him betrayed by Judas, bound by the souldiers, Condemned by Pilate, scourged, crowned with thorns, buffeted and spit upon, Forsaken by all his followers and led away to be crucified … I heard his dying groans, and saw him laid in a cold grave.[27]

---

[23] 4 Oct. 1737, 1, p. 339; 12 Dec. 1736, 1, pp. 133-4; see also 12 Sep. 1736, 1, p. 67; 19 Jun. 1737, 1, p. 256.

[24] 7 Oct. 1736, 1, p. 76.

[25] [West], *Memoirs*, p. 77. See M.D. Brock, *Satan and the Scots: The Devil in Post-Reformation Scotland, c.1560–1700* (Abingdon, 2016), pp. 97–124; D.B. Hindmarsh, *The Evangelical Conversion Narrative: Spiritual Autobiography in Early Modern England* (Oxford, 2005), pp. 215–16; J. McCallum, *Exploring Emotion in Reformation Scotland: The Emotional Worlds of James Melville, 1556–1614* (Cham, 2022), pp. 25–41; Yeoman, 'Heart-Work', pp. 198–204.

[26] 6 Mar. 1737, 1, p. 190. Other examples include [West], *Memoirs*, pp. 28, 79, 81–2, 155; Elizabeth Blackadder, 'A Short Account of the Lord's Way of Providence towards me in my Pilgrimage Journeys', in *Women's Life Writing*, p. 391; Cairns, *Memoirs*, p. 103; Mistress Rutherford, 'Mistress Rutherford's Conversion Narrative', ed. David Mullan, *Miscellany of the Scottish History Society XIII* (Edinburgh, 2004), p. 159. See L.E. Schmidt, *Holy Fairs: Scotland and the Making of American Revivalism*, 2nd edn (Grand Rapids, MI, 2001), esp. pp. 32–41.

[27] 1 Aug. 1736, 1, p. 36.

On a happier occasion she saw the Lord on his throne of glory, praised by saints and angels, and her own family in 'Robes of Glory'.[28] There was a handful of individuals – mostly women – who publicised prophecies in Restoration Scotland, but after Presbyterianism was re-established, religious authorities typically discouraged visionary activity. Jonet Fraser, a Dumfries visionary who described a glorious visit to Heaven in 1684–5, was compelled in 1691 to confess to her presbytery that she had 'pretended to prophecying and seeing of visions and that she had sinned greatly in being deluded by Satan'.[29] Elizabeth Cairns (1685–1741), a working-class woman who mostly recorded her memoirs in the 1730s, wrote of obtaining 'a distinct view of the sufferings of Christ' and 'a view of the promised land'. However, an 'experienced Christian' scolded her: 'sensible manifestations were reserved for eternity'.[30]

Brown's interactions with God were yet more questionable. Typically, God communicated with diarists by causing them to recall pertinent passages of scripture, or directing ministers to deliver particularly apt sermons. The biblical language was proof against diabolic trickery.[31] Cairns noted at one point: 'I sought that the Lord would shew me his mind conform to his word, for fear of a delusion.'[32] God frequently courted Brown in the impassioned language of the Song of Songs: 'Thou art all fair, My love, and there is no spot in the[e]' (Song 4:7); 'Thou hast Ravished my heart, My sister, My spouse' (Song 4:9).[33] However, he also addressed her more freely. He promised her that 'I will make you a wonder to your self and to others, I will let out so much of my love to you', and that 'I'le tell you as much of the secrets of my providence as ever I told a creature.'[34] When Brown was assailed by religious doubts, he became 'A Smiting and a frowning Beloved'. He protested that 'You never believe a word that I say', and bemoaned her inconstancy: 'Who but a God, whose patience is infinite, would have born with you?'[35] He underlined that it was only a point of principle that kept him from punishing her more severely: 'were it not That I regard my own honour and Glory which is so much concerned in my making out my promises to you, I would

---

[28] 25 Jul. 1736, 1, pp. 27-8.
[29] L. Yeoman, 'Away with the Fairies', in L. Henderson (ed.), *Fantastical Imaginations: The Supernatural in Scottish History and Culture* (Edinburgh, 2009), pp. 29–46, at p. 40.
[30] Cairns, *Memoirs*, pp. 36, 47. See also Schmidt, *Holy Fairs*, pp. 145–53.
[31] See Hindmarsh, *Evangelical Conversion Narrative*, pp. 206–8; Mullan, *Women's Life Writing*, pp. 17–18; Webster, 'Writing to Redundancy', at p. 49.
[32] Cairns, *Memoirs*, p. 94.
[33] For example, 4 Jul. 1736, 1, p. 16; 23 Jul. 1736, 1, p. 25; 11 Jan. 1737, 1, p. 152; 25 Jun. 1737, 1, p. 261; 19 Jul. 1736, 1, p. 23; 24 Jul. 1737, 1, p. 282. On the erotic elements in women's spiritual writing, see S.M. Dunnigan, 'Spirituality', in G. Norquay (ed.), *The Edinburgh Companion to Scottish Women's Writing* (Edinburgh, 2012), pp. 11–21, at pp. 14–17.
[34] 10 Oct. 1736, 1, p. 80; 31 Jul. 1736, 1, p. 34.
[35] 19 Dec. 1736, 1, p. 137; 10 Jul. 1736, 1, p. 18.

never speak more to you, But glorify my Justice in your eternal damnation'.[36] In the end, he always came back to avowals of love, explaining on one occasion that 'the more vile and undeserving you are, The more The riches and freedom of my love will be seen in loving the like of you'.[37] Brown spoke with 'more freedom, then I could have done to A friend' in their conversations, and did not hesitate to 'complain' and 'argue' about the hardships befalling herself and Drummond.[38]

Sometimes Brown's conversations with God took a more practical bent. God was not above courting her, avowing on one occasion that 'If all the fulness of a God will satisfy you, Then all is Yours, I can refuse you nothing That you ask.'[39] She declined his offers to give her proofs of his devotion, but allowed him to tell her secrets, and welcomed his promise to 'hold comunion with you about every thing that concerns you, Both about your self and others'.[40] He gave her advance warning of the deaths of two acquaintances, and promised the deliverance of numerous others.[41] One member of Brown's social circle was Jane (or Jean) Campbell of Aberuchill, the wife of Drummond's colleague Sir James Campbell. Brown and Jane Campbell were often at odds, and God could be relied upon to take Brown's side. When Brown complained that 'Mrs C.' had 'taken up a new pett' at her and refused to see her, he vowed that 'I will speak more fully to you about all her concerns then ever, and I will make her acknowledge that she has wronged you'.[42]

Brown did not only become God's confidant; she also emerged as a saviour of Scotland. It was common for spiritual diarists in the Covenanting tradition to pray for the Presbyterian Church of Scotland. Cairns again went further than most of her fellow spiritual writers. She explained that in one prayer session 'I felt a power, that made me wrestle and plead with sovereignty, and would not quit the poor church of Scotland'. She then heard something like a voice, which said 'Come hither, and I will shew you things to come'. She wondered whether to ask God about the Church of Scotland, but hesitated, reflecting that the Lord had not revealed his mind to 'any of the female sex' since the times of the Old Testament. However, the Lord proceeded to show her (by unspecified means) 'that both church and land were in great danger, yet he would bring about a deliverance'.[43] Brown's dealings on behalf of the Scottish nation were yet more explicit. She made frequent prayers for the 'poor land', crying in one diary entry 'No matter what become of all my concerns if A Redeemer but abide in Scotland!'[44] God was swayed by Brown's pleas, declaring that 'I am not able to withstand the voice of thy weeping

---

[36] 25 Sep. 1737, 1, p. 329.
[37] 10 Sep. 1738, 2, p. 104.
[38] 20 Nov. 1736, 1, p. 119; for example, 26 Jan. 1737, 1, p. 181; 23 Jan. 1737, 1, p. 179.
[39] 10 Oct. 1736, 1, p. 80.
[40] 11 Jan. 1737, 1, p. 151; 16 Apr. 1737, 1, p. 203; 5 Dec. 1736, 1, p. 127.
[41] 13 Aug. 1736, 1, p. 57; 7 Apr. 1737, 1, p. 201.
[42] 23 Jul. 1736, 1, p. 25.
[43] Cairns, *Memoirs*, pp. 92 and 94.
[44] 12 Dec. 1736, 1, p. 133.

supplications', and later vowing: 'If you ask my abiding in Scotland while Sun and Moon endures, I'le do it.'[45]

Within the world of Brown's diary, she shines as a figure of exceptional spiritual eminence. Her diary exemplifies the impossibility of realising the ideal of the subsumed self within spiritual writing. In the practice of self-loathing there was often an assertion of individuality; diarists found themselves not only sinful, but the most sinful of all mortals. Dictating in 1729, the celebrated Covenanter Helen Alexander declared: 'O what a fearful sight got I of myself! that I thought there was none upon the earth like me, and wondered that I was out of hell'.[46] Brown wrote in very similar terms: 'What a wonder it is that I am out of hell! Did ever, Mortal, do, as I do!'[47] Furthermore, spiritual diaries generally evidenced their authors' standing as members of the elect. Steven Rendall has argued that no single, consistent self can emerge from a diary; it is a genre of fragments and discontinuities, in which the entries speak with a plurality of voices.[48] Brown described rapid fluctuations in her own identity: one moment she considered herself a saint, the next she was convinced of her own damnation. However, the diary brought an overarching coherence to her experiences. While Brown as a character was in doubt as to her spiritual standing, Brown as the author clarified. In an entry from October 1736, Brown described dropping to her knees and begging to be shown if her experiences were not of the Lord, as 'I was fully content to drop all of them, and hence forward, never to open my mouth, on the subject, of Religion'. She was promptly assailed by 'a flood of Blasphemous thoughts'. Recording this experience, she might have interpreted the thoughts as a sign that she was indeed deluded. Instead, she determined that they were pressed upon her by 'the enemy'. The Lord, meanwhile, continued to avow his 'Truth and Faithfullness'.[49] Thus, although Brown expressed doubts about her religious status on a near daily basis, her written work arranged these doubts into a schema of diabolic attacks, preserving for her a consistent identity as a chosen vassal of God.

Some women who used religion to navigate marginality did so by assuming quasi-masculine roles. Female prophets – especially Quakers – spoke with authoritative voices modelled on biblical patriarchs.[50] Brown's religious reflections were couched in a language of emotion and supplication, and awash with avowals of love and metaphors about matrimony with God. This

---

[45] 1 Aug. 1736, 1, pp. 37–8.
[46] Helen Alexander, 'Passages in the Life of Helen Alexander', in *Women's Life Writing*, p. 192.
[47] 30 Jun. 1736, 1, p. 13.
[48] S. Rendall, 'Review: On Diaries', *Diacritics*, 16:3 (1986), 56–65, at 60–4.
[49] 3 Oct. 1736, 1, p. 75.
[50] See E. Bouldin, *Women Prophets and Radical Protestantism in the British Atlantic World, 1640–1730* (Cambridge, 2015), p. 62; DesBrisay, 'Lilias Skene', at pp. 168–9; D. Watt, *Secretaries of God: Women Prophets in Late Medieval and Early Modern England* (Cambridge, 1997), p. 123; P. Mack, *Visionary Women: Ecstatic Prophecy in Seventeenth-Century England* (Berkeley, CA, 1992), pp. 172–8.

style was not uniquely feminine. Covenanting men's spiritual writing was often similarly emotional and impassioned, even to the point of framing God as a husband.[51] It is notable, nevertheless, that Brown assumed a place of religious authority without adopting an overtly masculine voice. Her writing probed at gendered constraints, rather than transcending them altogether. This point is further evidenced when we consider Brown's engagement with broader society. In a study of religion and early modern women's writing, Diane Willen suggests that 'women found in godliness an ideology of sorts which inherently mixed public and private: they could be saints and affect the state in that capacity long before they were to become citizens'.[52] Brown framed herself as a defender of Scotland's Covenanting past. But while she wrote of God's anger at the Church, she made no comment on specific disputes or political milestones. Despite her doubts about whether God would speak to women, Cairns reflected readily on the detrimental effects of the Union, Act of Toleration, patronage, and the oath of abjuration.[53] Brown was comparatively reticent. She may have imagined – as did Drummond – that her work might one day be published, but in practice it offered her no meaningful pathway to political involvement.

Nor does her writing seem to have significantly impacted her dealings with her social circle. God at one point observed that 'my love to you has been very great, So that others have been made to observe it, And to wonder at my setting such marks of my favour on you as I have done'.[54] However, there is little evidence that anybody except Drummond was significantly impacted by Brown's spiritual journey. When she thanked God for a particularly inspiring sermon by Neil McViccar, he suggested that she tell the minister, explaining that he was 'sunk, many atime with the fear that his ministry be not blest, and what know ye but it may be a mean of strengthning his hands'.[55] Brown did not dare do so, however, and ended by asking Drummond to relay the message. On another occasion, God informed her:

> I have A Message to send you ... to JP, to tell her, she is upsitten, and backslidden in my way, and I am angry at her. The time has been when she prized oppurtunity's for prayer, both alone, and with others, and Now when she has time to get both, she slights them, And if she go on in this way, I will deprive her of both.

Brown wrote: 'I came off my knees in great perplexity. I could not resolve to tell it her, I knew she had the pett at me, and would not take it well.' After

---

[51] See McCallum, *Exploring Emotion in Reformation Scotland*, pp. 25–41; Mullan, *Narratives of the Religious Self in Early-Modern Scotland*, pp. 309–59; Yeoman, 'Heart-work', pp. 171–207.
[52] D. Willen, 'Religion and the Construction of the Feminine', in A. Pacheco (ed.), *A Companion to Early Modern Women's Writing* (Oxford, 2002), pp. 22–39, at p. 36.
[53] See Mullan, 'Scottish Women's Religious Narrative', at p. 187.
[54] 25 Sep. 1737, 1, p. 330.
[55] 6 Aug. 1738, 2, p. 98.

days of wavering, she finally passed on the communication. The best she could say of the outcome was 'she said nothing to break me'.[56] Brown's diary might have allowed her to develop her own sense of her identity and social role, but the only appreciable broader impact stemmed from her influence on Drummond.

Relationship with Drummond

George Drummond was educated in Edinburgh, and became accountant-general of excise in 1707. He remained in public service throughout his life, with brief forays into trade. He was first appointed lord provost in 1725, and served another five terms later in life.[57] The period covered by his diary (24 June 1736 to 26 November 1738) was a difficult one. His second wife had died in 1732, and he was providing for ten children. He had run afoul of Archibald Campbell, 1st earl of Ilay (1682–1761), the foremost Scottish politician at the time. When Drummond's diary commenced, he was working as a commissioner on the board of customs. In June 1737, his salary was cut from £1,000 to £500 at Ilay's behest, and in October 1737 he was fired altogether, leaving him convinced that he would be 'immediately torn to peices' by his creditors.[58] The following January he was appointed as a commissioner of the board of excise, with pay backdated to October, but he continued to declaim that 'I am on the brink of ruin, and no hope of deliverance'.[59] His own conversion experience had taken place when he was seventeen, and he continued to chase the sensation of being 'sensibly breathd on' by God, but his financial difficulties inspired a crisis of faith.[60] When he heard that he might be fired he wrote: 'Is there anything real in Religion?' On the day of his dismissal he railed: 'how can you have any dependence on any promise in the bible!'[61] Although he acknowledged that Abraham, Joseph, and David might have had greater trials, he added that 'I knew no other whose tryals were darker.'[62]

The diaries give no indication as to how Drummond and Brown became acquainted. When Drummond began writing they had known each other for a few years. Brown frequently rode over to Drummond's home to join his family for their evening prayers, or spent time with him in his room. Her

---

[56] 27 May 1738, 2, p. 71; 30 May 1738, 2, p. 71.
[57] See A. Murdoch, 'Drummond, George (1687–1766), Accountant-General of Excise in Scotland and Local Politician', *ODNB*, https://doi.org/10.1093/ref:odnb/8065 [accessed 1 March 2023].
[58] 8 Oct 1737, 1, p. 296.
[59] 21 Jun. 1738, 2, p. 26.
[60] 26 Jul. 1736, 1, p. 9.
[61] 7 Oct. 1737, 1, p. 295; 13 Oct. 1737, 1, p. 298.
[62] 9 Oct. 1736, 1, p. 53.

standing in his life is evidenced by a prayer he made during private worship in July 1736, when he accepted God's covenant 'for my self, for RB, for all my children, for all their seed, throughout all their Generations, for my mother, for all my family, and for all my friends, by nature and grace'.[63] He felt that it was 'no small honour' to transcribe 'the words of the Most high to a poor Earth worm', and speculated that her diary would be seen more widely after their deaths.[64] Although he acknowledged that his friends would think him mad for the faith he placed in Brown, he had himself become quite convinced of her spiritual eminence.[65] On 6 December 1736 he explained:

> For the first two or 3 years of our acquaintance it was the habitual exercise of my mind, To examine, if what she got was really from The Lord. The many outmakings of The Lords word both about my self and others, which I have seen, hath put that matter past all doubt, what succeeds to it, is, What construction I am to put on the promises, and what am I to expect to see, in the outmaking of them.[66]

On 6 September 1738, he told himself: 'The Quakers are as high in their pretensions, And you are satisfyed, all theirs is delusion, May not all hers be so too?' However, he quickly dismissed the idea as coming from a 'hellish quarter'.[67] On 23 April 1737, he wrote: 'I can solidly believe every thing else she has from The Lord, but what relates to my self, as to that, I am fully convinced that its from The Lord, But then I dread there may be something: with Respect to its accomplishment … which I silently leave as a mistery'.[68] On 26 September 1738, he mourned:

> while I am writing either in or from RB.s book my attention is fixed, and spiritual things employ my mind, but at present I don't feel the smallest degree of hope taking place in my soul that ever I shall see any one promise about me, in it, made out.[69]

But Drummond was deeply invested in his faith in Brown, and for the most part he found the friendship to be 'exceedingly strengthning and confirming to me, about the truth and reality of Religion'.[70]

Drummond related all of his affairs to Brown, and showed her letters from his creditors.[71] She prayed to God for Drummond's well-being almost every day, and received hundreds of promises of divine aid, blessings for each of Drummond's children, and a few assurances that Ilay would be damned to

---

[63] 4 Jul. 1736, 1, pp. 2-3.
[64] 26 Jul. 1737, 1, p. 233; 7 Nov. 1736, 1, p. 88; 2 May 1737, 1, p. 174.
[65] 9 Aug. 1737, 1, p. 287.
[66] 6 Dec. 1736, 1, p. 94.
[67] 6 Sep. 1738, 2, p. 37.
[68] 23 Apr. 1737, 1, p. 172.
[69] 26 Sep. 1738, 2, p. 161.
[70] 2 May 1737, 1, p. 174.
[71] 17 Jan. 1738, 2, p. 3.

eternal suffering.[72] God frequently told Brown that 'I will make you bear [Drummond's] burdens', and on one occasion declared: 'I can deny you nothing that you ask. If you ask Honour, Power, and Riches, for your friend, I'le give it'. Sadly for Drummond, she asked only that God should cleanse her of sin.[73] Drummond questioned whether he should buy a ticket for the Thames Bridge lottery, to allow the Lord to 'work a compleat deliverance for me'. God rejected the idea, but did recommend that Drummond seek the post of commissioner of the excise.[74] He also advised on a vexatious aunt of Drummond's who had inserted herself into the household. Drummond wanted her gone, but the woman had nowhere else to go, and he found that 'I cannot say a hard thing to her, her distress would lead me to comfort her'.[75] Brown was less concerned; the message she relayed from the Lord was: 'cast out this bond woman. 21 Gen. 10. There is an accursed thing in the midst of thee O Israel'.[76] Drummond wrote the next day that this command cleared his way – although in practice he continued to struggle to expel the aunt.[77]

Brown and Drummond typically referred to one another by initials, or as 'my friend'. As Katie Barclay has explored, the language of friendship was adopted by married couples from the 1720s, and the term implied a considerable intimacy between Drummond and Brown.[78] Drummond recorded that the possibility of marriage was first hinted at by God on 2 December 1734, perhaps indicating the existence of an earlier diary.[79] By 1736, God was not so much hinting as assuming. In July of that year, Brown relayed a vision in which God described the happiness that she and Drummond would later enjoy, and showed her their future children in a glorified state:

> So shall his seed be, And your seed, By him, are among that Number, I'le make you, mutual blessings to one another, and bring you together with much of my presence, and A Remarkable Blessing. All that ever you have enjoyed, is Nothing to what, Both, shall Enjoy, when, Together.

He added that their children would include men of God and men of great renown, and would be blessed with uncommon gifts, honour, and riches.[80] Drummond acknowledged that 'I view RB. as my partner by Gods designation and appointment, she is therefore my choice'. However, he was waiting for God to make the marriage a 'reasonable measure' by clearing their way

---

[72] 26 Jun. 1737, 1, p. 263; 23 Dec. 1736, 1, p. 141; 19 Jul. 1737, 1, p. 274; 10 Oct. 1737, 1, p. 348.
[73] For example, 23 Jul. 1736, 1, p. 25 and 1 May 1737, 1, p. 212; 1 Aug. 1736, 1, p. 38.
[74] 12 Jul. 1736, 1, p. 5; 25 Jul. 1736, 1, p. 28; 17 Oct. 1737, 1, p. 352.
[75] 16 May 1737, 1, p. 216; 3 Aug. 1737, 1, p. 234.
[76] 26 Jun. 1737, 1, p. 264.
[77] 27 Jun. 1737, 1, p. 225.
[78] K. Barclay, *Love, Intimacy and Power: Marriage and Patriarchy in Scotland, 1650–1850* (Manchester, 2011), pp. 134–6.
[79] 20 Sep. 1736, 1, p. 49.
[80] 25 Jul. 1736, 1, p. 27.

on the financial front.[81] The delay did not distress him. On 13 August 1738, he reflected:

> Were lust suffered to be my tryal, at the rate it sometimes has been, my present situation which is – The Lords having pointed out RB. for my partner, and making it utterly unreasonable for us to think of uniting now – yea, putting the most distant prospect of the time when, quite out of view, would create great uneasiness. But Blessed be God, he has heard prayer and answered it with respect to this, for I see her every day with no more desire, then if we were of the same sex, so it has been for two years past. Thus blessed be his name we converse together in a holy innocence.[82]

If this boded ill for Brown, there was worse to come. On 16 October 1738, a friend of Drummond's called Mrs Fenton suggested that he should remarry. She had in mind a widow, Hannah Parson, whose estate would bring an end to Drummond's financial woes. Drummond was doubtful: 'I dare not make one step towards deliverance … unless the Lord opens my way.'[83] On 22 October, he owned: 'Its true an agreeable partner, bringing great relief to me in my present overwhelming distresses … is a thing much to be desired'. However, he reminded himself that the Lord had pointed out another partner, and it would be 'ridiculous' to give any consideration to Mrs Fenton's proposal.[84] Brown seems to have agreed with this judgement. On 26 October, Drummond noted that 'somethings RB had [from the Lord] on the 22th about this marriage affair cools me to it, it is dropt out of my mind'.[85]

However, Mrs Fenton struck upon a particularly effective method of persuasion. On 22 November, she told Drummond that she had prayed about the matter, and heard 'What do you know if this womans money is not given to her, to be a Blessing to him, and, If he is not to be a blessing to her by being the means of her conversion?' Drummond consented to meet with Parson the next day, and found 'nothing disagreeable either in her manner or person'.[86] On 25 November, he wrote: 'tho this marriage would probably relieve me out of these distresses, yet, however desireable that would be, upon looking into my heart, I find I dare not take one step in it till I can see the Lord calling me to it'.[87] Besides a few lines from the next morning about how his 'mind was calm' in prayer, this was the final entry in his own diary, and his transcription of Brown's stops on 24 September.[88] Drummond and Parson were married in January 1739. It was a short-lived union: Parson died in February 1742. Drummond's fourth and final marriage took place in 1755, to a Quaker called

---

[81] 24 Jul. 1737, 1, p. 232.
[82] 20 Sep. 1736, 1, p. 49; 13 Aug. 1738, 2, p. 35.
[83] 16 Oct. 1738, 1, p. 165.
[84] 22 Oct. 1738, 1, p. 166.
[85] 26 Oct. 1738, 1, p. 167.
[86] 22 Nov. 1738, 2, p. 169; 23 Nov. 1738, 2, p. 169.
[87] 25 Nov. 1738, 2, p. 170.
[88] [26 Nov. 1738], 2, p. 170.

Elizabeth Green. Drummond's diary scorned the 'pretensions', 'delusion', and 'Enthusiasm' of Quakers. Perhaps he grew more tolerant with time, or decided that a bit of delusion was forgivable in someone with a £20,000 fortune.[89] Brown's brother Ebenezer became minister of Penicuik in 1745 under the patronage of John Clerk of Penicuik, a connection possibly facilitated by Drummond, who had worked for Clerk himself.[90] But if he had any further dealings with Rachel Brown, they are not recorded. She thus disappears from the historical record.

In the seventeenth century, it was possible for women to get involved in negotiating marriage contracts. This changed in the eighteenth century, as part of a growing distaste for 'mercenary' marriage and a shift towards idealising marriages based on romantic love. Katie Barclay argues that this development 'silenced' women during the courtship process.[91] Brown's diary gave her a means of challenging this marginalisation. The suggestion of marriage came originally from her pen. So, too, did suggestions to better Drummond's financial situation by casting out his aunt and seeking a post on the board of excise. This is not to suggest that Brown fabricated her conversations with God. She doubtless believed that the Lord inspired her thoughts and dreams, and guided her wishes when it came to Drummond. She interpreted her own desires through a religious lens, and found in religion a justification for expressing them, even to a man of higher social standing. And yet, her efforts were ultimately in vain. While Drummond wrote of his faith in Brown's communications, he hesitated in practice to follow the divine guidance she relayed. It is perhaps unfair to say that worldly considerations prevailed for Drummond; he certainly comforted himself with the reflection that, after all, a marriage to Mrs Fenton might be God's will. But it is clear that religious imperatives alone could not override his prudence or practicality.

Conclusion

The patriarchal structure of the Kirk notwithstanding, religion offered women opportunities to negotiate marginality. Spiritual union with God was a rebirth, and permitted women to reenvisage their social roles. Within her diary Brown became a blessing to her friends and to the local minister, a heaven-sent helpmeet for Drummond, and the driving force behind the deliverance of Scotland's Church. She constructed her identity in relation to the male figures of God and Drummond, but was by no means passive herself. She advised Drummond and 'bore his burdens' as an equal, or as one more advanced in grace. She also effectively proposed to him, defying the usual constraints of courtship. Her curious relationship with God demonstrates the

---

[89] 6 Sep. 1738, 2, p. 37.
[90] NRS, CH2/297/33, Penicuik Kirk Session: Appointment of Minister.
[91] Barclay, *Love, Intimacy and Power*, p. 95.

potential for idiosyncrasy within a genre often considered formulaic: the deity was an assiduous lover to Brown, eager to please and allegedly unable to deny her wishes.

Brown's identity as formulated through her writing did not always align with her identity as understood by her wider social circle, however. She hesitated to pass on God's guidance to her friends, and they do not seem to have appreciated the reprimands she did relay. At various points in the seventeenth century, devotion to the Presbyterian cause necessarily entailed political activism, but the situation was different by the 1730s. Brown's criticism of the direction of the Kirk was confined to her prayers, and she made no comment on the Secession or the religious disputes surrounding it. While she discussed Drummond's job prospects, there is no suggestion that she engaged in any serious way with the political world he inhabited. Eighteenth-century Scotland had its share of female prophets and mystics, and women were prominent in the evangelical revivals, but it was not until the nineteenth-century development of missionary work, philanthropic organisations, and Sunday schools that mainstream religion offered women a path to community leadership.[92] When it came to Drummond, Brown clearly had influence, but it could not outweigh the charms of a wealthy widow. For all her devotion, she remained unable to escape poverty. The persistent importance of religion within eighteenth-century society is not always sufficiently appreciated: for both Brown and Drummond, religion was a means of understanding their own thoughts and feelings, as well as determining their roles within their communities.[93] But however far her spiritual journey might have elevated Brown in her own perception, its practical impact remained limited. The marginalisation of women – especially poor women – was encoded in eighteenth-century social structures, and could not be escaped solely by reimagining the self.

---

[92] On the nineteenth-century developments, see Brown, 'Religion', p. 97; W.W.J. Knox, *Women and Scottish Society, 1700–2000* (London, 2021), pp. 198–204; A. Stott, 'Women and Religion', in H. Barker and E. Chalus (eds), *Women's History: Britain 1700–1850: An Introduction* (Abingdon, 2005), pp. 100–23, at pp. 110–14. For an argument about how religion might draw eighteenth-century women into the 'public sphere', see K. Glover, *Elite Women and Polite Society in Eighteenth-Century Scotland* (Woodbridge, 2011), pp. 134–8.

[93] On historians' tendency to downplay the importance of religion, see D. Allan, 'Protestantism, Presbyterianism and National Identity in Eighteenth-Century Scotland', in T. Claydon and I. McBride (eds), *Protestantism and National Identity: Britain and Ireland, c.1650–c.1850* (Cambridge, 1998), pp. 182–205, esp. at pp. 182–3 and 193–6.

12

Queering the Castalian: James VI and I and 'Narratives of Blood'

Lucy R. Hinnie

This work began life as a call to arms for the discussion of bisexuality in the era of James VI and I. In the process of development, it has come to be a consideration of early modern Scottish scholarship itself, and the ways in which the truth can be obfuscated, made wilfully opaque, implied in the margins. It is an examination of the ways in which marginalised histories are maintained in the status quo through decades of scholarship which elides the obvious, shies away from the reality of lived queer experiences, and dares not to label or name that which is discusses.

Throughout this work, the term 'queer' will be utilised. In considering the use of this term, the following definition becomes useful:

> Queer works as an umbrella term for a range of sexual and gender identities that are not 'straight,' or at least not normative. In a second sense, queer functions more as a verb than a noun, signaling a critical stance ... skeptical of existing identity categories and more interested in understanding the production of normativity and its queer companion, nonnormativity.[1]

When we erase queerness, we do more than just flatten our historical understanding. In the case of James, we eliminate the potential for consideration of the influence of his parents, Mary, Queen of Scots and Lord Darnley. We further limit the potential for deeper analysis of the complex and stylistically nuanced work of poets such as Alexander Montgomerie. We deny the full lived experience of the people who shape these narratives. We wilfully push to the margins.

Indeed, there is an ever-present pushback against the retrospective labelling of concepts such as homosexual or indeed bisexual. Michael B. Young states in *James VI and the History of Homosexuality* that 'strictly speaking, in early modern Britain, no one was a homosexual because the word, and arguably the connotations that went with it, did not exist'.[2] As such, at no point does Young's initial study of James, one of the only studies in which James' sexuality is the focus rather than a hushed sidenote, name James as a

---

[1] S.B. Somerville, 'Introduction', in S.B. Somerville (ed.), *The Cambridge Companion to Queer Studies* (Cambridge, 2020), pp. 1–14, at p. 2.
[2] M.B. Young, *James VI and I and the History of Homosexuality* (Basingstoke, 2000), p. 3.

homosexual. Nor, it should be said at the outset, will this chapter. Instead of focusing on the labels of homosexual or bisexual, I wish to reclaim and instate the concept of queerness at the court of James and in his personal life. Previous accounts have rendered James as simply a homosexual man living in a time where this was understood within the acceptable norms of courtly society, while others have adhered to a strictly heterosexual understanding of his life.[3] In utilising the term and framework of queerness, particularly in relation to the literary culture of the period, a new understanding can be reached.

Queerness is a lived experience that transcends eras and epochs. It is both a retaliation and resistance to the norm. It can be argued that James' experience with his favourites, such as George Villiers, duke of Buckingham, was, in fact, the norm of his era, but the queerness I see within James' story abides in the stringent resistance to the scandal that encompassed his biological parents, and the way in which scholarship itself has flattened James' life to a state of unspoken queerness, silenced through emphasis on his rule, his politics, and his extant heirs rather than investigation or consideration of his relationships. His queerness has become, at best, a side note, which has remained unnamed in scholarship for years, and to this day carries a certain taboo. Young's work is vitally important, following in the lineage of Caroline Bingham[4] and David Bergeron,[5] not least because it devotes time to the discussion of the conception of sodomy, effeminacy, and manliness in the Jacobean era. Throughout scholarship, not only is James' queerness eradicated, but so too is that of his father, Henry, Lord Darnley. What is being discussed in this chapter is the 'influence of meaning' queerness holds for our understanding of James, of his parents, and of his court poets.

In the twenty years that have passed since Young's work, the articulation and discussion of queerness has changed. Young himself has revisited his work, 'reconsidering' a queer history of James in 2012.[6] The focus of his 'Reconsideration' is the material reality of whether or not James and his favourites engaged in sex. While this work is useful in surveying and contrasting the different approaches of historians, and, vitally, highlighting the regression of historical accounts which shy away from James' sexuality, further questions bear consideration. Wherein lies the influence of his mother, Mary, Queen of Scots, and her scandalous legacy? Does her legacy encourage a softening of the harder edges of James' life, a hangover from an era where stability of rule was keenly sought? How can Scottish literature of the late sixteenth and early seventeenth century aid our understanding of James' life and our relationship to queerness as modern readers? Moreover, what is the role of queerness not just in the rule of James VI and I but also in our accounts

[3] D.M. Bergeron, *King James & Letters of Homoerotic Desire* (Iowa City, IA, 1999).
[4] C. Bingham, *James I of England* (London, 1981).
[5] Bergeron, *King James*.
[6] M.B. Young, 'James VI and I: Time for a Reconsideration?', *Journal of British Studies*, 51:1 (2012), 540–67.

and understanding of this period in history and literature? It is time to bring these questions into sharper focus, and out of the margins.

Context

This essay is largely, and necessarily, speculative, exploring criticism directly addressing the queerness of James and his relationships to those around him. It is born of two aspects of research conducted in the early 2020s. Firstly, the curation and execution of a graduate seminar on medieval women, and the questions it raised about matrilinear inheritance and the erasure of women. Secondly, it draws upon the editing work undertaken on the Bannatyne Manuscript (c.1568), in which poems are curated to deftly circumvent the influence of Mary's reign. It is argued by Alasdair MacDonald, amongst others, that George Bannatyne's editing process was influenced strongly by the contemporary political climate in the 1560s.[7] Specifically, it is believed that the collection began as a series of love poems celebrating the marriage of Mary and Darnley, but upon the dissolution of the marriage, and the emerging disrepute of the queen, a sharp editorial shift was initiated by Bannatyne. References to the queen, to Catholicism, and to the royal marriage were removed and the collection expanded to become a generic and greatly expanded collection of Scots verse. This act of redaction and reshaping speaks to a need to conform to a stable and acceptable set of social norms, flattening and actively disregarding the scandal of the Marian reign, an act that wilfully pushes perceived sexual transgression to the margins.

Despite this deliberate curation, provocative remnants endure within the manuscript, such as a curious five-stanza poem attributed to James' father, Lord Darnley, examined within this chapter. This chapter then culminates in reflection on Montgomerie's work and style. The language deployed by Montgomerie and its relation to James' own poetic sensibilities adds further intrigue to a queer understanding of this Castalian exchange. Historical and critical context will be given, alongside an examination of two poems in particular: 'gif languor makis men licht' from the Bannatyne Manuscript, and Montgomerie's 'Solsequium', which alludes to and deploys outright much of James' favoured imagery of the crown.

Utilising the theoretical framework proposed in Rebecca Solnit's 2014 work *Men Explain Things To Me*, and offering close literary analyses of works by Darnley and Montgomerie, this chapter recontextualises our understanding of James' unique and abundant queerness, and the ways in which historical account, and to a large extent James himself, reframed his life in direct response to the scandal and turmoil of his family line.

---

[7] A.A. MacDonald, 'The Bannatyne Manuscript: A Marian Anthology', *Innes Review*, 37 (1986), 36–47.

JAMES VI AND I AND 'NARRATIVES OF BLOOD'

The Political Elimination of Matrilineal Influence

Eliminate your mother, then your two grandmothers, then your four great-grandmothers. Go back more generations and hundreds, then thousands disappear. Mothers vanish, and the fathers and mothers of those mothers. Even more lives disappear as if unlived until you have narrowed a forest down to a tree, a web down to a line. This is what it takes to construct a linear narrative of blood or influence of meaning.[8]

So says Rebecca Solnit in her essay 'Grandmother Spider', part of her seminal 2014 collection *Men Explain Things To Me*. If we follow Solnit's suggested thought experiment, and apply this prism of understanding to the life of James VI, we find key female figures from Scottish history instantaneously marginalised. Mary, Queen of Scots, his mother, Mary of Guise, his grandmother, and Margaret Tudor, his great-grandmother, would all disappear from criticism and historical accounts of his life. What Solnit invites is the dissolution of matrilineal influence, and in its absence, the realisation of its loss: the 'influence of meaning' we are denied. The centrality of matrilineal influence in James' life is evident, and we know from historical accounts that this matrilinear influence expanded beyond the ties of blood to his relationship with his godmother, Elizabeth I. In this sense, the impact of Mary's legacy not only on James' life, but also on the historical accounts thereof, is profound.

James is in many ways an unusual case for such a thought experiment, considering how much we know about the women who preceded him. This emphasises their absence even further, an inherent poignancy. The blood, influence, and meaning of his mother's life is threaded throughout his existence, whether through her scandalous legacy, or the lack of her bodily presence. It is the elephant in the room of his correspondence with Elizabeth I. I raise Solnit's idea at the fore because the connection between James and the blighted legacy of his mother is integral. It is integral in understanding the queerness of James' life and the tendency of historical accounts to flatten the queerness that pervades his cultural and personal legacy, and to consign it to the margins. After the turbulent reign of Mary, a wilful peace was sought, a union of crowns, a move towards a time of stability.

Michael B. Young asks 'how could a queer history of Britain not include James VI and I?'[9] Young goes on to offer a direct and comprehensive answer. Through a retrospective of historical criticism, with a particular focus on the twentieth century, Young's incisive analysis of the practice of queer erasure offers a distinctive mode of understanding the way in which James' sexuality has been commented upon, evaded, and explained away throughout critical discourse, giving breadth and context to the earlier work of historians, and dimension to queerness.

[8] R. Solnit, 'Grandmother Spider', in *Men Explain Things To Me* (London, 2014), p. 72.
[9] Young, 'James VI and I', at p. 540.

Most historians of an earlier era struggled with the subject of James's sexuality. Some treated it better than others, of course, but the general tendency was to make light of it, express disapproval (even repugnance), or dodge the subject altogether.[10] Attempts to desexualise the implications of historical accounts and to pigeonhole James into the category of homosexuality, heteronormativity, or asexuality serve to circumvent the discussion of what, to many, seems to be a blindingly obvious liminal queerness. Young's paper concludes with a searing analysis of the discourse between George Villiers, duke of Buckingham, and James regarding mutual masturbation and the king's 'large bountiful hand'. Bergeron does not shy from this topic, stating that 'by all sensible accounts, Buckingham became James's last and greatest lover'.[11]

Bergeron and Young are the most outspoken in their analysis and acceptance of James' queerness. With their works coming towards the end of the twentieth century and into the twenty-first, they follow in the footsteps of a number of varied critiques of James' life and work, and ride a wave of a more oblique understanding of James' sexuality. Indeed, in 2022's *Bad Gays: A Homosexual History*, James is afforded his own chapter. Taking their scholarship through an England-specific lens, Huw Lemmey and Ben Miller create a vivid picture of an England in political turmoil, and the ongoing impact of James' reign as one 'that shaped the growth of colonialism and capitalism'.[12] They trace this back to 'the ongoing intrigue of [James'] royal court, not least the fallout from his persistent, foolhardy habit of falling head over heels for beautiful, arrogant, and reckless favourites – for James had realised that the unease of the crown-wearing head could be eased significantly if it lay beside a beautiful young man'.[13]

Steven Reid's 2023 monograph *The Early Life of James VI: A Long Apprenticeship 1566–1585* addresses the historical lacunae of overt academic comment, stating in relation to James' relationship with Esmé Stuart that 'most political historians ... have avoided discussing the emotional and possible sexual dimensions to their relationship, or have couched this in ambiguous terms while simultaneously projecting a strong tone of disapproval'.[14] Reid rightly looks to the work of David Harris Willson in a footnote to this remark: in the 1950s Willson alluded to the pull of Esmé Stuart for the young king, couching his remarks by describing Stuart as 'fascinating but sinister',[15] symptomatic of the aforementioned queerphobia in literary criticism of the period. By 1981, Caroline Bingham was able to refer to James' sexual preferences, speaking openly not only about Esmé Stuart and

---

[10] Ibid., at p. 546.
[11] Bergeron, *King James*, p. 98.
[12] H. Lemmey and B. Miller, *Bad Gays: A Homosexual History* (London, 2022), p. 57.
[13] Ibid., p. 57.
[14] S.J. Reid, *The Early Life of James VI: A Long Apprenticeship, 1566–1585* (Edinburgh, 2023), p. 16.
[15] D.H. Willson, *King James VI and I* (London, 1956), p. 32.

the king's infatuation,[16] but also about James' keen interest in Robert Carr, earl of Somerset.[17] Somerset features strongly in Alan Stewart's 2003 work *The Cradle King*, alongside remarks on James' 'intimacy with D'Aubigny [Stuart]',[18] the 'passion and violence' of Buckingham in contrast to Somerset's 'gentle and fulfilling' companionship.[19] *The Cradle King*, therefore, sits alongside other early 2000s work, such as Jenny Wormald's extensive entry in the *Oxford Dictionary of National Biography*, in which Wormald concedes that 'at the very least James was bisexual'.[20] Pauline Croft is explicit in her discussion, spending time analysing the phoenix metaphor that would come to stand for Esmé Stuart in James' cultural lexicon, building on his 'passionate adolescent crush [which] permanently stamped his bourgeoning sexuality'.[21] A clear trajectory towards a widespread acceptance of James as a queer man, and attendant literary analyses, is evident, with Young's work the jewel in the crown. It is Reid, however, who gives the most measured and fluent interpretation of James' sexuality, when he says that 'it is impossible to extrapolate from such a limited range of material, when viewed objectively, whether this relationship [between James and D'Aubigny] can be categorised as familial, homosocial or sexual'.[22] Where Reid's work truly shines is in its willingness to accept, and indeed highlight, James as a 'pivotal figure in the history of early modern sexuality' despite this lack of material evidence.[23] It is here that the boundaries between literary scholarship and historical research can become porous and allow for generative thinking around queerness.

Young's research is pivotal in ensuring that discussion of James' sexuality is no longer evaded, but it was a short remark regarding James' own son, Charles I, which caught my eye. Young describes Charles in the 1630 as 'trying to lead an exemplary life in contrast to his father'.[24] I found myself considering the ways in which parental influence, and in the case of James maternal erasure, hold sway over the modes of living adapted by children defining themselves as other, breaking free of expectations. How does this relate not only to James' adversarial relationship to Mary's legacy, but furthermore to his association by blood to Lord Darnley?

James was the child of two scandalous figures, and also the man who would unite the crowns of Scotland and England. Of James' immediate family, Darnley is the figure whose personal history remains most nebulous. From the murky circumstances surrounding his death at Kirk O' Field, to the uncertainty and speculation about his part in the death of David Rizzio, Darnley's

[16] Bingham, *James I of England*, p. 3.
[17] Ibid., pp. 80–1.
[18] A. Stewart, *The Cradle King: A Life of James VI and I* (London, 2007), p. 54.
[19] Ibid., p. 314
[20] J. Wormald, 'James VI and I (1566–1625), King of Scotland, England, and Ireland', ODNB, https://doi.org/10.1093/ref:odnb/14592 [accessed 5 June 2024).
[21] P. Croft, *King James* (Basingstoke, 2003), p. 16.
[22] Reid, *Early Life of James VI*, p. 132.
[23] Ibid., p. 16.
[24] Young, 'James VI and I', p. 571.

voice is marginalised (he is, after all, rarely remembered as 'King Henry'), relegated to second fiddle to that of his wife, underscoring the way in which royal narratives will trump and subsume the personal history of those in their orbit, particularly in the case of spouses. Moreover, Darnley himself is subject to the same obfuscation and oversight regarding his sexuality. John Guy's *My Heart Is My Own* pulls no punches in its assessment of Darnley's sexuality:

> While Darnley was polished and urbane, his character was tainted by recklessness, sexual excess, pride and stupidity. He was almost certainly bisexual, as was the vogue of young hedonistic courtiers in France ... when Darnley was described as a 'great cock chick', the pun was intentional.[25]

Guy remains a lone voice in attesting to Darnley's sexuality. The lack of evidence to which Reid refers regarding James' sexuality is even more pronounced when it comes to Darnley.

Bingham is more circumspect in her assessment, in particular Darnley's relationship to David Rizzio, who Elizabeth I's ambassador Sir Thomas Randolph claimed Darnley shared a bed with.[26] In her work *Darnley: A Life of Henry Stuart*, Bingham focuses on the conflict that arose between Darnley and Rizzio: 'the person to whom [Rizzio] was most objectionable was his former patron the King, who saw Rizzio first as undermining his influence, but soon imagined him as alienating the affections of his wife'.[27] If Guy's account is to be believed, there are clearly many layers of intrigue into the motivations and jealousy of Lord Darnley, complicated further by the brutal murder of Rizzio at the Palace of Holyroodhouse in 1566. The chance to examine the poetic representation of Darnley, and arguably his own expression through poetic means, is a unique opportunity to analyse and consider his status as lover, suitor and husband to Queen Mary and the way in which this is performed through poetry.

The Literary Darnley

To see Darnley's name attached to a poem in the Bannatyne MS is a curious thing, yet in poem 305 we see a clear attribution of 'gif languor makis men licht' to 'king hary stewart'.[28] Darnley's name is not one traditionally associated with poetry, but this Bannatyne attribution was accepted by the late John MacQueen in his 1970 edition of 'Ballatis of Lufe'.[29] By 1980, this

---

[25] J.A. Guy, *My Heart is My Own: The Life of Mary Queen of Scotland* (London, 2004), p. 198.
[26] Ibid., p. 211.
[27] C. Bingham, *Darnley: A Life of Henry Stuart, Lord Darnley, Consort of Mary Queen of Scots* (London, 1995), p. 214.
[28] W.T. Ritchie (ed.), *The Bannatyne Manuscript: Writtin in Tyme of Pest* (4 vols, Edinburgh, 1928), vol. 3.
[29] J. MacQueen, *Ballatis of Luve* (Edinburgh, 1970), p. xxvi, p. 132.

was regarded as inaccurate by the Fox and Ringler facsimile.[30] Bannatyne of course cites Darnley as the author of this poem, which leads readers to believe this was a widely-held understanding, or at the very least one that was not outwardly contentious. Considering the arguments of MacDonald and MacQueen that the manuscript started as a collection of love poems for Mary and Darnley's marriage, it is curious that this poem did not bear deletion or reattribution in Bannatyne's later editing and collation.

Though the attribution is contentious, it is important that it exists: two provocative scenarios follow. One is that this is the true work of Darnley, and the other is that it is a performative, assumed voice from another poet. Both scenarios are valuable. If it is the true work of Darnley, as MacQueen accepts, we acquire unique and exciting insight into Darnley's performance of love. If, as Fox and Ringler argue, Darnley is not the author of this poem, we are invited to see the fascination in which Darnley and his plight were held by the poetic imagination of a contemporary. Someone has taken on the burden of representation in acting out these projected emotions, giving an idea of the impact and public perception of the Darnley and Mary scandals.

'Gif languor makis men licht' is, in many senses, a simple poem, numbered 305 in the Bannatyne. It is a lament of love's wondrous pain, the possession of the heart and the torturous ordeal of romantic love. The narrator prostrates himself before the female beloved, 'that lady pure / the well of womanheid'. The lack of her presence pains the narrator, who claims to be 'in sorrowfull siching soir / til tyme scho be present'. Though categorised as one of the poems celebrating love, 'in prayis of wemen' no less, inverted power dynamics dominate this poem.

MacQueen discusses the poem in the context of exploring the overt courtliness of certain Bannatyne lyrics. Darnley's complaint is part of a larger discussion in which MacQueen states that '[courtly love lyrics] make up the bulk of the fourth part of Bannatyne's anthology'.[31] In particular, he draws attention to the beginning of the final stanza:

> Schaw, schedule, to that sweet
> My pairt so permanent
> That no mirth quhill we meet
> sall cause me to be content.
>
> (ll. 33–36)[32]

The language of servitude and labour is not uncommon in courtly love poetry, yet when the identity of the poet is revealed as 'king hary stewart', discomfort is evoked. Knowing as we do his grisly end, the performance of devotion takes a turn that is, if not overtly sinister, at the very least deeply melancholic, with

---

[30] D. Fox and W.A. Ringler (eds), *The Bannatyne Manuscript: National Library of Scotland Advocates' MS.1.1.6* (London, 1980), p. xxxv.
[31] MacQueen, *Ballatis of Luve*, p. xxxvi.
[32] Ritchie, *Bannatyne Manuscript*, vol. 4.

something of a dramatic irony about it. As previously noted, the inclusion and exclusion of poems within the Bannatyne is the focus of many larger scale studies. The inclusion of this poem in the section 'prayis of wemen' can be read as an attempt to assuage any lingering Marian sympathies, heightening Darnley's status as a victim of feminine wiles.

As pointed out by Fox and Ringler, one other poem exists that is attributed to Darnley.[33] In the Devonshire Manuscript, folio 57r contains a short two-stanza verse in a beautiful hand.[34] This was likely appended to the manuscript in the early 1560s. It is quoted here in its entirety:

> My hope is yow for to obtaine,
> Let not my hope be lost in vaine.
> Forget not my paines manifoulde,
> Nor my meanynge to yow vntoulde.
> And eke withe dedes I did yow craue,
> Withe swete woordes yow for to haue.
> To my hape and hope condescend,
> Let not Cupido in vaine his bowe to bende.
> Nor vs two louers, faithfull, trwe,
> Lyke a bowe made of bowynge yewe.
> But nowe receaue by your industrye and art,
> Your humble seruant Hary Stuart.[35]

The short poem speaks of hope of love's success: 'let not Cupide in vain his bow to bende', 'for us two lovers, faithfull, true'. It is signed 'your humble servant Hary Stewart'. Read in tandem with the Bannatyne verse, there is a striking difference in its optimistic tone, standing in sorrowful juxtaposition to the more jaded narrator of 'langour'. Once again MacQueen's comments on courtliness come to light. If 'my hope' is the optimistic voice of a desirous lover, 'langour' is the language of complaint of one struggling in love's plight, the object of affection unattainable and the pain overwhelming. 'The nar the fyre I go / The grittar is my heit' (ll. 23–24) states the poet, emphasising the intensity of his desire and the temptation he feels towards his beloved.

Within the Bannatyne, the content of 'langour' dwells in the mournful, the speaker recounting images of his 'labour all in vane' (l. 20) and evokes language of oppression, absence and possession. The 'torture' of the speaker is drawn from the 'hairt lament' of love's experience. Conversely, the tone of the Devonshire verse is altogether optimistic, a shining tribute to the potential of romantic love and the optimism of a prosperous union. The courtly trajectory of Darnley's lived experience is easily mapped onto these verses,

---

[33] Fox and Ringler, *Bannatyne Manuscript*, p. xxxv.
[34] R. Siemens and C. Crompton, 'A Social Edition of the Devonshire MS (BL Add. MS 17492)', 2012, https://en.wikibooks.org/wiki/The_Devonshire_Manuscript.
[35] Ibid., fol. 57r.

something that has not been done yet in critical literature. What is evident is an emotional inheritance writ large for the court audience, a failing of romantic love, perhaps performative, but nonetheless enshrouded in scandal that endured.

Looking to Darnley's son, James' contribution to the poetic flourishing of the court is well documented. Central to James' court, scholars such as Jack argue, was his 'Castalian Band', a group comprised of Montgomerie, John Stewart of Baldynneis and Thomas and Robert Hudson and others.[36] Recent scholarship by Sebastiaan Verweij has contested the concept of the Castalian band, 'an inward-looking group of courtiers playing to the royal tune',[37] looking to the work of Priscilla Bawcutt to argue that the relationships of the so-called band were 'far more fragmented than Castalian literary activity might make believe'.[38] Irrespective of the nature of the group, the ongoing influence of his poetic interest was consolidated in the ethos of James' 1585 cultural manifesto 'Reulis and Cautelis', in which, Jack argues, '[James] visualize[d] a forward-looking renaissance in Scottish vernacular literature, led by him and centred in the Edinburgh court'.[39] His passion for poetry and culture is a lasting legacy of his reign.

In the practice described by Solnit as 'construct[ing] a linear narrative of blood or influence of meaning'[40] emerges the notion of James as the child of not one, but two poets. It is true, and poignant, that the title of poet is nebulous for both Mary and Darnley. The authorship of Mary's casket sonnets remains contentious,[41] and Darnley's poetic output is limited to the two attributions discussed above. Yet the influence of parental interest, this 'narrative of blood', adds a further dimension to our understanding of James.

The singularity of what he achieved in his reign sits alongside a bi-curiosity that extends beyond his sexuality. Both Scottish and English, VI and I, belonging to Elizabeth and also to Mary, both Darnley's and the queen's, the chimeric James is not easily hemmed into traditional categories of historical understanding. Yet his life has been flattened and robbed of this dimensionality in many accepted accounts of his existence, an act of queer erasure and marginalisation. In examining more closely these fleeting examples of 'hary Stewart' on the page, Darnley is pulled from his own obscurity, a victim of the greater Marian narrative, and adds a new dimension to our understanding of his son. Just as the scandal of Mary's life put pressure on the accepted narrative of James' reign to be one of peace and unity, so too

---

[36] R.D.S. Jack, *The Italian Influence on Scottish Literature* (Edinburgh, 1970), p. 54.
[37] S. Verweij, *The Literary Culture of Early Modern Scotland: Manuscript Production and Transmission, 1560–1625* (Oxford, 2016), p. 32.
[38] Ibid. P. Bawcutt, 'James VI's Castalian Band: A Modern Myth', *SHR*, 80:2 (2001), 251–9.
[39] Jack, *Italian Influence*, p. 54.
[40] Solnit, 'Grandmother Spider', p. 72.
[41] R. Smith, 'Reading Mary Stuart's Casket Sonnets: Reception, Authorship, and Early Women's Writing', *Parergon*, 29:2 (2012), 149–73.

did the emotive poetry and queerness of his father put unspoken pressure on James to live a life free of overt scandal.

Montgomerie's Sunflower

It is important at this point to note that the reluctance of criticism to engage with questions of queer desire is not limited to the field of Scottish history. Queer-focused studies of late medieval and early modern Scottish literature are scant, with the most notable exception being Evelyn Newlyn's 2004 work on the Maitland Quarto manuscript, in particular poem 38, arguing that the poem 'subtly employs rhetoric and conventions in veiled discourse that suggests not only that a woman is speaking of love for a woman, but also that [the poem] may have been written by a female poet'.[42] Though Newlyn proposed a new and transgressive methodology of reading poetry in the late medieval era, the time that has lapsed since her call to arms has seen little in the way of queer literary study specific to Older Scots material.

Newlyn's suggested methodology proposes that one should 'read against the culture' to identify and celebrate women poets.[43] I propose to take this further, and read against a culture of a system of homosocial 'favourite' relationships, to read through that matrilinear erasure, in order to uncover the radical queer potential therein. To revisit the work of Alexander Montgomerie within this context is not simply to seek a tangible revelation of homosexuality or erotic desire. To approach it in this way is both reductive and counterproductive. Examining Montgomerie's verse, considering the constraints of both queer and matrilinear erasure, sheds new light on how conflicted emotions are expressed. The liminal understanding of James' multiple identities, benefactor, poet, king, friend, and son of Mary, is negotiated in Montgomerie's work. Montgomerie himself is a poet who traversed both the Marian and Jacobean reigns. His Catholic sympathies within a Protestant court are well documented,[44] and result from Montgomerie's 'triple career as a soldier, courtier and poet',[45] a liminal state which Ronald Jack explores in some detail.[46] This struggle is reflected in his work. A handful of verses attributed to Montgomerie exist in the Bannatyne's fourth section, placing him temporally in the pre-James era, and emerging again as a key member of James' court.

---

[42] E. Newlyn, 'A Methodology for Reading Against the Culture: Anonymous, Women Poets and the Maitland Quarto MS (c.1586)', in E. Newlyn and S.M. Dunnigan (eds), *Women and the Feminine in Medieval and Early Modern Scottish Writing* (London, 2004), pp. 89–103, at p. 96.
[43] Ibid., p. 100.
[44] See R.J. Lyall, *Alexander Montgomerie: Poetry, Politics, and Cultural Change in Jacobean Scotland* (Tempe, AZ, 2005).
[45] R.D.S. Jack, *Alexander Montgomerie* (Edinburgh, 1985), p. 4.
[46] Jack, *Italian Influence*, pp. 4–6.

Jack describes Montgomerie's poetic approach as 'direct'[47] and having a 'simple sincerity',[48] adding a sense of earnestness to his poetry. Furthering Jack's work on Montgomerie, Sarah Dunnigan writes of the erotics and representation in the work of Montgomerie in her 2002 monograph *Eros and Poetry*. She states that 'love, above all for the king, entails sacrifice, and Montgomerie is the most willing and poignant of love's martyrs'.[49] Further to this, Dunnigan directly addresses the wilful erasure of queer subtext, noting that 'the delicate eroticisation of James within the Scottish Jacobean court has not [been recognised]'.[50] In the case of Montgomerie, there is a unique focus on what Dunnigan terms 'profane love poetry for the topoi of sovereignty'.[51] When queerness is no longer elided but actively analysed, in the vein of this scholarship, a richness compounds our understanding of the relationship between courtier and monarch.

A poem which bears further analysis is Montgomerie's 'Solsequium'.[52] The art of rule is euphemised in images of sun, flourishing flora, and planetary gods, emphasising the favoured imagery of James as Apollo or the sun itself.[53] Montgomerie's reference in line 20 to 'my lamp of licht, my Lady, and my love' would not be out of place in a traditional love poem. Here it serves in a narrative of larger, political devotion.

Throughout this poem a sense of transience, of mutability and change are writ large. Day and night, decay and growth, grief and joy co-exist on the page. The joy felt by the narrator is mutable and dependent on the presence of Apollo, the narrator pleading for sunset to delay:

> O happie day
> Go not auay
> Apollo stay
> Thy chair from going doun into the West.
>
> (ll. 49–51)[54]

The conflicted feelings behind Montgomerie's narrative voice are implicit. The problematic nature of his devotion to James are a likely source of this tension. Devotion to James and his rule is counterintuitive. How can such a viable, strong, and lauded ruler co-exist with this scandalous matrilinear inheritance, and with Montgomerie's own chequered past with religion?

---

[47] Ibid., p. 90.
[48] Ibid., p. 110.
[49] S.M. Dunnigan, *Eros and Poetry in the Courts of Mary Queen of Scots and James VI* (Basingstoke, 2002), p. 125.
[50] Ibid., p. 132.
[51] Ibid.
[52] I wish to thank David Parkinson for the discussion this elicited in the Older Scots seminar class that ran during my time at the University of Saskatchewan, which prompted much of this research.
[53] See Bergeron, *King James*, p. 98.
[54] D.J. Parkinson (ed.), *Alexander Montgomerie, Poems* (2 vols, Edinburgh, 2000).

Through imagery of marigolds and clear crystal skies, Montgomerie's sorrow is piquant. The poem concludes with a sense of stoicism: 'fareweill with patience perforce till day'. Though the road may be rocky, previous lines having dealt with such hyperbolic language as 'thy presence me restores / to lyf from death / thy Absence also shores / to cut my breath' (ll. 57–8),[55] the narrator will stay the distance.

The nature of Montgomerie's relationship with James is not often explored in critical discourse. It is not mentioned in the work of Young, who focuses on historical accounts and epistolary exchange rather than literary works. A further Montgomerie sonnet entitled 'Against the God of love' opens with a damning indictment of Cupid as a 'blind brutal boy that w(t) they bou abuses / leill leisome luve'[56] (ll. 1–2), evoking what Dunnigan terms a 'charge of duplicity' that undermines an idealised image of James and may allude to his queer identity. Resentment and frustration are palpable in this verse. Contrasted with the devotional melancholy of 'Solsequium', this spectrum of emotion offers yet another dimension to a relationship that is too often a casualty of heteronormative critical practice.

Montgomerie's poetry offers an intense evocation of emotion, shrouded in poetic imagery and courtly platitudes. His feelings towards James fluctuate, from the devotion of a subject to his monarch, a lover to his beloved, to an almost familial discourse. The vibrancy of these emotions, and the language in which they are rendered, transcends the norm into what Dunnigan fittingly describes as 'the typically baroque excesses of Montgomerie's poetry bring[ing] erotic pleasure and the sacramental together, a fusion witnessed in the haunting presences and representations of the erotic poems'.[57] What is now clear is that absences, too, haunt these poems, with desires implicit but unspoken.

James in the Media: Queer Afterlives

The occlusion of queerness in our understanding of Scottish history is endemic, and yet it is a source of fascination for creatives. A number of cultural moments in the last ten years stand out that draw the public consciousness towards the queer potential of court life in the late sixteenth century. In 2018, a flamboyant, acerbic and self-aggrandising James VI burst onto screens across the UK. Scotland's own Alan Cumming took on the role in an episode of the BBC's *Doctor Who*: 'you may prostrate yourselves before me, God's chosen ruler and Satan's greatest foe, come to vanquish the scourge of witchcraft across the land!'[58] Joy Wilkinson's tongue-in-cheek script references James' attitudes towards women, and of course, witches. With James pitted

---

[55] Ibid.
[56] Ibid.
[57] Dunnigan, *Eros and Poetry*, p. 148.
[58] 'The Witchfinders', directed by S. Aprahamian, *Doctor Who*, BBC, 2018.

against Jodie Whittaker's female Doctor, the result is an historically questionable yet thoroughly entertaining romp. Cumming's James sparks with life, his feathered cap saturated in camp, and his moustache-twirling antagonism exacerbated against Whittaker's Doctor. Cumming's pantomimic James offers the offhand remark that 'my father was killed by my mother, who was then imprisoned and beheaded',[59] nonchalantly summarising the intricacies of Mary's scandalous reign. It is entertaining, certainly, but speaks moreover to the ongoing fascination with the historical trauma and drama of James' life, and the potential of queering the past.

This overtly queer depiction came hot on the heels of Josie Rourke's 2018 film *Mary Queen of Scots*, in which James' father, Henry, Lord Darnley, became the subject of scrutiny. This led to such headlines as *Out* magazine's pithy 'The Gay Stuff in "Mary Queen of Scots" Is Actually Pretty Accurate.'[60] Jack Lowden's louche lothario Darnley swaggered and flirted his way into the beds of both Mary and Rizzio, shocking general audiences and reinforcing the bisexuality that has long been hinted at in historical accounts of courtly spaces, building on the work of John Guy cited earlier in this chapter. 2018 also saw the Oscar-winning film by Yorgos Lanthimos *The Favourite*, which drew attention to sexual practices and favours at the court of Queen Anne, further highlighting this liminal, sexually fluid courtly space. The release of both films within a year did not evade comment, with magazine articles such as Michael Cuby's drawing overt, and well-reasoned, comparisons between the two depictions of early modern queerness.[61] Even historical fiction has taken a recent interest in the queer culture of the Jacobean court. In 2022, Neil Blackmore published *The Dangerous Kingdom of Love*, in which Francis Bacon attempts to find a young suitor for the king, in defiance of Robert Carr.[62] Time and time again, audiences ask 'Was this real? Can this have happened?', reflected in these clickbait headlines. We continue to deal with the thorny impact of heteronormative, patrilinear accounts of Western history, exposing the fault lines between traditional, limited understandings of history, and the expansion of understanding through queerness. As mentioned at the outset, works like *Bad Gays* are a clear sign that there is a voracious public appetite to understand not just queer histories, but complex queer figures, who encompass all too human flaws and become, in this sense, real people. Works such as that by Lemmey and Miller open up these histories to new, intersectional audiences, and our understanding of history is

---

[59] Ibid.
[60] J. Feder, 'The Gay Stuff in "Mary Queen of Scots" is Actually Pretty Accurate', *Out Magazine*, 14 December 2018, www.out.com/popnography/2018/12/14/gay-stuff-mary-queen-scots-actually-pretty-accurate [accessed 5 June 2023].
[61] M. Cuby, 'Gay Royalty: The Favourite and Mary Queen of Scots are Must-See Period Films', 10 December 2018, www.them.us/story/the-favourite-mary-queen-of-scots [accessed 5 June 2023].
[62] N. Blackmore, *The Dangerous Kingdom of Love* (London, 2022).

richer for it.[63]

It is notable also that traditional accounts, questions, and observations circumvent the definition of bisexuality, a recurring theme in the lives of both Darnley and his son James, with the notable exception of Wormald.[64] This is not unique to Scottish studies by any stretch: in a study as recent as 2020, conducted by Kirby, Merritt et al. it was concluded that:

> Although negative attitudes toward the gay and lesbian community have declined in recent years, attitudes toward bisexual individuals have not followed suit, perhaps due to questions around the legitimacy of their identity.[65]

This idea of legitimacy of queer desire permeates much of the discussion today. Yet some hope endures: the National Museum of Scotland holds matching stained glass panels depicting James and Buckingham,[66] displayed alongside other accoutrements related to the king. On the outside of its display case is a QR code, beneath an LGBTQ+ flag, prompting the visitor to listen to a minute-long explanation of the relationship between the king and his favourites. It is a small step, but an important one for making queer history visible in the narrative of a nation.

Conclusion: Marginality and Queerness

Dunnigan and Young posit crucial questions about the elusive nature of queer history in homoerotic discourse and behaviour, and in turn, queer identities across the spectrum. As Dunnigan asks, 'who formulates this injunction to elusiveness or silence?'[67] Thinking about the inheritance of James in terms of his parents, his poetic prowess, and the united crowns of England and Scotland provokes myriad issues of erasure and obfuscation. The time for flattened understanding is surely past: limiting our understanding of James and his court dulls our ability to read deeper meaning into these works. Solnit implores us to avoid the disappearance of lives 'as if unlived'[68] – we must allow these lives to be examined in the full spectrum of human emotion and lived queer experience.

The 'narrative of blood'[69] described by Solnit requires an active

---

[63] Lemmey and Miller, *Bad Gays*.
[64] Wormald, 'James VI and I'.
[65] T.A. Kirby, S.K. Merritt, S. Baillie, L.W. Malahy and C.R. Kaiser, 'Combating Bisexual Erasure: The Correspondence of Implicit and Explicit Sexual Identity', *Social Psychological and Personality Science*, XX(X) (2020), 1–10.
[66] Unknown, George Villiers, Duke of Buckingham, 1619, NMS, A.1966.175; Unknown, James I, 1619, NMS, A.1966.174. My thanks to Peter Burke for pointing out this display, in May 2023.
[67] Dunnigan, *Eros and Poetry*, p. 138; Young, 'James VI and I'.
[68] Solnit, 'Grandmother Spider', p. 72.
[69] Ibid.

engagement with context, and poses a disruptive potential for meaningful understanding of a history that flourishes in queerness, where femininity and queerness are no longer the casualties of marginalisation, but rather the locus of our interest. The influence of Mary, of Darnley, can and should be read large in James' life, for he existed not solely as a monarch, but as the son of a troubled and scrutinised marriage. The resistance of historical accounts to reflect any disruption or queerness in James' reign can easily be read as resistance to further disruption. In examining the poetry of Darnley and Montgomerie, the relationship that readers have to queerness has been brought into focus, allowing for examination of what is implicit in the devotion of Montgomerie and the performative complaint and delight of 'hary Stewart'.

In expanding and enriching our understanding of James and his queerness, we resist the suffocating marginalisation of a vital part of not only James' life, but of social history writ large. In reclaiming and commenting upon that which has gone unremarked and unspoken, we extend a kindness to those who will go on to study James in future years, by showing that to live a life of queerness and to embody this practice in your rule and cultural influence is a powerful and impactful thing.

Afterword

Understanding life at the margins matters. It matters in part because the very delineation of 'mainstream' as against 'marginal' tells us a great deal about a given society's self-perception and dominant value-systems. Similarly, reconstructing the mechanisms used to police these borders offers significant insights into the nature of power and the ordering structures underpinning it. More importantly, however, we should heed the central lesson emerging from the growth of 'history from below': ordinary people, including those living at the margins, matter quite simply because they were, and are, part of their community. If we overlook their experiences by constantly diverting our attention towards noisier, showier elites, then we cannot hope to achieve a full or comprehensive understanding of past societies. The margins are part of the picture, and they demand our attention for that reason.

The essays in this collection have suggested a number of recurring dynamics in the experience of social marginality in early modern Scotland. The first of these is the challenge of observable difference. Whenever a group or individual was visibly distinctive, suspicion and unease tended to accompany them, particularly when that variation was of a kind that challenged accepted social standards or expectations. In this volume, we have seen such dynamics emerge from Holmes' study of disability, Tyson's work on the Romani, Lee's analysis of enslaved Black children, and Kennedy's discussion of itinerants. Something similar, moreover, emerges from Doak's work on executioners, another group that was very publicly singled out, albeit by their work rather than their identities, and from Hall's discussion of the consequences of behavioural irregularity. In none of these cases was the handicap of visible difference necessarily insurmountable; other considerations or pressures often mitigated it. Nonetheless, it is clear that people pushed to the margins of early modern society in Scotland often ended up in this position because of the anxiety and discomfort with which visible difference was instinctively met.

Legal disadvantage is an equally prominent recurring theme. As Tyson and Kennedy remind us, the marginalised position of itinerants and migrants was enshrined and reinforced through legislation and regulation, much of it designed to quarantine the 'other'. Allen and Weston have shown that the world of work was heavily regulated, ensuring that those labouring on the 'wrong' side of the divide faced not just stigma, but active legal disadvantage, up to and including criminal prosecution. The legal constraints endured by coal mine workers, forced to live under a system of indenture, were more striking still, and Tree has shown very clearly how this basic fact of their existence shaped not only how such individuals performed their jobs, but how they lived, loved, and worshipped. The law, it can confidently be said, was a powerful engine of marginalisation.

Into this mix can also be added economic status. Hunter and Kennedy very much place this centre stage, demonstrating the role of poverty in curtailing opportunity, but balancing this with recognition that, through both formal and informal relief, attempts were often made to keep the poor socially engaged. Tyson, too, reminds us how a perception that they were a net economic drain helped drive forward the marginalisation of the Scottish Romani. But while economic factors could isolate, they could also help build new, self-contained social and/or economic communities, a dynamic that shines through strongly in the contributions of Allen, Weston, and Tree. Indeed, it was in some cases possible for economic considerations to counterbalance other marginalising forces, as can be seen from Kennedy's discussion of how migrants might leverage rare or useful skills into greater social acceptability. What emerges from all of this is a complex situation in which economic status could both deepen and shape marginal experiences, but not necessarily in a straightforward fashion, and also, in the right circumstances, having the power to do the precise opposite.

Running through all of this was a deeper, more fundamental factor: gender. Across many of contributions to this volume, we have seen how gendered standards or expectations shaped individual and collective experiences of marginality, particularly for women. This was true for people with disabilities (as shown by Holmes), the poor (Hunter and Kennedy), the Romani (Tyson), unlicensed workers (Allen), and indentured coal workers (Tree). But men, too, had to grapple with gender, as is clear from Hinnie's exploration of queerness and Hall's case study of how 'masculine' behaviour could run disastrously out of control. But gender is most obviously at the fore in the essays of Weston and McGill. Their studies have very different subjects – sex workers for the former, a middle-ranking diarist for the latter – but both grapple with the same fundamental question: how, in the context of a patriarchal society that deliberately curtailed female activity, could women exercise agency and find a way of negotiating the limits imposed upon them by gendered standards? The intersection between marginality and gender was potent indeed.

**

This collection was always intended as a conversation starter. The editors and authors fervently hope that the new insights, approaches, methodologies, and source-bases showcased in these pages will inspire further research, deepening our understanding of the marginalised groups and individuals whose lives we have centred. If we return to the hitherto under-discussed axes of marginality outlined in the introduction – itineracy, race, economic function – all of them now appear slightly less opaque as a result of this book. Nonetheless, gaps remain, and perhaps the most fitting way to close the volume would be to highlight some of the key ones, thereby mapping out the possible contours of future research. On migration, Tyson and Kennedy have shed light on some of the challenges facing various types of itinerant on the conceptual or nationwide levels, but detailed, local studies are now required to add texture to this picture. Especially welcome in this regard would be analysis of rural Scotland – while it is all too easy, given the comparatively richer source-base, to concentrate on towns, most Scots continued throughout early modernity to live in the countryside, but we remain, as yet, almost entirely in the dark when it comes to the nature of rural mobility, or the way it was perceived.

With regard to race and cultural distinctiveness, again this book has advanced our understanding, not least through Lee's discussion of enslaved and formerly enslaved young people and Tyson's work on the Romani. These contributions show what might be achieved through careful analysis, and future research could build on their example, perhaps especially through focused case study work. More is certainly needed on Black people, especially before the later eighteenth century, and investigation into the Jewish presence, hinted at by Hunter and Kennedy, might also be rewarding. Still more glaring as an ongoing lacuna, however, is the foreign-born community. A huge array of other cultures were present in Scottish society (we have come across French, Dutch, German, Fleming, Italian, and Greek settlers in this book alone), but virtually nothing is known about them. And that is before we even consider our astonishing dearth of knowledge about the English-born community, which was clearly substantial, and influential, by the later seventeenth century, if not before. As research priorities go, this, surely, must rank as an urgent one.

The complex relationship between economic function and social position has been addressed repeatedly in this book, but again, new research directions are not hard to identify. Discussion of other 'marginalising' work, whether unlicensed (as identified by Allen), illicit (as analysed by Weston), indentured (the focus of Tree's contribution), or stigmatised (on which Doak concentrates), would be welcome. The comparative richness of gender historical approaches means we know a reasonable amount about the nature and implications of women's work, but further investigation into non-elite women would still be useful. And what about farm and domestic service? This was a vital sector for young people, particularly young women, and it had clear implications for social position, but we currently know very little about it indeed. Just as importantly, attention needs to move away from Edinburgh. The capital, through its size, wealth, and political function, was an anomaly, and if we are to develop our understanding of early modern work, we need to spread our attentions out, not just to the other developing cities like Aberdeen or Glasgow, but to the small towns, villages, and hamlets in which the majority of Scots lived, worked, and died. In all this, we could do worse than replicate the in-depth case study approach deployed here to such effect by Hall.

Even for themes previously better served in terms of scholarly research, this book has helped map out potential future directions. Through the work of Hunter and Kennedy, we have seen how analysis of ecclesiastical records in particular can offer insights into the lives of the poor, but it is probably time to bring this more firmly centre stage, which would help rebalance a historiography that, for very good reasons, has tended so far to privilege the mechanics of relief over the actual experience of poverty. In making this conceptual pivot, we would also be better placed to take up Holmes' challenge of paying greater attention to the place of disability in early modern society.

This book has also suggested some avenues for further exploration in the comparatively richly served fields of women's and gender history. The multiple intersections between gender and other forms of marginality uncovered in various of the essays underline how vital it is for scholars to make gender a prominent part of their conceptual toolkit – early modern Scotland was manifestly not a society that can be understood in any of its details unless gender dynamics are borne explicitly in mind. But we might also return to the approaches offered by Weston and McGill, wherein gender emerges not as a straitjacket to be endured, but as a space to be negotiated. Starting from this assumption will allow scholars to reinforce an already developing trend within Scottish scholarship (perhaps most clearly observable in witchcraft studies) towards recognising that women habitually fought for agency in every area of their lives. Conversely, Hall's work in particular reminds us that gendered expectations – and the negative personal consequences of flouting them – affected men, too, and this should act as a spur for further investigation into the construction and performance of masculinity.

One final theme needs to be mentioned. As Hinnie notes in her impassioned call to arms, queer perspectives on pre-modern Scotland remain very thin on the ground, and almost all of those that do exist focus on the uniquely well-documented case of James VI – as of course, following the most important sources, does Hinnie herself. Much more work from this standpoint, delving below the level of the elite, is needed, not just in the obvious form of exploring 'deviant' sexual behaviours (one might be forgiven for inferring from the current literature that nobody was ever anything but heterosexual before the nineteenth century), but also through considering fluid and non-standard identities. The available source-base, it is true, presents a challenge for scholars interested in these questions. But as the essays in this volume have shown, that is always the case when exploring marginal lives. The effort is worthwhile, however, because, as we expand our understanding of the overlooked, the downtrodden, and the side-lined, so too does our picture of early modern Scotland grow infinitely richer.

Index

Abandonment (of spouses)   34, 134–5, 169
Abercromby, Alexander   169
Aberdeen   9, 44, 68n, 83, 102, 105, 108, 116, 165, 174, 175, 176, 213
  presbytery   51
Aberdeen infirmary   82
Aberdeenshire   58, 82, 83
Abernethie, George   44
Abjuration, oath of   187
Abraham (biblical patriarch)   188
Accounts, account books   21, 123, 145, 146, 150–1, 156–7
Acts *see* Legislation and acts
Adamson, Elspeth   44
Admiralty   169
Africa   82
Africans   82, 92
Agency   2, 7, 13, 80, 86, 93, 94, 112, 145–6, 153, 154, 155, 159, 160, 211, 213
Agriculture   101
Aikenhead, Thomas   125
Alcohol, drunkenness   68, 69–70, 138, 142, 148, 152, 155, 157, 165, 170, 174
Alexander, Helen   186
Alexander, John   39
Algiers   43
Allegiance, oath of   154
Alloa   22, 145
Americas
Amersone, Thomas
Anchovy Valley estate   87, 88, 89, 90
Anderson, Archibald   88–90
Anderson, Cornelius   118n
Anderson, Janet   140
Andersone, Christian   151

Anglo-Dutch Wars   34
Anglophobia   169
Angus (Forfarshire)   56
Ann (enslaved person)   84–5
Anna of Denmark   176
Anne, Queen   207
Anneis, Zeocham   175
Anstruther Easter   33n, 35, 36, 39, 40, 41, 42, 43, 44, 45, 175
Apprenticeship, apprentices   10, 27, 64, 87, 98, 104, 106, 107, 109, 132, 175
Argyll   119
Argyll, justiciary court of,
Ariés, Philippe   91
Artisans   11, 45, 62–78, 97–113, 138
  barbers   173
  baxters   69, 97
  bonnet-makers   102
  brewers   101, 139, 173
  candlemakers   101
  clockmakers   176
  cobblers   108–11, 112, 126
  coopers   173
  cordiners   64, 65, 67, 69, 70, 72, 73, 76, 99, 100, 102, 104–7, 108, 109–11, 112, 130, 175
  glassmakers   173, 176
  hammermen   102, 173
  horners   170, 174
  joiners   86
  lace-makers   132
  leather-workers   169, 177
  litsters   71, 73, 76, 173, 175
  paper-makers   176
  porters   101
  shoemakers *see* Artisans, cordiners
  silk-making   27, 176

INDEX

skinners   115, 176
slaters   173
tailors   53, 101, 102
weavers   104n, 106n, 169
wool-dressers   176
wrights   63, 98n, 171, 173
Assimilation   92, 174, 177, 178
Atchisone, John   43
Atlantic   87, 90
Auchtermuchty   33n, 40, 43
Ayr   37n, 67n, 116, 123
Ayrshire   9, 82, 118

Bacon, Francis   207
Bailies *see* Magistrates
Baillie family   48
Baillie, Alison   71-2
Baillie, George, of Jerviswood   28
Baillie, James   172
Baillie, John   172
Baillie, Mary   172
Baillie, Patrick   172
Baillie, William   172
Baird, William   109
Balcarras   175
Banff   170
Banishment, transportation   47, 56, 60, 61, 62, 63, 71, 118, 125, 130, 133, 134-5, 140-2, 153, 158, 168, 170-1, 172, 196, 200-2, 204
Bannatyne manuscript   196, 200-2, 204
Bannatyne, George   196
Banquhill, Archibald   123
Baptism   52, 62n, 171, 173, 182
Barclay, Katie   190, 192
Barclay, Robert   26
Barrie, Alexander   119
Bawds, bawdy houses   130, 133, 134, 135, 136-9, 140, 142-3
Begging, beggars   3, 27, 31, 32-3, 52, 56, 57, 66n, 114, 119, 126, 138, 148-9, 164, 165, 166, 167, 170
Belhelvie   68n
Bellchester   117
Bells   29, 173
Bennet, Racheal   128
Bergeron, David   195, 198
Berry, Charlotte   64

Bible   180-1, 182, 184, 186, 188
Bickering   77
Bingham, Caroline   198, 200
Bisexuality   194-5, 199, 200, 207-8
Black people   10-11, 79-94, 210
Blackcoat   21
Blackmore, Neil   207
Blair, Hugh, of Borgue   21
Bolt, Thomas   87-91
Bo'ness   165
Book of Discipline, First   33
Booths *see also* stalls
Boots   109, 110
Borders, borderers   49, 53, 57, 58, 59, 67, 117
Botany Bay   62
Bothwell, Adam   70, 73
Boyd, Thomas   99
Bressay   91
Bridge of Dee   105n
Bridgend   103, 104, 106-7
Bridges, Helen   175
Bristol   86
Brodie, Francis   62
Brodie, Patrick   53
Brodie, William (Deacon)   62-3
Broken men, masterless men   64, 167-8
Brothels   131, 136-7, 134, 137, 139
Brotherstanes, Patrick   172
Brown, Callum   180
Brown, Ebenezer   182, 192
Brown, Gilbert   182
Brown, Hugh   182
Brown, James   39-40
Brown, Jane   182
Brown, Jean   182
Brown, John   182
Brown, Mary   182
Brown, Patrick   182
Brown, Rachel   13, 179-93
Brown, William   122
Bruce, George   159
Bruce, Peter   176
Bryan, Charles   89
Bryson, Alexander   73
Bryson, Katherine   72
Buchan, William   22, 28
Buchanan, Thomas   154

INDEX

Burgesses 12, 62–78, 97–8, 99, 103, 104, 105, 109, 132, 173, 175, 176
   daughters of 132
Burghs 63, 102–3, 104, 105, 106, 121, 123, 128, 132, 173 *see also* individual burghs
Burns, Janet
Burntisland 42, 68n, 183

Cairns, Elizabeth 184–5, 187
Calder, Laurence 124
Callander 167
Calvinism 180, 183, 191
   conversion 183, 188, 191
   election, 186
Cameron 175
Campbell, Anna 142
Campbell, Anne 132
Campbell, Archibald, 1st earl of Ilay, 3rd duke of Agyll 119, 188
Campbell, Archibald, bishop of Aberdeen 28, 29
Campbell, Duncan 21
Campbell, Duncan 23–4
Campbell, James, of Aberuchill 185
Campbell, Jane, of Aberuchill 185
Campbell, John, 1st earl of Breadalbane 21, 24, 121, 123
Campbell, Margaret 133
Candles 101
Canongate 26, 64, 65, 66, 67, 71, 72, 76, 77, 85, 134, 137n, 138, 139, 140, 141, 176
   kirk session 25, 65, 66, 67, 70, 71, 73, 140
Capitalism 145–6, 147, 160, 198
Capp, Bernard 136
Cargill, Janet 134
Caribbean 81, 83, 87, 88, 91
Carlisle 134
Carmichael, Alexander 106
Carnbee 35, 175
Carnbo 175
Carnegie, Margaret 142
Carr, Robert, 1st earl of Somerset 199, 207
Carts 173
Castalian Band 196, 203
Castle o' Clouts 107

Cathcart 153
Catholicism 8, 51, 196, 204
Cato (enslaved person) 82–3, 93
Cautioners 66, 68, 72, 74, 76, 77, 134
Chalmers, William 137
Changelings 20–1
Charity, philanthropy 32–46, 132, 177–8, 193
Charles I 117, 171, 199
Charming, charms 53, 55, 165
Chazelon, Pierre 176
Children, childhood 17, 19, 20, 22, 26, 30, 35, 39, 41, 45, 59–60, 67, 79–94, 124, 136, 146, 148, 150, 151, 152, 167, 173, 177, 182, 188, 189, 190, 199, 210
Christmas 148
Church of Scotland 8, 18, 29, 32, 33, 46, 51, 142, 152, 154, 169, 179, 183, 185, 187, 192
   courts 5, 25, 27, 33, 35–6, 38, 43, 44, 45, 54, 60, 135, 140, 146, 152, 158, 171, 179 *see also* individual presbyteries and kirk sessions
Clark, Agnes 72
Cleall, Esme 18
Clergy 44, 101, 131 *see also* Ministers
Clerk, David 35
Clerk, John, 1st baron Penicuik 148, 151–2, 153, 156–8, 159
Clerk, John, 2nd baron Penicuik 61n, 148, 192
Clerk family 145
Clerks 22, 25, 27
Clouters 107–8, 109
Clubs 98, 112
Coal 37, 101, 121, 145–60, 166
Coal mines 145–60
   Carden 152, 153, 156
   Cassingray 150
   Dunfermline 151, 152
   Fawside 153
   Grange 156
   Kinglassie 156
   Loanhead 145(n), 146, 150, 151–3, 159, 160
   Sheriffhall 150, 151, 153, 157, 160

Torry 150-1
Tranent 158, 160
Coal mining 145-60
Cockburn, Alexander 116, 120
Collace, Katharine 182
Colonel, John 125-6
Common weal 102-3, 112
Commonwealth and Protectorate 9
Communion 24, 126, 183, 185
Comrie, James 169
Condon, William 175
Constables 48, 56, 57, 70-2, 73, 130, 137, 142
Corporatism 12, 97-113
Correction houses 27, 133, 135, 140, 141, 149
Corse, William 166
Coupar Angus 105
Court (royal) 194-209
Court, John 134, 137n
Courts 18, 29, 51, 56, 60, 65, 66, 69, 75, 97, 111, 115, 126, 131, 145, 146, 147, 158
  Burgh 71, 77
  ecclesiastical *see* Church of Scotland
  franchise 4, 26, 58, 76, 116, 152, 155-6, 165
  justiciary 21, 48, 53, 55-6, 60, 61, 155-6, 168, 169, 172
  sheriff 55-6, 118
Covenanters 9, 148, 179-80, 182-3, 185, 186-7, 189
Covenants (National, Solemn League and Covenant) 174n, 183
Cowan, Margaret 73
Craftsmen *see* artisans
Craig, James 177
Craig, John 39n, 41
Craig, John 72-3
Crail 33n, 35, 36, 37-8, 42, 44, 45
Creech, William 136-7
Creich, Agnes 36
Cressy, David 49
Crieff 123
Crime, criminality 7-8, 29, 47, 51-5, 60-1, 63, 114-16, 119, 120, 121, 123, 130-1, 135, 137, 138, 141-3, 142, 167-8
  adultery 51, 60, 61, 67

assault 28, 73, 142n, 164, 168, 169
banditry 167-8
bestiality 116, 175
blackmail 167
blasphemy 61, 125
conventicling 153
culpable homicide 116
fornication 68, 115-16, 171
fraud 125, 140
incest 51, 60, 74, 168
infanticide 8, 119
kidnap 167
murder 60, 116, 120, 123-4, 128, 168, 200
rape 119, 142
reset 54, 55, 57-8, 60-1, 68, 71, 134n, 166, 167, 172
robbery 42, 48, 55, 59, 120, 136, 137, 138n, 167, 168
sabbath-break 69-72, 164
sorning 167, 168
theft 50, 51, 53-4, 55, 56, 59, 60, 119, 125
treason and rebellion 54, 114, 116, 117, 118, 125, 126, 154, 156
usury 124, 169
witchcraft 6, 7, 21, 28, 51-3, 56, 61, 69, 72-6, 116, 213
Criminals 7-8, 10, 63, 116, 119, 123, 126, 128, 168
Croatia 120, 125n
Cromarty, Jacqueline 181
Cruickshanks, Elizabeth 138
Culloden, battle of (1746) 134
Culross 101, 102, 159
Culter, John 172
Culzean 82
Cuming, Isobel 175
Cumming, Alan 206-7
Cunninghame, Frederick 166
Cupar 175
Currier, Jean 44
Cuthbertson, William 67-78

Dairsie 33n, 39n, 40
Dalgleish, John 124, 125
Dalkeith 86
Darien 111
David, king of Israel 188

Davidson, George 45
Davidson, James 76
Deacons 65-6, 101, 110, 111
Defoe, Daniel 149
Derbyshire 149
Devinport, Robert 176
Dewar, George 45
Dickson, John 63
Dickson, John, of Bellchester 117
Dingwall, Helen 4
Disability 12, 17-31, 35, 38, 39, 210, 213
  autism 21
  blindness 20, 23, 26, 27, 29, 35, 38, 39
  deafness 23, 28, 29, 39
  intellectual 21, 24, 34, 39
  lameness 20, 21, 25, 27, 29, 39-40
  nonverbal 23, 39
  physical 22, 34, 39
Disease, illness 19-20, 22, 30, 38, 83, 93, 147, 153, 166
  cancer 39
  gonorrhoea 83
  leprosy 26, 39
  measles 20
  mental 21, 28-9, 39
  pox 20
  rickets 19
  scurvy 83
  venereal 138
  see also Plague, pestilence
Dishington, Agnes 36-7
Disorder 50, 65, 164-5, 166, 167
Disorderly houses see Brothels
Doctor Who 206-7
Domestic sphere 12, 17-31, 82, 99, 101, 103, 131
Donaldsone, William 118
Douglas, Margaret 135
Douglas, Mary 147
Dragge, Cornelius 169
Dremellan 154
Drinking establishments 63, 138, 139, 143
Drummond, George 179-93
Dryburgh, Janet 130, 138
Dryburgh, Michael 72
Duckham, B.F. 150

Duff, George 175
Dumbarton 122, 123, 163, 165, 170, 173
Dumfries 68n, 103, 104, 106-7, 115, 184
  kirk session 165, 171, 175
Dunbar 124
Dunbar, battle of (1650) 40-1, 43
Dunbog 33n, 40, 42, 44
Duncan, Margaret 43
Duncan, William 39
Dundee 9, 56-7, 105, 142, 170-1, 177
  kirk session 142, 166
Dundonald 53
Dunfermline 68(n), 124
  kirk session 42, 164, 171
Dunino 33n, 35, 38, 40, 42, 43, 44
  kirk session 37, 39, 41
Dysart 68n, 69, 173

East Lothian 176
Easter 148
Aberly, Susan Schoon 20
Edinburgh 5, 9, 10, 12, 25, 27, 48, 53, 56, 57, 58, 59, 62-78, 85, 87, 97, 99, 103, 105, 106, 108, 109, 111, 114, 116, 120, 121, 123, 124-8, 131-44, 164, 166, 170, 172, 175, 176, 177, 181, 182, 183, 188, 203, 212
  burgh council 20, 25, 27-8, 110, 120, 132, 133, 139, 167, 171
  castle 136
  presbytery 74, 77
Edison, Betty 39
Egyptians see Gypsies
Elders 26, 36, 48, 71, 152
Elgin 122, 130, 165, 171, 172, 173
  kirk session 177
Elizabeth I 197, 201, 203
Emigration 10
Engagement (1648) 171
Engineer 176
England 3, 4, 10, 32-3, 40, 49, 61, 117n, 120n, 174n, 176, 198, 199, 208
Enlightenment 18
Episcopalianism 8, 158

INDEX

Erskine, George, of Innerteill   59
Erskine, James   119
Erskine, John, of Carnock   148
Essex Peter (enslaved person)   85
Eviction   66-7, 76-7, 78
Execution   47, 56, 59-60, 61, 63, 114-29, 172, 207
Executioners *see* lockmen
Exodus   168

Faa *see* Faw
Fairfull, David   45
Fairs and markets   65, 98, 99, 103, 104, 105, 107, 112, 107, 112, 114-15, 124, 132, 143, 173 *see also* hiring fairs
Falkirk   165
Family   5, 30, 47, 67, 68, 71, 73, 76, 78, 85, 86, 89, 91-2, 99, 118, 119, 125, 132, 134, 136, 139, 142, 143, 149, 168, 169, 174n, 181, 184, 188, 189, 196, 199 *see also* Kinship
Famine   9, 57, 65, 68-70, 77, 106, 167
Fanny (enslaved person)   83, 93
Faw family   47-8
Faw, Alexander   56
Faw, David   47
Faw, Harrie   56
Faw, James   56
Faw, John   47
Faw, Katherine   60
Faw, Moses   47-8, 55
Faw, Robert   47
Fawside   153
Fearnan   24n, 25
Fees   98, 102, 104n, 105n, 106, 107, 107, 111, 113, 148, 164, 169, 173
Fenton, Henry   71
Fenton, Mrs   191, 192
Ferryport   33n, 35, 38, 39, 40, 42, 44, 45
  kirk session   41
Fife   12, 32-46, 69, 150, 152, 175
Fines, fining   60, 66, 68, 74, 139, 152, 172
Finlay, Kirkman   123
Finnison, John   119

Fishing   176
Flawt, Robert   119
Fleming, Grisel   38-9
Fleming, John   70-1
Flooker, Katherine   37
Forbes, Alexander   57-8
Fordyce   22
Forest of Dean   149
Forfar   56, 119
Forrat, Margaret   99
Forrester's Wynd   133
Fortoun, Charles   67, 69
Fortune-telling   52-3, 55, 168
Fox, Adam   125
France   116, 120, 124n, 127, 129, 169, 200
France, Lues de   176
Fraser, Janet   140-1
Fraser, John   23
Fraser, Jonet   184
Frazer, Robert
Freedom-seeking   83-6, 93-4
Freemen   97-113
Friedland, Paul   119-20
Friendship, friends   27, 30, 68, 71, 71, 86, 87, 88, 89, 123, 125, 142, 169, 175, 185, 189, 190, 191, 193
Frith, Uta   21
Fruit sellers   133
Fuird, Robert   170
Furdie, George   152
Futhie, Henry   73, 75

Gaelic   5, 11
Gaels   11, 53
Gender   6-8, 34, 80, 99, 112, 136, 143, 160, 179, 180, 187, 195, 211, 212, 213
General Assembly   27, 44, 154
Germany   115, 116, 120, 129, 146
Ghretson, Henry   164
Gibson, Alexander, 2nd Lord Durie   152
Gibson, George   42
Girdles   100, 101
Glasgow   43, 85, 90, 91, 102, 103, 118, 121, 123, 135, 153, 155, 158, 164, 166, 169, 170, 171, 172, 174, 177, 213

220

INDEX

burgh council   156, 173, 177
Glen, David   122
Goatherd (Dumfries)   104
God   22-3, 27, 28, 32, 51, 52, 61, 66, 136, 148, 179-93, 206
Gold, Hugh   154
Gold, Peter   154
Goodare, Julian   7, 50
Goodey, C.F.   24
Gorbals   103
Gordon, David   40
Gordoune, Thomas   170
Gowdie, Thomas   20
Graeme, Patrick   118
Graham, James, of Kilmannan   123
Graham, Michael   6
Grahame, Walter   43
Grainger, James   81
Grant, Alexander   181
Grant, John, of Freuchie   57
Gray, Andrew, 7th Lord Gray   56-7, 60
Gray, George   124
Gray, John   71-2
Green, Elizabeth   191-2
Greenock   87
Grub, Isobel,
Guardbridge   119
Guards and watches   121, 123, 128, 139, 142, 143n, 165-6, 170
Guilds *see* Incorporations
Gust, Onni   18
Gypsies, Egyptians   10, 12, 47-61, 138, 168, 170, 172, 178, 210, 211
   definitions of   48-9
   laws and proclamations against   49-54
   enforcement of legislation against   55-9, 168, 172
   toleration of   59-61

Haa of Cruister, Bressay   91
Hackston, David   117n
Haddington   63, 101, 105, 106, 109, 122
Halkerston Wynd   134, 138
Halket, Anne   20, 30
Hamilton   123
Hamilton, James   169

Hamilton, John, archbishop of St Andrews   119
Hamlet (enslaved person)   84
hangmen *see* lockmen
Harbours   173, 176
Hartman, Saidya   80
Hay, John   133
Hay, Richard Augustine   58
Heaven   184, 192
Heich, Jock   126
Hell   186, 189
Henton, Alexander   44
Highlands   22, 58, 165, 167
Hiring fairs   101 *see also* fairs
Hitchcock, David   3-4
Holy Spirit   180
Holyroodhouse, palace of   136, 200
Homosexuality   194-5, 198, 199, 204, 207, 208
Horse Wynd   62
Hospitality   68, 70, 170
Hospitals, infirmaries   20, 27, 82-3
Houston, William   90
Houston, Rab   6, 18, 21, 26
Hudson, Richard   203
Hudson, Thomas   203
Hume, Baron David, of Ninewells   54
Hume, George, of Kimmerghame   28
Hunter, Anna   176
Hunter, John   176
Husbands   17, 25, 60, 67, 68, 71, 73, 74, 75, 76, 99, 101, 112, 134-5, 136, 137, 138, 142n, 156, 169, 179, 187, 200
Hutcheson, Alexander   111

Illegitimacy   67, 91, 177
Illness *see* Disease
Immigrants   3, 10, 164, 172n, 174, 175, 178
   English   42, 169, 175, 176, 212
   Irish   169, 172, 177
   Dutch   169, 175, 212
   German   169, 176, 212
   French   42, 169, 212
   Flemish   176, 212
   Greek   177, 212
   Italian   176, 212
   Jewish   10, 42-3, 212

Impairment *see* Disability
Incorporations   25, 62, 63, 67, 69, 72, 97, 98n, 101-2, 104-7, 108, 109, 110, 111, 143
Indenture, indentured labour   148-9, 150
Industrial action   155-7
Innes, James (junior)   80, 87-93, 94
Innes, James (senior)   87, 88, 89, 92
Innkeepers   119, 139, 142n, 170
Intermarriage   174-5, 178
Inveraray   84, 116, 121, 165
   kirk session   165
Inverness   42, 122, 124, 173, 174
   kirk session   171
   burgh council   164, 166, 170
Ireland, Irish   10, 49, 169, 170, 172, 177
Ireland, David   39n
Irvine   123, 174
Italy   120, 127

Jackson, John   127
Jacobites, Jacobitism   134
Jailers   70, 76
Jamaica   80, 85, 87-92, 135, 141
James (enslaved person)   84
James IV   52
James V   52
James VI   12, 13, 48, 50, 51, 53, 55, 57, 59, 60, 61, 148, 169, 194-209, 213
'James VIII'   155
Jamesone, Alexander   175
Jedburgh   101, 105
Jesus Christ   98, 183, 184
Joseph, son of Jacob   188
Journeymen   27, 98, 101, 102, 108, 109, 110, 111, 134
Justices of the peace   56, 57, 172

Kay, Nans   37-8
Keith, James   27
Kellos, Elizabeth   139
Kells, Katherine   67-8, 69, 71-2
Kelso   68n, 176
   kirk session   177
Kemback   33n, 35, 43
Kennedie, Hew   40

Kennedy, Scipio   82
Ker, Thomas   151
Kerr, William   63
Ketch, Jack   117
Kilconquhar   33n, 35, 36, 39, 40, 41, 43, 44, 173, 175
   kirk session   45
Kilday, Anne-Marie   7
Kilmadock   154-5
Kilmarnock   102
Kingston   87, 90
Kinship   18, 30, 31, 47, 56, 58, 91, 92, 93 *see also* Family
Kirk sessions *see* Church of Scotland
Kirkcaldy   43, 68n, 105
Kirkcudbright   125
Kirkgunzean   171
Kirkliston   169
Kirkwall   102, 109, 118, 120, 127
Knox, John   179

Labourers   27, 99-102, 122, 145, 148
Lamb, David   90
Landward   103, 105
Langley, Christopher   17-18, 20, 29
Langton, Margaret   135
Lanseman, James   177
Latae, Margaret   37, 44
Lauder, John, of Fountainhall   21, 54, 126
Leather   104, 108n, 109, 111
Legislation and acts   3-4, 20, 106-7, 110, 111, 139, 210
   poor relief   32-3, 46, 52, 106, 107, 110, 143,
   Egyptians   48, 49, 50, 52, 53-4, 55, 56, 57, 61
   miners   147-50, 160
   toleration   187
Leitch, Dugald   119, 121
Leith   86, 110n, 175, 183
Leith Wynd (Canongate and Edinburgh)   66-7, 138, 139, 141
Lemmey, Hew   198, 208
Leneman, Leah   6, 131
Lerwick   91, 120
Leslie, Beatrix,
Leuchars   33n, 35, 39n, 41, 42, 43, 44
Lewis   126, 176

INDEX

Liberton 183
Liberty lands (of burghs) 103-4
Lightoune, Riachel 26
Linlithgow 122, 127
Liverpool 166
Livesay, David 89
Livingston, kirk session 177
Livingston, Henry 74-5
Loanhead 105n
Loch Maree 29
Lochfoot 104
Lockheart, George 177
Lockhart, George, of Carnwath 148
Lockmen 12, 114-29, 141, 146, 210
Logan, William 45
London 42, 44, 85, 86, 92, 137-8, 149, 166, 172n
Longmuir, Matthew,
Lord Advocate 47, 56, 58, 59, 142
Lothians 166
Lottery 190
Love 46n, 136, 146, 183, 184-5, 186-7, 192-3y, 196, 200, 201-2
Lowlands 11, 56, 59
Lowrie, Archibald 72
Lowrie, Thomas 72-6
Lowrie, William 68, 72
Lynch, Michael 105, 107
Lyndsey, Jonet 170

MacClerich, Donald 116
MacDonald, Alasdair 196, 201
Macfarlane, Christian 24
Macgoun, Donald (alias John Smith) 172
Mackenzie, George, of Rosehaugh 54, 55-6, 142, 156
MacKenzie, Rachel 133
MacKinnon, Dolly 79
MacNeil, Neil 86
MacQueen, John 201, 202
MacRitchie, David 58n
Magistrates 44, 47, 48, 49, 52, 53, 54, 56, 57, 58, 59, 60-1, 67-8, 69, 73, 74, 78, 103, 112, 118, 119, 121, 122, 123, 124, 130, 133, 137, 138, 140, 141, 142, 152, 156, 164, 166, 170, 172, 174, 175, 181, 188

Makgie, Archibald 170
Malcolm, Margaret 130
Malcolmson, James 118
Manufactories 149, 177
Manumission 79, 87, 88, 89, 90
Markets see Fairs
Marriage 21, 65, 68, 70, 91, 100n, 107, 133, 134-5, 149, 169, 173, 174-5, 178, 181, 190-2, 196, 201, 209
Mary I 194, 195, 196, 197, 199, 200-1, 203-4, 207, 209
Mary of Guise 197
Marson, John 106
Martin, Thomas 152-3
Maxwell, Elizabeth 135
Maxwell, Elspeth 56
Maza, Sara 80
McCallum, John 9, 33, 34
McCarie, Donald 123
McCaul, Marion 116
McClelland, John 118, 121
McDonough, Susan 131
McFarlane, Jean 141
McEwen, John 121-4, 126, 128
McGrigor, Calum Oig 167-8
McKenzie, Donald 122
McKiachan, Dugland 165
Mcmollen, George 171
McNair, Elspeth 68
McNiccoll, John 123
McPherson, Jean 133
McViccar, Neil 187
Meal 26, 37, 115, 124
Medicine 18n, 27, 132, 172
Meggat, John 73, 75
Merchants 22, 25, 64, 85, 90, 109, 166, 169, 175, 176
Midlothian 150
Migration, migrants 2, 10, 13, 163-78, 210-12
Miller, Alexander 72
Miller, Barbara 134
Miller, Ben 198, 208
Mills 99
Milner, Stephen 147
Mine workers 13, 145-60, 211
  bearers 98, 146, 147-8, 150-3, 156, 157, 158

223

INDEX

gatemen 148
grieves 150-3, 157
hewers 147, 148, 150-3, 154, 155, 156, 157, 158, 159
overseers 150, 157
oversmen 150, 151, 152-3, 157
watermen 148
windmen 148
Ministers 11, 30, 36, 39, 43, 44, 77, 136, 140, 146, 152, 154, 155, 171, 173, 175, 179, 183, 184, 187, 192 *see also* Clergy
Mint Close 130
Mintz, Steven 92
Mitchell, James 175
Mitchison, Rosalind 6, 9, 32, 137
Mobility 10, 13, 40, 139, 153, 163-78, 212
  attitudes towards 164-8
  regulation of 168-73
  acceptance of 173-8
Moffet, Anna 151
Molly houses 137-8
Monteagle estate 87
Montgomerie, Alexander 194, 203, 204-6, 209
Moor, Elizabeth 175
Moray 172
Morison, John 44
Mosstowie 57, 172
Mouat, John 118-21, 122, 126, 127, 128
Mowbray, Robert 27
Mugdock 123
Muirton 85
Mullan, David 179-81
Mullen, Stephen 147
Mundy, James, of Malsetter 169
Munro, Robert 123-4
Munro, William 137
Murray, John 27-8
Murray, Colonel John 137
Murray, Patrick 30
Muir, William 133
Muirhead, Andrew 155
Munro, Robert 123-4
Munro, William 137
Mutilation
  judicial 116, 117n

  branding 116, 121, 172
  tongue-boring 116
Mystics 193

Nairn 172
Naturalisation 175, 176
Nawken 49
Nef, J.U. 149
Neptune (enslaved person) 84, 86
Netherbow 97-8
Netherlands 127
Networks 4, 12, 13, 18, 26, 30, 64, 66, 69, 66, 69, 73, 131, 142, 143, 166, 169, 172, 178
Newall, John 125
Newbattle 136
Newbiggin 151
Newcastle 85, 149
Newspapers 5, 82, 83-6, 93
Newton of Douglas 154
Nungate, Haddington 106
Nuremberg 117

Oatcakes 100
Officers 68, 71
Old Aberdeen 100n, 105, 165, 170
Old Rayne 82
Old Statistical Account 136
Oliphant Kinloch 85
Orkney 42, 114n, 118, 120, 122
Ormistoun, George 124-5
Ormistoun, Harry 117, 124-8
Osnall, John 68
Outlandmen 104, 107, 112

Packing and peeling 107
Paisley 169
Parliament 20, 47, 50, 52, 55, 57, 146, 147, 148, 155, 156, 165, 170, 176
Parliament, British 3
Parliament, English 3
Parliament House 127
Parson, Hannah 191
Pascall, Peter 177
Paterson, Laura 119
Patrick Street Close 137n
Patriquin, Larry 32
Patronage 183, 187, 192
Patterson, Margaret 133-4

224

Paul, apostle   183
Pearson, Agnes   67
Pedie, John   155-6
Pedie, Robert   153, 155-6
Peebles   119, 166, 172
Peebles Wynd   133
Penicuik   192
Perth   68n, 85, 103, 105, 107, 109, 175
   presbytery   29
Perth and Stirling, synod   154
Perthshire   58, 119, 121-4
Peter (enslaved person)   84, 86
Pilate, Pontius   183
Pitlochry   122
Pittenweem   33n, 40, 41, 43
Plague, pestilence   120, 165-6, 167, 172
Plainstone Close   137
Plantations, colonies   4, 80-1, 82, 91, 134, 141
Plot, Robert   159
Politics   1-2, 3, 6, 20, 32, 51, 58, 62, 97, 112, 127, 131, 143, 147, 154-5, 159, 160, 171, 187, 188, 193, 195, 196, 197-8, 205, 212
Pool, Elspeth   68
Poor, poverty   3, 4, 5, 9-10, 12, 22, 24, 26, 27, 28, 30, 32-46, 50, 52, 53, 68-9, 111, 122, 132, 140, 149, 164, 166, 167, 169 170-1, 172, 177, 181, 193, 211, 213
Poor relief   9-10, 12, 32-46, 52, 132, 135, 166, 177 *see also* Legislation and acts
Port Glasgow   174
Porteous, John   72
Porteous, John   101
Porthole, Dumfriesshire   104
Portpatrick   42
Prayer   18, 30, 179, 180, 185, 187, 188-9, 191, 193
Prejudice   4, 50, 146-7, 168, 169, 210
Presbyterianism   8, 148, 154-5, 179, 182-3, 184, 185, 193
Presbyteries *see* Church of Scotland
Prestone, John   157
Prestonpans   28
Print, printing   63, 117

Prisons, prisoners, imprisonment   39, 40-1, 43, 56, 59, 60, 62, 64, 69, 70, 85, 111, 125, 130, 133, 134, 135-6, 138n, 140, 141, 149, 153, 163, 207 *see also* Correction houses
Privy Council   43, 47, 50n, 51-2, 53, 54, 55-7, 58, 59, 60, 73, 75, 136, 153, 164, 166, 169
Prophecy   184 *see also* Second sight
Prosecution   7, 51, 54, 56, 57, 58, 61, 67, 139, 140, 141, 172, 211
Protectionism   166, 173
Providence   22-3, 184
Provosts *see* Magistrates
Pryd, Isobel   35
Punishment *see* Fines, fining; Execution; Mutilation; Scourging; whipping
Purcell, Bessie   69, 72-6
Purdie, John   169
Purdie, William   153-4

Quakerism, Quakers   186, 189, 191-2
Queerness   13, 194-209

Race, ethnicity   11, 12, 49, 80, 91, 212 *see also* Black people; Gaels; Gypsies
Raffe, Alasdair   180
Ramsay, Andrew   85
Ramsay, Helen   70
Randolph, Thomas   200
Ranke, Leopold von   1
Ranken, Walter   123
Recipe books   19-20, 28, 29
Reformation   5, 8, 9, 33, 48, 51, 52, 61, 155, 180
Remissions   60
Rendall, Steven   186
Repairs   99, 107-11, 112, 176
Reputation   12, 50, 67, 68, 75, 146, 158, 160, 171, 172
Restoration   2, 34, 116n, 156, 158, 184
Restrictions
   poor relief   37-8
   mobility   165-6, 168-73
   sex work   140-3

work   99, 101, 107, 109
Revivalism   180, 193
Revolutions
    industrial   17n, 160
    of 1688-9   131, 136, 137, 139, 154, 155
Riddel, Martha   133
Riddel, John   65-7, 76, 77
Risings and rebellions
    Argyll's, 1685   117n
    Covenanter, 1679   154
    Pentland, 1666   117n
    Radical, 1820   117
Ritchie, James   175
Rizzio, David   116, 200, 207
Robertson, Bessie   73
Robertson, John   73
Robertson, Robert   121
Robeson, Agnes   74, 75
Robinson, Thomas   70
Rochead, Thomas   175
Roma, Romani *see* Gypsies
Roslin   58
Ross, Katherine   53
Ross-shire   172
Rowat, Jane   182
Royal College of Physicians   27
Royal Mile   66
Royal Society   159
Rumbold, Richard   117, 125
Rutherford, Samuel   182
Rymer, Thomas   38

Sabbath   65, 66, 69, 71, 164
Salt   149, 150, 155, 159, 160
    saltpans   28, 150, 160
Salters   98, 147, 148, 149, 154, 155
Sanderson, Margaret   6
Sanquhar   171
Sart, John   29-30
Satan, devil   74, 116, 152, 184, 206
Schmidt, Franz   117
Schools, schooling   28, 176, 193
    schoolboys   77
    schoolmasters   27, 77, 175
Scollay, Robert   87-91
Scoonie   152
Scotstarvit   175
Scourging   51-2, 56, 71, 115-16, 118,
    121, 123, 125, 135, 141, 183
Secession, Secession Church   183, 193
Second sight   23 *see also* Prophecy
Selkirk   5
Selkirkshire   47, 56
Serfdom   98, 175 *see also* Mine workers; Indenture
Servants, service   11, 17, 19, 24, 26, 27, 28, 53, 68, 72, 98, 102, 106, 107, 110, 111, 132, 133, 139, 148-9, 171, 175, 212
Sewage, waste   173
Sewing   109, 132
Sex work, sex workers   13, 125, 130-44
Shallit, Paul   42
Sharp, James, archbishop of St Andrews   36
Sharpe, James   115
Shetland   5, 60, 80, 87-93, 94, 118-22
Shoemakers *see* Artisans
Shoes   37, 45, 99, 103, 104, 106, 107, 108-11, 112, 122
Simpson, James   108
Sinclair, George   158-9
Sinclair, James   122
Sinclair, William, 14th baron Roslin   58
Sinclair, William, 16th baron Roslin   58
Skene, James   127
Skene, Laurence   70
Skippers   42, 135, 163, 175
Slavery, enslavement   2, 12, 43, 79-94, 136, 147, 210
Sleich, Alexander   72
Smith, Alexander   63
Smith, Barbara   141
Smith, David   92
Smith, John (alias Donald Macgoun)   172
Smith, Laurence   70
Smith, William   73
Smout, T.C.   5-6, 32
Smyth, Olaw   119
Smyth, William   76
Society for the Reformation of Man-

ners 138
Soldiers, veterans 20, 34, 39-41, 119, 134, 135, 137, 174, 176, 204
Solnit, Rebecca 196, 197, 203, 208-9
Somerset 149
Sorcery *see* Crime, criminality
Soutars *see* Artisans
Spain, Spaniards 127
Spindler, Erik 64
Spithill 105
Sprot, Agnes 28
St Andrews 75, 105, 119
  archbishop 103 *see also* Sharp, James; Hamilton, John
  presbytery 40, 42, 174
  university *see* Universities
St Giles Cathedral
St Leonards 33n, 39
St Monans 33n, 36-7, 39, 40, 42, 43, 44
Stallangers 98, 112, 113
Stalls *see also* Booths 98, 99, 108, 132
Stampeild, James 169
State 1, 4, 7, 50, 51n, 55, 154
Stewart, Alan 199
Stewart, Alexander, of Clarie 175
Stewart, John, of Baldynneis 203
Stirk, Isobel 38
Stirling 56, 68n, 109, 123, 127, 173, 174
  synod 154
Stirling, Archibald 38
Stornoway 5, 125
Stowe, kirk session 58n
Strangers 26, 42, 42-3, 45, 61, 163-78
Straton, Philip van der 176
Streetwalkers 133, 137, 139
Stuart, Esmé, 1st duke of Lennox 198-9
Stuart, Henry, Lord Darnley 193-209
Stuart, Kathy 146
Suburbs 104-7, 109, 110n, 111, 112, 137, 140, 142
Sutherland 58
Sweet, John 70
Symson, James 110

Tannenbaum, Frank 63
Taverns *see* Drinking establishments
Taxation, taxes 4-5, 105, 166
Taylor, Becky 49
Testimonials 10, 41-2, 43, 140, 148, 171-2
Theft *see* Crimes, criminality
Thomason, Thomas 155
Thompson, E.P. 2
Thomson, James 28
Thomson, James 155
Thomson, Jean 28
Thurso 122, 123, 171
Tobacco 134, 166
Todd 6
Tolbooths
  Canongate 70, 139
  Dundee 56
  Edinburgh 59, 62, 138n
Toleration, Acts of, *see* Legislation and acts
Tont (enslaved person) 86
Torphichen 99
Torthorwald 165
Toshach, Duncan, of Monzievaird 123
Towns *see* Burghs
Transportation *see* Banishment
Travellers *see* Gypsies
Trotter, Gavin 59, 60
Trumbach, Randloph 137
Tudor, Margaret 197
Tulliallan 154-5
Turpie, James 152
Turnbull, George 22-3
Tyninghame 22

Unfreemen 12, 97-113
Union of 1707 61, 155, 176, 187
United Societies 154
Universities 158
Unst 118, 121
Urie 26

Vagrancy, vagrants 2, 3-4, 27, 31, 50, 52, 53, 57, 120, 126, 141, 148, 164, 166, 172, 178
Veitch, Jon 66
Villiers, George, 1st duke of Bucking-

ham   195, 198, 199, 208
Vincent, John   1
Violence   51, 53, 59, 65, 66, 67, 77, 81, 83, 128, 138, 139, 142, 143, 156, 167, 169, 199
Visions   182-3, 184, 190

Walker, Andrew   44, 45
Walls, town   103, 105-6, 127
Walls, Janet   139
Wann family   119
Ward, Edward   135-6
Wardrope, Alexander, of Carntyne   155-6
Warrock, Elizabeth   56, 60
Wars of the Three Kingdoms   1-2, 3, 20, 34, 39
Watt, James   82
Wells   29, 174
Wemyss, Elizabeth   133
Wemyss, Jean, countess of Angus and Sutherland   19
West, Elizabeth   182, 183
Westkirk   183
Whipping *see* Scourging
Whit, Arthur   44
White, Isobel   65
White, William   65
Whyte, Ian   6
Whyte, John   127*n*
Whytt, Marion   177
Wide, Andrew   45

Willen, Diane   187
William II   137
Williams, Eric   147
Williamson, Findlay   72
Willie, Anne   134
Willson, David Harris   198
Wilson, Helen   67
Wilson, Robert   150-1
Witchcraft *see* Crime, criminality
Wood, Andy   147
Wood, John   35
Women   1, 3, 6-8, 10, 13, 56, 59, 75, 81, 115, 116, 130-44, 146, 179-81, 184, 186, 211, 212, 213
  single   132, 136, 171
  widows   34, 45, 98, 100(n), 101, 112, 134, 135, 139, 172, 176, 191, 193
  work   13, 99-101, 112, 130-44, 148, 150, 211
Wricht, William   175
Wright, John   165
Wright, Robert   153
Writers   25, 62*n*, 133, 175
Writing
  self   5, 20, 180
  spiritual   20, 180-2, 183, 186-7, 193
Wryght, Patrik   172

Yeoman, Louise   179
Yule *see* Christmas

St Andrews Studies in Scottish History
Previously published

I
Elite Women and Polite Society in Eighteenth-Century Scotland
Katharine Glover

II
Regency in Sixteenth-Century Scotland
Amy Blakeway

III
Scotland, England and France after the Loss of Normandy, 1204–1296
'Auld Amitie'
M. A. Pollock

IV
Children and Youth in Premodern Scotland
Edited by Janay Nugent and Elizabeth Ewan

V
Medieval St Andrews: Church, Cult, City
Edited by Michael Brown and Katie Stevenson

VI
The Life and Works of Robert Baillie (1602–1662)
Politics, Religion and Record-Keeping in the British Civil Wars
Alexander D. Campbell

VII
The Parish and the Chapel in Medieval Britain and Norway
Sarah E. Thomas

VIII
A Protestant Lord in James VI's Scotland
George Keith, Fifth Earl Marischal (1554–1623)
Miles Kerr-Peterson

IX
The Clergy in Early Modern Scotland
Edited by Chris R. Langley, Catherine E. McMillan and Russell Newton

X
Kingship, Lordship and Sanctity in Medieval Britain
Essays in Honour of Alexander Grant
Edited by Steve Boardman and David Ditchburn

XI
Rethinking the Renaissance and Reformation in Scotland
Essays in Honour of Roger A. Mason
Edited by Steven J. Reid